The Theatre Student

GUIDE TO BROADWAY MUSICAL THEATRE

 # THE THEATRE STUDENT SERIES

In *"The Lady or the Tiger"* sequence from **The Apple Tree**, *Sanjar must choose between two doors. Behind one is a Bride. Behind the other—Death. The same is true in selecting a musical for production—only the choice is much wider. The only solution is to become familiar with all the musicals that are available.*

The Theatre Student

GUIDE TO BROADWAY MUSICAL THEATRE

Tom Tumbusch

WITH ADDITIONAL RESEARCH AND COMPILATION

BY MARTY TUMBUSCH

Foreword by Richard Rodgers

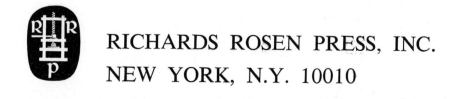

RICHARDS ROSEN PRESS, INC.
NEW YORK, N.Y. 10010

Standard Book Number: 8239-0243-9
Library of Congress Catalog Card Number: 71-153811
Dewey Decimal Classification: 792

Published in 1972 by Richards Rosen Press, Inc.
29 East 21st Street, New York City, N.Y. 10010

Revised Edition

Manufactured in the United States of America

To My Wife, Marty

ABOUT THE AUTHOR

TOM TUMBUSCH first became seriously interested in the musical theatre during his college years at the University of Dayton, when he appeared in productions of *Finian's Rainbow, The Boy Friend,* and *Guys and Dolls.* After graduation in 1962, he remained at the University as choreographer for *Little Mary Sunshine, The Fantasticks,* and *Wonderful Town.*

While still an undergraduate, he began to think about writing a book on musical theatre and initiated serious research on the subject. In the process he became involved in a special study of musicals in their prior-to-Broadway runs and became associated with other high-school and little-theatre groups involved in musical production.

From the former he learned the little things that spell the difference between making a musical work or flop; from the latter the need to adapt the techniques of Broadway to the local level. His theories first appeared in a series of eight articles in *Dramatics* magazine. After additional research and testing in production situations these ideas were expanded into his previous contribution to this series, *The Theatre Student—Complete Production Guide to Modern Musical Theatre,* a work that deals extensively with recreating a Broadway musical in a high school, college, or little theatre.

He is the author of numerous articles on musical theatre and lectures on the subject. He is also performing arts editor of *Dayton USA,* the Chamber of Commerce publication, and Dayton correspondent for *Variety.*

7

CONTENTS

PREFACE

This book is for people who enjoy musical theatre, especially those who participate in productions of Broadway book musicals. It is based on the premise that history alone is not enough; that there must be a better way to "visualize" the actual productions of the past. To that end it provides the most complete record of the musicals covered.

High-school, university, and little-theatre groups have the additional problem of selecting a musical for production. Hopefully this book will make their job easier (1) by providing insight to more shows available for production and (2) by presenting the material compiled from over 2,300 catalogs, programs, magazine articles, scripts, souvenir programs, recordings, newspaper clippings, photographs, and other research sources in one handy reference source, plus notes taken during performances and firsthand experience on the Broadway scene.

To illuminate the high point of musical theatre achievement I have gone back and reviewed 114 musicals. These reviews are presented in a standardized format I believe will be most useful for producers considering a revival production of the show. For the most part I have tried to view each musical through the eyes of an "out-of-town" critic offering first, informative insight on each show and second, in many cases, constructive suggestions on how a show could be improved.

Being of the opinion that drama critics and critics of musical theatre should be separate specialists, it follows that I also believe the critics have called a number of musicals wrong—that rash or biased opinions have sometimes clouded or destroyed substantial musical theatre achievements. The main criterion I have used for judging the shows reviewed was: How good does it work as a musical?

In doing so I was not encumbered by the pressures of the more celebrated newspaper and magazine critics who must submit their hastily prepared reviews within a few minutes or hours of departing from the theatre—a job a mere handful of men in the last fifty years have been able to manage. In most cases I have had the test of time, acceptance of non-New York audiences, and extensive study to guide an admitted light hand of criticism. The purpose here is to provide a foundation to build upon, not to probe for defects.

Each show spotlighted is broken down into seventeen information categories that are described in detail at the beginning of Section I. The spotlighted musicals follow, focusing on the author's pick of the best musicals available for production.

A comprehensive list of *all* musicals available through major leasing agents up to January 1, 1971, is included in Section II. Section III provides information on how to obtain production rights for shows that are not generally available in the United States, and Section IV fills in information on most other operettas, comic operas, and other forms of musical theatre that remain available for production. The Index is cross referenced by title and authors.

Even though the producers' share in subsidiary rights income is minimal, a number of them have taken the trouble to supply photos of their original Broadway productions. These have been credited as requested. My special thanks to The Lynn Farnol Group for the complete collection of photos from the Rodgers and Hammerstein shows.

For additional photos and research I am indebted to Paul Meyers and the staff of the Lincoln Center Performing Arts Library, Kay Johnson and the staff of the

Wisconsin Center for Theatre Research, Ron Longstreth of the International Thespian Society, and the many personalities, composers, authors, rights-leasing agents, and others who cooperated in making this book possible.

Last but not least, my thanks to Betty Traylor and especially my wife, Marty, for the massive typing and secretarial job involved.

Tom Tumbusch
Dayton, Ohio

FOREWORD

The American musical theatre has become an imposing body of collaborative endeavor comprising a genuine, indigenous American art form. Although it has its roots in the operetta of Middle Europe, the American musical has evolved during the first half of the 20th century into a native born and bred theatrical product, marketed at home, but also exported throughout the world.

I am proud and grateful to have been an architect of the musical theatre, and I am anxious that it should be perpetuated. For this to happen, constant injections of new blood are needed. These infusions must eventually come from America's young people, who must first be made to feel a certain pride of ownership in the art form.

This book, I think, should afford them the opportunity of getting to know the musical theatre Broadway has traditionally offered, and of taking the first steps toward its further development. But more important, Broadway needs the people for whom this book is written. *The Theatre Student—Guide to Broadway Musical Theatre* is a much-needed bridge between an accepted art form and its future.

Richard Rodgers

SPOTLIGHTED MUSICALS

Every night new people sit in a theatre somewhere in the world and discover the wonderments of musical theatre. For many the joy is the added dimension the music brings to a characterization. For others it is the spectacle of seeing a mammoth production work like a precision Swiss watch. Still others become attracted to the charm or excitement of the show.

The spirit of a good musical is an infectious one—unless perhaps you are a great dramatic actor who cannot sing or dance. But even that fear is soon dispelled by the many juicy dramatic parts in musical theatre.

To appreciate a musical fully it is necessary to understand all the elements that go into one. Many people are content to enjoy (or detest) musicals for what they see on the surface. Others want to know why the construction of the show is good or bad; to see the beauty of professionalism that goes over the heads of most of the audience; to weigh the contributions of each collaborator; to be knowledgeable on the many facets of musical theatre; and/or to help produce intelligently a revival production of a musical. For this relatively small percentage of musical theatre connoisseurs the art form must be studied. A thorough examination must be made of what has gone before.

Of course, the optimum research would be to visit a good revival production of each important musical. To some degree this is possible, thanks to the summer-theatre movements and outstanding work by some colleges—and even some high-school groups.

The next best way is to have a permanent record of print and sound. This section is an attempt to fulfill the print part and provides guidance to the sound and what full scripts are generally available.

In addition to a synopsis of each musical, other production data is included to help the enthusiast visualize the original production and the revival producer to judge requirements of the show.

In respect to the latter, it should also be pointed out that a show not spotlighted could be equally rewarding under the proper circumstances. Such shows as *Wizard of Oz, Our Miss Brooks,* and other Broadway and non-Broadway musicals have been produced in high schools, colleges, and little theatres with great success.

Unfortunately, in an undertaking such as this, a line must be drawn between the musicals that can be featured with photos and full production data and those that are simply listed. It is the author's considered opinion that the spotlighted musicals are the best that modern musical theatre has produced. A comprehensive list of other musicals available for production is found in Section II.

Data on each spotlighted musical is broken down into the following elements:

Title
Authors
What it is based on
When it opened
Number of performances
Agent for production rights
Recordings
Published text
Musical numbers
Digest of plot
Instrumentation
Principal characters and casting guide
Scenes and sets
Period and costumes
Choreography
Lighting and special effects
Notes concerning the individual show

All of these elements are important or helpful in understanding a musical. Although some listings tend to impart a certain amount of historical and inside information, this is not its purpose. The object is to allow the reader to visualize each show.

In standardizing these listings "certain words"

were found "creeping into his vocabulary" as Professor Harold Hill would say. In an attempt to eliminate misunderstanding, a brief discussion of each element is in order.

THE MUSICAL SHOW TITLE

The title of the show often represents the entire sales value when enticing the public to buy tickets. Most musicals have been well named and are thoroughly known inside and outside theatrical circles. Lesser known and misnamed shows, such as *Goldilocks* (about making silent movies), *The Gay Life* (turn-of-the-century society life), and *A Family Affair* (the chaos of preparing for a wedding) possess no such asset, but could be every bit as interesting as *Hair, Hello, Dolly!*, or *My Fair Lady*.

Musical theatre entries in this spotlighted section are almost exclusively musicals or musical comedies. Operettas, comic operas, and grand opera are not treated in any detail. A comprehensive list of titles, complete with author(s), composer, and rights-leasing agent, can be found in Section IV—Other Musical Shows.

AUTHORS

Nearly all musicals are a collaboration. Three major creative functions are involved—music, book, and lyrics. Each has been designated behind the names of the person(s) responsible for those functions as credited in the show's official billing.

In several cases a show has been doctored by uncredited writers and/or composers, many of whom are famous for other shows. Who really wrote a song is a lively game played freely by Broadway insiders and gossips.

As a side note, many people are interested to learn that the lyrics for a song are usually written first.

WHAT WAS THE SHOW BASED ON

A large percentage of musicals are based on a book, straight play, screenplay, comic strip, or collected works—and in a few cases (*Say Darling, Girl in Pink Tights, Little Mary Sunshine, The Boy Friend,* and *Dames at Sea*) on other musicals. Several highly successful musicals have had original books, but this is largely stifled by producers who put together costly musical productions. They like to know that at least one major element is success-proven. They are also keenly aware of the effect this has on advance ticket sales.

The value of knowing the original creative work is chiefly one of reference for details. How did the original author describe this scene or that character's dress? Is there more information that will provide further insight into the character? What other background can be gained? Sometimes it's just plain fascinating to go back to the original effort and compare how the ideas were handled differently.

The caution is, of course, that of the difference in media. Something that doesn't work as a play might work great as a musical. The book might have been ponderous, but onstage as a musical it flies. (Often, too, it is the other way around.)

One has merely to compare the metamorphoses of *Pygmalion* to *My Fair Lady,* the Academy Award-winning film *The Apartment* to *Promises, Promises,* and/or Shalom Aleichem's stories to *Fiddler on the Roof* to get a good perspective of translation into the musical idiom.

On the other hand, *Sherry* was assassinated by the critics for merely inserting songs in the proven play *The Man Who Came to Dinner*.

Many hit musicals have subsequently been made into movies. Very rarely has this been done successfully. In most cases the transition has been a total disaster. *Guys and Dolls* and *The Sound of Music* were two of the best done. However, even in those there were many unnecessary changes. Film companies should have been shot for what they did to *Bells Are Ringing, Pajama Game, Damn Yankees, Gypsy, My Fair Lady, West Side Story,* and many others. The titles have been tarnished. People who saw only the movie versions are likely to feel the stage version of the show could be no better.

WHEN IT OPENED

The opening night is listed for two main reasons.

First, to place it in the correct creative period. Over the years writing and production techniques have changed slowly but steadily. Shows of the 1940's tend to require fewer sets, and writing construction is usually loose. In the early 1950's construction began to tighten, set-drop-set-drop production style permitted more sets. *My Fair Lady* firmly established the mechanical stage in 1956, and most productions since that time have seemed to stage about any kind of sets willed by the authors or designers—many playing an integral part in the writing achievement.

Secondly, if the number of performances is used as an indication, it should be remembered that older shows (before air travel) played mostly to New York audiences. In modern mobile society, the Broadway musical production probably plays to more visitors than to New York area theatregoers.

NUMBER OF PERFORMANCES

One of the first questions asked about any Broadway musical is, "How many performances did it run?" For that reason the official number of paid performances for each show is included.

This is a poor yardstick to use between shows. The producer, size of theatre, opening date, ethnic audience appeal, starring names, and many other factors contribute to the total. Likewise, grouchy critics, an ill or departed star, theatre schedule conflicts, union strikes, and other circumstances have shuttered many a new or successful musical before its time. Likewise, homier shows such as *I Do! I Do!* couldn't sell out six performances a week in New York, but packed theatres of twice the size eight times a week on the road.

The number of performances refers only to the "official" opening and paid post-review performances. The figure does not include the out-of-town tryouts, benefits, New York previews, or road-show companies.

Many Broadway musicals had short runs because they were poor shows. In other short-run musicals there lies a lot of good (sometimes great) material. Poor direction, undercapitalization, unfair reviews, miscasting, or a number of other problems occasionally kill a potentially great musical. *Hot Spot*, the musicalization of the Peace Corps, underwent extensive surgery in New York previews. Finally most of the numbers were whipped into shape, but the book needed more work. It could have been fixed, but management was forced to open the show. When the reviews were written, *Hot Spot* was relegated to a small corner of oblivion.

A year and a half before, another show suffered the same difficulties. Out-of-town prior-to-Broadway business was dismal. Critics kept reminding the producer that nothing worked and never would. Opening night was delayed while rewriting continued. The gossip of doom flowed from the experts—many of whom had not even seen the show. Advance ticket sales were nil. However, in the last few days of reworking, *How to Succeed in Business Without Really Trying* was salvaged. It went on to win just about every award available, including the Pulitzer Prize for drama. Had it been forced to open a week earlier, chances are it would be filed right beside *Hot Spot*.

Golden Boy on the other hand faced the same tedious tryouts and delayed opening experience. There were three major versions of the script. The first was justly discarded in Detroit. The second script was excellent, but the decision was made to appeal more to the Negro audience, and the existing version was generated. Not only was the show overly rewritten but it also failed to at-

tract the hoped-for Negro audience. Had the second script been used, the number of performances could have been much greater.

In some cases the *official* script may be quite different from the show as it ran on Broadway. In one show (which shall remain nameless for obvious reasons) a name film director (husband of the star) was staging his first musical. Be he ever so effective on film he was clearly killing the production. (Film directors are often redeemed in the editing room.) The producer, realizing his misjudgment (producers never make errors), hired a director with a long track record of successful productions to advise. When advice didn't work, changes were made behind the director's back, only to be changed again when he discovered them. The battle was on. To make a long story short, the musical that opened on Broadway was a compromise. The reviews were mixed. The director departed town following the opening, the changes that made it a much better production were inserted, and the show ran a little over nine months on good word of mouth. But the published and acting scripts are that of opening night.

RECORDINGS

The first original-cast album was *Oklahoma!* in 1943, and just about every major musical since then has been recorded. Most of the smash hit show albums are kept in "print" and remain available. As a special service to theatrical interests, Columbia Records keeps all its musical theatre titles (smash or flop) in its catalog. On occasion RCA Victor has rereleased some shows or sold masters to those interested in pressing a new edition.

In the same league with original-cast albums are recordings of revival productions, which in many cases add songs or dance music that were not included on the original disc because of lack of space. With the invention of "microgroove" recording it became possible to include much more material. Often the revival productions are much better recordings, yet faithful to the concepts of the original production.

For musicals that have been made into motion pictures there is also a film or sound track recording. For the most part they are poor references. However, they are sometimes valuable for dance music or other material as done in New York that does not appear on the original-Broadway-cast album. Beware of new songs and orchestrations used in film recordings.

Studio and television cast recordings are also available for many shows. Studio-cast albums are valuable when none other exists, but as with TV recordings, stars signed for such ventures tend to stylize or otherwise distract from the dramatic impact as written. Television productions are notorious for "experimenting" with musicals because they can neither afford the commercial-less time to present the entire work properly nor is the small screen suitable to theatrical choreography or the spectacle of a big musical. In rare cases of some small musicals such as *Who's Ernest?* (*Ernest in Love*), TV productions have been done with great success.

The catalog numbers shown with each featured musical are for the most recent releases as of January, 1971. Some albums may no longer be available from the listed companies. However, many public libraries have reference or circulating copies. Depending on the show, a purchased copy might be available from out-of-print dealers in New York or other large cities, but at collectors' prices ranging from $15 to $50 for a popular album.

PUBLISHED TEXT

Acting scripts are not available for most musicals. Leasing agents furnish one director's script and a set of sides (lines and cues for each speaking part, typed individually). This, of course, is impractical and should be corrected in due course.

The postage cost to receive and return bulky perusal scripts can be avoided since a large percentage of musicals have been published in one form or another. These are identified for each spotlighted show.

Unless otherwise indicated the reference is for a hardbound volume. Paperbacks are designated by a (P) following the publisher and year. The now-defunct *Theatre Arts* magazine published a large number of musicals between the years 1949 and 1964, which are available in most libraries.

The *Best Plays* series has published cuttings from several musicals over the years and could be helpful. The opening-night date indicates which volume of *Best Plays* would have the cutting, if applicable.

There may be some discrepancies between a published and production script, but they are usually minor. A published script will usually include several photographs, which can be useful. And while on the subject be sure to check the *Theatre World* annuals and theatrical year books for other photo guidance.

LEASING AGENTS

Obtaining rights for musicals differs from the payment of flat fee rates customary with plays. Production rights are also more expensive. In addition to the royalty fee, certain materials such as orchestrations, director's script, sides, and chorus books must be rented. (In some cases, as with Samuel French musicals, acting editions and chorus books may be purchased.)

An abbreviated reference for the leasing agent is given for all musicals spotlighted in this section. Explanation of the abbreviation and the agent's complete address appear at the beginning of Section II on page 187.

MUSICAL NUMBERS

All songs (except reprises) are listed in this section. Hit songs (as nearly as can be defined by nightclub usage, recordings, and air play) are shown in capital letters. Musical numbers added in revival productions or otherwise connected with the title are also listed.

An attempt has been made to indicate major dance numbers (the numbers not in "quotes") but this is not all-inclusive for every show. Also, many songs evolve into a dance or production number.

DIGEST OF PLOT

In trying to synopsize a musical one gets the same feeling as reading the lyrics to a song without knowing the melody. The words on the paper can only provide a sparse glimpse on how the show will play—or the added dimension the music will bring.

Hair is "three" shows. The record gives one impression. Reading the script makes you wonder if it's the same show. Once the original production is seen, there's a question whether the music and book really matter at all, as they are simple fragments of a production concept.

Yet the plot provides the framework into which all the other elements are fitted. Therefore an attempt has been made to capture the spirit of each show in the plot synopsis. In doing so, emphasis has been placed on the show's major story construction. Subplots have been included only if they affect the construction of the show.

Many musicals, such as *Brigadoon* and *The Fantasticks,* build a beautiful show around a simple idea. Others, such as *How to Succeed . . .* seem to become better with each surprising new twist. The synopses vary accordingly.

INSTRUMENTATION

This is the information the musical director needs before he can give his blessing to any musical. Since this information is not always provided in catalogs, it is presented here for each show featured. Instrumentations for other shows are available from the leasing agent.

The instrumentation is given as it was orchestrated for the original production. All instruments are listed with the exception of the individual items for the percussion part. To provide some idea of this area, the following is a typical percussion part:

Percussion I–II
   Timpani (2 drums)
   Snare Drum (brushes and sticks)
   Bass Drum
   Tom-Toms (2 pitches)
   Toy Drums (3 pitches)
   Bongo Drums
   Cymbals (small and large suspended)
      Hi-hat Cymbal
      Choke Cymbals
      Hand Cymbals
      Finger Cymbals
   Anvil
   Tam Tam
   Temple Blocks (4 pitches)
   Wood Blocks (2 pitches)
   Celeste
   Glockenspiel
   Xylophone
   Chimes
   Tambourine
   Triangle
   Cow Bell
   Sistrum (small metal rattle)
   Train Whistle
   Slide Whistle
   Ratchet
   Siren
   Castanets
   Slap Stick
   Glass Tree
   Raspberry

Simplified or updated orchestrations are available for many shows. If these are known they are so noted. In either case, if instruments are doubled, the parts can be played by separate musicians as long as they can be individually arranged in the orchestra pit.

For the sake of brevity, certain instruments have been abbreviated thus: baritone saxophone: bari sax; clarinet: clar; electric (guitar): elec; English horn (cor anglais): Eng. horn; piccolo: pic; saxophone: sax.

CHARACTERS

The total speaking parts refers to the number of sides for the musical. Often the smaller parts can be doubled. The number of principals generally refers to those parts that received billing in the original productions. The casting characteristics are based on the original concept for each part shown, except when musical or acting range dictates otherwise (a big-name star who cannot sing can carry a part whereas a lesser known cannot). First emphasis is given to the talent most important for the part. The chorus size is usually flexible; however, it is not recommended to exceed the maximum cast size given unless an unusually large stage is involved.

Any special talents such as juggling, playing a musical instrument onstage, etc., are listed in this section. Likewise the need for any animals or other unusual "casting" is noted.

SCENES AND SETS

This section lists the number of acts followed by the number of scenes. Some scenes are recurrent and thus the set requirements are further refined to the number of full stage, partial stage, painted scenic drops or curtains, and important set pieces. Most musicals also have a "show curtain," which is revealed during the playing of the overture. These are not included in the listing unless they recur throughout the production, as was often the case in earlier days.

The requirements described refer to the original Broadway production.

PERIOD AND COSTUMES

The time, period, or other costuming data are the description of the author. The types of dress mentioned are an identification of the costumes required and in no sense are a complete costume plot. The compilation was taken from script descriptions, souvenir programs, and other photos from the original or road productions.

If this is a particular problem area, inspection of the complete costume plot, available from major costume suppliers, is advisable.

CHOREOGRAPHY

In this section an attempt is made to label the particular dance required for each musical. Not all people, or choreographers for that matter, describe dance movement alike. Nor does the dance movement in many musicals lend itself to specific description.

However, the dance music in a musical's score was usually written to match specific dance patterns created by the shows original choreographer. If you are not prepared to rescore, it is helpful to know the original dance styling.

Keep in mind that the description of standard ballroom dance music such as fox-trot, tango, waltz, etc., takes on a slightly different meaning when applied to the musical theatre stage. The footwork style is the same, but the steps are bolder and more dramatic. There are lifts and patterns that are not seen on most dance floors.

The scripts of many musicals simply call for a ballet. Rarely is this classic ballet á la "Swan Lake." Rather the term refers to a dance sequence. Check the choreography section for each musical for a more specific description of the dance movement of the original production.

Other terms used are as follows: modern ballet—not necessarily containing classic ballet steps—a free-flowing movement often contemporary and dramatic. Example: the "Jets' Song" dance from *West Side Story*. Jazz—related to free-form modern ballet, but with quicker, shorter, and more animated steps. The "Steam Heat" number from *Pajama Game* is a widely known example of jazz. Modern jazz—a freer form, yet most often used in large chorus numbers. It could be stylized as in the case of *Li'l Abner*, interpretive as in the "Tick Tock" female dance solo in *Company*, or stand on its own as in the "Rich Man's Frug" from *Sweet Charity*. Tap requires special metal tap shoes—the taps are emphasized and steps somewhat limited. Soft shoe (no metal taps) is more relaxed, with more personable body movement. There are many clichéd steps, but possibilities are unlimited. Production numbers usually build, perhaps from a solo or dance specialty with more members of the cast gradually joining in. A production number might also include moving scenery, a stream of showgirls on various levels, an energetic total cast dance bash, and other elements that almost always build up to a smashing ending. Dance specialties or fads, such as the "Sword Dance" from *Brigadoon*, the Charleston, the coronation pageantry in *Camelot*, are examples of special cases in which individual research by the choreographer will be required.

LIGHTING AND SPECIAL EFFECTS

Obviously no one could accurately present *Peter Pan* without the flying technique. Certain other effects such as the rainbow in *Finian's Rainbow*, the projections in *Your Own Thing*, the movie in *Fiorello!*, or the balloon ascending in *Ben Franklin in Paris* are essential to the production and are listed. Nonessential special effects and general guidelines to lighting are also listed.

Most musicals require some nonorchestral sound effects. Such effects can be important to actual production, but their value in visualization was questionable. Therefore, the space was devoted to extra photographs and other details considered more important.

NOTES

An artistic form as dynamic as musical theatre defies standardization. Every musical is unique.

Not all are the smash successes that the ads proclaim. Even the huge blockbusters age. There is gold in many shows that have been forgotten or pushed rapidly from the Broadway scene. Comments regarding these intangibles are found under the "Notes" heading. Recommendations for direction, style, updating, editing, and rewriting are indicated where required. Special facts of interest are also included for some shows.

ONE LAST WORD

One of the major purposes of this book is to lift the mystique from a number of musicals—through pictures, synopsis, and detailed information of each spotlighted show. The hope is that the reader becomes familiar with the most enduring musicals—and that today's producers choose the shows to best suit current production abilities and facilities instead of just automatically selecting the latest available "hit musical." Careless selection of even a top hit can be disastrous.

Groups that specialize in the production of musical theatre are wise to present and/or study other forms of the art. Much may be learned from operettas, comic operas, and, in some cases, grand opera.

*

ALLEGRO

Richard Rodgers (Music),
Oscar Hammerstein II (Book, Lyrics)
Opened Oct. 10, 1947
315 Performances

BASED ON: Original

AGENT: R & H

PUBLISHED TEXT: Knopf, 1948, Modern Library #200

RECORDINGS: RCA LOC (LSO) 1099

DIGEST OF PLOT: *Allegro* is the life of Joseph Taylor, Jr., from his country doctor parentage in 1905 to his major decision in life at age 35. Following how he grows up, enters school, and meets his future wife, then through medical school and marriage. Against his will and the lifelong desire of his family, he is driven by his wife's ambitions to take on a big-city practice. His success as a society doctor is personal failure. Enter Emily, a big-city nurse with small-town ideas, the girl Joe needed all along. Leaving his wife to the medical stars with whom she has become all too familiar, Joe returns with Emily to the home-town practice to which his father had dedicated his life.

MUSICAL NUMBERS: "Joseph Taylor, Jr.," "I Know It Can Happen Again," "One Foot, Other

COURTESY OF THE LYNN FARNOL GROUP, INC.

Ending of "Joseph Taylor, Jr." number in Allegro. *Platforms, projections, and set pieces carried by cast constituted the only scenery used in original production.*

Foot," "A FELLOW NEEDS A GIRL," "Freshman Dance," "As They Imagine They Are," "A Darn Nice Campus," "The Purple and Brown," "SO FAR," "You Are Never Away," "What a Lovely Day for the Wedding," "It May Be a Good Idea for Joe," Wedding, "To Have and to Hold," "Wish Them Well," "Money Isn't Everything," Hazel Dances, "Yatata, Yatata, Yatata," "THE GENTLEMAN IS A DOPE," "Allegro," "Come Home."

INSTRUMENTATION: Violin A, B, C, D, viola, cello, bass, flute, oboe, clar I–II, bassoon, horn I–II, trumpet I–II, trombone I, II, tuba, percussion, piano, conductor.

CASTING: 37 parts, 10 principals plus singing and dance specialties. Large vocal chorus (singing chorus is used frequently to interpret the mental and emotional reactions of the principals, after the manner of a Greek chorus). All principals are actor-singers. Legitimate voices required. Total cast, 30–45.

SCENES AND SETS: 2 acts, continuous action. 3 locations—home town, college town, and large city. The original production used only lighting and movable set pieces.

PERIOD AND COSTUMES: From 1905 to 1940: everyday wear from the turn of the century, the 1920's, and the late 1930's. Society dress of late 1930's (male and female).

CHOREOGRAPHY: Modern and ballet styles, free-floating movement. Slow-building production numbers with a lot of sign and prop carrying.

LIGHTING AND SPECIAL EFFECTS: Area lighting very important. If done as the original, lighting becomes more important as it must provide substantial interest.

NOTES: Ideal for little-theatre or college groups. More musical drama than comedy. Moving music, should be done more often than it is. The original staging concept proved to be the show's weak point. An imaginative setting could only help. The show was revised for a 1968 production at the Goodspeed Opera House, East Haddam, Conn., utilizing changes suggested by Oscar Hammerstein II. A delicate show that can be rewarding if done well.

ANNIE GET YOUR GUN

Irving Berlin (Music, Lyrics),
Herbert and Dorothy Fields (Book)
Opened May 16, 1946
1,147 Performances

BASED ON: Original

AGENT: R & H

Ethel Merman as Annie, with her medals from European tour, in the Lincoln Center revival of Annie Get Your Gun.

PUBLISHED TEXT: Irving Berlin Music Corp.

RECORDINGS: RCA LOC (LSO) 1124
Metro (5)548 (F)
DECCA DL (7)9018

DIGEST OF PLOT: Annie Oakley emerges from the hills of Ohio to become the crack rifle shot of the country. She joins the Buffalo Bill Wild West Show and falls in love with Frank Butler, the show's featured champion sharpshooter. Over a billing conflict about whose picture should go where, Frank and Annie have words. Frank departs to join a rival show. Annie assumes top spot, and her show strikes out for Europe. Playing nothing but command performances, the company returns home on a freighter seeking to join forces with Frank's show in order to survive. Things have been anything but easy for the rival group, and the merger is quickly concluded to the immortal show business anthem, "There's No Business Like Show Business." All is well with the show, but tempers flare, and each star challenges the other to a shooting match. Annie's friend, Chief Sitting Bull advises that she miss on purpose, which she does, losing the match and winning Frank as a consolation prize.

MUSICAL NUMBERS: "Buffalo Bill," "I'm a Bad, Bad Man," "Doin' What Comes Natur'lly," "THE GIRL THAT I MARRY," "You Can't Get a Man With a Gun," "THERE'S NO BUSINESS LIKE SHOW BUSINESS," "THEY SAY IT'S WONDERFUL," "Moonshine Lullaby," "I'll Share It All With You," Ballyhoo, "My Defenses Are Down," Wild Horse Ceremonial Dance, "I'm an Indian Too," Adoption Dance, "Lost in His Arms," "Who Do You Love I Hope," "SUN IN THE MORNING," "ANYTHING YOU CAN DO," "Old Fashion Wedding" (added in 1966).

INSTRUMENTATION: Violin A, B, C, D, viola, cello, bass, flute I–II, oboe (Eng. horn), clar I–II, bassoon, trumpet I–II, III, trombone I, II, III, percussion, harp, guitar, piano, conductor.

CASTING: 50 parts, 8 principals. Annie, onstage 90 percent of running time, strong voice. Frank, matinee idol type with strong singing voice. Tommy and Winnie, song-and-dance team. Buffalo Bill and Chief Sitting Bull, comic character actors. Large singing and dancing chorus, children (3 having featured parts). Total cast, 40–60.

SCENES AND SETS: 2 acts, 10 scenes, 9 sets, including drops.

ACT I
Scene 1: The Wilson House, a Summer Hotel on the Outskirts of Cincinnati, Ohio. July.
Scene 2: A Pullman Parlor in an Overland Steam Train. Six Weeks Later.
Scene 3: The Fair Grounds at Minneapolis, Minn. A Few Days Later.
Scene 3a: The Arena of the Big Tent.
Scene 4: A Dressing-Room Tent. The Same Day.
Scene 5: The Arena of the Big Tent. Later That Night.

ACT II
Scene 1: The Deck of a Cattle Boat. Eight Months Later.
Scene 2: Ballroom of the Hotel Brevoort. The Next Night.
Scene 3: Aboard a Ferry. En Route to Governors Island. Next Morning.
Scene 4: Governors Island. Near the Fort. Immediately Following.

PERIOD AND COSTUMES: 1885: days of the Wild West when Easterners were anxious for an "imported" piece of the action. Backwoods rags, flashy Wild West garb, traveling and everyday clothes of the times, evening clothes, and Indian costumes.

CHOREOGRAPHY: Indian dance, soft shoe, ballroom, and production numbers.

LIGHTING AND SPECIAL EFFECTS: General lighting. Trick shooting effects (originally done with Annie on flashy motorbike—very fast pass across stage with guns blazing—follow spot only).

NOTES: Each version of *Annie Get Your Gun* varies in polish, but such a strong show always seems to come across a hit. Irving Berlin wrote a new song, "Old Fashion Wedding," for the 1966 Lincoln Center Production at which time "Who Do You Love I Hope" was deleted. Both scores are available.

ANYONE CAN WHISTLE

Stephen Sondheim (Music, Lyrics),
Arthur Laurents (Book)

Opened April 4, 1964
9 Performances

BASED ON: Original

AGENT: Music Theatre

Ray Middleton (Frank Butler) and Ethel Merman (Annie), the original leads in Irving Berlin's Annie Get Your Gun.

PUBLISHED TEXT: Random House, 1965

RECORDINGS: COL KOL-6080
KOS-2480

DIGEST OF PLOT: Cora is the mayoress of a town willed to her by her late husband. The town is going bankrupt because its only industry makes a product that never wears out. Her town council, headed by Comptroller Schub—assisted by conservative Treasurer Cooley and ignorant Police Chief Magruder (who is always handcuffed to a teen-age girl), create a miracle of water flowing from a rock. Its religious significance is immediately recognized, and the pilgrim tourist traffic begins to flow. Nurse Apple arrives with her "cookies" from the Cookie Jar, the town's mental institution and only going concern. The town council refuses the cookies the right to partake of the miracle, but they mix with the crowd. In an attempt to separate the sane pilgrims from the insane cookies, the services of Dr. Hapgood are employed. He proceeds to divide the people into groups, but no one can understand who is who or what is what. Hapgood also persuades Nurse Apple to compromise her uptightness and they fall in love. By the time it is discovered that Hapgood is really only another cookie, a new miracle is discovered in a nearby town, and the crowds depart leaving the principals to manage themselves instead of trying to run people.

MUSICAL NUMBERS: "I'm Like the Bluebird," "Me and My Town," "Miracle Song," "Simple," "A-1 March," "Come Play Wiz Me," "Anyone Can Whistle," "A Parade in Town," "Everybody Says Don't," Ballet, "I've Got You to Lean On," "See What It Gets You," Waltzes, "With So Little to Be Sure Of."

INSTRUMENTATION: Cellos A (2), B (2), C bass, reed I (flute, pic I, alto flute I), reed II (oboe, Eng. horn, clar), reed III (clar I, E♭ clar, flute II, pic II, alto flute II (bari sax), reed IV (clar II, bass clar, flute), reed V (bassoon, clar, bass sax), horns I, II, trumpets I, II, trombone I, II (tuba), percussion (2), accordion, piano-conductor (celeste).

CASTING: 17 parts, 7 principals, 4-man song/dance team, which backs female leads nightclub style. Cora, character lead who sings and dances. Her "people," Treasurer Cooley, Chief Magruder, Comptroller Schub, good character men who sing or dance a little. Fay Apple, versatile actress who sings and dances (does French accent as major bit). Hapgood, good actor who sings but dances little.

SCENES AND SETS: 3 acts (could be done in 2), 1 back drop against which 4 major units are moved: City Hall (front flies to reveal interior), Hotel Superbe, Miracle Mountain, which revolves to reveal hoax, 1 cave ceiling fly-in to mask mountain interior, and Fay's bedroom insert set.

ACT I
The Town.
The Miracle.
The Interrogation.

ACT II
The Celebration.
The Romance.
The Parade.
The Release.

ACT III
The Conspiracy.
The Confrontation.
The Cookie Chase.
The Farewell.
The End.

PERIOD AND COSTUMES: Present, in "a not too distant town": modern suits, dresses, lingerie, hats executed in colorful fabrics. A feeling of a circus atmosphere is what is desired. Preacher-cut black suit for Treasurer Cooley, Western-flavored sheriff's outfit for Magruder, pinstriped business suit for Comptroller Schub. Doctor and nurse uniforms. Usher uniforms for song/dance boys. Mayoress costuming slightly out-of-date.

CHOREOGRAPHY: Unorthodox modern ballet ranging to modern jazz in rare instances. Two major ballets—"The Cookie Release" and "The Cookie Chase," in which men wear toe shoes, people are thrown through the air, etc., wild sequences in which all the rules are discarded. Both are interworked with dialogue and have a story line. Also, there are waltzes, a parade, pure ballet, and song-and-dance bits.

LIGHTING AND SPECIAL EFFECTS: Dramatic and some tightly controlled lighting throughout.

NOTES: *Anyone Can Whistle* (originally titled *Side Show*) was ahead of its time. At least some material offended every critic. Many people walked out. But nevertheless it was a masterpiece; an attempt to shake up the musical theatre formula, which, of course, *Hair* eventually did. Sondheim later perfected some of the concepts used for *Whistle* and the result was the successful *Company*. The following production notes are Stephen Sondheim's own instructions:

"A Note on the Scenery: The play is written to be performed on a revolving stage against suggestive pieces rather than full, literal sets. The style should be bright, warm, and gay; the colors should be almost primary.

"A Note on the Cast: If the demands of the script were to be taken literally, the play would have to be performed by a cast of hundreds in an enormous arena—where it would die. Like the scenery, the staging should suggest, rather than duplicate literally.

"The many small parts should be performed by a small 'stock company' of five or six versatile musical actors. Although every possible zany costume device should be used, from wigs and eyeglasses to beards and false noses, there should not be any serious attempt to fool the audience. The 'stock company' plus the seven principals should be able to take care of all speaking parts (except mere bits) and musical soloists.

"The many extras—rather loosely described as 'townspeople, cookies, tourists, pilgrims'—should be suggested by a small group of good singers and dancers; and, perhaps, by the imaginative use of dummies.

"A Note on the Play: Because the style is obviously unconventional, do *not* look for symbols and/or hidden meanings: there are none. What is meant, is said. The main attempt is simply to tell a good story in farcical terms with wild (if sometimes vicious) humor and music."

ANYTHING GOES

Cole Porter (Music, Lyrics), Guy Bolton, P.G. Wodehouse, Howard Lindsay, Russel Crouse (Book)

Opened Nov. 21, 1934
420 Performances

BASED ON: Original

AGENT: Tams-Witmark

PUBLISHED TEXT: Manuscript Only

RECORDINGS: EPIC FLM 13100
FLS 15100
DEC 8318 (F)

DIGEST OF PLOT: *Anything Goes* is a tuneful ocean crossing on the S.S. *America*. Billy Crocker comes to the ship for instructions from his Wall Street boss, E. J. Whitney. While there he discovers that the love of his life, Hope Harcourt (chaperoned

The grand lounge of the S.S. America as it appeared in the original 1934 production of Anything Goes.

by her mother) and her fiancé, Sir Evelyn Oakleigh, are on board. Also on board is dance-hall sweetheart Reno Sweeny and her chorus girls. Billy decides to stow away and somehow win Hope. He runs into public enemy No. 13 disguised as Rev. Dr. Moon and his moll, Bonnie Le Tour. Moon has an extra ticket intended for public enemy No. 1, Snake Eyes Johnson, who has failed to show up for the crossing. Someone on board suggests that Billy is No. 1, and the chase is on. Incorporating various disguises, Billy continues to woo Hope. Back on shore the real No. 1 is captured in the company of the real cleric Dr. Moon, but Billy and Moon do not get the message and escape from the brig, where they have been placed for their suspicious actions. Like all 1930's musicals the end is utopian with Billy getting Hope, Reno gets Sir Evelyn, E. J. Whitney gets Mrs. Harcourt. Moon gets a pardon and is free to express openly his love for Bonnie.

MUSICAL NUMBERS: "YOU'RE THE TOP," "Bon Voyage," "IT'S DELOVELY," "Heaven Hop," "FRIENDSHIP," "I GET A KICK OUT OF YOU," "ANYTHING GOES," "Public Enemy Number One," "Let's Step Out," "LET'S MISBEHAVE," "BLOW, GABRIEL, BLOW," "ALL THROUGH THE NIGHT," "Be Like the Bluebird," "Take Me Back to Manhattan."

INSTRUMENTATION: Flute (clar, alto sax), oboe (tenor-bari sax), trumpet, trombone, bass, guitar-banjo, percussion, piano-conductor.

CASTING: 23 parts, 7 principals. Hope, sings and tap dances. Billy, good actor, good voice helps. Moon, character comic who sings comic number, good voice not required. Reno, strong musical comedy type who belts songs and hoofs well. Sir Evelyn and E. J. Whitney, mostly straight acting roles with little singing. Bonnie, dance-hall-girl type. Dance-hall chorus line and other chorus roles very flexible—can vary from 6 to 24. Total cast, 30–46.

SCENES AND SETS: 2 acts, 16 scenes, 8 sets including drops.

ACT I
Scene 1: Weylin Caprice Bar.

Scene 2: Afterdeck. Midnight Sailing.
Scene 3: Mr. Whitney's and Dr. Moon's Cabins.
Scene 4: The Afterdeck.
Scene 5: Sir Evelyn's Cabin.
Scene 6: The Deck.

ACT II
Scene 1: The Lounge.
Scene 2: The Brig.
Scene 3: Conservatory of Sir Evelyn's Home, England.

PERIOD AND COSTUMES: The 1930's with all the fashions of the day as worn by the ship's passengers, including girls' pants, slumber helmets, pleated skirts, and chorus costumes. Also sailor dress white uniforms, deck shorts/tunic outfits, entertainer gowns, black parson's suit, collar and hat, evening wear, and various business suits and disguises.

CHOREOGRAPHY: Tap, kick line, "Heaven Hop," soft shoe, and production numbers.

LIGHTING AND SPECIAL EFFECTS: General lighting.

NOTES: The above describes the 1962 revival in which additional songs from other Cole Porter shows were slickly included with great success. It is this version that is generally available for stock and amateur productions. For the record, the original production had only 12 songs of which several were reprised. In this revival "The Gypsy and Me" has been deleted. The songs added are "It's Delovely" from *Red Hot and Blue*, "Friendship" from *DuBarry Was a Lady*, "Let's Do It" and "Heaven Hop" from *Paris*, "Take Me Back to Manhattan" from *The New Yorkers*, and "Let's Step Out" from *Fifty Million Frenchmen*.

APPLAUSE

Charles Strouse (Music), Betty
Comden, Adolph Green (Book), Lee
Adams (Lyrics)
Opened March 30, 1970

BASED ON: "All About Eve" and Original Story by Mary Orr

AGENT: Tams-Witmark

PUBLISHED TEXT: Random House, 1971

RECORDINGS: ABC-OCS-11

DIGEST OF PLOT: Veteran actress Margo Channing is really acting as she presents the Tony Award to Eve, a new star at Margo's expense. They first met after opening night of Margo's last show a year and a half ago. Eve seemed to be just a delightful girl down on her luck. She played Margo's ego just right, stepping in just as Margo's director and fiancé, Bill Sampson, was departing for Rome to do a film. Soon Eve and Margo were inseparable. Margo's friends were now Eve's friends. When Eve helped sway Margo from taking Christmas week off to visit Bill in Rome, she attracted the eye of Eve's producer, Howard Benidict. She was so eager to learn and found Howard's company stimulating. At Bill's welcome home party Margo began to feel the drift in the wind. Eve had muscled in as her understudy and Margo was suffering an acute case of self-preservation. Bill's lack of concern and compassion led to a bitter quarrel and Bill's exit from their marriage plans. Following the breakup, Margo was in Connecticut visiting playwright-friend Buzz Richards and wife Karen. Karen felt Margo behaved unfairly toward Eve and arranged for Margo to get stranded in the country. Eve went on in her place to become an overnight star. Eve's press interviews were anything but kind to Margo. Reading them, Bill realized that Margo's fears of Eve were well-founded and returned to her for an unsuccessful attempt at forgiveness. Eve wanted all the status symbols, including Bill. Coldly rejected she turns to Buzz to promote a play she could call her own. She won the play and now the Tony Award. However, the award winner is claimed by Howard. Margo is sober to the occasion until her mind finally focuses on her release from the rigor of maintaining star status. At last there is a chance for happiness with Bill.

Lauren Bacall, Sammy Williams, and the boys of Applause.

MUSICAL NUMBERS: "Backstage Babble," "Think How It's Gonna Be," "But Alive," "The Best Night of My Life," "Who's That Girl?," "APPLAUSE," "Hurry Back," "Fasten Your Seat Belts," "Welcome to the Theatre," "Inner Thoughts," "Good Friends," "She's No Longer a Gypsy," "One of a Kind," "One Hallowe'en," "Something Greater"

Bonnie Franklin sings the title song from Applause.

INSTRUMENTATION: Violins 1–5, viola, cello, bass violin (fender bass), alto sax (clar, flute, piccolo, alto flute), alto sax (clar, flute, piccolo), tenor sax (clar, Eb clar, soprano sax), tenor sax (clar, bass clar, flute), bari sax (bassoon, clar, flute), trumpets (3, 1st trpt plays Maestro electronic unit), tenor trombones (2), bass trombone, percussion (2) guitar (banjo, mandolin), harp, piano, organ.

CASTING: 20 parts, 8 principals. Margo Channing—actress who sings and dances well, carries show. Eve—actress who sings well, minor dances. Bill—versatile actor-singer. Duane Fox—dancer who acts. Buzz and Karen—light comedy roles, good voices help. Howard—mature, straight role. Bonnie—strong song-and-dance gal, sings show's two best numbers. Chorus of 18 dancers, 8 singers. Total cast, 30–40.

SCENES AND SETS: 2 acts, 16 scenes, 7 full stage sets, 1 curtain drop, (Village Bar and Backstage sets are fly-ins. All other sets full stage wagon units.)

ACT I
Scene 1: The Tony Awards.
Scene 2: Margo's Dressing Room.
Scene 3: Village Bar.
Scene 4: Margo's Living Room.
Scene 5: Margo's Dressing Room.
Scene 6: Joe Allen's.
Scene 7: Margo's Bedroom.
Scene 8: Margo's Living Room.
Scene 9: Backstage.

ACT II
Scene 1: Buzz and Karen's Conn. Home.
Scene 2: Margo's Dressing Room.
Scene 3: Joe Allen's.
Scene 4: Margo's Living Room.

Scene 5: Backstage.
Scene 6: Margo's Dressing Room.
Scene 7: Backstage.

PERIOD AND COSTUMES: The present—latest wild evening fashions, "in" gowns and men's wear, rehearsal clothes, casual clothes for Bill, coats, dresses, suits, everyday wear. Lounging robes, winter casual clothes, waiter uniforms, leather jackets, and far-out garb for "Village boys."

CHOREOGRAPHY: Modern, jazz, "Applause" and "She's No Longer a Gypsy" production numbers, feature solos in several numbers.

LIGHTING AND SPECIAL EFFECTS: Video-tape of Tony Awards wired to several monitors around theatre (could be sound only). Mostly general lighting. Colored lighting effects in Village Bar scene.

NOTES: *Applause* is a good example of a formula musical geared to the "in" sophisticates of New York. It received unanimous rave reviews at a time when not so "in" formula shows were being bombed by the critics at every turn. Outstanding female lead required.

APPLE TREE, THE

Jerry Bock (Music), Sheldon Harnick, Jerry Bock (Book), Sheldon Harnick (Lyrics)
Opened Oct. 18, 1966
463 Performances

BASED ON: Stories by Mark Twain, Frank R. Stockton, and Jules Feiffer

AGENT: Music Theatre

PUBLISHED TEXT: Random House, 1967

RECORDINGS: COL KOL-6620
COL KOS-3020

DIGEST OF PLOT: *The Apple Tree* consists of 3 one-act musicals. *The Diary of Adam and Eve* is a charming and beautiful twist to the Bible story with Eve dominating Adam's right to name all living things as she interjects herself into Adam's heretofore uncomplicated life in Eden. *The Lady and the Tiger* presents the age-old tale of the victorious warrior Sanjar, who makes the supreme mistake of loving the King's daughter, and getting caught. For his trial he must choose between two doors—behind one a beautiful girl; behind the other a ferocious tiger. Barbara learns which door is which. After a tormented decision (love for him—life; jealousy of the other woman—death), she gives Sanjar a sign. Which door did she choose—lady or tiger? *Passionella* is a chimney sweep rendered unemployed by automation. She whiles away her time in front of her TV set yearning to be a movie star. Her TV-oriented neighborhood fairy godmother appears and grants her every wish—between the hours of the evening

news and the late late show. As a star she finds fame hollow until she meets an earthy rock 'n' roll singer named Flip. She adopts a new humble image and wins an Oscar. Passionella and Flip are married, only to discover that they both subscribe to the same neighborhood fairy godmother.

MUSICAL NUMBERS: "Here in Eden," "Feelings," "Eve," "Friends," "The Apple Tree," "Beautiful, Beautiful World," "It's a Fish," "Go to Sleep, Whatever You Are," "What Makes Me Love Him," "I'll Tell You a Truth," "Make Way," "Forbidden Love," "I've Got What You Want," "Tiger, Tiger," "Which Door?," "Oh, to Be a Movie Star," "Gorgeous," "(Who, Who, Who, Who,) Who Is She?," "Wealth," "You Are Not Real," "George L."

INSTRUMENTATION: Violin, viola, cello, bass, flute (pic, clar, melodica, alto sax, E♭ clar), G flute (C flute, clar, pic, alto sax), oboe (bass clar, clar, Eng. horn, tenor sax), flute (clar, tenor sax), bassoon (clar, bass clar, bari sax), trumpet I–II, III, trombone I, II, III, guitar, harp, percussion I–II, piano-conductor.

CASTING: 6 parts, 3 strong leads (two males, one girl) versatile enough to play three parts or nine people to be type-cast in the three independent sequences. The girl and younger male must have good strong singing voices. Chorus, 10–16 members.

SCENES AND SETS: Three parts, Part I: *The Diary of Adam and Eve*. Symbolized garden-post-like tree for climbing, mound of flowers, 2 portable lean-to shelters (1 plain, 1 decorated), a more permanent shelter, apple tree in distance (scrim optional). Assorted set pieces. Part II: *The Lady and the Tiger*. 2 stylized doors, partitioned, feather drop, steps, doors, and set pieces. Part III: *Passionella*. Rooftop and chimney and Ella's room, tinsel drop, painted Hollywood drop, and large Oscar statue.

PERIOD AND COSTUMES: Adam and Eve, plain modern-day dress, sports shirt, slacks, plus tux for devil. Lady and the Tiger, brief, feathered and jeweled, Arabian-Nights-like. Passionella, special gowns, evening wear, leather jackets and pants, costumes for doubles.

CHOREOGRAPHY: Adam and Eve, none. Lady and the Tiger, 1 wild whip-cracking number, choreographed pantomiming of the two-door justice of the land. Passionella, modern, discothèque.

LIGHTING AND SPECIAL EFFECTS: Scrim helpful in Adam and Eve. Passionella loaded with flash pots, doubles, rear projected film in background, etc. The original sets for *The Apple Tree* were cast plastic with self-contained lights similar to modern gasoline service station signs.

NOTES: Three one-act musicals is a novel approach, which works well in *The Apple Tree*. Probably works better if the same actors play all three segments.

Flip (Alan Alda) sings "You Are Not Real" to Passionella (Barbara Harris) from The Apple Tree.

BAKER STREET

Marian Grundeff, Raymond Jessel (Music, Lyrics), Jerome Coppersmith (Book)

Opened Feb. 16, 1965
313 Performances

BASED ON: Stories by Sir Arthur Conan Doyle

AGENT: Tams-Witmark

PUBLISHED TEXT: Doubleday, 1966

RECORDINGS: MGM (S)7000-OC

DIGEST OF PLOT: *Baker Street* is an evening with Sherlock Holmes—a sequence of events that begins with an attempt on the master sleuth's life. The bullet fells a dummy, and Holmes appears from underneath a beggar's disguise to accost his would-be killer. Next it is a quest for love letters, which brings him in contact with one of the rare Holmes romantic interests, actress Irene Adler. Beneath all this diversion Holmes begins to sense an underlying plot to keep him occupied while something bigger is taking place. Holmes and Irene embark, disguised once again, on a search of London's underworld. They are getting too close to Professor Moriarty's plot to steal the Crown Jewels. Holmes is captured, but Irene escapes with the aid of a Holmes agent, who is then killed. The vicious Professor also captures Dr. Watson and leaves them to be destroyed by a tamper-proo. .me bomb. Irene manages to get the word of Holmes's danger to the Baker Street Irregulars, a band of teen-age boys that he employs from time to time. They come to his aid moments before the bomb is to go off. Once freed, Holmes quickly sizes up the device and discovers a way to keep it from going off. He tracks down Moriarty on the Cliffs of Dover and engages the Professor in hand-to-hand combat. The Professor is overcome and falls from the foggy heights. Holmes's next deduction is the hideout where the jewels are hidden. He arrives there with the police, who capture Moriarty's gang and recover the gems.

MUSICAL NUMBERS: "It's So Simple," "I'm in London Again," "Leave It to Us, Guv," "Letters," "Cold Clear World," "Finding Words for Spring," "What a Night This Is Going to Be," "London Underworld," "I Shall Miss You," "Roof Space," "A MARRIED MAN," "I'd Do It Again," "Pursuit," "Jewelry."

INSTRUMENTATION: Violins (3), viola, cello, bass, flute (pic, clar), flute (pic, clar, alto flute, E♭ clar), oboe (Eng. horn), clar (bassoon), horns I–II, trumpets I–II, III, trombone I, II (euphonium), percussion I–II, harp, organ-celeste (organ-conductor).

CASTING: 19 parts, 6 principals. Sherlock Holmes, actor who sings. Dr. Watson, character man. Irene Adler, legit soprano, good lead voice. Professor Moriarty, the heavy, sings but voice is not required. Baker Street Irregulars, 6 to 8 spirited teen-age boy dancers. Chorus of 10 to 20. Total cast, 35–45.

SCENES AND SETS: 2 acts, 16 scenes, 8 full stage sets, 2 drops, 1 coach set piece, Cliffs of Dover insert set. In the New York production the sets were a large part of the show.

ACT I
Prologue: Baker Street, London.
Scene 1: Baker Street Flat.
Scene 2: Stage of the Theatre Royal.
Scene 3: Backstage at Theatre Royal.
Scene 4: An Alley in Baker Street.
Scene 5: Irene's Flat.

Scene 6: Baker Street Flat.
Scene 7: London Underworld.
Scene 8: Moriarty's Ship.

ACT II
Scene 1: A Street in London.
Scene 2: Moriarty's Ship
Scene 3: Interior of a Carriage.
Scene 4: The Cliffs of Dover.
Scene 5: A Part of London.
Scene 6: Baker Street Flat.
Scene 7: A Hall in London.
Scene 8: Baker Street.

PERIOD AND COSTUMES: Late 19th-Century London: traditional Holmes costumes, clever disguises, class and peasant wear of the times, house coats, costume dress wear for "Jewelry" number.

CHOREOGRAPHY: Modern, 2 production numbers, some ballet.

LIGHTING AND SPECIAL EFFECTS: Fog, tightly controlled lighting, gunshots, horses' hoofs and bouncing carriage interior, numerous rigged set pieces. Day and night exteriors. One drop in New York production displayed rooftop view of a parade —all the figures in the parade were marionettes by Bil Baird.

NOTES: There is a lot of extraneous material in *Baker Street;* however, proper pruning, timing, and a spectacular production can make it a memorable experience. Truly a set designer's show.

BELLS ARE RINGING

Jule Styne (Music), Betty Comden, Adolph Green (Book, Lyrics)
Opened Nov. 29, 1956
925 Performances

BASED ON: Original

AGENT: Tams-Witmark

PUBLISHED TEXT: Random House, 1956; *Theatre Arts,* April, 1959

RECORDINGS: COL OL 5170
COL OS 2006

DIGEST OF PLOT: Ella, a charming and heartwarming switchboard operator, gets tangled up with her clients' private lives as she performs her duties for Susanserphone Answering Service. She falls in love with Plaza O-double 4-double 3, a writer named Jeff Moss who is currently battling the bottle and blank sheets of paper. Jeff believes the person on the other end of the line is an old lady, whom he trusts for guidance. For all her flirtations with the clients, Ella is suspected of running a vice ring. Under pressure of the police, Ella is forced to go personally to Jeff's apartment to wake him up for an important appointment. Meanwhile, Sue, the owner of the answering service, rents part of the building to her boy friend Sandor's Titanic Record Company. It turns out the record company is the front for a bookmaking ring. All goes well until Titanic receives an order for Beethoven's Tenth Symphony. By this time Jeff is in love with Ella and escorting her to the best parties. Ella realizes that she can't lead this kind of life and runs off into the night. Searching for her, Jeff comes upon Dr. Kitchell and Blake Barton, who have also been straightened out by Ella. When they come to this realization, Jeff bolts for Susanserphone just in time to express his love and prevent Ella from leaving town.

MUSICAL NUMBERS: "It's a Perfect Relationship," "On My Own," "You've Got to Do It," "It's a Simple Little System," "Is It a Crime?," "Hello, Hello There," "I Met a Girl," "LONG BEFORE I KNEW YOU," "Mu-cha-cha," "JUST IN TIME," "Drop That Name," "THE PARTY'S OVER," "Salzburg," "The Midas Touch," "I'm Goin' Back."

INSTRUMENTATION: Violins A-C, B-D, viola, cello, bass, clar (alto sax, flute), clar (alto sax, flute, pic), clar (sax, oboe, Eng. horn), clar (bass clar, sax, bass sax), clar (tenor sax, bassoon), horns I–II, trumpets I–II, III, trombone I, II, percussion, harp, piano, guitar.

CASTING: 17 parts, 10 principals. Ella, comic lead, sympathetic, good voice. Jeff, handsome leading man, good voice. Sandor, good character man required. Carol and Carl, lead dancers. 5 other principals, mostly straight acting with some singing and character work. Large chorus and substantial choral work. Total cast, 45–55.

SCENES AND SETS: 2 acts, 22 scenes, 6 full stage sets, 5 drops, 2 partial sets (1 set and 1 drop could be eliminated by doubling with slight changes in decor), telephone booth.

ACT I
Opening
Scene 1: Office of Susanserphone. Late Afternoon.
Scene 2: Jeff Moss's Living Room.
Scene 3: An Alley at Night.
Scene 4: The Office. Early Morning.
Scene 5: A Street in Front of the Office.
Scene 6: Jeff Moss's Living Room.
Scene 7: A Street.
Scene 8: A Subway Car.
Scene 9: A Street.
Scene 10: Dr. Kitchell's Office.
Scene 11: A Street.
Scene 12: A Drugstore.
Scene 13: A Street.
Scene 14: The Office. A Week Later.
Scene 15: Jeff Moss's Living Room.

ACT II
Scene 1: The Office. The Next Night.
Scene 2: The Park.

Scene 3: Larry Hastings' Penthouse.
Scene 4: The "Crying Gypsy" Café.
Scene 5: The "Pyramid" Nightclub.
Scene 6: Bay Ridge Subway Platform.
Scene 7: The Office.

PERIOD AND COSTUMES: The present, New York City: office clothes, evening wear, leather jackets, various uniforms (10–20), dentist smock, *La Traviata* dress, and brief nightclub chorus girl costumes.

CHOREOGRAPHY: Jazz, cha-cha, production numbers, soft shoe, the works.

LIGHTING AND SPECIAL EFFECTS: Crossfade essential, day and night exteriors, moving subway effects.

NOTES: A great show totally destroyed in the movie version. Some minor book updating of topical material might be helpful.

BEN FRANKLIN IN PARIS

Mark Sandrich, Jr. (Music)
Sidney Michaels (Lyrics, Book)
Opened Oct. 27, 1964
215 Performances

BASED ON: Original

AGENT: Samuel French

PUBLISHED TEXT: Random House, 1965

RECORDINGS: CAP VAS(SVAS)-2191

DIGEST OF PLOT: Ben Franklin arrives in Paris with his two grandsons seeking support for the Colonies' war against England. He quickly wins the friendship and popularity of the French court, but winning the King's recognition and support is another matter. Ben learns that an old friend, Madame La Comtesse Diane de Vobrillac, is close to the King. He appeals to her romantic nature, but now as a confidante to King Louis XVI, Diane is more practical. She demands more proof that America is not a losing proposition—it must win a battle. Franklin's hopes seem dashed when the British capture Philadelphia. Diane won't see or talk with Franklin, but he manages to trick her up into a hot-air balloon. Alone in the gondola, he gets her to agree to winning a battle of a different sort—to get another major power to split the cost of financing America's war effort. Believing it impossible, she agrees. The Spanish ambassador hears of Franklin's mission to involve Spain as the second ally and avoids him at all costs. The persistent Franklin arranges an encounter at the Abbey de Morellet amid a flowing grape harvest. After several toasts, the ambassador becomes friendly and agrees to fund arms and supplies. With this help the tide of the war begins to change. The Colonists defeat the British at Saratoga. This is all Ben needs to sway the King. But the

British have countered by winning over Ben's son William, the governor of New Jersey. The traitorous act pulls the rug from under Ben's plan. To regain the upper hand he offers to marry Diane, but is rejected. As a final effort Ben prepares to go to England where he knows he will be hanged—an act of martyrdom he feels sure the French could not overlook. However, Diane learns of the plan and intercedes with the King. Soon thereafter the King summons Benjamin Franklin, not the Philadelphian, but the Ambassador of the United States of America.

MUSICAL NUMBERS: "We Sail the Seas," "I Invented Myself," "Too Charming," "Since Last We Talked Alone," "Half the Battle," " 'Tis Incredible as Love," "Whatever Became of Old Temple?," "A Balloon Is Ascending," "To Be Alone with You," "You're in Paris," "How Laughable It Is," "Hic Haec Hoc," "God Bless the Human Elbow," "When I Dance with the Person I Love," "We've Got the British Lion by the Tail," "Diane Is," "Look for Small Pleasures," "I Love the Ladies."

INSTRUMENTATION: Violins A, B, C, viola, cello, bass, reeds I–V, horn I–II, trumpet I–II, III, trombone I–II, harp, percussion.

CASTING: 23 parts, 10 principals. Ben Franklin, must act, sing, and move well. Onstage most of the time. Diane, sings and acts. Temple Franklin, acting and singing are not rigorous. Same for Benny Franklin Bache, a boy of 7 or 8. Janine, teen-age girl who sings. Other principals have minor roles. Ben carries almost everything. Large chorus of 20 to 30 members. Total cast, 30–50.

SCENES AND SETS: Prologue, 2 acts, 14 scenes, 7 full sets, 3 drops (including one that rolls off batten to give the illusion of a balloon ascending), and the balloon.

ACT I
Prologue
Scene 1: The Docks.
Scene 2: Versailles.
Scene 3: A Paris Street.
Scene 4: Ben's House.
Scene 5: The Park.
Scene 6: Sky Over Paris.
Scene 7: The Pont Neuf.
Scene 8: Paristown.
Scene 9: The Pont Neuf.
Scene 10: Ben's House.
Scene 11: The Vineyards.

ACT II
Scene 1: The Spanish Embassy.
Scene 2: A Paris Street.
Scene 3: Versailles.
Scene 4: Diane's House.
Scene 5: Ben's House.
Scene 6: Versailles.

PERIOD AND COSTUMES: France, 1776–77: powdered wigs, satin hoop skirts, breeches, vests, and long coats befitting the French court. Sailor outfits, maiden dresses, monks' robes, more casual dress for the townsfolk, and a large cast for Ben's leg.

CHOREOGRAPHY: Mostly choreographed movement, some soft shoe, waltz, and precision marching extending into some dance rhythms. Frolic when Ben gets the Spanish ambassador drunk at the monks' abbey.

LIGHTING AND SPECIAL EFFECTS: Ascending balloon with its two passengers. Versatile lighting equipment. Exterior lightning and thunderstorm.

NOTES: Like the musical *1776, Ben Franklin in Paris* is the spirit of factual history. Although Diane represents four ladies whom Franklin used to America's advantage, and a certain amount of dramatic license has been taken, the play is mostly historically correct—with much of the dialogue interpolated from Franklin's own words. It was not a smash hit, but certainly deserves many, many more performances than it has been getting. The show can be tightened in many areas. Several "in-one" scenes can be trimmed drastically—also suggest eliminating the "You're in Paris" number (Act I, Scene 8) and the opening dance in Scene 9, which are not only extraneous, but damaging.

BLOOMER GIRL

Harold Arlen (Music), E. Y. Harburg (Lyrics), Sig Herzig, Fred Saidy (Book)

Opened Oct. 5, 1944
653 Performances

BASED ON: A play by Dan Lilith James

AGENT: Tams-Witmark

PUBLISHED TEXT: Manuscript Only

RECORDINGS: DEC(7)9126

DIGEST OF PLOT: Horatio Applegate, hoop-skirt manufacturer, cleverly marries five of his six daughters to hoop-skirt salesmen. However, the sixth daughter, Evelina, falls under the influence of her Aunt Dolly Bloomer, passionate suffragette and the originator of bloomers. Horatio decides the best way to straighten Evelina out is to get her married. He selects handsome Jefferson Lightfoot Calhoon of his Kentucky sales district. Evelina is interested in Jeff but is suspicious of any hoop-skirt salesmen. To test him, she has him free his personal slave, Pompey. While this is getting Jeff into trouble, Evelina is off leading a parade of Aunt Dolly's bloomer girls and she herself lands in jail. It takes Aunt Dolly's old suitor, the governor, to set everything straight. Evelina and Jeff settle down to romance just as the first shots of the Civil War are sounded.

On the village green with the original cast of Bloomer Girl.

MUSICAL NUMBERS: "When the Boys Come Home," "Evelina," "Welcome Hinges," "Farmer's Daughter," "It Was Good Enough for Grandma," "The Eagle and Me," "RIGHT AS THE RAIN," "T'morra' T'morra'," "Rakish Young Man with the Whiskahs," "Pretty as a Picture," Waltz, Style Show Ballet, "Sunday in Cicero Falls," "I Got a Song," "Simon Legree," "Liza Crossing the Ice," "I Never Was Born," "Man for Sale," Civil War Ballet.

INSTRUMENTATION: Violin A, B, C, D, viola, cello, bass, flute I, II (pic), oboe, clar I–II, bassoon, trumpets I–II, trombone I, II, percussion, piano, piano-conductor.

CASTING: 31 parts, 11 principals, several featured dancers. Serena, actress who sings. Evelina and Jeff, romantic leads who sing, minor dancing. Dolly, powerful character woman, minor singing. Horatio, good character man who sings. Daisy, good singer-actress. Pompey, Negro slave who sings and dances. Sheriff, Hamilton, and Gus, straight roles. Alexander, sings one number. Large singing and dancing chorus. Total cast, 45–55.

SCENES AND SETS: The action takes place in Cicero Falls, a small eastern manufacturing town. 2 acts, 10 scenes, 5 full stage sets, 2 partial stage sets, 3 scenic drops.

ACT I
Scene 1: Conservatory of the Applegate Mansion.
Scene 2: Applegate Bathroom.
Scene 3: The Lily.
Scene 4: Hedge Outside Applegate Estate.
Scene 5: Yellow Pavilion.
Scene 6: Applegate Garden.

ACT II
Scene 1: The Village Green.
Scene 2: Corridor of the Town Jail.
Scene 3: Cicero Falls Opera House.
Scene 4: Conservatory of the Applegate Mansion.

PERIOD AND COSTUMES: Spring of 1861: hoop skirts, bloomer ensembles, male suits, and casual wear of the time. Appropriate dress for the sheriff and three deputies, the governor, and the slave, Pompey.

CHOREOGRAPHY: Waltz, Civil War and Style Show ballets, dance specialties, parades.

LIGHTING AND SPECIAL EFFECTS: Mostly general lighting, tight lighting on partial stage set.

NOTES: Probably one of the first musicals to touch on the racial issue, it remains somewhat timely. The show is historical in nature, but entirely fictional.

Bobby asks Maisie "Won't You Charleston With Me?" in the 1969 revival production of
The Boy Friend.

THE BOY FRIEND

Sandy Wilson (Music, Book, Lyrics)
Opened Sept. 30, 1954
485 Performances

BASED ON: Original

AGENT: Music Theatre

PUBLISHED TEXT: Manuscript Only

RECORDINGS: RCA LOC-1018

DIGEST OF PLOT: A spoof of 1920's musicals. Polly, the daughter of a millionaire in Madam DuBonnet's fashionable finishing school on the French Riviera, falls in love with Tony, who delivers her costume for the school's big masquerade ball. Feeling Tony would be interested in her only for her money, Polly assumes the role of the school's secretary. About this time, Lord and Lady Brockhurst arrive on the Riviera searching for their long-lost son, who

is, of course, Tony. Subplots find Lord Brockhurst having a delightful time with all the young ladies, a rekindled romance between Polly's father and Madam DuBonnet, and all the girls and their boy friends finding a utopian ending in fun and romance.

MUSICAL NUMBERS: "Perfect Young Ladies," "The Boy Friend," "Won't You Charleston with Me?," "Fancy Forgetting," "I Could Be Happy with You," "Sur la Plage," "A Room in Bloomsbury," "You Don't Want to Play with Me Blues," "Safety in Numbers," "Riviera," "It's Never Too Late to Fall in Love," Carnival Tango, "Poor Little Pierrette," "It's Nice In Nice" (added in 1970 revival.)

INSTRUMENTATION: Violin A, B, clar (sax), bass clar (bass sax), trumpet, trombone, percussion, bass, banjo.

CASTING: 25 parts, 10 principals. Polly, legitimate voice, some dancing. Tony, legitimate voice, some dancing. Maisie, cute comic, dances. Dulcie, sexy comic, dances. Bobby, song-and-dance man. Lord Brockhurst, character man. Three other principals, straight roles. Chorus of 20–24. Total cast, 30–34.

SCENES AND SETS: 3 acts, 3 sets.

ACT I
The Drawing Room of the Villa Caprice, Madam DuBonnet's Finishing School on the Outskirts of Nice, 1926.

ACT II
The Plage. That Afternoon.

ACT III
The Terrace of the Café Pataplon. That Night.

PERIOD AND COSTUMES: The French Riviera, the roaring 20's: flapper dresses, blazers, white pants, suits, long swim suits, big hats, masquerade costumes, maid and bellboy uniforms, and tango costumes.

CHOREOGRAPHY: Charleston, cake walk, tango, "The Riviera" (as described in the song), soft shoe, waltz, overacted movement.

LIGHTING AND SPECIAL EFFECTS: General lighting.

NOTES: Direction MUST be very stylized. The show is nothing if played straight. All the old bits . . . you're right when the audience say "Oh, no!" to themselves and then laugh . . . overacting, cartoon makeup, etc.

BRIGADOON

Fredrick Loewe (Music),
Allan Jay Lerner (Lyrics, Book)
Opened March 13, 1947
581 Performances

BASED ON: Original

AGENT: Tams-Witmark

PUBLISHED TEXT: *Theatre Arts,* August 1952; Coward-McCann, Inc. 1947

RECORDINGS: COL CL-1132
RCA LOC-1001 (OC)
MGM E-3135 (F)

DIGEST OF PLOT: On a hunting expedition in the Scottish Highlands, Tommy and Jeff come upon a small village, unlisted on their map. They discover that it's an enchanted village that comes to life for only a single day each 100 years. They arrive amid a wedding feast and join in the festivities. The American, Tommy, falls deeply in love with Fiona, and laughter finds its way to this strange land as Meg pursues the attentions of Jeff. All is nearly lost as Harry Beaton tries to cross the bridge that would doom Brigadoon forever. But Jeff saves the day, stopping Harry at the foot of the bridge. In the struggle that follows, Harry strikes his head on a boulder and is killed. As Brigadoon's day ends, Tommy leaves his love to return to New York and his fiancée. But he is haunted by his love for Fiona. He breaks his engagement and returns to the Highlands, where, by the power of his love, he reawakens the slumbering town long enough to rejoin Fiona.

MUSICAL NUMBERS: "Once in the Highlands," "BRIGADOON," "Down on MacConnachy Square," "Waitin' for My Dearie," "I'll Go Home with Bonnie Jean," Dance, "THE HEATHER ON THE HILL," "The Love of My Life," "Jeannie's Packin' Up," "COME TO ME, BEND TO ME," Dance, "ALMOST LIKE BEING IN LOVE," The Wedding Dance, Sword Dance, "The Chase," "There but for You Go I," "My Mother's Weddin' Day," Funeral Dance, "From This Day On."

INSTRUMENTATION: Violin A, B-C, viola, cello, bass, flute (pic, alto flute), oboe, clar I, II, bassoon, horn, trumpets I–II, III, trombone, percussion, piano, piano-conductor.

CASTING: 18 parts, 7 principals. Tommy Albright and Fiona MacLaren, romantic leads; both must sing well. Jeff Douglas, comic, does not sing. Meg Brockie, female comic, sings. Harry Beaton, dancer with dialogue. Mr. Lundie, straight role. Charlie, Irish tenor, excellent voice with control. Strong choral work; several good voices required. Total cast, 30–46.

SCENES AND SETS: 2 acts, 11 scenes, 9 sets in original production, could be done with 7. Use of a painted scrim advisable. New York bar set rolls in front of scrim.

ACT I
Prologue
Scene 1: A Forest in the Scottish Highlands, About 5 on a May Morning.
Scene 2: A Road in Brigadoon, Then the Village Square—MacConnachy Square—Later the Same Morning.
Scene 3: An Open Shed, About Noon.
Scene 4: The MacLaren House, Midafternoon.
Scene 5: Outside Mr. Lundie's House.
Scene 6: The Churchyard, Dusk.

ACT II
Scene 1: A Forest Inside Brigadoon, Later at Night.
Scene 2: A Road in Brigadoon.
Scene 3: The Glen, Immediately After.
Scene 4: A Bar in New York City, Four Months Later.
Scene 5: The Forest—Same as Scene 1 of Act I —Three Days Later.

PERIOD AND COSTUMES: Modern English hunting and day wear, plus 18th-Century Scottish Highlands: kilts, dresses, peasant wear, wedding garments.

The Sword Dance in MacConnachy Square from the original production of Brigadoon.

CHOREOGRAPHY: Sword ritual dance, chase, and Highland Fling. Research should be done on sword dance, wedding dance, and funeral.

LIGHTING AND SPECIAL EFFECTS: Fog, City appearing and disappearing (scrim). Tight control colored lighting changes during the chase to catch Harry Beaton.

NOTES: *Brigadoon* is a large-looking musical with a very flexible cast size. It can be performed well by just about any group without the casting looking out of place. To add to its attractiveness it is a relatively easy production to mount. Drops carry a large portion of the scenery. And good *Brigadoon* drops can be rented. Bagpipe players were used in the original and revival productions, but are not at all necessary.

BYE BYE BIRDIE

Charles Strouse (Music), Lee Adams (Lyrics), Michael Stewart (Book)
Opened April 14, 1960
608 Performances

BASED ON: Original

AGENT: Tams-Witmark

PUBLISHED TEXT: D. B. S. Publications, 1968

RECORDINGS: COL-5510
COL OS-2025
RCA LOC-1081 (F)
RCA KOS-3040 (F)

DIGEST OF PLOT: The long-postponed wedding of theatrical agent Albert Peterson and his fiancée, Rosie, finally looms a reality when Conrad Birdie, Albert's idol rock 'n' roll singer-client is drafted. Once Conrad departs, Albert is planning to give up show biz in favor of a steady job and the security of being an English teacher. Before Conrad's induction, however, Albert plans a spectacular publicity-minded goodbye kiss to a typical American girl on the country's most popular TV variety show. The entourage departs for Sweet Apple, Ohio, where the chosen girl, Kim MacAfee, has trouble convincing her steady boy friend, Hugo, that this kiss doesn't mean anything. In fact, Hugo crashes the TV show and knocks Conrad cold. Birdie's idol image shattered, he takes off for a night on the town to see what it's really like to be a teen-ager. Rosie sees her chance of marriage going down the drain and likewise departs for the freedom of a natural life. Albert is stuck with his defeatist, ailment-ridden mother who has followed him from New York. The parents of Sweet Apple call out the guards to protect their children from Conrad's big-city ideas. Actually it's Conrad who is shying from the girls' advances. Albert has it out with Mama and arrives at the ice house hideout just in time to come to Conrad's aid. The parents, police, and Rosie are close on Albert's heels. Conrad is arrested. Albert orders Rosie to pack all their bags and meet him at the railway station at 6:30 A.M. At the appointed time Rosie arrives to find Albert has packed the released Conrad and Mama off to New York on the 6:25 and has two tickets for Pumpkin Falls, Iowa, where he will become an English teacher at last.

MUSICAL NUMBERS: "An English Teacher," "The Telephone Hour," "How Lovely to Be a Woman," "We Love You, Conrad," "PUT ON A HAPPY FACE," "Normal American Boy," "One Boy," "Honestly Sincere," "Hymn for a Sunday Evening," Ballet: "How to Kill a Man," "One Last Kiss," "What Did I Ever See in Him?," "A Lot of Livin' to Do," "KIDS," "Baby, Talk to Me," Shriners' Ballet, "Spanish Rose," "Rosie."

INSTRUMENTATION: Violin A–B, C, cello, bass, alto sax (clar, flute, pic), alto sax (clar), tenor sax (clar, bass clar), bari sax (clar), horn, trumpets I–II, III, trombone I, II, guitar-bass guitar (banjo), percussion, piano-conductor.

CASTING: 20 parts, 8 principals. Albert, situation comic who must also sing and dance well. Rosie, sings and dances. Kim, sings. Mr. MacAfee, nervous comic, strong character man. Mae, solid, grim comedienne. Conrad Birdie, rock 'n' roll singer who acts slovenly, helps if he can play (or beat) the guitar.

Dick Gautier as Conrad Birdie dazzles the crowd on the courthouse steps of Sweet Apple, Ohio.

COURTESY OF DRAMATICS MAGAZINE

Large teen-age singing and dancing chorus and other adults. Total cast, 30–60.

COURTESY OF DRAMATICS MAGAZINE

Chita Rivera (Rose) and Dick Van Dyke (Albert) in front of Birdie poster notify Kim MacAfee that she has won Birdie's last kiss.

SCENES AND SETS: 2 acts, 18 scenes, 9 full stage sets (including 2-room office, 2-story house, and 3-level telephone set, others are flown in), 2 partial sets, 2 drops, railway car (rear only).

ACT I
Scene 1: Office of Almaelou Music Corp., New York.
Scene 2: Sweet Apple, Ohio.
Scene 3: MacAfee Home.
Scene 4: Pennsylvania Station, New York.
Scene 5: Railroad Station, Sweet Apple.
Scene 6: Courthouse Steps.
Scene 7: MacAfee Home.
Scene 8: Stage of Central Movie Theatre, Backstage Office.
Scene 9: Stage of Central Movie Theatre.

ACT II
Scene 1: MacAfee Home, Kim's Bedroom.
Scene 2: MacAfee Home.
Scene 3: Streets of Sweet Apple.
Scene 4: Maude's Roadside Retreat.
Scene 5: Maude's Private Dining Room.
Scene 6: Back Door, Maude's.
Scene 7: The Ice House.
Scene 8: Railroad Station.

PERIOD AND COSTUMES: The present: suits, dresses, current teen-age fashions (both slacks and dresses), well-worn mink coat, skin-tight gold lamé motorcycle costume and boots for Conrad, cheerleader uniforms, Shriners' fezzes, Spanish Rose costume, Conrad's casual clothes. Trench coats, bathrobes, pajamas, and one elaborate teen-age evening gown.

CHOREOGRAPHY: Latest rock dance fads, production numbers, modern ballet, modern, soft shoe.

LIGHTING AND SPECIAL EFFECTS: Tight lighting required on a few scenes. Self-contained, individual lights in telephone number set. Day and night lighting. Train effects.

NOTES: *Bye Bye Birdie* was a "sleeper" when it opened. Ever since, it has been a major musical attraction, particularly among high-school groups by whom it has been the most often produced musical for several years running. The show is highly topical—dealing with a rock music fad as applied to a generation gap. Rock is no longer just a fad, and a growing number of parents with teen-agers were part of the original rock movement. At this writing *Birdie* is still winning large appreciative audiences.

CABARET

John Kander (Music), Joe Masteroff (Book), Fred Ebb (Lyrics)
Opened Nov. 20, 1966
1,165 Performances

BASED ON: *I Am a Camera* by John van Druten and stories by Christopher Isherwood

AGENT: Tams-Witmark

PUBLISHED TEXT: Random House, 1967

RECORDINGS: COL KOL-6640
COL KOS-3040

DIGEST OF PLOT: Cliff, a young American writer, comes into the garish depravity of 1929–30 Germany—the eve of the Nazi takeover. He visits the Kit Kat Klub where he meets Sally Bowles, an English singer. She is impressed with Cliff and moves in on him. Their love affair is a fiery one—Sally's search for carefree pleasure versus Cliff's integrity. Romance also finds its way into the lives of Fraülein Schneider, Cliff's landlady, and Herr Schultz, Jewish fruit store owner. Their tender and fragile love results in an engagement party. At the party Fraülein Schneider is warned against marrying a Jew. Meanwhile Sally has become pregnant. Cliff teaches English and does petty smuggling, but money is still a problem. Sally wants to return to the job at the Klub. Their argument on the subject is interrupted by Fraülein Schneider who has

Prologue to Cabaret.

come to return their engagement gift. She has decided to sacrifice her love for the security of her rooming-house business. This is the last straw for Cliff, who tells Sally they will return to America. For Sally, life is her career in Berlin. She has an abortion and, despite last-minute pleas from Cliff, returns to the Cabaret. Throughout the show the perverted little Master of Ceremonies of the Kit Kat Klub keeps popping up for musical sequences. These numbers underscore the dramatic scenes that precede them—replaying the essence of the scene with added dramatic emphasis.

MUSICAL NUMBERS: "Willkommen," "So What?," "Don't Tell Mamma," "Telephone Song," "Perfectly Marvelous," "Two Ladies," "It Couldn't Please Me More," "Tomorrow Belongs to Me," "Why Should I Wake Up," "The Money Song," "Married," "Meeskite," "If You Could See Her," "What Would You Do?," "CABARET."

INSTRUMENTATION: Violins I–II (3), viola, cello, bass, pic (flute, E♭ clar, clar, alto sax, soprano sax), pic (flute, clar, soprano sax, alto sax), oboe (Eng. horn, clar, tenor sax), bassoon (clar, bass clar, bari sax), horn, trumpets I–II, trombone I, II, guitar (banjo), percussion, accordion-celeste, piano.

CASTING: 28 parts, 7 principals. Master of Ceremonies, dirty little man with good voice and acting ability. Cliff, good voice. Fraülein Schneider, actress. Sally Bowles, acts, sings, dances. Herr Schultz, simple character man. 2 other minor principals, 4-member female stage band (drums, trombone, sax, piano), accomplished singing-dancing chorus of 10 or 14. Several good male voices required for a cappella harmony number. Total cast, 40–56.

SCENES AND SETS: 2 acts, 4 full sets, 1 large mirror, 1 insert set (train compartment), plus permanent spiral staircase on stage left proscenium arch.

ACT I
Scene 1: Emcee's Welcome.
Scene 2: Compartment of a European Railway Train.
Scene 3: A Room in Fraülein Schneider's Flat.
Scene 4: Kit Kat Klub.
Scene 5: Cliff's Room.
Scene 6: Emcee's Comment.
Scene 7: Fraülein Schneider's Living Room.
Scene 8: Spiral Staircase.
Scene 9: Cliff's Room.
Scene 10: Emcee's Comment.
Scene 11: Fraülein Schneider's Living Room.
Scene 12: Herr Schultz's Shop.

ACT II
Scene 1: Emcee's Comment.
Scene 2: Herr Schultz's Shop.
Scene 3: Emcee's Comment.
Scene 4: Cliff's Room.
Scene 5: Kit Kat Klub.
Scene 6: Cliff's Room.
Scene 7: Compartment of a European Railway Train.
Scene 8: Emcee's Goodnight.

PERIOD AND COSTUMES: Berlin, Germany (1929–30), before the start of the Third Reich: coats and streetwear of the time, cabaret costumes, gaudy female evening wear, period sailor suits of various nations, Emcee costumes, chorus line, scant girlie costumes, gorilla suit with pink tutu.

CHOREOGRAPHY: Tap, modern, waltz, cabaret production numbers, kick line.

LIGHTING AND SPECIAL EFFECTS: Dramatic lighting required, cabaret set lighting, telephone effects, audience-aimed footlights (optional), large mirror, cabaret sign (optional), traveling train effects.

NOTES: *Cabaret* is a brilliant work with an innovative twist in that the cabaret musical numbers "instantly replay" the dramatic scenes preceding them. This is not obvious, however, and may confuse much of the audience who miss the connection. Tailoring the Emcee's lead-in lines to these segments may add some clarity. Also, much of *Cabaret* could be considered objectionable to those not understanding the degradation of Germany during this period.

CALAMITY JANE

Sammy Fain (Music), Charles Freeman (Book), Paul Webster (Lyrics)
Movie and TV

BASED ON: Screenplay by James O'Hanlon

AGENT: Tams-Witmark

PUBLISHED TEXT: Manuscript Only

DIGEST OF PLOT: Deadwood City's two most famous peace officers, Calamity Jane and Wild Bill Hickock, get involved in saving the neck of Henry Miller, the local saloon operator. It seems that "Millie" has been promoting a beautiful actress named Frances Fryer, but Frances turns out to be a boy, Francis. Millie's attempt to cover up is soon unmasked by the angry miners, and only Calamity can cool the crowd with her trusty pistols. To keep the peace, Calamity sets out for Chicago to bring back the miner's real heart-throb, Adelaide Adams. In Chicago Calamity mistakes Adelaide's maid, Katie Brown, for the actress and hauls her back to Deadwood. Onstage Katie is greeted warmingly, but breaks down and confesses that she is not the famous star. Calamity once more has to restore order and persuades the audience to give Katie a chance. They do, and she wins the heart of every male in town—including Calamity's dashing love hope, Lt. Danny Gilmartin. Calamity reluctantly overcomes her jealousy over losing Danny and discovers her true love for Wild Bill.

MUSICAL NUMBERS: "Deadwood Stage," "Adelaide," "Everyone Complains About the Weather," Weather Dance, "Men," "Careless with the Truth," "A Hive Full of Honey," Adelaide's Ballet, Weather Dance lesson, "I Can't Do Without You," " 'Tis Harry I'm Planning to Marry," "Windy City," "Keep It Under Your Hat," Exaggeration Ballet, "Higher Than a Hawk," "A Woman's Touch," "Love You Dearly," "The Black Hills of Dakota," "SECRET LOVE."

INSTRUMENTATION: Violin I (2), II, viola, cello, bass, clar (alto sax, flute), clar (alto sax), clar (tenor sax), clar (bass clar, bari sax), horns I–II, trumpets I–II, III, trombone I, II, guitar, percussion, piano-celeste.

CASTING: 17 parts, 6 principals. Calamity Jane, comic lead who sings and dances. Wild Bill Hickock, rugged he-man who sings, minor dance steps. Lt. Danny Gilmartin, handsome leading man who sings. Katie Brown, attractive gal who sings and dances. Francis Fryer, does female impersonation, sings, and dances. Henry Miller (Millie), character man. Total cast, 36–46.

SCENES AND SETS: 2 acts, 18 scenes, 5 full stage sets (including elaborate "Golden Garter" Saloon set complete with stage), 2 partial sets, 2 featured drops. (Note: Exterior of "Golden Garter" should revolve or fold into the interior for a smoother flow of action.)

ACT I
Scene 1: The Golden Garter—Daytime.
Scene 2: The Same—Nightime.
Scene 3: Later That Night.
Scene 4: The Golden Garter—Following Morning.

Scene 5: Chicago Street.
Scene 6: Adelaide's Dressing Room, Chicago.
Scene 7: Outside the Golden Garter.
Scene 8: Katie's Dressing Room at the Golden Garter.
Scene 9: The Golden Garter—Night.

ACT II
Scene 1: Outside the Golden Garter—Morning.
Scene 2: Outside and Inside Calamity's Cabin.
Scene 3: The Road to the Fort.
Scene 4: Ballroom of the Fort.
Scene 5: A Corner of a Garden Outside Ballroom.
Scene 7: Outside the Golden Garter—Night.
Scene 8: The Same—Morning.
Scene 9: The Golden Garter.

PERIOD AND COSTUMES: Old West, Deadwood City, Dakota Territory, 1876: buckskins, cowboy outfits, Western suits and hats of the period, frilly dresses, dance-hall girls' costumes, Army and Cavalry uniforms.

CHOREOGRAPHY: Modern, modern ballet, Western folk, barroom brawl.

LIGHTING AND SPECIAL EFFECTS: Calamity's cabin is transformed from ruin to a well-kept womanly home in the course of one number ("A Woman's Touch"). Trick shooting effects.

NOTES: The widely acceptable Western setting of *Calamity Jane* can be helped by pruning of extraneous material. A 90-minute television version, done in the mid-1960's, lost none of the show's impact. It's a wonder the recorded score for this exciting show is not available. The score will not disappoint anyone who would like to do the show but has refrained because of the music's being unknown.

CALL ME MADAM

Irving Berlin (Music, Lyrics) Howard Lindsay, Russel Crouse (Book)
Opened Oct. 12, 1950
644 Performances

BASED ON: Original

AGENT: Music Theatre

PUBLISHED TEXT: Manuscript Only

RECORDINGS: DEC-(7)9022

DIGEST OF PLOT: Sally Adams, Washington's "hostess with the mostes," is named Ambassador to the Grand Duchy of Lichtenburg—a tiny kingdom steeped in royal custom and rapidly changing coalition governments. Kenneth Gibson, an eager young diplomat, is assigned to be her aide. True to her almost total disrespect for protocol, Sally arrives late in Lichtenburg. There she encounters foreign minister Cosmo Constantine, not, however, to the degree her romantic nature would like. Worse yet, Cosmo refuses American foreign aid. Sally gets talked into a scheme to get Cosmo elevated to Prime Minister to make way for a new foreign minister eager to accept American money to "save" the country. When the loan is all but consummated, Cosmo finds out about it and resigns. This ruins all possibilities for another coalition, and the country must hold its first general election in twenty years. Sally openly campaigns for Cosmo, forcing her recall to Washington for becoming involved in another government's internal affairs. Kenneth, too, commits a grave diplomatic error by falling in love with the Princess Maria and arranging secret meetings with her. However, a spirit of democracy is over Lichtenburg. The princess is granted permission to ask Kenneth to marry her. Elected Prime Minister, Cosmo visits Sally in Washington to grant her the royal order of Dame—and revive their "acquaintance."

MUSICAL NUMBERS: "Mrs. Sally Adams," "The Hostess with the Mostes' on the Ball," "WASHINGTON SQUARE DANCE," "Lichtenburg," "Can You Use Any Money Today?," "Marrying for Love," "THE OCARINA," "IT'S A LOVELY DAY TODAY," "The Best Thing for You Would Be Me," "Something to Dance About," "Once Upon a Time Today," "They Like Ike," "YOU'RE JUST IN LOVE."

INSTRUMENTATION: Violins A–C, B–D, viola, cello, bass, pic (flute, clar, alto sax), alto sax (bass clar, clar), tenor sax (clar, oboe, Eng. horn), tenor sax (flute, clar), bari sax (alto sax, bass clar, bassoon, clar), horn, trumpet I–II, III, trombone I, II, percussion, guitar, piano-conductor.

CASTING: 20 speaking parts, 8 principals. Sally, carries the show with good acting and powerful voice. Kenneth, strong, handsome singer. Cosmo, warm character actor, sings little. Princess Maria, good voice. Three touring senators, mostly straight roles, but lead one number. Pemberton Maxwell, straight role. Four principal dancers. Several ocarina players. Separate singing and dancing choruses. Total cast, 30–45.

SCENES AND SETS: 2 acts, 13 scenes, 5 full stage sets, 3 drop sets, which are a series of painted cloth panels rather than 1-piece drops, and 1 partial stage set (Sally's sitting room in Lichtenburg).

ACT I
Scene 1: Office of the Secretary of State.
Scene 2: Sally's Living Room in Washington.
Scene 3: Public Square in Lichtenburg.
Scene 4: Reception Room in the American Embassy.
Scene 5: Public Square in Lichtenburg.
Scene 6: The Lichtenburg Fair.
Scene 7: A Corridor in the Palace.
Scene 8: Sally's Sitting Room in the Embassy.

ACT II
Scene 1: The Public Square.

COURTESY OF LELAND HAYWARD

Sally Adams (Ethel Merman) is the "Hostess With the Mostes' " on the ball in Call Me Madam.

Scene 2: The Embassy Garden.
Scene 3: The Public Square.
Scene 4: Sally's Sitting Room.
Scene 5: Sally's Living Room in Washington.

PERIOD AND COSTUMES: The mid-1950's in two mythical countries; one is called Lichtenburg, the other the United States of America: Washington party gowns and formal wear, bright folk costumes, royalty everyday dress, festival costumes, potato bug costumes (2).

CHOREOGRAPHY: Square dance, folk, dance specialties, couples dance interludes during the festival, brief passages of waltz, tango, Charleston, blues, rumba, fox trot.

LIGHTING AND SPECIAL EFFECTS: General lighting. Sliding door to secret passageway.

NOTES: A great show if you have a great Sally. Comes across as the delightful show that most every-

one has forgotten. Very topical. Time is no longer the present, but the 1950's. Now done as a period piece. If not, "They Like Ike" must be updated. Strongly suggest, however, doing it as 1950's.

CAMELOT

Frederick Loewe (Music)
Alan Jay Lerner (Book, Lyrics)
Opened Dec. 3, 1960
873 Performances

BASED ON: *The Once and Future King* by T. H. White

AGENT: Tams-Witmark

PUBLISHED TEXT: Random House, 1961; Dell, 1967 (P)

RECORDINGS: COL KOL-5620
                  COL KOS-2031

DIGEST OF PLOT: King Arthur and his new bride, Guinevere, institute a new form of government ministered by the Knights of the Round Table. Hearing of this new justice, Lancelot, a French knight, arrives in Camelot during a May Day celebration. His manner is disagreeable to everyone except Arthur. After defeating Arthur's three best knights, Lancelot joins the Round Table only to fall hopelessly in love with Guinevere. Not wishing to come between Guinevere and his best friend, Arthur, he departs Camelot for a foreign mission—only to return later with his love burning stronger than ever. In the meantime Arthur's evil illegitimate son, Mordred, comes upon the scene seeking absolute power. He exposes the romance and has Guinevere arrested to be burned at the stake. Lancelot frees Guinevere, and the two escape to France. Arthur is forced to declare war on his old friend as an act of chivalry. On the battlefield he tells a small boy to go unto the world and tell everyone of Camelot's quest for right, honor, and justice.

MUSICAL NUMBERS: "I Wonder What the King Is Doing Tonight," "The Simple Joys of Maidenhood," "CAMELOT," "Follow Me," "C'est Moi," "The Lusty Month of May," Dance, "Then You May Take Me to the Fair," "HOW TO HANDLE A WOMAN," "Before I Gaze at You Again," "IF EVER I WOULD LEAVE YOU," "The Seven Deadly Virtues," "What Do the Simple Folk Do?," "Fie On Goodness!," "I Loved You Once in Silence," "Guinevere."

INSTRUMENTATION: Violins A, B, viola, cello, bass, flute, pic, oboe (Eng. horn), clar I, clar II, E♭ bass clar (flute or clar, bass clar), bassoon, horns I, II, III, trumpets I, II, III, trombones I, II, percussion, guitar (lute mandolin), harp. (Special condensed orchestration for 11 or 12 pieces also available.)

CASTING: 22 speaking parts, 5 principals. Arthur, first an actor, but should sing well. Guinevere and Lancelot, must have excellent voices and acting ability. Morgan LeFey, must have an outstanding voice for her 1 number. Pellimore, comic character inserted without much need. Mordred, nasty little man, minor singing. Strong choral work. Total cast, 40–50.

SCENES AND SETS: 2 acts, 19 scenes, 8 full stage sets (all incorporating a back drop). 5 painted scene drops. 3 partial sets (Arthur's study, tents, Queen's bedchamber). Floor mats (optional).

ACT I
Scene 1: A Hilltop near Camelot.
Scene 2: Near Camelot.
Scene 3: Arthur's Study.
Scene 4: Countryside Near Camelot.
Scene 5: A Park Near the Castle.
Scene 6: A Terrace of the Castle.
Scene 7: The Dressing Tents Outside the Jousting Field.

Scene 8: The Grandstand of the Field.
Scene 9: The Terrace.
Scene 10: The Corridor Leading to the Great Hall.
Scene 11: The Great Hall.

ACT II
Scene 1: Main Terrace of the Castle.
Scene 2: The Terrace.
Scene 3: A Forest near Camelot.
Scene 4: The Forest of Morgan LeFey.
Scene 5: Corridor of the Castle.
Scene 6: The Queen's Bedchamber.
Scene 7: Camelot.
Scene 8: The Battlefield Outside Joyous Gard.

PERIOD AND COSTUMES: Camelot, a long time ago: tunics, tights, robes, capes, flowing court gowns, painted conical female hats with streaming veils. Chain mail, knights' armor, etc. Regal robes for King and Queen. Pages. Jousting horse costume strapped onto individual man on shoe stilts. Some special footwear.

CHOREOGRAPHY: Not a strong dance show. Most movement is pageantry. Some lively acrobatic dancing in "Lusty Month of May" number and jestering at the joust.

LIGHTING AND SPECIAL EFFECTS: Some dramatic lighting required. Fog.

NOTES: When *Camelot* opened it was expected to be another *My Fair Lady*. It wasn't and it has never seemed to rise above this stigma. Had it been written before *Lady* it would have enjoyed a stature similar to *Brigadoon*. As time passes *Camelot* should stand more on its own. The production must be a splendid one to carry the show's several pageant scenes. It need not be as opulent as the original, but it must be big and bold.

CAN-CAN

Cole Porter (Music, Lyrics)
Abe Burrows (Book)
Opened May 7, 1953
892 Performances

BASED ON: Original

AGENT: Tams-Witmark

PUBLISHED TEXT: Manuscript Only

RECORDINGS: CAP W-452

DIGEST OF PLOT: La Mome Pistache is the proprietress of Bal du Paradis, café in the Montmartre exhibiting the then scandalous and illegal Can-Can dance. To the delight of Paris, 1890's Bohemians, and society female fanciers, Pistache's club flourishes with the help of sympathetic police and

Gwen Verdon and original cast dancers from Can-Can.

judges. That is, until young Aristide Forestier is named to the bench. Claudine, principal Can-Can dancer, is having man problems with her temperamental artist/boy friend, Boris Adzindzinadze, whom she keeps. Their love spats provide a portion of comedy and a reason for the Quatz' Arts Ball "Adam and Eve" ballet, the show's major dance sequence.

Sensing the danger, Pistache trys to seduce Aristide. Apparently for the first time in her life, she fails. Aristide orders the police to raid the Can-Can. However, when the case comes before him, none of the witnesses can remember seeing the dance, and the case is dismissed. So Aristide ventures into the Montmartre to get the necessary evidence himself. This time he and Pistache discover their mutual love. During their preoccupation with each other a new raid is launched, catching the high judge in a scandal for which he is disbarred. Freed from his regi-

mentation as lawyer and judge, Aristide joins Pistache in the freedom and excitement of Montmartre.

MUSICAL NUMBERS: "Maidens Typical of France," "Never Give Anything Away," "C'EST MAGNIFIQUE," "Quadrille," "Come Along with Me," "Live and Let Live," "I Am in Love," "If You Loved Me Truly," "Montmart'," "The Garden of Eden," "Allez-Vous-En," "Never, Never Be an Artist," "IT'S ALL RIGHT WITH ME," "Every Man Is a Stupid Man," The Apaches, "I LOVE PARIS," "CAN-CAN."

INSTRUMENTATION: Violin A–C (2) (accordion), B–D, (guitar), viola, cello, bass, flute (pic, clar), oboe (Eng. horn), E♭ clar (B♭ clar, bass clar, alto sax), flute (clar), clar (bassoon), horn I–II, III, trumpets I–II, trombone (euphonium), percussion, piano-celeste.

CASTING: 34 parts, 8 principals. Aristide, handsome actor who should sing well. Pistache, powerful singing voice—very attractive and sexy. Boris, comic character man. Hercule, Theophile, Etienne, Boris' foils. Claudine, lovely girl and accomplished dancer. 12 to 16 above-average dancers required, mostly female. Total cast, 40–54.

SCENES AND SETS: 2 acts, 16 scenes, 7 full stage sets (including some drops), 2 partial sets, 3 scenic drops.

ACT I
Scene 1: Correctional Court.
Scene 2: A Street in Montmartre.
Scene 3: Bal du Paradis.
Scene 4: Pistache's Office.
Scene 5: Sidewalk Café.
Scene 6: Jail.
Scene 7: The Atelier.
Scene 8: The Street.
Scene 9: Quatz' Arts Ball.

ACT II
Scene 1: The Atelier.
Scene 2: The Café.
Scene 3: "La Blanchisserie."
Scene 4: The Street.
Scene 5: Roof of "La Blanchisserie."
Scene 6: Prison.
Scene 7: Court of Assizes.

PERIOD AND COSTUMES: Paris, 1893: police uniforms, judge robes and white powdered wigs, Can-Can dresses (ruffles under skirt with scoop neck leotard tops, plus garters and black silk stockings), apache dress, striped and plaid suits, sailor uniform, double-breasted coats, artist smocks, men's velvet coats, tux, feather boas, top hats, capes, form-fitting satin sheath gowns. Skimpy Quartz' Arts Ball animal costumes: snake, penguins, kangaroos, flamingos, inchworms, frogs, sea horses, cats, plus Adam and Eve.

CHOREOGRAPHY: Can-Can, ballet, dance specialty, modern, apache.

LIGHTING AND SPECIAL EFFECTS: Some dramatic lighting and special effects during Adam and Eve ballet. Lights on several set pieces and drops (Paris, "city of lights").

NOTES: Can-Can is a big, bawdy, and winning musical, not a production that can easily be skimped on. The production is designed for a set-drop, set-drop production sequence.

CANTERBURY TALES

Richard Hill, John Hawkins (Music) Martin Starkie, Nevill Coghill (Book), Nevill Coghill (Lyrics)

Opened Feb. 3, 1969
121 Performances

BASED ON: Translation from Geoffrey Chaucer by Nevill Coghill

AGENT: Music Theatre

PUBLISHED TEXT: Manuscript Only

RECORDINGS: CAP SW 229

DIGEST OF PLOT: Chaucer sets the mood, and the host of Tabard Inn, Harry Bailey, the plan for a pilgrimage to the shrine of Thomas à Becket at Canterbury. Harry proposes that each pilgrim tell a tale as they ride, and to insure the merriment of the trip he will go along as guide. The group is off next morning, and the Miller is the first to offer his story —a tale of Alison's seduction from her Carpenter husband by a young Oxford lad. The telling fires the Steward (once a Carpenter), who unreels a sordid tale of a pilfering Miller duped by two Cambridge students who seduce both his wife and daughter. The Merchant's tale spins yet another yarn of young Damian who outwits his rich old master for his new wife's hand. The mental ability of young lovers versus older duly proven, the Wife of Bath sets forth her thoughts of woman over man and offers proof with a tale of a doomed Knight in King Arthur's court who must find out what women really want. The answer he needs comes from an old hag whom he must then marry. However, when he denies despair and pledges his undying love, she becomes young and beautiful. But it is the Knight whose words do conquer when he presents his personal ideas, in lieu of a tale:
"Where courtesy and reason say their say,
    The greater strength may lie in giving way;
    In married love, obedience interlocks
    With courtesy—and that's love's paradox!"
The journey is ended at Canterbury Cathedral and Chaucer steps forward for a few humble last words and a fond good night.

MUSICAL NUMBERS: "Song of Welcome," "Good Night Hymn," "Canterbury Day," Pilgrim Riding Music, "I Have a Noble Cock," "Darling, Let Me Teach You How to Kiss," "There's the Moon," "It Depends on What You're At," "Love Will Conquer All," "Beer Is Best," "Come On and Marry Me, Honey," Mug Dance, "Where Are the Girls of Yesterday?," "Hymen, Hymen," "If She Has Never Loved Before," "I'll Give My Love a Ring," "Pear Tree Quintet," "I Am All A-Blaze," "Love Pas de Deux," "What Do Women Want?," "April Song."

INSTRUMENTATION: Trumpet I–II, III, trombone I–II, horn (bass tuba), piano, elec organ, guitar I–II, bass, percussion I–II.

CASTING: 45 parts (many written to be doubled in several tales), 7 principals, 9 major supporting roles. Chaucer, straight role. Host, winning character man. Miller, song, some dancing. Wife of Bath, char-

Basic unit-beamed set of Canterbury Tales *adapted to Tabard Inn.*

acter woman who sings. Alison and other young girls, young, pretty, yet naughty and sing, diversified acting ability. Nicholas and other spirited young men, the male counterpart to Alison's requirements. Steward and older men, diversified character actors who sing. Nun and older women, actresses, little singing. Other supporting roles of Merchant, Knight, Prioress, Priest, Clerk, Friar, Cook, Pardoner, and Summoner, actors who also sing. Singing and dancing chorus of pilgrims, villagers, bridesmaids, attendants, etc. Total cast, 30–50.

SCENES AND SETS: 2 acts, 14 scenes, 1 basic beam structure with various fly-ins and inserts to form the numerous resting places and settings for the tales.

The action passes between the Tabard Inn, London, and Canterbury Cathedral in the spring during the latter part of the 14th century.

ACT I
Scene 1: Tabard Inn.
Scene 2: Orchard.
Scene 3: The Miller's Tale.
Scene 4: Orchard.
Scene 5: Golden Goose (Alehouse).
Scene 6: Steward's Tale.
Scene 7: Same.

ACT II
Scene 1: Inn-Chapel.
Scene 2: Merchant's Tale—House.
Scene 3: Merchant's Tale—Garden.
Scene 4: Bridge.
Scene 5: Wife of Bath's Tale.
Scene 6: Canterbury.
Scene 7: The Cathedral.

PERIOD AND COSTUMES: April, 1387: tights, tunics, robes, buccaneer shirts, shantung dresses, nun's habit, priest's cassock, special footwear, wimples, hats, Knight's traveling garb, wedding dress, Chaucer's scholarly robes and headwear, nightcaps and gowns.

CHOREOGRAPHY: Parade, acrobatics, folk.

LIGHTING AND SPECIAL EFFECTS: Some dramatic lighting required, but general lighting for most.

NOTES: *Canterbury Tales* is writen almost completely in rhyme. However, it is played as straight dialogue. Nonprofessionals may have to work hard to avoid stressing the rhyme cadence rather than the intent of the script. The music is rock-oriented pageantry and suffers from a certain sameness. The show does provide an interesting evening in communicating the wisdom and works of Chaucer. It also offers a rare proof of the contrast between the worth, the performance, and the critical reception a show is given. *Canterbury Tales* opened March 3, 1968, in London almost a year prior to the Broadway production. The latter ran only 121 performances, whereas the London production continues in its fourth smash hit year as this book goes to press. A musical production is what you make it.

CARNIVAL!

Bob Merrill (Music, Lyrics),
Michael Stewart (Book)
Opened April 13, 1961
714 Performances

BASED ON: Material by Helen Deutsch

AGENT: Tams-Witmark

PUBLISHED TEXT: D. B. S. Publications, 1968

RECORDINGS: MGM (S)39460C

DIGEST OF PLOT: Lili comes to a third-rate European carnival in search of her late father's friend who she hopes will give her a job, but learns that he, too, has died. Alone in the world, she catches the eye of Marco, the carnival's aging roué magician, who decides to help her find a job. Unsuccessful as a souvenir vendor and magic assistant, Lili is near despair. She is tempted to take her own life, but is talked down from the high ladder by Carrot Top, the right puppet hand of Paul Berthalet, an angry, young, disabled dancer turned puppeteer. She joins Paul and his assistant, Jacquot, to form a new act, which is an immediate success and in time lifts the image of the entire carnival. Paul develops a secret love for Lili, relaying it through the words of his puppets. But he is constantly confounded by her naive adoration of Marco. Angered, too, is Rosalie, Marco's partner and spurned lover. Rosalie lands a contract that will take Marco away from the carnival and Lili. Double-crossing Marco tries to talk Lili into leaving with him, but is rejected as Lili realizes her true love for Paul.

MUSICAL NUMBERS: "Direct from Vienna," "A Very Nice Man," "Fairyland," "I've Got to Find a Reason," "Mira," "Sword, Rose and Cape," "Humming," "Yes, My Heart," "Everybody Likes You," "Magic, Magic," "Tanz mit Mir," Carnival Ballet, "LOVE MAKES THE WORLD GO 'ROUND," "Yum Ticky," "The Rich," "Beautiful Candy," "Her Face," "Grand Imperial Cirque de Paris," Dance, "I Hate Him," "Always, Always You," "She's My Love."

INSTRUMENTATION: Violin A–B, C, cello, bass (tuba), flute (pic), flute (clar, bass clar, alto sax), oboe (clar, tenor sax), bassoon (clar, bari sax), horn, trumpets I–II, trombone I, II, percussion I–II, harp, guitar, accordion, piano (celeste).

CASTING: 36 roles, 6 principals. Lili, legitimate voice, excellent actress, little dancing. Paul, strong baritone, must also supply voices for and operate two hand puppets. Jacquot, warm, sympathetic character, voice not essential, operates puppets, should be nimble dancer. Marco, voice desirable, must move well, slick, moderate dancing, performs magic. Rosalie, comedienne, booming voice if possible. Mr. Schlegel, straight man role. Chorus of 4 or 5 roustabouts. Cyclist, dog trainer, stilt walker, jugglers, clowns, strongman, aerialist (simple spin on rope), clowns, small band, and other carnival-type characters. Midget helps if available. (Roustabouts are dancers who also position all the set pieces during the performance.) Total cast, 36–46.

SCENES AND SETS: 2 acts, continuous action divided into 10 centers of activity. 4 drops, partial large circus tent, 6 portable side show panels, 4 puppet stages, stick trees, ladder unit, 4 carnival wagons, combination office and stage unit, and 2 magic illusion cabinets. All units, with the exception of tent and ladder unit, must roll.

ACT I
Scene 1: The Carnival Area.
Scene 2: The Puppet Booth.
Scene 3: Inside Schlegel's Office.
Scene 4: The Carnival Area.
Scene 5: The Carnival Area.
Scene 6: Interior of Main Tent.
Scene 7: Carnival Area at Night.

ACT II
Scene 1: The Midway.
Scene 2: Trailer Camp.
Scene 3: Outside Main Tent.

PERIOD AND COSTUMES: The peak of horse-drawn traveling circus days near a small town in southern Europe (1930's): carnival costumes, clowns. Harem girls, ringmaster, vendors, bearskin, tights, fringe-trimmed costume leotards, etc. Full dress suits, matching magician and assistant wardrobe, vests, leather roustabout togs, boots, special footwear, long blue coat and blue jumper for Lili, striped shirts, dark slacks, European-cut shirts, and leisure-time clothes.

CHOREOGRAPHY: Opening parade during which all the carnival people arrive, set up the tent, and prepare the carnival site, modern dance with some Spanish, Slavic overtones (very athletic and spirited), jiglike steps and leaps for the "Bluebird girls," many of the same spirited steps converted to graceful ballet movements when the carnival becomes magical, acrobatics.

LIGHTING AND SPECIAL EFFECTS: Pin lights, colored filters, highly dramatic lighting (day

Prelude—Amusement Park. Carousel.

and night), numerous cross-fades, strings of light bulbs onstage, distant ferris wheel with lights, dance-hall-type revolving mirror reflecting small light dots over the set and audience, shadowing techniques, magic effects.

NOTES: The show also requires the use of four lovable hand puppets, who are actually important characters in the story. They must be handled skillfully. *Carnival!* is a unique musical for versatile performers. The production must be well oiled and run smoothly. No show could be more worthwhile, but it takes a special effort to do it right.

CAROUSEL

Richard Rodgers (Music),
Oscar Hammerstein II (Lyrics, Book)
Opened April 19, 1945
890 Performances

BASED ON: *Liliom* by Ferenc Molnar

AGENT: R & H

PUBLISHED TEXT: Alfred A. Knopf, 1946; Modern Library #200

RECORDINGS: DEC(7)9020
CAP W(SW)-694(F)
RCA LOC(LSO)-1114(R)

DIGEST OF PLOT: Carousel barker Billy Bigelow could have any girl he wants and knows it. Julie Jordan knows it, too, but is drawn by Billy's good looks, brashness, and coy interest in her. Their flirtation then gets them both fired—leaving them little else than each other. They marry, but to Billy, who has always relied more on muscle and a cunning wink than on brains or tenderness, it soon seems an impossible adjustment. Jigger appears on the scene to suggest a robbery to get money. Billy refuses in favor of returning to the carousel, but reconsiders when Julie tells him he's to be a father. A born loser, Billy gambles away almost all his share before the job is done. Still he goes through with it, and when everything goes wrong it is Jigger who escapes. Confused, frightened, and faced with jail, Billy stabs himself. Julie reaches him and he dies in her arms. Elevated to the backyard of Heaven, Billy is confronted by his faults and errors in life by the Starkeeper. He grants Billy a return to earth for one day to do some good for somebody. Already it's 15 years later and Billy's daughter is displaying his arrogance of old. After failure, typical of days of old, Billy finds a way to persuade her to have the courage, faith, and hope in the future that he never had.

MUSICAL NUMBERS: CAROUSEL WALTZ, "You're a Queer One, Julie Jordan," "WHEN I MARRY MISTER SNOW," "IF I LOVED YOU," "JUNE IS BUSTIN' OUT ALL OVER," "When the Children Are Asleep," "Blow High, Blow Low," Soliloquy, "THIS WAS A REAL NICE CLAM BAKE," "Geraniums in the Winder," "There's Nothin' So Bad for a Woman," "WHAT'S THE USE OF WOND'RIN," "YOU'LL NEVER WALK ALONE," "The Highest Judge of All," Young Louise Ballet.

INSTRUMENTATION: Violins A–B (2), C, viola, cello, bass, flute I–II, oboe (Eng. horn), clar I, II, bassoon, horn I–II, III, trumpet I–II, trombone I, II, tuba, harp, percussion, piano, conductor.

CASTING: 29 parts, 6 singing principals, 2 dancing principals. Legitimate voices required. Separate singing and dancing choruses. Strong choral work: Ballet training required for principal dancers, helpful for others. Carousel is one of the more dramatic musicals requiring concentrated acting by every member of the cast. A line of children used in walk-on. Total cast, 35–45.

SCENES AND SETS: Prelude, 2 acts, 9 scenes, 9 sets including revolving carousel and drops in each set. Fishnets, sails, and other set pieces used in front of a sky drop, with different ground row sets can be very effective.

PRELUDE: An Amusement Park on the New England Coast, May.

ACT I
Scene 1: A Tree-Lined Path Along the Shore. A Few Minutes Later.
Scene 2: Nettie Fowler's Spa on the Ocean Front, June.

ACT II
Scene 1: On an Island Across the Bay, That Night.
Scene 2: Mainland Waterfront. An Hour Later.
Scene 3: Up There.
Scene 4: Down Here. On a Beach. Fifteen Years Later.
Scene 5: Outside Julie's Cottage.
Scene 6: Outside a Schoolhouse. Same Day.

PERIOD AND COSTUMES: 1873–1888: New England fishing mainland. Striped shirts, sweaters, denim slacks, sea coats, floor-length frilly dresses, suits, streetwear of the times, go-to-meetin' clothes, graduation dresses, carnival costumes, policemen uniforms, plus sea captain and appropriate dress for the Starkeeper and heavenly friends.

Act I, Scene 2. Nettie Fowler's Spa. Carousel.

COURTESY OF THE LYNN FARNOL GROUP, INC.

CHOREOGRAPHY: Choreographed opening prologue, modern ballet, the "hornpipe" mariners' dance, large ballet sequence requiring at least two highly trained dancers.

LIGHTING AND SPECIAL EFFECTS: Fog for heavenly clouds, working carousel, day and night dramatic lighting.

NOTES: Many critics claim *Carousel* will be Rodgers and Hammerstein's most lasting work. It is highly dramatic, and the construction is a masterpiece. Then add the score and the emotion the show generates and it's easy to understand that sooner or later almost every group does this show.

CELEBRATION

Harvey Schmidt (Music),
Tom Jones (Words)
Opened Jan. 22, 1969
100 Performances

BASED ON: Original

AGENT: Music Theatre

PUBLISHED TEXT: Manuscript Only

RECORDINGS: CAP SW-198

DIGEST OF PLOT: The Narrator introduces a symbolic celebration of the theatre in the makeup of a New Year's Eve party given by the rich establishment. The party is a stage where Young Orphan seeks only the garden of the orphanage that Edgar Allan Rich, through his formula for money making, has torn down. The Narrator has become Potemkin, an opportunist with an eye for young men with bright ideas. Potemkin gets Orphan invited to Rich's party where he meets Angel, a soulful girl, yet compromising enough to avoid a gray existence. Rich is bored by everything at his own party: the masked antics of his Revelers—all the artificial things that have made him rich. Sensing an opening, Potemkin hatches a plot whereby Orphan and Angel fall in love to prey upon the romanticism of Rich. Orphan can then trade Angel for the garden. The plan works to perfection. But the rejuvenated Rich, playing the role of Adam to Angel's Eve, seeks to renege on his promise to Orphan and keep the garden. Orphan claims the garden belongs to him, but Rich orders Potemkin to throw him out. However, Orphan hides during the ensuing smoke screen of pageantry, following which he also emerges as Adam to do hand-to-hand combat with Rich's aging portrayal. It's the stroke of 12 and Rich's time has run out. He dies in Orphan's arms as Potemkin, as Father Time, counts him out. Returning to the Narrator, he proclaims that Orphan and Angel must now cast aside their familiar and winning roles to

Clockwise: Susan Watson (Angel), Ted Thurston (Rich), Keith Charles (Potemkin), Michael Glenn-Smith (Orphan) were the original cast of Celebration.

strive bravely for the chance at reality and change for which they have fought and won.

MUSICAL NUMBERS: "Celebration," "Orphan in the Storm," "Survive," "Somebody," "Bored," "My Garden," "Where Did It Go?," "Love Song," "To the Garden," "I'm Glad to See You've Got What You Want," "It's You Who Makes Me Young," "Not My Problem," "Fifty Million Years Ago," "The Beautician Ballet," "Saturnalia," "Under the Tree," "Winter and Summer," "Celebration" finale.

INSTRUMENTATION: Piano I, II, guitar*, bass*, harp*, electric piano*, percussion A, B, C, (or solo percussion).

CASTING: 4 parts, all principals, plus group of 12 Revelers who are onstage almost the entire time. All play hand musical or rhythm instruments. Potemkin, actor who sings and dances. Orphan, actor/singer who dances, legit voice. Angel, legit voice actress who dances. Rich, fat character man who dances and sings. Revelers, pantomime, sing and dance. Total cast, 16–24.

SCENES AND SETS: A unit set of basically two levels—a major crudely built platform playing area (could be stage floor or large raked platform) and an upper level. Various small carry-ons, placards, posters, boxes, mirrors, tinsel curtain, and chairs.

* May be eliminated.

ACT I
The City.

ACT II
The Country, the Boy's Garden.

PERIOD AND COSTUMES: New Year's Eve: black suit, tattered orphan's rags, angel costume with breakaway wings over mesh bra and bikini with rhinestone "pasties" and spangles covering vital areas, devil girl costume, rich people's dresses and suits, white fox stole, long underwear, Adam and Eve fig-leaf costumes, costume accessories to create beauticians, barbers, body-builders, Father Time costume, scant belly dancer outfits and masks, masks, masks (some special, but most novelty store items).

CHOREOGRAPHY: Modern, whip dance, exotic dances, modern ballet, processions, decorator's dance (placing of strings of artificial flowers around stage in dance), dance of machine puppets, mirror dance by Rich and Orphan, slow ritualistic battle dance.

LIGHTING AND SPECIAL EFFECTS: Dramatic lighting required. "Visual effects," written prop actions for specific dramatic effects. Large, full sun (and overlays for eclipsing same), large shadows of earth-moving machines.

NOTES: *Celebration* is a highly stylized show. The author offers ten pages of notes with the production script detailing the reasoning, the original production, and suggested script alterations after the fact. He describes the show as a "ritual experience" —an off-beat musical that is definitely not a musical comedy. It employs masks, "visuals," cast members playing rhythm instruments, and so on. A highly dramatic impact piece. Good show for sophisticated little-theatre groups.

COMPANY

Stephen Sondheim (Music, Lyrics),
George Furth (Book)
Opened April 26, 1970

BASED ON: Original

AGENT: (not yet announced)

Larry Kert and the original cast of Company.

PUBLISHED TEXT: (not yet available)

RECORDINGS: COL OS-3550

DIGEST OF PLOT: Bobby, an aging playboy of 35, keeps company with five married couples who are each undergoing various pains of matrimony. As he visits each he is drawn into their hang-ups, joys, and sorrows. Sarah and Harry are fighting booze and diets and enjoying the little things they do together—such as a karate match. Susan and Peter need each other, but feel more secure when divorced. Jenny and David are material faddists. It's the latest of everything for them, including "pot." As long as there are new status symbols and a good income, their marriage will last. Amy and Paul have been living together for several years. They are to be married just to make it legal, but the wedding almost blows up their relationship until Bobby steps in. Larry and Joanne are worldly and have been married frequently. Marriage for them is a convenient arrangement and hedge against loneliness. Bobby is always the life of the party, the first to be called on in time of need, the would-be lover of wayward wives and the constant target of matchmaking. The regular girls in Bobby's life are tired of waiting. The pleasure of his company is no longer enough. Bobby tells himself he is looking for a particular kind of girl (who is safely impossible to find). To him April is interesting, but lacks self-assurance. Kathy comes pretty close to ideal but he assumes she'd only turn him down if he asked. Marta is loads of fun, but she's a kook with too many theories. With Bobby the safe number is three. His "crazy" married couples are all the friendship and exposure to marriage that a man could want. When he does lure a girl to his love nest it's all he can do to fight off boredom. However, Bobby is confused by the anguish he sees in his beloved married friends and, equally, by their reluctance to give up marriage. As they help Bobby mature in his thinking it becomes clear to him that part of man's being is to be shared with a woman. And with the sharing comes not only the happiness, but the unhappiness as well. He must stop clinging to the lives of his friends and start building a life of his own. He begins. They will miss him, but they are confident he will make an excellent husband.

MUSICAL NUMBERS: "Company," "The Little Things You Do Together," "Sorry-Grateful," "You Could Drive a Person Crazy," "Have I Got a Girl for You," "Someone Is Waiting," "Another Hundred People," "Getting Married Today," "Side by Side by Side," "What Would We Do Without You," "Poor Baby," "Tick Tock," "Barcelona," "The Ladies Who Lunch," "Being Alive."

INSTRUMENTATION: A, B–C violins, cello (2), bass, alto sax (E♭, B♭ clar, flute, piccolo, alto flute), tenor sax (B♭, bass clar, flute, piccolo, alto flute), tenor sax (bass clar, B♭ clar, flute), baritone sax (B♭, contrabass clar, oboe, Eng. horn), baritone sax (B♭ clar, bassoon), French horn (2), trumpet 1–2 (flugelhorn), 3, trombone, bass trombone, roxichord, guitar I–II, percussion I–II.

CASTING: 14 parts, all principals. All act, sing, and dance. One exceptional female dancer required. Four female pit voices. Two girls must have flawless diction for machine-gun lyrics. Total cast, 14.

SCENES AND SETS: 1 major set with several levels and elevators; what might be a series of garden apartments. Insert roll-on sets are a park bench, large table, two living-room motifs, a bedroom, a kitchen counter and cabinets, and moving platforms. None is elaborate.

PERIOD AND COSTUMES: Modern: latest chic fashions. Few costume changes, almost one to a character. Specials are the airline stewardess costume with many zippers at the "right" spots, formal wear, wedding veil, lingerie smock for dancer, terry cloth robes.

CHOREOGRAPHY: "Side by Side by Side" production number—top-hat-and-cane type of number bridging into modern, modern jazz, interpretive dance solo.

LIGHTING AND SPECIAL EFFECTS: Tight area and dramatic lighting required throughout to shrink various portions of the large set as each scene requires. Original production used rear projections on a slatted screen arrangement. This was not visible to one fourth of the downstairs audience and most of the balcony, and was not really necessary.

NOTES: *Company* will undoubtedly be recorded as a major breakthrough in musical theatre. It's not a show that the audience can just sit back and watch pass them by. They must become involved to thoroughly enjoy and appreciate this tremendous creative achievement.

DAMES AT SEA

James Wise (Music),
George Haimsohn, Robin Miller (Book, Lyrics)
Opened Dec. 20, 1968
575 Performances

BASED ON: Original

AGENT: Samuel French, Inc.

PUBLISHED TEXT: Samuel French, 1969

RECORDINGS: COL OS-3330

DIGEST OF PLOT: Mona Kent is the temperamental star of a 42nd Street theatre musical—"Dames at Sea." Hennessy, the show's hard-luck producer with 12 straight flops to his credit, makes a great referee. Ruby arrives via bus from Centerville, Utah, to become a star. She auditions and is hired for the chorus. The suitcase she left on the bus is returned by Dick, a sailor on liberty who just happens to be from Ruby's home town. He's also an aspiring songwriter and proves it on the spot with a special song for Ruby. Mona has been watching and decides he's a prize worth having. Dick's buddy, Luckey, shows up and is an instant hit with Joan, the show's leading dancer. Dick disclaims his earlier weakness to Mona's flirtations and makes up with Ruby. However, Hennessy receives word the theatre has been sold out from under him, and the show must vacate. The next logical place? Dick and Luckey's ship, where else? And the boys' commanding officer is none other than "Kewpie Doll" Courageous, one of Mona's old flames. Mona makes it appear that Dick has weakened again, which makes another reconciliation necessary. To fix the matter once and for all, Joan and Luckey plot to get Mona seasick. With Mona safely retired in Captain Courageous' quarters, Hennessy finally sees the light and puts Ruby in the starring role. Ruby is a smash. Arrived on the bus this morning and the toast of Broadway tonight—complete with congratulations from the President of the United States. The Hollywood dream comes true. There's a new star and budding romances at every turn—Ruby and Dick, Joan and Luckey, Mona and the Captain, who are all married to a tuneful 21-gun salute.

MUSICAL NUMBERS: "Wall Street," "It's You," "Broadway Baby," "That Mister Man of Mine," "Choo-Choo Honeymoon," "The Sailor of My Dreams," "Singapore Sue," "Good Times Are Here to Stay," "Dames at Sea," "The Beguine," "Raining in My Heart," "There's Something About You," "The Echo Waltz," "Star Tar," "Let's Have a Simple Wedding."

INSTRUMENTATION: Pianos and percussion.

CASTING: 7 parts, 7 principals. Mona, character actress who sings and dances. Ruby, actress who sings and dances. Dick, singer/dancer, good actor. Joan and Luckey, sing, dance, and act. Hennessy and Captain, older character men, minor tap dance (in the original Off-Broadway production both parts played by same actor). Chorus optional (original production did not use one, but it would be an easy and helpful addition). Total cast, 6–20.

SCENES AND SETS: 2 acts (could be done as one), 2 full stage sets, 2 fly-in set pieces, 2 mirror-backed panels in second act set revolve to create illusion of a gigantic cast as per old movie musicals.

ACT I
Backstage at a 42nd Street Theatre.

ACT II
On Board a Battleship.
Scene 1: Battleship Deck.
Scene 2: Before Scenery Mountain.
Scene 3: Backstage Curtain.
Scene 4: Same.
Scene 5: Show Traveler Opening to Battleship Deck.

PERIOD AND COSTUMES: Early 1930's: fashions of the times: raincoat, dance rehearsal clothes, sailor uniforms, Oriental robes, sailorette uniforms, captain's uniform, slicker, cellophane umbrellas, tutus, wedding dresses, dress white Navy uniforms.

CHOREOGRAPHY: Tap, couples numbers (à la Fred Astaire and Ginger Rogers), waltz, production numbers.

LIGHTING AND SPECIAL EFFECTS: Mostly general lighting, follow spot required, shadow curtain, falling brick wall, exploding smoke pots, full rainbow projection for finale.

NOTES: *Dames at Sea* is a spoof of the movie musicals of the 1930's—the era of the Great Depression when the only requirement of entertainment was diversion from the troubles of reality. No one had to feel the plot was relevant, believable, or even possible —but it had to be fun, and fun in those days was often ridiculous. This is the spirit that *Dames at Sea* recaptures. It is not to be confused with the operetta parody of *Little Mary Sunshine*. The technique is about the same, but the subject matter is quite different. With any work of this type it helps if a large percentage of the audience either lived during the period or is familiar with it. Its beauty would probably go right over the heads of most younger audiences—save perhaps a large promotional buildup and explanation along these lines prior to each presentation.

DAMN YANKEES

Richard Adler, Jerry Ross (Music, Lyrics), George Abbott, Douglass Wallop (Book)
Opened May 5, 1955
1,022 Performances

BASED ON: *The Year the Yankees Lost the Pennant* by Douglass Wallop

AGENT: Music Theatre

PUBLISHED TEXT: Random House, 1956; *Theatre Arts,* November, 1956

RECORDINGS: RCA LOC(LSO)-1021
RCA LOC-1047(F)

DIGEST OF PLOT: Joe Boyd, lifelong Washington Senators fan, offers to sell his soul if his team could only beat those damn Yankees. Mr. Applegate appears and offers him the opportunity to become Joe Hardy, the greatest player baseball ever knew. Insurance Man Boyd accepts, but gets Applegate to agree to an escape clause. As Joe Hardy, he is accepted by the team, and the Senators start winning, but Joe longs for his wife. Applegate calls on his chief seductress, Lola, to return Joe to his selfish ways. But this is the first time Lola has come up against true love and she flops miserably. Applegate turns to scandal to force Joe back in line. Joe's fans come to his aid in a hearing that alleges he took a bribe under another name. In the meantime, however, the deadline for Joe to exercise his escape clause has passed. Lost souls, Joe and Lola spend one last wonderful evening together before the pennant-winning game that Applegate plans for the Senators to lose—to the consternation of all. But Lola drugs her boss, and he doesn't get to the ballpark until the last of the 9th inning. Infuriated, he turns Joe back on the spot just as he is running to make the catch for the final out. As Joe Boyd, he makes the winning catch and disappears to return to his wife. Applegate tries to tempt Joe into returning to play in the World Series and be with Lola, but he fails.

MUSICAL NUMBERS: "Six Months Out of Every Year," "Goodbye, Old Girl," "HEART," "Shoeless Joe from Hannibal, Mo.," "A Man Doesn't Know," "A Little Brains—a Little Talent," "WHATEVER LOLA WANTS," "Who's Got the Pain?," "The Game," "NEAR TO YOU," "Those Were the Good Old Days," "TWO LOST SOULS."

INSTRUMENTATION: Violin A–C, B–D, viola, cello, bass, clar (flute, pic, alto sax), alto sax (clar, flute), tenor sax (oboe, Eng. horn), tenor sax (bass clar), bari sax (clar, bassoon, bass clar), trumpet I–II, III, trombone I, II, III, horn, percussion, guitar, piano-conductor.

CASTING: 20 roles, 11 principals. Lola, sexy, excellent dancer who acts and sings. Joe Hardy, young, handsome baritone, legit voice helpful, minor dance. Applegate, good comic character actor, good with hands for a few feats of magic, 1 song. Sohovik, Smokey, Vernon, and Van Buren, a quartet, comic baseball player roles. Gloria, girl sports reporter, sings 1 number. Joe Boyd, Meg, and others are straight roles with minor singing. Separate singing and dancing chorus. Total cast, 28–40.

SCENES AND SETS: 2 acts, 22 scenes, 7 full stage sets (including 2 drops), 2 scene drops, 2 partial sets.

ACT I
Scene 1: Suburban Front Porch and Living Room, Hannibal, Mo.
Scene 2: A Corridor Under the Stands of the Washington Baseball Park.
Scene 3: Dugout of the Washington Baseball Park.
Scene 4: Billboard Near the Ballpark.
Scene 5: Welch's Office.
Scene 6: Billboard.
Scene 7: Meg's House, Same as Scene 1.
Scene 8: Corridor at Baseball Park.
Scene 9: The Locker Room.
Scene 10: In Front of Black Curtain or Billboard.
Scene 11: Hotel Ballroom.

ACT II
Scene 1: Locker Room.
Scene 2: Billboard.

Scene 3: Applegate's Apartment.
Scene 4: Commissioner's Office.
Scene 5: Billboard Drop.
Scene 6: Nightclub.
Scene 7: Joe Hardy Billboard.
Scene 8: Same as Before.
Scene 9: Dugout and Stands.
Scene 10: Corridor at Ballpark.
Scene 11: Meg's House.

PERIOD AND COSTUMES: Washington, D.C., sometime in the near future: baseball uniforms, current fashions (streetwear and housedresses), business suits, purple bathrobe, Lola's strip costume, two mambo costumes, party dresses, evening clothes, several warm-up jackets (optional).

CHOREOGRAPHY: Modern jazz on baseball themes, light strip-tease ("Whatever Lola Wants" not offensive), jazz mambo, patter choreography for "Heart" and "Those Were the Good Old Days."

LIGHTING AND SPECIAL EFFECTS: Flash pots, set provisions for the exchange of young for old Joe. Floodlight (ballpark lights) facing into audience.

NOTES: The set-drops sequence of set makes this show easy to stage. Should the Washington Senators baseball team ever begin to win or the club franchise be sold to another city, the show might not have the same impact. The name of the baseball team could be that of any loser except the Yankees.

DESTRY RIDES AGAIN

Harold Rome (Music, Lyrics),
Leonard Gershe (Book)
Opened April 23, 1959
473 Performances

BASED ON: Story by Max Brand

AGENT: Tams-Witmark

PUBLISHED TEXT: Manuscript Only

RECORDINGS: DEC(7)9075

DIGEST OF PLOT: Wash, the town drunk of Bottleneck, is named sheriff after his predecessor is killed while trying to protect a rancher who lost his spread to the town gambler, Kent, and his gal, Frenchy. Wash realizes that he needs help and sends for Tom Destry, Jr., son of a famous gunfighter. Destry arrives at the Last Chance Saloon carrying a bird cage and parasol for Rose Lovejoy's new Paradise Alley girl, who arrives on the same stagecoach. He becomes a laughingstock when it's discovered that he doesn't even tote a gun. However, Destry soon makes headway in solving the sheriff's murder. Kent feels the heat and orders Frenchy to do a little sidetracking. Instead of being drawn off the track by Frenchy's advances, Destry tricks Kent into disclosing the location of the sheriff's body. This provides enough evidence to jail Gyp Watson as the murderer. But when Destry learns that the town justice is a barroom trial he leaves town to get a Federal Justice. Kent decides a jail break is necessary to keep Gyp from talking. Destry returns in the heat of the attempt to free Gyp, during which Wash is killed. Destry is saved by a repentant Frenchy. Destry then wipes out the badmen and he and Frenchy embrace at last.

MUSICAL NUMBERS: "Bottleneck," "Ladies," "Hoop-de-Dingle," "Tomorrow Morning," "Ballad of the Gun," "The Social," "I Know Your Kind," "I Hate Him," "Paradise Alley," "Anyone Would Love You," "Once Knew a Fella," "Every Once in a While," "Fair Warning," "Are You Ready, Gyp Watson?," "Not Guilty," "Only Time Will Tell," "Respectability, "THAT RING ON THE FINGER," "I Say Hello."

INSTRUMENTATION: Violin A (2), B, viola, cello, bass, clar (alto sax, flute, pic), clar (alto sax), clar (tenor sax), clar (tenor sax), clar (bari sax), horn, trumpets I–II, III, trombone I, II, guitar, percussion, piano-celeste.

CASTING: 20 parts, 11 principals. Destry, warm, gentle, likable, takes command when necessary, good voice. Frenchy, disarming, flashy dance-hall star, powerful voice. Gyp Watson, Bugs Watson, and Rockwell, bad guys, dance trio, excellent dancers, must be able to handle bullwhips. Wash, comedy character man, sings. Kent, ringleader of bad guys, straight role. Large chorus of dance-hall girls, girls from Paradise Alley, cowboys, and townspeople. Total cast, about 40.

SCENES AND SETS: Prologue, 2 acts, 12 scenes, 4 full stage sets (including elaborate Last Chance Saloon), 1 partial set, 3 scene drops.

ACT I
Scene 1: The Last Chance Saloon.
Scene 2: Same.
Scene 3: A Street.
Scene 4: A Corral.
Scene 5: Frenchy's House.
Scene 6: Paradise Alley.
Scene 7: A Road in Bottleneck.
Scene 8: Last Chance Saloon.

ACT II
Scene 1: Outside the Jailhouse.
Scene 2: Frenchy's House.
Scene 3: Sheriff's Office.
Scene 4: Last Chance Saloon.

PERIOD AND COSTUMES: Turn of the century, Bottleneck (the Old West): cowboy outfits (hats, shirts, vests, slacks, boots, gun belts), dude suits, three all-black outfits for bad-guy trio, dance-hall girls (plume headpiece, pink-corset-type tops, black mesh elbow-length mitts, removable can-can skirt, pink tights, high-button shoes). Paradise Alley girls, lacy turn of century floor-length fancy dresses and

parasols. Frenchy, skin-tight dresses and costumes with flared bottoms, removable skirt from one. One union suit and other garb of the Old West for townspeople, etc.

CHOREOGRAPHY: Dance-hall show, modern square dance, whip dance (villains' jazzy ballet with three cracking bullwhips).

LIGHTING AND SPECIAL EFFECTS: Some dramatic lighting required. Day and night lighting. Chinese lanterns in party scenes. Blank guns. Whip handling.

NOTES: *Destry Rides Again* is a classic of the Old West and has been made into films several times. Although connoisseurs may look askance at the musical version, it stands on its own rather well. If not permitted to drag, it can be a smash success.

DO I HEAR A WALTZ?

Richard Rodgers (Music),
Arthur Laurents (Book),
Stephen Sondheim (Lyrics)
Opened March 18, 1965
220 Performances

BASED ON: *The Time of the Cuckoo* by Arthur Laurents

AGENT: R & H

PUBLISHED TEXT: Random House, 1966

RECORDINGS: COL KOL-6370
COL KOS-2770

DIGEST OF PLOT: Tourist Leona Samish, a mid-thirties secretary, arrives in Venice seeking the adventure and romance that are passing her by in America. She is staying in a *pensione* (tourist home) run by Signora Fioria along with other American visitors: Eddie and Jennifer, who are trying to convince themselves that their marriage is happy, and a planned-tour couple, Mr. and Mrs. McIlhenny. While shopping Leona meets shopowner Renato DiRossi. They are attracted to each other, but she becomes suspicious when he turns on the charm. He gives her a lesson in shopping in Venice that helps break the ice, but she remains aloof. That evening she is alone again and regrets her action. The next morning she returns to DiRossi's shop to buy a garnet goblet, but he is not there. That afternoon he personally delivers a mated goblet and asks for a date. Reluctantly she agrees, only to discover that he is married. Sulking in the courtyard that evening she sees a rejected Eddie seducing Fioria and leading her off to a gondola. DiRossi arrives and uses the occasion to illustrate the realities in romance. He suggests an affair and Leona concedes. The result isn't everything that Leona had always imagined it would be, but when DiRossi arrives with a garnet necklace she begins to hear the romantic waltz of

Elizabeth Allen and Sergio Franchi in Venice street scene from Do I Hear a Waltz?

her dreams. To share her happiness, Leona throws a party but is shattered when DiRossi must borrow from her to pay for her necklace. She throws him out, gets drunk, and betrays Eddie's affair with Fioria. The next morning all the guests are leaving. Leona realizes her mistakes and is ready to begin again. And she can, much wiser from her experience.

MUSICAL NUMBERS: "Someone Woke Up," "This Week Americans," "What Do We Do? We Fly!," "Someone Like You," "Bargaining," "Here We Are Again," "Thinking," "No Understand," "Take the Moment," "Moon in My Window," "We're Gonna Be All Right," "DO I HEAR A WALTZ?," "Stay," "Perfectly Lovely Couple," "Thank You So Much."

INSTRUMENTATION: Violins A–B (4), viola, cello, bass, flute (pic, alto flute, clar), flute (pic, clar), oboe (Eng. horn, clar, flute), bassoon (clar, bass clar, flute), trumpet I (flugel horn), II, trombone I, II, III (bass), percussion, harp (celeste), guitar (mandolin).

CASTING: 12 parts, 8 principals, 2 small boys, 6 featured dancers. Leona, actress who sings. DiRossi, broad-range singer, actor. Signora Fioria, actress who sings. Eddie, Jennifer, Mr. and Mrs. McIlhenny, actors who sing. Giovanna, comic part, a voice helps. Separate singing and dancing choruses. Strong choral work. Total cast, 30–50.

SCENES AND SETS: 2 acts, 11 scenes, all sets are full stage (however, these require only one Venice backdrop plus fly-in panels, major bridge unit, portable shop, step and platform unit).

ACT I
Scene 1: Venice.
Scene 2: Garden of Pensione Fioria.
Scene 3: DiRossi's Shop.
Scene 4: Piazza San Marco.
Scene 5: Interior of Pensione Fioria.
Scene 6: Garden of Pensione Fioria.

Act II
Scene 1: Façade of Pensione Fioria.
Scene 2: Outside Garden of Pensione Fioria.
Scene 3: The Piazza.
Scene 4: Garden of Pensione Fioria.
Scene 5: Same.

PERIOD AND COSTUMES: The present: traveling dress, sweater, tourist clothes from other lands: Indian, German, French. Sailors, dress guards, vendors, craftsmen, suits, sports coats, casual dresses, nuns' habits, conservative evening dresses.

CHOREOGRAPHY: Waltz, modern ballet, featured couples number.

LIGHTING AND SPECIAL EFFECTS: Some dramatic lighting required.

NOTES: *Do I Hear a Waltz?* promised to be a style-setter of musicals. Richard Rodgers had been looking for a lyric partner since the death of Oscar

Hammerstein II, and Stephen Sondheim was definitely an equal match. The show was considered the first of many the new team would do. It was rumored that Sondheim did not work well with Rodgers' style of music and almost mechanically kept his side of the bargain. The bittersweet show did not catch on well, nor was there another collaboration. The show is loosely constructed. Cutting would not be difficult. Songs are engaging. Could be tightened to about two hours.

DO RE MI

Jule Styne (Music),
Garson Kanin (Book),
Betty Comden, Adolph Green (Lyrics)
Opened Dec. 26, 1960
400 Performances

BASED ON: Original

AGENT: Tams-Witmark

PUBLISHED TEXT: Manuscript Only

RECORDINGS: RCA LOCD-2002

DIGEST OF PLOT: Hubie Cram, a would-be VIP has lived his life in wait of the big deal. His wife, Kay, is playing her familiar waiting game at the worst table at the Casacabana. Hubie arrives with news of a jukebox scheme. Kay points out young tycoon John Henry Wheeler, the king of the entire jukebox and record industry, who is at ringside to catch one of his acts. During the performance Hubie is asked to move, jolted about, and nearly trampled. In defiance he moves his table to ringside and is promptly thrown out. At home later, Kay suggests that Hubie get a legitimate job. He hears not, but is fired with a brainstorm to bring his old slot-machine gang in on the jukebox deal. He sells his plan to the aging hoods. Wheeler learns of the competition but laughs it off. With good reason—Hubie's group is thrown out of the Zen Pancake Parlor while trying to wrap up their first placement. The hoods want to use muscle, but Hubie has a new flash to turn the singing waitress, Tilda Mullin, into their own recording star. For once they succeed. Tilda is a smash. That is, until Wheeler walks into her recording studio by mistake. It's love at first sight. The hoods resent Wheeler's underhanded takeover and want to solve the problem in the traditional gangland manner. Hubie manages to hold the line, save a major knockdown dragout brawl. It's a dim moment, but faithful Kay joins in to convince Tilda that Wheeler has a large collection of women. But the plan fails, and Tilda and Wheeler are married. This triggers a jukebox war that destroys, among other things, Hubie and Kay's marriage. There's a big investigation, and Hubie is in the spotlight he's always wanted. When the light goes out Hubie is forced to face bare reality. There's not a big deal in miles; only a forgiving Kay

waiting to take him back. Hubie is quick to realize it's the biggest break of his life.

MUSICAL NUMBERS: "Waiting, Waiting," "All You Need Is a Quarter," "Take a Job," Dance: The Juke Box Hop, "It's Legitimate," "I Know About Love," The Auditions, "Cry Like the Wind," "Ambition," Success, "Fireworks," "What's New at the Zoo?," "Asking for You," "The Late, Late Show," "Adventure," "MAKE SOMEONE HAPPY," "Don't Be Ashamed of a Teardrop," Dance: The Juke Box Trouble, "V.I.P.," "All of My Life."

INSTRUMENTATION: Violin A–B (2), C, cello, bass, alto sax (clar, pic, flute, alto flute), alto sax (clar, pic, flute), tenor sax (clar, oboe, Eng. horn), tenor sax (clar, bass clar), bari sax (clar, bass clar, bassoon), horn, trumpets I–II, III, trombone I, II, III, guitar, percussion I–II, piano-conductor.

CASTING: 28 parts, 7 principals. Hubie, carries show with tour de force comic performance, sings and dances confidently. Kay, comedienne who sings and dances. Tilda, attractive actress with legit singing voice, minor dance. Wheeler, legit voice, acts, minor dance. Fatso, Skin, Brains, good character men who sing. Total cast, 40–50.

SCENES AND SETS: 2 acts, 16 scenes, 4 full stage sets, 8 partial stage sets (some fly-ins), 2 drops (one has 8 jukeboxes that light up).

ACT I
Scene 1: The Casacabana.
Scene 2: Hubie and Kay's Bedroom.
Scene 3: Fatso's Ice Cream Parlor.
Scene 4: Brains's Chicken Farm.
   A Box at Hialeah.
   A Street.
Scene 5: John Henry Wheeler's Office.
Scene 6: Zen Pancake Parlor.
Scene 7: Music Enterprise Associates.
Scene 8: Zen Pancake Parlor.
Scene 9: All Over Town.
Scene 10: A Recording Studio.
Scene 11: Imperial Room.

ACT II
Scene 1: Hubie and Kay's Bedroom.
Scene 2: John Henry Wheeler's Office.
Scene 3: Music Enterprise Associates, Inc. (Redecorated).
Scene 4: The City.
Scene 5: Hearing Room in the Senate Office Building.

PERIOD AND COSTUMES: The present (1960): evening clothes, formal wear, well-dressed dummies, exotic chorus-girl costumes, uniforms for waiters, busboys, head waiter, housecoats, soda jerk jacket, teen-age kids fashions, movers' coveralls, Japanese kimonos, hippie outfits, eight animal costumes, white tie and tails, pajamas, street clothes, expensive suits.

CHOREOGRAPHY: Nightclub chorus line, featured dance duo, modern, ballroom, brief Venezuela dance (by chorus girls), production numbers, Hubie and Kay final dance sequence—polka, samba, tango, and waltz.

LIGHTING AND SPECIAL EFFECTS: Dramatic lighting required. Fireworks effects, breakaway door in 1 set, bomb explosion, riot effects.

NOTES: Another good show that doesn't seem to be done too often. A fun show that demands a great comic actor for Hubie's part and tight, fast-paced direction. Can be a very funny show.

ERNEST IN LOVE

Lee Prockriss (Music),
Anne Croswell (Book, Lyrics)
Opened May 4, 1960
103 Performances

BASED ON: *The Importance of Being Earnest* by Oscar Wilde

AGENT: Music Theatre

PUBLISHED TEXT: Manuscript Only

RECORDINGS: COL OL 5530
COL OS 2027

DIGEST OF PLOT: Jack Worthing, a country gentleman known to his London friends as Ernest, is preparing to propose to Gwendolyn Fairfax. She has always wanted to marry a man named Ernest,

WISCONSIN CENTER FOR THEATRE RESEARCH

Leila Martin in Ernest in Love.

Jack especially, but her mother, Lady Bracknell, is more insistent on a proper family background. Jack visits his friend, Algernon Moncrieff, and confides the assumed name is really that of a fictitious wicked younger brother, a proper guise created for his lovely ward, Cecily—thus enabling him to get to town at a whim. The tale is as familiar to Algy, who has created a mythical Mr. Bunbury, who gets ill whenever Algy wants to visit the country. As they take pride in each other's deceptions Gwendolyn and her mother arrive. Jack proposes at the first opportunity. Gwen is willing, but mother demands proof of family, which Jack cannot supply—explaining only that he was found in a handbag in a railway station. Before Lady Bracknell can drag Gwen away, Jack tells her his address in the country. Overhearing, Algy decides to investigate young Cecily. Arriving before Jack, he introduces himself as Ernest Worthing. Miss Prism, Cecily's governess, is distracted long enough by her highly refined flirtation with the local rector, Dr. Chasuble, to allow Algy and Cecily to fall hopelessly in love. Meanwhile Jack has arrived and announced the death of his brother Ernest. Gwen appears in search of Jack only to discover Cecily. The girls are taken with each other until they learn of their mutual interest in "Ernest." Lady Bracknell turns up in search of Gwen but is even more alarmed to discover Miss Prism, who disappeared 28 years ago with an infant baby boy. Prism owns up and reveals a confusion with handbags. In the realization of truth Jack discovers he is Algy's older brother. Not that there can be any doubt, but Dr. Chasuble recalls his christening as Ernest.

MUSICAL NUMBERS: "Come Raise Your Cup," "How Do You Find the Words?," "The Hat," "Mr. Bunbury," "Perfection," "A Handbag Is Not a Proper Mother," "A WICKED MAN," "Metaphorically Speaking," "You Can't Make Love," "Lost," "My Very First Impression," "The Muffin Song," "My Eternal Devotion."

INSTRUMENTATION: Bass, flute (clar), oboe (clar), bassoon (bass clar), piano-conductor.

CASTING: 16 parts, 7 principals. Jack and Algernon, good actors who sing. Gwendolyn and Cecily, good actresses with legit voices. Lady Bracknell, good character woman who sings 1 number. Miss Prism, character woman, minor singing. Dr. Chasuble, character actor who sings. Lane and Effie, manservant and maid, sing 1 number, minor dancing. Total cast, 16.

SCENES AND SETS: 2 acts, 9 scenes, 5 full stage sets, 3 partial stage sets. Mechanical sets advisable. First scene could be cut, reducing cast to 11 and sets to 3 (Algy's flat, garden, and Jack's house in the country).

ACT I
Scene 1: A London Street.
Scene 2: Jack's Flat.
Scene 3: Gwendolyn's Room.

Scene 4: Algy's Flat.
Scene 5: Garden of the Manor House.

ACT II
Scene 1: One of the Guest Rooms in the Manor House.
Scene 2: The Garden.
Scene 3: The Morning Room of the Manor House.
Scene 4: Church Lawn.

PERIOD AND COSTUMES: 1895: work clothes for dancing master, piano teacher, bootmaker, tobacconist, and greengrocer. Servant uniforms. Rector's black suit and collar, undergarments, dressing robes, society dresses, hats, gloves, walking sticks, plumed female hats, mourning suit with black accessories, hounds-tooth suit, bowler hat, jacket with Oxford crest, straw hats.

CHOREOGRAPHY: Brief light soft shoe numbers during song interludes.

LIGHTING AND SPECIAL EFFECTS: General lighting.

NOTES: Most little-theatre groups will find this musical farce just the thing they have been looking for—small cast, great music, and delightful book. The show, under the title of *Who's Ernest?*, was aired on the "U.S. Steel Hour" as a TV special. The cutting was an exceptionally good one.

FAMILY AFFAIR, A

John Kander (Music),
James and William Goldman (Book),
James Goldman and John Kander (Lyrics)
Opened Jan. 27, 1962
65 Performances

BASED ON: Original

AGENT: Music Theatre

PUBLISHED TEXT: Manuscript Only

RECORDINGS: U.A. 4069

DIGEST OF PLOT: Gerry Siegal has asked Sally Nathan to marry him. Sally's family is small, and her uncle, Alfie, wants a small, intimate wedding. Gerry's family is large, and mother Tilly and father Morris would like to see something a *little* larger. Alfie begins to become suspicious at the preliminary planning meetings. Discussions become tedious as large lawn parties begin to break out. As the groom's parents continue the planning for a large country club affair, Uncle Alfie and his friends declare war. A wedding consultant is hired. She has her own ideas. Meanwhile, the Nathans and Siegals are no longer speaking. Morris chastises Tilly for taking over, and Alfie is plotting revenge. Finally, they realize that they have almost destroyed the wedding. However, the bride and groom have retained their sanity and step in to announce their own intentions for a quiet family affair. In the end there is a wedding.

MUSICAL NUMBERS: "Anything for You," "Beautiful," "My Son, the Lawyer," "Every Girl Wants to Get Married," "Right Girls," "Kalua Bay," "There's a Room in My House," "Siegal Marching Song," "Nathan Marching Song," "Harmony," "Now, Morris," "Wonderful Party," "Revenge," "Summer Is Over," "I'm Worse Than Anybody," "What I Say Goes," "The Wedding."

INSTRUMENTATION: Violin, cello, bass, alto sax (E♭ clar, pic, flute), alto sax (flute, pic, clar), tenor sax (clar, oboe, Eng. horn), bari sax (bass clar, flute, clar), trumpet I–II, III, trombone, horn, percussion, guitar, harp, piano-conductor.

CASTING: 33 parts, 6 principal, 6 supporting roles. Alfie, comic actor who sings and dances. Gerry and Sally, the bride and groom, actors who sing and dance. Tilly, character actress who sings. Morris, character actor who sings. Miss Lumpe, comedienne who sings and dances. Some intricate choral work. Total cast, 33–50.

SCENES AND SETS: 2 acts, 22 scenes, 5 full stage sets, 8 partial stage sets, 4 drops, 1 wedding canopy.

ACT I
Scene 1A: A Bare Area.
Scene 1B: Nook of Alfie's Den and Siegals' TV room.
Scene 1C: Foyer in Nathan Apartment.
Scene 2: The Siegals' Bedroom.
Scene 2A: A Telephone Traveler.
Scene 3: In Front of Traveler, Alfie's Office, Bookshop, Flowershop, and Bakery.
Scene 4: Bridal Shop at Marshall Field.
Scene 5: Country Club Gym.
Scene 6: Siegals' Backyard.
Scene 7: Alfie's Backyard.
Scene 7A: A Football Field.
Scene 8: Old Oaks Country Club.
Scene 9: Nook of Alfie's Den.

ACT II
Scene I: Siegals' Kitchen.
Scene 2: Nook of Alfie's Den.
Scene 3: Bachelor Dinner.
Scene 4: Nook of Alfie's Den.
Scene 5: Corridor at Country Club.
Scene 6: In Front of Traveler.
Scene 7: Nook of Alfie's Den.
Scene 8: Corridor at Country Club.
Scene 9: The Wedding.

PERIOD AND COSTUMES: The present: suits, dresses, casual clothes, bathrobes, bridal fashions, gym suits, ridiculous cook-out aprons, frivolous clothes of affluent suburbia, uniforms for Country Club staff, sleazy evening dresses, wedding ensembles for all.

CHOREOGRAPHY: Ballroom, hula, modern, football game/cheerleader dance.

LIGHTING AND SPECIAL EFFECTS: Flexible area lighting required, onstage luau lanterns.

NOTES: Show is strongly Jewish-oriented and stretches one gag rather thin. Script is well-written, fast-paced comedy for seven/eighths of show. Ending with wedding is weak, but the women love it. Should be a great show for Jewish community center groups.

FANNY

Harold Rome (Music, Lyrics),
S. N. Behrman, Joshua Logan (Book)
Opened Nov. 4, 1954
888 Performances

BASED ON: Trilogy by Marcel Pagnol

AGENT: Tams-Witmark

PUBLISHED TEXT: Random House, 1955

RECORDINGS: RCA LOC(LSO)-1015

DIGEST OF PLOT: The teen-age love of Marius and Fanny has matured under the rueful guidance and encouragement of Cesar, Marius' arrogant yet appealing tavern-keeper father. Fanny loves Marius with all her heart, but he cannot fully accept her devotion. He is continually torn between his yearning for Fanny, his duty as an only son, and adventure calling him to sea. Marius gives in to the mystery of the sea and signs for a five-year voyage. His father disowns him, but Fanny bravely yields to her rival. In the passion of their goodbye Marius almost changes his mind. However, Fanny sends him on his way, knowing it is the only way to save their love. Soon thereafter Fanny discovers she is to bear a child. Panisse, an older man and wealthy sailmaker, has made previous marriage proposals to Fanny. In desperation she turns to him, and they are married. Having suspected the situation all along, Panisse is delighted at the prospect of the child's arrival. Convinced it will be a boy, Panisse digs out letters to make his store-front sign read "& Son." Cesar and Panisse, dedicated old-world (often fiery) friends, band together to see to the boy's rearing. On Cesario's first birthday, Marius returns and attempts to claim both Fanny and his son. Fanny finds it difficult to spurn her lover once more, but Cesar discovers them and drives him off. It is twelve years later. Like his true father before him, Cesario yearns for the sea and runs away to join Marius. This proves to be a final blow to an aging and ill Panisse. Marius returns the boy to the Panisse home. The final moments are happy, and Panisse's dying wish is that Fanny and Marius be reunited.

MUSICAL NUMBERS: "Never Too Late for Love," "Cold Cream Jar Song," "Octopus Song," "Restless Heart," "Why Be Afraid to Dance?," "Shika, Shika," "Welcome Home," "I Like You," "I Have to Tell You," "FANNY," "The Sailing," "Oysters, Cockles and Mussels," "Panisse and Son," "Wedding Dance," "Birthday Song," "To My Wife," "The Thought of You," "Love Is a Very Light Thing," "Other Hands, Other Hearts," "Montage," "Be Kind to Your Parents," "Cesario's Party."

INSTRUMENTATION: Violin A–C (2), D–B (mandolin), viola, cello, bass, flute (pic), oboe (Eng. horn), clar (bass clar), flute (clar), clar (bassoon), horns I–II, trumpets I–II, III, trombone I, II, harp, percussion, concertina, piano-celeste.

CASTING: 28 parts, 9 principals. Fanny and Marius, young lovers who act and sing. Panisse and Cesar, men of the world who must act very well and sing respectably. Honorine, Fanny's mother, must sing and act. Other principals and small ensemble carry a comparatively light load. Total cast 20–40.

SCENES AND SETS: 2 acts, 16 scenes, 8 full stage sets, 2 partial sets, fishnet drop (Hakim's cellar), 2 scene drops, plus large ship model in full sail as it glides off into the mist. Scrim helpful on wedding scene.

ACT I
Scene 1: Waterfront of Marseille.
Scene 2: Harkim's Cellar.
Scene 3: Cesar's Bar. Night.
Scene 4: Dock.
Scene 5: Cesar's Bar. Daytime.
Scene 6: Honorine's Kiosk.
Scene 7: Panisse's Sail Shop.
Scene 8: The Wedding.
Scene 9: Waterfront of Marseille.

ACT II
Scene 1: The Nursery.
Scene 2: Panisse's Living Room.
Scene 3: Vignette 1.
        Vignette 2.
        Vignette 3.
Scene 4: Cesario's Room.
Scene 5: Circus.
Scene 6: A Garage in Toulon.
Scene 7: Panisse's Bedroom.

PERIOD AND COSTUMES: The action takes place over a period of years in and around the Old Port of Marseille. The precise period is not mentioned or important. Styles should reflect the "Old World" flavor in dresses, men's suits, and sailor uniforms. Arabs, a Moroccan drummer, belly dancer, saloon girls, nuns, a young boy, a maid, a priest, and two acolytes.

CHOREOGRAPHY: Belly dance, choreographed couples number as sweethearts kiss their sailors goodbye, folklike town dancing, wedding dance, circus ballet.

LIGHTING AND SPECIAL EFFECTS: Ship sailing off into the distance, fog for mist, lighting effect during circus number, and good dramatic lighting throughout.

NOTES: *Fanny* is delicately written and one of the most dramatic musicals available. When the film was made the score was used for background music only with all songs deleted. However, onstage they capture a character depth that can't be projected on the motion picture screen.

FANTASTICKS, THE

Harvey Schmidt (Music),
Tom Jones (Book, Lyrics)
Opened May 3, 1960

BASED ON: Suggested by the Play, *Les Romantiques,* by Edmund Rostand

AGENT: Music Theatre

PUBLISHED TEXT: Drama Book Shop, 1964

RECORDINGS: MGM (S)38720C

DIGEST OF PLOT: Two crafty fathers want their children to marry each other, but know if the boy and girl were aware of this desire they would surely hate each other. So they have built a wall between their homes to keep them apart. Sure enough, they find this highly romantic and fall hopelessly in love. The fathers, noting their plan has been fulfilled, hire a band of actors to fake an abduction so the boy can fight them off and become a hero—thereby providing a reason for tearing down the wall and consummating the marriage. The plan succeeds, but with the mystique of romance removed, the realities of life are quick to cause problems. Both the boy and girl turn to things worldly and are hurt. Finding mutual need in hurt and disillusionment, their love is strengthened, and the pretty picture of romantic love is once more completed—this time on solid ground.

MUSICAL NUMBERS: "TRY TO REMEMBER," "Much More," "Metaphor," "Never Say No," "It Depends on What You Pay," "SOON IT'S GONNA RAIN," Rape Ballet, "Happy Ending," "This Plum Is Too Ripe," "I Can See It," "Plant a Radish," "Round and Round," "They Were You."

INSTRUMENTATION: Piano, harp, percussion, bass.

CASTING: 8 roles, 5 singing principals, 2 actors, and 1 mute/handyman. The Narrator, Boy, and Girl must sing well. Total cast, 8–15 with chorus added.

SCENES AND SETS: 2 acts, 1 set consisting of platform, 4 poles, and banner reading *The Fantasticks* in logo script.

PERIOD AND COSTUMES: The present: boy and girl wear casual clothes, fathers wear colorful suits, El Gallo wears black suit and hat, as does the mute, who also carries a large bag as part of his dress. Actors wear discarded costume tatters over brightly dyed union suits.

CHOREOGRAPHY: No dancing as such, but the whole production is almost choreographed rather than directed.

LIGHTING AND SPECIAL EFFECTS: Dramatic and flexible lighting is essential.

NOTES: *The Fantasticks* is a very charming and delicate show written to be performed intimately. When done on proscenium stage, every effort should be made to shrink the playing area. Build up orchestra pit and use as playing area. Use orchestra onstage. Use light towers and lowered batten lights in full view. The set—platform and four poles—is a boon to the set construction department, but an unprepared director's nightmare. Direction should be extremely graphic and tight, yet not overdone. As the book and lyric writer, Tom Jones, says, "Less is more."

COURTESY OF LORE NOTO

Original cast of The Fantasticks. *Top: Jerry Orbach; 2nd row: Hugh Thomas, Rita Gardner, William Larsen; bottom row: Richard Stauffer, Kenneth Nelson, and George Curley.*

FIDDLER ON THE ROOF

Jerry Bock (Music),
Joseph Stein (Book),
Sheldon Harnick (Lyrics)

Bottle Dance from Fiddler on the Roof.

Opened Sept. 22, 1964

BASED ON: Shalom Aleichem's Stories

AGENT: Music Theatre

PUBLISHED TEXT: Crown, 1964; Pocket Books, 1965(P)

RECORDINGS: RCA LOC(LSO)-1093
COL OL-6610
COL OS-3010

DIGEST OF PLOT: Tevye is the dairyman for the poverty-ridden Jewish settlement of Anatevka in Tsarist Russia. He has five daughters who ponder the future men in their lives at the very time Yente the matchmaker is arranging a marriage between Tevye's eldest, Tzeitel, and the town's wealthy butcher Lazar Wolf. On the way home Tevye meets Perchik, a student and would-be social reformer. He invites him to Sabbath dinner and to stay on to teach his daughters the Scriptures. Later he meets Lazar Wolf and agrees to the wedding. But Tzeitel is in love with Motel, a poor and lowly tailor. Tzeitel pleads their love, and Tevye gives his blessing. He stages a fake dream for his wife, Golde, to gain her support for the change in grooms. The wedding takes place, but is marred by a Tsar-ordered demonstration. Hodel has now expressed her wish to marry Perchik. Tevye agrees, even though he knows it will take her far from home. Pondering this new kind of love, Tevye questions Golde if she really loves him. Their third daughter, Chava, tells Tevye she wants the same freedom to marry. Only her choice is Fyedka, a gentile. This blow Tevye cannot accept and when he learns of their marriage, denies her existence. Word is received that all Jews must evacuate Anatevka for homes outside Russia. The villagers have already begun to scatter to the safe sectors of the world as Tevye's family pack their few belongings and begin the long journey to America.

MUSICAL NUMBERS: "Tradition," "MATCH-MAKER, MATCHMAKER," "If I Were a Rich Man," "Sabbath Prayer," "To Life," "Miracle of

Miracles," "The Tailor, Motel Kamzoil," "SUN-RISE, SUNSET," Bottle Dance, Wedding Dance, "Now I Have Everything," "Do You Love Me?," "I Just Heard," "Far from the Home I Love," "Anatevka," Epilogue. (The music of "Tradition" was a hit record under the title "Fiddler on the Roof Theme.")

INSTRUMENTATION: Violin, viola, cello, bass, flute I (alto flute, clar, pic), oboe (Eng. horn), clar I (E♭ clar, flute III), clar II (flute II, pic I), bassoon (bass clar), horns I–II, trumpet I–II, III, trombone I, II, percussion, plectrum, accordion, piano-conductor. (Modified version available.)

CASTING: 22 roles, 9 principals. Tevye, exceptional actor, sings, minor dancing, carries show. Golde, winning actress, sings. Tevye's daughters, Tzeitel, Hodel, Chava, sing. Motel and Lazar Wolf, actors who sing. Perchik, legit voice. Yente, straight character role, 1 minor song. Male dancing chorus. About 20 to 30 villagers (mostly sing) and the Fiddler who plays or fakes playing the violin. Total cast, 40–50.

COURTESY OF HAROLD PRINCE

Tevye (Paul Lipson) and Golde (Peg Murray) depart from Anatevka to seek a life in the New World.

SCENES AND SETS: 2 acts, 18 scenes, 4 full stage sets (interior and exterior of Tevye's house are the same unit), 4 drops, 1 partial set, 1 partial drop. In the original production Tevye's house was mounted on a small turntable offset on a large center turntable.

ACT I
Prologue
Scene 1: Kitchen of Tevye's House.
Scene 2: Exterior of Tevye's House.
Scene 3: Interior of Tevye's House.
Scene 4: The Inn.
Scene 5: Street Outside the Inn.
Scene 6: Outside Tevye's House.
Scene 7: Tevye's Bedroom.
Scene 8: Village Street and Motel's Tailor Shop.
Scene 9: Part of Tevye's Yard.
Scene 10: Tevye's Entire Yard.

ACT II
Prologue
Scene 1: Exterior of Tevye's House.
Scene 2: A Village Street.
Scene 3: Exterior of Railroad Station.
Scene 4: Village Street.
Scene 5: Motel's Tailor Shop.
Scene 6: A Road.
Scene 7: Tevye's Barn.
Scene 8: Outside Tevye's House.

PERIOD AND COSTUMES: 1905, Anatevka, a village in Russia on the eve of the revolutionary period: peasant costumes for the fathers, mothers, sons, and daughters, including waist prayer shawls and boots. Also skull caps, nightgowns and caps, constable and soldier uniforms, and the Fiddler's costume.

CHOREOGRAPHY: March opening, little strut, Jewish folk dancing, bottle dance, wedding dance, choreographed dream sequence, treadmill ending. Choreographic manual available.

LIGHTING AND SPECIAL EFFECTS: Dramatic lighting and flexible lighting equipment essential.

NOTES: *Fiddler on the Roof* is a sparkling musical, but all costumes, scenery, and lighting reflect the poverty of the Russian Jews.

FINIAN'S RAINBOW

Burton Lane (Music),
E. Y. Harburg, Fred Saidy (Book),
E. Y. Harburg (Lyrics)
Opened Jan. 10, 1947
725 Performances

BASED ON: Original

AGENT: Tams-Witmark

PUBLISHED TEXT: Random House, 1947; Berkley, 1968 (P); *Theatre Arts,* January, 1948

RECORDINGS: COL OL-4062
COL OS-2080
RCA LOC(LSO)-1057 (R)

DIGEST OF PLOT: Finian McLonergan arrives in Rainbow Valley, Missitucky, with his daughter,

Original cast of Finian's Rainbow *as they sang "Great Come and Get It Day."*

Sharon, and a "borrowed" pot of gold. His theory is to plant the gold near Fort Knox. Surely it will multiply just as America's bullion burial has made all Americans rich. They encounter poor sharecroppers who are about to lose their land. Henchmen of Senator Billboard Rawkins are ready to pay back taxes and take over. However, his plan is foiled by Woody, who returns from the big city with the tax money, and by Finian, who covers the hidden charges when Woody cannot. In exchange, Finian gets property rights for enough land to sow his golden dream. While Sharon and Woody are falling in love, Og, a leprechaun, confronts Finian and demands the return of his pot of gold. But Finian ignores him, as a figment of his imagination. Geologists, working on a secret dam project, detect gold on the sharecroppers' land. Learning this, Rawkins moves in to take the land by force. As he is manhandling a Negro sharecropper, Sharon wishes that Rawkins was black. Unwittingly, she is standing over the magical pot, and her wish is granted. Rawkins dashes into hiding. A telegram arrives from Shears and Robust granting unlimited credit to the people of the gold-rich valley. Woody persuades them to use the credit to buy tractors and equipment to improve the harvest. Without his gold, Og will become mortal. However, his search for the pot is interrupted by Sharon with whom he immediately falls in love. When Shears and Robust arrive to collect for all the merchandise, Woody satisfies them with proof of future profit. The McLonergan economic theory is working, but Sharon is charged with witchcraft and the mysterious disappearance of Rawkins. Og encounters Billboard in the woods and magically improves his disposition. Arriving back in the Valley, Og encounters Susan the Silent. Love strikes again, only harder. He also learns Sharon is to be burned as a witch unless a white Rawkins can be found. Og believes Susan can tell him where the gold is hidden and so wishes. She talks. He is sitting above the crock. He unearths the pot and makes the final wish that saves Sharon for Woody, but renders himself completely mortal. But Og has Susan. Finian, having proven his theory without a shadow of doubt, moves on to Oak Ridge, Tennessee, to proclaim the miracles of a small rock given him by Nicholas the Nucleus.

MUSICAL NUMBERS: "This Time of the Year," Dance, "HOW ARE THINGS IN GLOCCA-MORA?," "Look to the Rainbow," Dance, "OLD DEVIL MOON," "Something Sort of Grandish," "IF THIS ISN'T LOVE," Dance, "Necessity," "Great Come-and-Get-It Day," Dance, "When the Idle Poor Become the Idle Rich" Dance, Dance o' the Golden Crock, "The Begat," "WHEN I'M NOT NEAR THE GIRL I LOVE."

Rudy Bond as Ben Marino and politicians deliver "Politics and Poker," in Fiorello!

INSTRUMENTATION: Violin, A, B, C, D, viola, cello, bass, flute (pic, clar), oboe (Eng. horn), clar I, clar II (flute, pic), bass clar (clar, bassoon), horns I–II, trumpets I–II, trombone I, II, harp, guitar, percussion, piano, piano-conductor.

CASTING: 30 roles, 11 principals, large chorus of separate singing and dancing ensembles. Susan, dances but does not speak. Finian, comic character man, straight role. Woody and Sharon, romantic singing leads. Og, likable leprechaun, sings and dances. Rawkins, a screaming bigot, straight comic role. Strong choral work. Featured chorus parts. Children required (4–8). Total cast, 40–52.

SCENES AND SETS: 2 acts, 10 scenes, 3 full stage sets, 3 scenic drops.

ACT I
Scene 1: The Meetin' Place, Rainbow Valley, Missitucky.
Scene 2: The Same.
Scene 3: The Colonial Estate of Senator Billboard Rawkins.
Scene 4: The Meetin' Place.
Scene 5: A Path in the Woods.
Scene 6: The Meetin' Place.

ACT II
Scene 1: Rainbow Valley.
Scene 2: A Wooded Section of the Hills.
Scene 3: The Meetin' Place.
Scene 4: Just Before Dawn.

PERIOD AND COSTUMES: The fabled area of Missitucky, a state in the U.S.A.: appropriate costumes for sharecroppers, sheriff, Irish immigrants, Og the leprechaun (with breakaway pants—for him to grow out of), geologists, Shears and Robust (formal morning coats, etc.), preacher and three gospelers, deputies, Senator Rawkins (white Kentucky Colonel suit), and outlandish Hollywood fashions for each sharecropper and their children.

CHOREOGRAPHY: Modern ballet, couples number, parade, one male quartet number, one female quartet number.

LIGHTING AND SPECIAL EFFECTS: General lighting. Flash pots, white Senator is turned black on stage, rainbow is projected, lightning strikes.

NOTES: *Finian's Rainbow* is a brilliant work that was timely, ahead of its time, and highly durable in content. Its seemingly innocent comedy really bites. In a way it's two separate shows. The less mindful of the audience see a happy and funny musical. The more sophisticated see it as a tightly constructed musical that makes a powerful social statement.

FIORELLO!

Jerry Bock (Music),
Jerome Weidman, George Abbott (Book),
Sheldon Harnick (Lyrics)
Opened Nov. 23, 1959
796 Performances

BASED ON: Original

AGENT: Tams-Witmark

PUBLISHED TEXT: Random House, 1960; *Theatre Arts,* November, 1961

RECORDINGS: CAP-WAO(S)-1321

DIGEST OF PLOT: Fiorello H. LaGuardia is a storefront lawyer who champions the causes of his poor clientele. He confides to his secretary, Marie, and his staff that he wants to run for Congress on the Republican ticket. The word is eagerly greeted by the headquarters politicos who are wondering whom to sacrifice to Tammany Hall this election. In the meantime Fiorello is called on to bail out Thea, leader of the lady garment workers' union, who was arrested while leading picketing of her sweat-shop employer. Thea and Fiorello find comfort in their mutual causes and become close friends. Fiorello takes his soapbox campaign to every street corner in the district. The multilinguist wins the vote of the people much to the surprise of everyone. In Washington he sees the need for the unpopular draft act and is one of the first to volunteer for America's participation in World War I. Unaware of Marie's love for him, Fiorello proposes to Thea before going overseas. Newsreels depict Fiorello's hero role in winning the war, and he returns home. It's ten years later, and Fiorello has challenged Gentleman Jimmy Walker in New York City's mayoral race. Thea dies during the nightmare campaign, and James J. Walker is returned to office in a landslide. Later, the years of corruption have caught up with Walker. Fiorello, having returned to his law practice, discovers faithful Marie at last. He fires her because he can't marry an employee and embarks on the campaign that makes him Mayor of New York.

MUSICAL NUMBERS: "On the Side of the Angels," "Politics and Poker," "Unfair," "Marie's Law," "The Name's LaGuardia," "The Bum Won," "I Love a Cop," "TILL TOMORROW," "Home Again," "When Did I Fall in Love?," "Gentleman Jimmy," "Little Tin Box," "The Very Next Man."

INSTRUMENTATION: Violins (3), viola, cello, bass, clar (alto sax, soprano sax, flute, pic), clar (flute, pic), clar (oboe, Eng. horn), clar (tenor sax, soprano sax, bass clar, flute), clar (bari sax, alto sax, flute, bass clar, bassoon), trumpets I–II, III, trombone I, II, guitar-banjo, percussion, piano-celeste.

CASTING: 39 speaking parts (most very small), 7 principals. Fiorello, polished actor, sings; physical stature resembling real-life counterpart important to many directors. Morris, Ben, Floyd, and Thea (LaGuardia's first wife), capable actors and actress who sing. Dora, light acting, sings and dances. Mitzi, powerful voice, heads kick line. Marie, actress with legit voice. Strong choral work requiring several good voices. Total cast, 40–56.

SCENES AND SETS: 2 acts, 19 scenes, 7 full stage sets, 3 scene drops. The original production used a center turntable.

ACT I

Prologue
New York City—1914
Scene 1: Fiorello's Law Office in Greenwich Village.
Scene 2: Ben Marino's Association.
Scene 3: Street Outside Strike Headquarters.
Scene 4: Fiorello's Office.
Scene 5: A Street Corner.
Scene 6: "The Bum Won."
Scene 7: Roof of Greenwich Village Tenement.
Scene 8: Street Cross-Over.
Scene 9: Ben Marino's Club.
Scene 10: Gangplank—for Returning Soldiers.

ACT II

Ten Years Later
Scene 1: The LaGuardia Home.
Scene 2: The Penthouse.
Scene 3: Fiorello's Law Office.
Scene 4: Madison and 105th Street.
Scene 5: Fiorello's Office.
Scene 6: Radio Announcer.
Scene 7: Ben Marino's Association.
Scene 8: Fiorello's Office.

PERIOD AND COSTUMES: New York City, shortly before World War I: suits, dresses, shawls, evening wear, WWI Army uniforms, hats, and coats. Flapper dresses for kick line. Dandy clothes for Jimmy's crowd. Fashions, 1920's into early 1930's.

CHOREOGRAPHY: Soft shoe, tap, kick line, modern jazz.

LIGHTING AND SPECIAL EFFECTS: Movie of WWI clips and LaGuardia shots as he departs for the war zone, fights, wins, and returns from battle. Good flexible lighting very important.

NOTES: *Fiorello* has the greatest impact on those familiar with the famous New York Mayor in real life. The show is a masterpiece of construction and one of the few musicals to win the Pulitzer Prize. However, promotion, program notes, and perhaps a curtain speech should be utilized to make sure the audience is well acquainted with the life and achievements of the title character.

Miyoshi Umeki sings "A Hundred Million Miracles" to Keye Luke, Juanita Hall, Rose Quong, and Conrad Yama, in Flower Drum Song.

FLOWER DRUM SONG

Richard Rodgers (Music),
Oscar Hammerstein II, Joseph Fields (Book),
Oscar Hammerstein II (Lyrics)

Opened Dec. 1, 1958
600 Performances

BASED ON: Novel by C. Y. Lee

AGENT: R & H

PUBLISHED TEXT: Farrar, Straus and Cudahy, 1959

RECORDINGS: COL OL-5350

COL OS-2009
DEC (7)9098(F)

DIGEST OF PLOT: Mei Li, a contract bride to Sammy Fong, and her father, Dr. Li, arrive in San Francisco to prepare for the wedding. Sammy, owner of the hip Celestial Bar, is madly in love with show-girl Linda Low and wants no part of his mail-order Chinese bride. In the interest of family honor he persuades Wang Chi Yang, the father of Wang Ta, and staunch Chinese traditionist, to take over the contract for his son. But despite his father's strict guidance in Chinese custom, Wang Ta has allowed himself to fall in love with a wildly Americanized girl—the same Linda Low. Later Mei Li and Wang Ta meet and are taken with each other. But Wang

Ta is still determined to announce his engagement to Linda at a party to celebrate the citizenship of Madam Liang, his aunt. When Ta declares his intentions, Mei Li is deeply hurt, but Sammy Fong is flabbergasted—he's lost both his girl and his star at the Celestial Bar. When Linda isn't listening, fast-thinking Sammy invites Ta's family to his club the next evening to toast the event. They are seated at ringside when the mystery of Linda's past quickly dissolves: She's a top strip-tease artist. A disillusioned Ta calls off the marriage and gets drunk. He turns briefly to an eager Helen Chao for comfort. However, blind to Helen's love for him, Ta seeks out Mei Li. But Mei Li is aware that Ta has turned to Helen, which serves to reinforce her earlier hurt.

She moves to hold Sammy to the original marriage contract. Meanwhile, Sammy and Linda have reconciled. Mei Li is also having second thoughts about Ta. The Three Family Association has decreed that Sammy must honor the contract, and all parties are miserable. But at the wedding ceremony, Mei Li reveals a new technicality that breaks the contract and permits a double wedding for the chosen lovers.

MUSICAL NUMBERS: "You Are Beautiful," "A HUNDRED MILLION MIRACLES," "I ENJOY BEING A GIRL," "I Am Going to Like It Here," "Like a God," "Chop Suey," "Don't Marry Me," "Grant Avenue," Ballet, "LOVE LOOK AWAY," "Fan Tan Fannie," "Gliding Through My Memoree,"

Pat Suzuki and "Fan Tan Fannie" girls at the Celestial Bar.

COURTESY OF THE LYNN FARNOL GROUP, INC.

"The Other Generation," "SUNDAY," Wedding Parade.

INSTRUMENTATION: Violin I (2), II (2), viola, cello, bass, flute I (pic), II (pic), oboe (Eng. horn), clar I (alto sax), II (alto sax), bass clar (tenor sax), trumpet I–II, III, trombone I, II, horns I–II, tuba, harp, guitar (banjo, mandolin), percussion, piano, conductor.

CASTING: 18 parts, 9 principals, 2 featured dancers. 3 to 6 children. Linda Low, dancer with powerful singing voice. Helen Chao, legit singing voice. Wang Ta, handsome leading man with legit voice. Mei Li, good actress, sweet voice. Dr. Li, Wang Chi Yang, and Madam Liang, act and sing. Sammy Fong, good character actor, minor singing and dancing. Large separate singing and dancing choruses. Total cast, 40–50.

SCENES AND SETS: 2 acts, 14 scenes, 6 full stage sets, 3 partial sets, 3 scene drops.

ACT I
Scene 1: House of Master Wang Chi Yang.
Scene 2: A Hill Overlooking San Francisco Bay.
Scene 3: The Wang Living Room.
Scene 4: Wang Chi Yang's Bedroom.
Scene 5: The Garden of the Wang House.
Scene 6: Linda's Celestial Bar Dressing Room.
Scene 7: The Celestial Bar.

ACT II
Scene 1: Helen Chao's Room.
Scene 2: The Wang Living Room.
Scene 3: Sammy Fong's Penthouse Apartment.
Scene 4: The Three Family Association.
Scene 5: Sammy Fong's Penthouse Apartment.
Scene 6: Grant Avenue, San Francisco's Chinatown.
Scene 7: The Three Family Association.

PERIOD AND COSTUMES: San Francisco's Chinatown, the present: Chinese-American streetwear, flashy American suits, various Chinese happy coats, ceremonial robes, satin dresses with side slits, headdresses, wedding garments, mandarin robes, brief showgirl costumes representing eight countries, brief costumes for nightclub chorus girls, baseball uniform, nightgown, Commodore uniform, tee shirts, slacks, leotards, smocks.

CHOREOGRAPHY: Soft shoe, modern jazz, cabaret production number (including strip), modern ballet, wedding parade.

LIGHTING AND SPECIAL EFFECTS: Some dramatic lighting required. Wind and fog during ballet (optional). Projected fish and Oriental designs (optional).

NOTES: *Flower Drum Song* can easily drag, a factor its complicated book can ill afford. Ending is not the greatest. Sure-fire direction and rapid pace essential.

FUNNY GIRL

Jule Styne (Music),
Isobel Lennart (Book),
Bob Merrill (Lyrics)
Opened March 26, 1964
1,301 Performances

BASED ON: Original

AGENT: Tams-Witmark

PUBLISHED TEXT: Random House, 1964

RECORDINGS: CAP (S)VAS-2059

DIGEST OF PLOT: Fanny Brice sits quietly in her dressing room pondering the return of her husband, Nick Arnstein, following his prison term. She recalls the events that have led up to this moment. She broke into show business with Keeney's Music Hall and her talent soon gained her a featured number. One evening, matinee idol Arnstein showed up backstage. But he was not an actor, rather, an elegant gentleman present only to pay off a gambling debt to Keeney. Awkward, funny Fanny had never met such a beautiful man. Florenz Ziegfeld broke the trance with an offer to appear in his *Follies*. She was a smash, Nick was there and at the party at Fanny's home afterward. They found love and need in each other, but Nick was due in Kentucky on business. Several months later their paths crossed in Baltimore. Once hurt, she reluctantly joined Nick for a private dinner and was overwhelmed. She left the show to marry Nick. Eventually, Fanny returned to the new *Follies* and her star rose high. Nick tried to keep pace but his luck turned at both gambling and business deals. Fanny tried to secretly underwrite an important venture, but Nick found out and was more resolute than ever to make it on his own. To Nick, pride was more important than involvement in a phony bond deal. Now, as Fanny waits she knows her future is in the balance. Where does Nick stand? Can he forgive and overcome? He arrives and is reluctant. He knows himself too well. As he leaves her, Fanny picks up her life and prepares to go onstage.

MUSICAL NUMBERS: "If a Girl Isn't Pretty," "I'm the Greatest Star," "Coronet Man," "Who Taught Her Everything?," "His Love Makes Me Beautiful," "I Want to Be Seen with You Tonight," "Henry Street," "PEOPLE," "You Are Woman," "DON'T RAIN ON MY PARADE," "Sadie, Sadie," "Find Yourself a Man," "Rat-Tat-Tat-Tat," "Who Are You Now?," "THE MUSIC THAT MAKES ME DANCE."

INSTRUMENTATION: Violins, cello, bass, flute (pic, clar, alto sax, alto flute), flute (pic, clar, alto sax, soprano sax), clar (bass clar, tenor sax, E♭ clar), clar (tenor sax, oboe), clar (bari sax, bassoon, bass sax), horn, trumpets I–II, III, trombone I, II, III, guitar-banjo, percussion I–II, piano-celeste.

Roger De Koven (Florenz Ziegfeld, Jr.) helps provide courage to Barbra Streisand (Fanny) shortly before Nick Arnstein returns. Scene from Funny Girl.

CASTING: 28 roles, 8 principals. Fanny, accomplished singer, actress, and comedienne who carries the show. Nick, handsome, good voice. Eddie, song-and-dance man. Mrs. Brice, good matronly actress, 2 vocals. Featured dancers, majestic show girls, and featured tenor, plus large separate singing and dancing choruses. Total cast, 40–50.

SCENES AND SETS: 2 acts, 24 scenes, 11 full stage sets including 4 or 5 drops (3 are backstage scenes of three theatres with flats against the wall, bare light, etc.), 3 partial sets, 1 drop, 1 scrim optional. Large set of steps.

ACT I
Scene 1: The New Amsterdam Theatre—Fanny's Dressing Room.
Scene 2: The Card Game.
Scene 3: The Stage of Keeney's Music Hall.
Scene 4: In Front of Keeney's Music Hall.
Scene 5: Fanny's Neighborhood.
Scene 6: Stage of Keeney's Music Hall.
Scene 7: Backstage at Keeney's Music Hall.
Scene 8: The Brice House.
Scene 9: Backstage at the New York Theatre.
Scene 10: The "Ziegfeld Follies" (Finale)—The New York Theatre.
Scene 11: Backstage at the New York Theatre.
Scene 12: Henry Street.
Scene 13: The Card Game.
Scene 14: A Private Dining Room.

ACT II
Scene 1: The New Amsterdam Theatre, Backstage.
Scene 2: New Amsterdam Theatre.
Scene 3: Fanny's Dressing Room and Backstage.
Scene 4: The Card Game.

Scene 5: The Arnstein Home.
Scene 6: Fanny's Dressing Room.
Scene 7: The New Amsterdam Theatre, Fanny's Dressing Room.
Scene 8: The Brice Home.
Scene 9: The New Amsterdam Theatre.
Scene 10: New Amsterdam Theatre, Fanny's Dressing Room.

PERIOD AND COSTUMES: 1915 to the 1920's: regular streetwear of the period, Dixieland band costumes, formal wear, brief showgirl costumes, maternity wedding dress, WWI Army uniforms, fringed dresses, party dresses, female evening wear, large hats, and other trimmings.

CHOREOGRAPHY: Tap, modern jazz, soft shoe, Ziegfeld production numbers, brief Jewish folk dancing.

LIGHTING AND SPECIAL EFFECTS: Dramatic and flexible lighting required to maintain the production's fast pace and to facilitate the large number of scenes and sets.

NOTES: One of the rare musicals to risk an unhappy ending, *Funny Girl* succeeded to a large degree on the talent of Barbra Streisand. It occasionally becomes ponderous and can stand some cutting. An outstanding girl to play Fanny is an absolute must. The Ziegfeld production numbers are virtually useless if they do not reflect the opulence, grace, and beauty of the originals.

FUNNY THING HAPPENED ON THE WAY TO THE FORUM, A

Stephen Sondheim (Music, Lyrics),
Burt Shevelove, Larry Gelbart (Book)
Opened May 8, 1962
966 Performances

BASED ON: The Plays of Plautus

AGENT: Music Theatre

PUBLISHED TEXT: Dodd, Mead and Co., 1963.

RECORDINGS: CAP-WAO(S) 1717
U.A. 4144(F)
U.A. 5144(F)

DIGEST OF PLOT: Hero agrees to free Pseudolus on the delivery of the courtesan Philia. Thinking the matter an easy task, Pseudolus presents himself at the house of Lycus, the dealer in courtesans in search of Philia, whom he is claiming for himself. However, she is not among Lycus' current wares. Just as he is about to leave, he spies Philia in an upstairs window, but soon learns that this new virgin from Crete has already been sold to the noble warrior Capt. Miles Gloriosus. Pseudolus convinces Lycus there is a plague in Crete and arranges for her to stay at Hero's house until the Captain arrives. Just as Hero and Philia find their true love for each other, Hero's father, Senex, unexpectedly returns from an aborted journey. Thinking Senex the Captain, Philia bravely seeks to do her duty in offering herself to him. Taking advantage of the situation, Senex moves her to the house of Erronius, an aging citizen who has been away for 20 years in search of his long-lost daughter and son. But alas, Erronius has now returned. Senex' slave Hysterium plays on the sounds coming from the house to make Erronius believe that it is haunted, and Pseudolus convinces him that the only way to exorcise the evil spirits is to circle the seven hills of Rome seven times. The calm is brief, however, as the Captain has arrived seeking his bride. Learning that the missing girl has been turned over to the charge of Pseudolus, Miles turns upon him, dagger raised. In desperation he cries—"Intermission!" When action resumes, Pseudolus sidesteps death by promising to deliver Philia. Faced with the problem of delivering Philia to both the Captain and Hero, Pseudolus gets Hysterium to masquerade as a dead version of Philia long enough to send the Captain back off to war. In the process of funeral ceremonies the masquerade is discovered, and it is trouble for all. At the darkest moment Erronius completes his seventh circumference of the hills to discover that the necklace worn by Philia and ring worn by Miles prove without a doubt that they are indeed his long-lost children—brother and sister. Learning the news, Miles is now happy to give his sister to Hero, her true love. Pseudolus, thanks to the gods of comedy, is at last a free man.

MUSICAL NUMBERS: "Comedy Tonight," "Love, I Hear," "Free," "The House of Marcus Lycus," "Lovely," "Pretty Little Picture," "Everybody Ought to Have a Maid," "I'm Calm," "Impossible," "Bring Me My Bride," "That Dirty Old Man," "That'll Show Him," Funeral Sequence and Dance.

INSTRUMENTATION: Violin, viola, cello, bass, clar (flute, alto sax), clar (alto sax), clar (tenor sax), bass clar (bari sax, clar), flute (clar), trumpet I–II, III, trombone I, II, III, percussion, harp.

CASTING: 19 parts, 10 principals, no chorus. (A few courtesans and warriors may be added for big scenes if desired.) Everyone sings and does comic bits, no dancing as such. Girls are all statuesque and glamorous. Prologue (Pseudolus), accomplished comic actor who sings well, minor dance. Hero and Philia, young lovers with legit voices. Miles Gloriosus, deep, powerful baritone or bass. Total cast, 19.

SCENES AND SETS: 2 acts, continuous action, 1 unit set consisting of 3 buildings (the houses of Erronius, Senex, and Lycus). The center stage, 1 atop 2 or 3 step platforms; all are 2 stories with action on the second level of the center structure. From time to time people appear at the second-floor windows of the other two.

John Carradine, Jack Gilford, David Burns, and Zero Mostel whoop it up in A Funny Thing Happened on the Way to the Forum.

PERIOD AND COSTUMES: Rome, 200 B.C.: togas, tunics, brief and exotic courtesan costumes with long flowing veils, robes, garb of the conqueror and his warriors, including armor and spears.

CHOREOGRAPHY: Opening comedy march, a chase, female seduction sequences, parade.

LIGHTING AND SPECIAL EFFECTS: General lighting for a day in spring.

NOTES: *Funny Thing* is a great burlesque in the true sense of the word. As done on Broadway, this show was a large treasure chest of sight gags, slapstick, and a bevy of old-time burlesque routines (a recurring artificial leg the most common). The bits for local productions need not necessarily be the same, but they must be funny and many.

GENTLEMEN PREFER BLONDES

Jule Styne (Music),
Joseph Fields, Anita Loos (Book),
Leo Robin (Lyrics)
Opened Dec. 8, 1949
740 Performances

BASED ON: Original

AGENT: Music Theatre

PUBLISHED TEXT: Manuscript Only

RECORDINGS: COL OL-4290
COL OS-2310

DIGEST OF PLOT: Dancers Lorelei Lee and

Carol Channing and the original cast of Gentlemen Prefer Blondes.

WISCONSIN CENTER FOR THEATRE RESEARCH

friend Dorothy have taken leave of the *Follies* and Prohibition for an ocean crossing on the *Île de France* and a booking in Paris. Lorelei is depressed at leaving her boy friend, Gus, behind, but recovers as soon as the ship is out to sea. She finds Dorothy a rich bachelor in Henry Spofford. This leaves Lorelei free to pursue Sir Francis Beekman, or, more specifically, Lady Beekman's diamond tiara. It's all legal. Lady Beekman wants to sell and Sir Francis wants to lend Lorelei the money to buy. Against the Paris skyline, Dorothy and Henry have fallen in love. Lorelei is already cultivating a new daddy in Josephus Gage. By this time Lady Beekman has discovered how Lorelei came by the money to purchase the tiara and sends her lawyers to collect. Gus arrives just as Lorelei is doing her best to coax the loan repayment money from Gage. Lorelei flees to make her nightclub debut with Dorothy. The girls are a great success, and later Lorelei makes up with Gus, who also agrees to repay the loan. They are to be married as all the dilemmas are solved and everyone is anxious to get back home to the U.S.A.

MUSICAL NUMBERS: "It's High Time," "Bye, Bye Baby," "A Little Girl from Little Rock," "I Love What I'm Doing," "Just a Kiss Apart," "It's Delightful Down in Chile," "Sunshine," "In the Champ de Mars," "I'm A-tingle, I'm A-glow," "House on Rittenhouse Square," "You Say You Care," "Mamie Is Mimi," "Coquette," "DIAMONDS ARE A GIRL'S BEST FRIEND," "Gentlemen Prefer Blondes," "Homesick Blues," "Keeping Cool with Coolidge," "Button Up with Esmond."

INSTRUMENTATION: Violins A–C, B–D, cello, viola, bass, pic (flute, clar, alto sax), clar (oboe, Eng. horn, alto sax), tenor sax (clar, bass clar), flute (pic, clar, bass clar, tenor sax), clar (bass clar, bassoon, alto sax, bari sax), trumpet I–II, III, trombone I, II, horn I–II, percussion, piano-conductor.

CASTING: 26 parts, 9 principals. Dorothy and Lorelei, song-and-dance leads, accomplished at both. Gus, light comic, sings. Henry, legit voice. Gage, strong baritone. Lady Beekman, straight role. Sir Francis and Mrs. Spofford, mostly straight roles, minor singing. Large separate singing and dancing choruses. Total cast, 45–55.

SCENES AND SETS: 2 acts, 12 scenes, 6 full stage sets (including 3 drops), 3 scene drops, large gangplanks.

ACT I
Scene 1: The French Line Pier in New York.
Scene 2: The Sun Deck of the *Île de France.*
Scene 3: The Boat Deck.
Scene 4: Lorelei's Suite on the *Île de France.*
Scene 5: Place Vendôme, Paris.
Scene 6: Champ de Mars—Under the Eiffel Tower.
Scene 7: The Place Vendôme.
Scene 8: Ritz Hotel in Paris—Lorelei's Suite.

ACT II
Scene 1: The Pre-Catelan in the Bois.
Scene 2: A Street in Paris.
Scene 3: The Ritz Hotel in Paris, Lorelei's Suite.
Scene 4: The Central Park Casino, New York.

PERIOD AND COSTUMES: 1924: flapper dresses, large hats, fringe skirts, plume headdresses, diamond tiara, deck dresses, brief girly production number costumes, evening dresses, double-breasted suits and overcoats, two white suits, diamond-studded flapper dress, white fur stoles, French streetwear, bathing suits, Olympic team blazers, policeman uniform, formal wear, flower girl, taxi driver.

CHOREOGRAPHY: Production numbers, tap, kick line, Charleston, dance specialties, some blues.

LIGHTING AND SPECIAL EFFECTS: Some dramatic lighting required.

NOTES: *Gentlemen Prefer Blondes* is a frivolous show; highly formula. Best presented as a light occasion or part of a running series of musicals as a change of pace. More than the average number of songs and a lot of material to squeeze in best performance time. Excellent direction required.

GEORGE M

George M. Cohan (Music, Lyrics),
Michael Stewart, John and Fran Pascal (Book),
Mary Cohan (Lyric and Musical Revisions)
Opened April 10, 1968
427 Performances

BASED ON: Original

AGENT: Tams-Witmark

PUBLISHED TEXT: Manuscript Only

RECORDINGS: COL KOS-3200

DIGEST OF PLOT: Following a brief prologue, Jerry Cohan learns of the birth of his son while on a vaudeville stage in Providence, R.I. It's years later and we find the four Cohans in Cedar Rapids working their way toward Broadway. Finally there's a big break—vaudeville impresario E. F. Albee will catch their act. Albee wants only sister Josie, but relents and agrees to use the whole act for an out-of-town circuit. George blurts out it's Broadway or nothing. Blowing their chance, the Cohans move to New York to try to make it their own way. In the process of building a name, George meets Ethel Levey. During the period of their courtship, the four Cohans and Ethel Levey achieve fame. She and George are married. Not satisfied with vaudeville success, George seeks a new form of entertainment. He writes his first musical comedy, but it is a flop. Unshaken, he starts to build *Little Johnny Jones.*

Joel Grey in his recreation of the life of George M. Cohan in George M sings "Give My Regards to Broadway" from Little Johnny Jones.

Auditions are held, numbers run through, scenery constructed, climaxing in the full production of "Give My Regards to Broadway." George M. Cohan has his first hit. Now a success on Broadway, George and his partner, Sam Harris, seek to become the kings. They sign the biggest star of the day, Fay Templeton. George is now on top, but wife Ethel is fed up, and the two are divorced. The event has a heavy impact on George's tremendous ego. Later he runs into Agnes Nolan from the cast of *Little Johnny Jones* and confides his troubles to her. Soon after she becomes the second Mrs. Cohan. With Agnes, George writes some of his more endearing works, including "Yankee Doodle Dandy," "Nellie Kelly," "Harrigan," "Over There," and "You're a Grand Old Flag." But then things begin to happen to the people that George has held most dear. His father has died, his sister Josie has married and left the theatre, and the actors whom he has always paid better than other producers have voted in Actors Equity and are presenting their "demands." Rather than recognize the union, he declares he will write no more shows. With the success of the union George retires from the Broadway scene. True to fact, George

comes out of retirement in the 1930's to help friend Sam Harris by starring in a new show, *I'd Rather Be Right*. Things have changed, and George is forced to eat a little crow by taking instead of giving orders. George confides to Agnes that he is a bit shaken by the experience but that he is happy about one fact—he is on Broadway again.

The show also has an epilogue of Cohan songs, which could be optional.

MUSICAL NUMBERS: "Musical Moon," "Oh, You Wonderful Boy," "All Aboard for Broadway," "Musical Comedy Man," "I Was Born in Virginia," "Twentieth Century Love," "My Town," "BILLIE," "Push Me Along in My Pushcart," "Ring to the Name of Rose," "POPULARITY," "GIVE MY REGARDS TO BROADWAY," "FORTY-FIVE MINUTES FROM BROADWAY," "SO LONG, MARY," "DOWN BY THE ERIE," "MARY," "All Our Friends," "YANKEE DOODLE DANDY," "NELLIE KELLY I LOVE YOU," "HARRIGAN," "OVER THERE," "YOU'RE A GRAND OLD FLAG," "The City," "I'd Rather Be Right," "Dancing Our Worries Away," "The Great Easter Sunday

Parade," "Hannah's a Hummer," "Barnum and Bailey Rag," "Belle of the Barber's Ball," "The American Ragtime," "All in the Wearing," "I WANT TO HEAR A YANKEE DOODLE TUNE."

INSTRUMENTATION: Violin I (2), II, viola, cello, bass, pic (flute, clar), clar (oboe, Eng. horn), flute (clar), clar (bassoon), horn, trumpets I–II, III, trombone I, II, percussion, piano-conductor.

CASTING: 25 parts, 6 principals (supporting parts play up to 7 walk-ons each). George M, highly versatile actor, singer, and tap dancer. Jerry, Nellie, and Josie Cohan, also versatile singers and dancers who act. Ethel Levey, actress who sings and dances. Agnes Nolan, actress who sings. Fay Templeton, sings "Mary." Sam Harris, actor who leads company in "All Our Friends" number. Extremely versatile cast. Chorus members sing and dance. Try to keep cast under 80.

SCENES AND SETS: 2 acts, 18 scenes, no sets repeated, practically all are full stage, but several are "stages," achieved with various curtains (Act II, Scene 8, is bare stage), 2 scenic drops, proscenium drape., Portable ship for "Give My Regards to Broadway" is built piece by piece as part of stage action and "sails" off mid-number, and large model of same sails in front of scenic drop to fire skyrocket. (Many of the sets fly in.)

ACT I
Scene 1: Prologue.
Scene 2: Providence, Rhode Island, 1878.
Scene 3: Onstage, Columbia Theatre, Cedar Rapids.
Scene 4: Street in Cedar Rapids.
Scene 5: Madame Grimaldi's Boarding House.
Scene 6: En Route to New York.
Scene 7: Adams Street Theatre, Various Other Theatres, New York, 1901–03.
Scene 8: General Area, New York, Then in Front of Savoy Theatre.
Scene 9: Stage of Liberty Theatre, New York.

ACT II
Scene 1: Office of Cohan and Harris, Fay Templeton's Apartment.
Scene 2: Onstage, New Amsterdam Theatre.
Scene 3: Rector's Restaurant, January 1, 1907.
Scene 4: Street Outside Rector's, Next Morning.
Scene 5: The Years till 1919.
Scene 6: The Years till 1937.
Scene 7: Midtown New York, February, 1937.
Scene 8: Stage of the Alvin Theatre.
Scene 9: Epilogue.

PERIOD AND COSTUMES: From 1878 to 1937: approximately 85 costumes for the major people in George M's life, plus a full set of chorus costumes for each of the following numbers, "Give My Regards to Broadway," "Down By the Erie," "All Our Friends," "Yankee Doodle Dandy," "Grand Old Flag" sequence, and "The City." Dancers' togs and rehearsal clothes used in prologue. Epilogue—full company mostly in costumes used previously, but principals have special wardrobe featuring George M in all-white formal wear. Several areas of under-dressing, fast changes, and other costuming shortcuts and problems.

CHOREOGRAPHY: Several group and solo tap numbers, large production numbers.

LIGHTING AND SPECIAL EFFECTS: Dramatic and versatile lighting required (quick massive changes and several cross-fades, etc.). Firing of sky-rocket. Twin player pianos to perform the entracte were used in the original production with great success.

NOTES: *George M* is a massive undertaking, but practically every song in the score is a hit with many classics included—familiar songs presented in a new and exciting way. Putting on this show takes detailed planning, building, and coordination. There are a fantastic number of places to go wrong, but the rewards of a great production make the effort truly worthwhile. Show must run at fantastic pace. Definitely not a show for beginners.

GOLDEN APPLE, THE

Jerome Moross (Music),
John Latouche (Book, Lyrics)
Opened April 20, 1954
125 Performances

BASED ON: Original

AGENT: Tams-Witmark

PUBLISHED TEXT: Random House, 1954

RECORDINGS: ELEK-5000

DIGEST OF PLOT: The engrossing tale of Ulysses and Helen is modernized to the town of Angel's Roost, Washington, on Mt. Olympus. Ulysses is leading the local boys home from war. Old Mother Hare, the town wizard, steals the scene at the welcome-home picnic given in the boys' honor by donating a golden apple to be presented to the winner of a baking contest. Paris, a traveling salesman, is elected to be judge of the contest and is promptly bribed by every contestant. In exchange for power over all women, he makes the appropriate award and steals Helen in his balloon. Brave Ulysses rounds up the boys to journey to the big city in pursuit. "He arrives, takes over the place, and sends poor Helen home in disgrace." Mayor Hector, never to take defeat lightly, plots his revenge by introducing the boys to the vices of the big city. One by one they are lost, and Ulysses is left alone. He overcomes a series of obstacles to return home eventually to Penelope and find true love.

MUSICAL NUMBERS: "Nothing Ever Happens in Angel's Roost," "Mother Hare's Seance," "My

Bibi Osterwald leads original cast of The Golden Apple *in "Goona-Goona" number.*

Love Is on the Way," "The Heroes Come Home," "It Was a Glad Adventure," "Come Along, Boys," "It's the Going Home Together," "Mother Hare's Prophecy," "Helen Is Always Willing," "The Church Social," "Introducin' Mr. Paris," "The Judgment of Paris," "LAZY AFTERNOON," "The Departure for Rhododendron," "My Picture in the Papers," "The Taking of Rhododendron," "Hector's Song," "Wind Flowers," "Store-bought Suit," "Calypso," "Scylla and Charybdis," "Goona-Goona," "Doomed, Doomed, Doomed," "Circe, Circe," "Ulysses' Soliloquy," "The Sewing Bee," "The Tirade."

INSTRUMENTATION: Violin I (2), II, viola, cello, bass, flute, oboe, clar I (alto sax), clar II (bass clar, tenor sax), bassoon, horns I, II, trumpets I, II, trombone, percussion, harp, piano-celeste, piano-conductor.

CASTING: 24 parts cast by voice type. All legitimate voices, 10 principals. Helen (mezzo-soprano), flighty. Lovey Mars (contralto), Mrs. Juniper (mezzo-soprano), Miss Minerva (soprano), competitive neighbors. Mother Hare (contralto), witch confined to wheelchair. Penelope (soprano), heroine. Ulysses (baritone), hero and strongest voice. Paris, ballet dancer, does not speak or sing. Hector (bass), bad guy, can soft shoe. Menelaus, tenor. 6 heroes, 3 tenors, baritone, bass-baritone, bass. Dancers, 6 boys, 6 girls. Chorus, sopranos, altos, tenors, basses (4 each).

SCENES AND SETS: 2 acts, 10 scenes, 6 full stage sets, 5 partial sets that must be mounted on wheels or turntables, 2 scene drops.

ACT I
Scene 1: In the Orchard.
Scene 2: The Village Green.
Scene 3: The Church Social.
Scene 4: At Helen's House.

ACT II
Scene 1: The Seaport of Rhododendron.

Scene 2: The Main Street of Rhododendron.
Scene 3: Back in Angel's Roost.
  Penelope's Home.
Scene 4: The Main Street.
Scene 5: The Big Spree.
  Madame Calypso's Parlor.
  Brokerage Office.
  A Waterfront Dive.
  The Hall of Science.
  The Wrong Side of Tracks.
Scene 6: Orchard at Angel's Roost.

PERIOD AND COSTUMES: 1900–1910, Angel's Roost, Washington, near Mt. Olympus: Sunday go-to-meetin' clothes, checkered suits, Yankee-type Army uniforms, black dress ensemble for Mother Hare, "store-bought" suits, seduction dresses, flower costumes, calypso, fancy dude suit, South Seas, Grecian banquet gowns, Circe's flowing veil dress.

CHOREOGRAPHY: Major dance sequence when Paris seduces Helen while she sings "Lazy Afternoon": slow modern ballet, waltz steps, two-step, folk steps.

LIGHTING AND SPECIAL EFFECTS: Descending then ascending balloon. Some dramatic and flexible lighting required, mostly in second act. Rocket, smoke, breakaway sets.

NOTES: *The Golden Apple* is written in two styles, the first act as an operetta, the second as a revue with much of the action in pantomime. The production is completely sung.

GOLDEN BOY

Charles Strouse (Music),
Clifford Odets, William Gibson (Book),
Lee Adams (Lyrics)
Opened Oct. 20, 1964
569 Performances

BASED ON: Odets' Play

AGENT: Samuel French

PUBLISHED TEXT: Atheneum, 1965

RECORDINGS: CAP (S)VAS-2124

DIGEST OF PLOT: Against his father's wishes, Joe Wellington takes up prize fighting because it gives him some prestige in the ghetto. Joe's white manager, Tom Moody, needs $500 to divorce his wife to marry his girl, Lorna. Tom knows Joe could be a better fighter if he would really put his heart into it. Sensing Joe's attraction to Lorna, Tom sends her into the ghetto to persuade Joe to fight harder. Joe questions her motives and asks why she cannot go for him. Meanwhile, Joe's brother-in-law, Ronnie, leads the ghetto dwellers in a mock of the deplorable living and environmental conditions. Following his talk with Lorna, Joe agrees to a road trip to gain expertise. As his reputation builds, Eddy Satin, an influential black promoter, becomes interested in Joe and wants to buy in. Tom is against the idea even though it would mean better fights for Joe. The decision, however, is Joe's. Eddy stages a big New York fight for Joe as a sample of how things can be under his management. In Joe's dressing room before the fight, he confesses his love to Lorna and declares he's fighting for her whether she likes it or not. He also gives her the choice of success with him, or Tom and nothing. Joe's father arrives to plead once more for Joe not to fight. Despite the internal wish to concede to his father, Joe is now driven by prize fighting's rewards. Following the fight, Eddie Satin throws a big party at his plush apartment and awards Joe luxuries far in excess of his winnings as a testament to future success. The influence Satin is building is obvious. Once again, Tom turns to Lorna to bail them out. She knows he's weakening and tries to convince him that there must be another way. But Tom is relentless in his wishes. Once again she seeks out Joe. This time, however, the interracial prejudices are stripped away, baring their mutual love. The next day when Lorna announces she is leaving the now-divorced Tom, he threatens suicide if she does. Knowing that he will, she denies Joe. Satin is now in complete control, which paves the way for a title fight with Lopez. Sensing Joe's personal defeat, his father finally gives him the word to fight just as he is to enter the ring with Lopez. Despite a drastic beating, Joe fights back in a desperate, ferocious daze to KO Lopez. In the midst of the dressing room celebration, Joe learns that Lopez is not only out, but dead. Immediately the warnings of his father and the weaknesses of his own personal drive appear before him. He never meant to injure or kill. His only goals were the rewards, now empty desires. In desperation, he turns to the high speed of his Ferrari, which adds his own life to his list of sacrifices.

MUSICAL NUMBERS: Workout, "Night Song," "Everything's Great," "Gimme Some," "Stick Around," "Don't Forget 127th Street," "Lorna's Here," The Road Tour, "This Is the Life," "Golden Boy," "While the City Sleeps," "Colorful," "I Want to Be with You," "Can't You See It?," "No More," The Fight.

INSTRUMENTATION: Violins, viola, cello, bass, reed I (E♭ alto sax, flute, pic, B♭ clar), reed II (E♭ alto sax, B♭ clar), reed III (B♭ tenor sax, B♭ clar), reed IV (B♭ tenor sax, B♭ clar, B♭ bass clar), trumpets I–II, III, trombone I, II, percussion.

CASTING: 23 parts, 8 principals. Joe Wellington, demanding Negro lead, must be accomplished actor who can sing and dance well. Lorna, white girl who has been around, sings. Mr. Wellington, concerned father, straight role. Tom, white fight manager, minor singing. Eddie Satin, ghetto king of vice, sings. Lopez, featured dancer. Tokio, trainer, straight role. Large singing and dancing chorus (Negro and white). Total cast, 40–50.

SCENES AND SETS: 2 acts, 20 scenes, the original Broadway production used projected scenery plus approximately 20 fly-ins to form the 11 settings. To achieve similar settings with solid scenery would require 7 full stage sets, 2 partial sets, and 4 drops. 2 scenes done on a black stage.

ACT I
Scene 1: A Gym.
Scene 2: Wellington Kitchen.
Scene 3: Tenement Rooftop.
Scene 4: Tom Moody's Office.
Scene 5: Schoolyard Playground.
Scene 6: Harlem Street Scene.
Scene 7: The Wellington Kitchen.
Scene 8: Railroad Depot.
Scene 9: The Road Tour.
Scene 10: The Madison Square Garden Marquee/ Joe's Dressing Room.

ACT II
Scene 1: A Bar.
Scene 2: Eddie's Penthouse Apartment.
Scene 3: River and Bridge Scene with Park Bench.
Scene 4: The Park.
Scene 5: Tom's Office.
Scene 6: Harlem Street "127th Street."
Scene 7: Dressing Room.
Scene 8: Boxing Ring.
Scene 9: Dressing Room.
Scene 10: Harlem Street.

PERIOD AND COSTUMES: New York City 1960–1964: current fashions, dresses, suits, sports clothes, streetwear, sweaters, jackets, boxing shorts and gloves, formal wear, evening dresses, Madison Square Garden attendant uniforms.

CHOREOGRAPHY: Modern ballet in boxing motif, modern jazz, rock 'n' roll, fight ballet.

LIGHTING AND SPECIAL EFFECTS: Special lighting effects, projected scenery, dramatic lighting required, follow spots used from wing loft positions.

NOTES: *Golden Boy* could have been a great musical. Instead, it is only a good one. The second script written in Detroit prior to Broadway tryouts was much better. In this version, Joe was a would-be surgeon, fighting only to pay his way through college. He won't fight harder for fear of injuring the hands he hopes someday will save the lives of Negroes who are turned away by white surgeons. Tom doesn't know the reason he won't hit harder and sends Lorna to bring Joe around. When Lorna finds him in a ghetto park, he is studying his medical books. She is drawn to him, but the racial barrier blocks further developments. The part of Joe's father is much stronger in this version as the man who has sacrificed everything to get Joe as far as he is. All

along, he's against Joe's fighting even if it does mean a faster education. Eddie Satin comes across a bigger heel in that such ideals mean nothing to him. When Tom sends Lorna to Joe the second time, the scene provided an understanding of interracial love that never really jells in the "official" version. Never were they closer than four feet until they ran off together at the scene-ending blackout, yet every member of the audience was pushing them together. And, of course, the fight, when the hands that were so painstakingly guided to save lives have killed, completes the paradox. The construction was magnificent. It might be well worth reconstructing.

GOLDILOCKS

Leroy Anderson (Music),
Walter and Jean Kerr (Book),
Joan Ford, Walter and Jean Kerr (Lyrics)
Opened Oct. 11, 1958
161 Performances

BASED ON: Original

AGENT: Samuel French

PUBLISHED TEXT: Doubleday & Co., Inc., 1958; Samuel French (P)

RECORDINGS: COL OL-5340
COL OS-2007

DIGEST OF PLOT: Maggie is concluding her farewell performance in show business. She is retiring to marry George Randolph Brown, a dashing young millionaire. Amid the farewell wishes, Max Crady enters waving an old movie contract. Despite George's offers to buy him out, Max is determined to hold Maggie to the agreement of one film. Actually, Max is shooting a series of one-reelers but manages to convince Maggie that they are all part of the same picture. This is all part of Max's plan to do a major spectacular on Egypt. He knows as soon as he agrees that Maggie has finished her picture she will depart to marry George. He'll be stuck with lovable but untalented Lois Lee. And besides, even hard-hearted Max is falling for Maggie. Max isn't releasing any pictures, however, and his limited capital is long gone. Pete, his right-hand man, solves the problem by getting George to finance the payroll. As an investor George is now on the site watching the proceedings. During the filming he gets carried away, thinking Maggie is in danger, and is injured while trying to save her. While in the hospital he is visited by Lois, and the two find much in common. Maggie arrives to chide George for getting involved with the production company she is trying to get rid of. George counters by announcing that he has purchased the company for her as a wedding present and that she is now Max's boss. The triumphant Maggie wastes no time to take out after Max, a sign that George interprets as her not truly loving him. Learning from his creditors that George has bought him out, Max plans to abscond to California with

Pat Stanley in fantasy ballet from Goldilocks.

the scenery he has been saving up for his big Egypt picture. However, Maggie shows up in time to stop him. They have it out over each other's intentions. As a result, Maggie agrees to let Max do the picture in New York. But he will have to find someone else to play the lead. She is leaving to marry George. Max should be jubilant, but is disturbed over losing Maggie. Shooting begins with Lois in the lead but Max can only find fault in her performance. Maggie shows up at a particularly discouraging moment, sending Lois off to comfort George. Interpreting this as a sign of love, Max proposes to Maggie. She turns him down, saying that only a sign from heaven could make her marry him. As filming resumes with Maggie starring, the sign comes as it begins to snow in the deserts of Egypt. Max hollers "Cut" as he and Maggie embrace.

MUSICAL NUMBERS: "Lazy Moon," "Give the Little Lady," "Save a Kiss," "No One'll Ever Love You," "If I Can't Take It with Me," "Who's Been Sitting in My Chair?," Dance, "There Never Was a Woman," "The Pussy Foot," Huckleberry Island Ballet, "Lady in Waiting," Dance, "The Beast in You," "Shall I Take My Heart and Go?," "Bad Companions," "I Can't Be in Love," "I Never Know When," "The Town House Maxixe," "Two Years in the Making," "Heart of Stone," Pyramid Dance.

INSTRUMENTATION: Violin A, B, viola, cello, bass, reed I, II, III, IV, V, horns I–II, trumpets I–II, III, trombone I, II, percussion, harp, piano-conductor.

CASTING: 13 parts, 7 principals. Maggie, actress, sings well, some dancing. Max, frustrated movie producer, comedy lead, sings. George, straight man, legit baritone voice. Lois, dancer, sings well. Pete, Andy, and Bessie, Max's assistants, comedy roles, sing. Featured dancers. Separate singing and dancing choruses. Total cast, 40–60.

SCENES AND SETS: 2 acts, 11 scenes, 9 full stage sets, 1 partial stage set, blue sky drop. Large flight of pyramid-type steps and several large idols required for the last scene.

ACT I
Scene 1: Onstage, New York City, 1913.
Scene 2: Maggie's Dressing Room.
Scene 3: Max's Lot.
Scene 4: Outside Max's Lot.
Scene 5: Max's Lot.
Scene 6: The Fat Cat Roof Garden.
Scene 7: Huckleberry Island.

ACT II
Scene 1: Rest Home on Mainland.
Scene 2: Bessie's Barn, Up the Hudson.
Scene 3: Ballroom, George's Town House.
Scene 4: Egypt on the Hudson.

WISCONSIN CENTER FOR THEATRE RESEARCH

Don Ameche (Max) and Elaine Stritch (Maggie) sing "No One Will Ever Love You (Like You Do)."

PERIOD AND COSTUMES: 1913: hussar's outfit, ice cream parlor suit, long spring dresses and parasols, clown suit, maid uniform, checkered and plaid suits of the day, dressing gown, frontier costumes, Indians, bear, pirate, and nightclub pussycat costumes, nurse uniforms, bathrobes, ball gowns, waiter uniforms, Egyptian costumes for everyone, Scottish Guard uniform.

CHOREOGRAPHY: Girl on the moon production number, soft shoe (with bear), modern jazz trio, modern ballet, ballroom (Maxine), Egyptian spectacle production number including a pyramid dance.

LIGHTING AND SPECIAL EFFECTS: Some dramatic lighting required. It snows during the finale.

NOTES: If there is truly a fun show, *Goldilocks* is it. The title is a real problem. All promotion should play up the idea of Goldilocks, "the hilarious Broadway musical about the silent movie days written by Walter and Jean Kerr." Using the title alone conveys the idea of a nursery-rhyme musical for children. The ending is also weak. Suggest adding reprise medley of "No One'll Ever Love You (Like *I* Do)" with slight lyric adjustment so each acknowledges they are now in love, which then segues into other major number reprises ending with full company presentation of "The Pussy Foot."

GUYS AND DOLLS

Frank Loesser (Music, Lyrics)
Jo Swerling, Abe Burrows (Book)
Opened Nov. 24, 1950
1,200 Performances

BASED ON: Story and Characters by Damon Runyon

AGENT: Music Theatre

PUBLISHED TEXT: *Modern Theatre* (Vol. 4), Anchor

RECORDINGS: DEC-(7)9023

DIGEST OF PLOT: The big shooters are in town, but Nathan Detroit is having a tough time finding a spot for his floating crap game. The cops have the lid on tight. There is one spot, but Detroit needs three grand front money. His only chance is Sky Masterson. Detroit tries to set up a pat bet, but Sky doesn't fall. But Sky has a soft spot for Detroit and his fiancée of 14 years, Miss Adelaide, the star of the Hot Box Revue. He offers Detroit another chance. Sky bets that he can get any girl that Detroit can name to fly with him to Havana. Detroit jumps at the bet and points out Sarah Brown, a solid Salvation Army reformer. Police Lieutenant Brannigan confronts Nathan in the company of suspicious characters. They detract attention by saying they have gathered to give Nathan a bachelor party in advance of his marriage to Adelaide. The only problem is Adelaide overhears and immediately takes Nathan up on the offer. Sky gets Sarah to agree to a deal. If she will join him for dinner, he will deliver twelve first-class sinners for a mission-saving prayer meeting. She's a good sport when she learns the restaurant is in Havana, and is eventually persuaded to go in

WISCONSIN CENTER FOR THEATRE RESEARCH

Sewer scene from Guys and Dolls.

order to save the mission. During the trip they fall in love. Nathan takes advantage of the situation by holding the crap game at the mission, not to be discovered until Sky and Sarah return. Sarah feels she has been used and won't speak to Sky. He admits defeat, but still feels obligated to make good on his marker for twelve sinners. Since Big Jule from Chicago is a big loser, the game has resumed in a nearby sewer. When Sky can't persuade the gamblers to attend Sarah's prayer meeting, he offers to roll them $1,000 each against their souls. The result is a full turnout. But Nathan has missed his date to elope and Sky has departed for points West. The jilted Adelaide and despondent Sarah meet and decide to apply feminine pressures. Nathan and Sky have reassembled and prepare to be willingly dragged to the altar.

MUSICAL NUMBERS: "Fugue for Tinhorns," "Follow the Fold," "The Oldest Established," "I'LL KNOW," "A BUSHEL AND A PECK," "Adelaide's Lament," "Guys and Dolls," "Havana," "IF I WERE A BELL," "MY TIME OF DAY," "I'VE NEVER BEEN IN LOVE BEFORE," "Take Back Your Mink," "More I Cannot Wish You," The Crap Game Dance, "Luck Be a Lady," "Sue Me," "SIT DOWN, YOU'RE ROCKIN' THE BOAT," "Marry the Man Today."

INSTRUMENTATION: Violins A–C, B–D, cello, bass, reed I (flute, alto sax, clar), reed II (alto sax, clar), reed III (tenor sax, clar, oboe, Eng. horn), reed IV (tenor sax, clar), reed V (bari sax, bass clar), trumpet I–II, III, trombone, horn, percussion, piano-conductor.

CASTING: 20 parts, 11 principals. Nicely Johnson, roly-poly nice hood, sings. Sarah Brown, the mission broad, legit voice. Arvide, fatherly type, one number. Nathan Detroit, weasel, small time sharpie, sings. Miss Adelaide, daffy nightclub girl, comedienne who sings and dances well. Sky Masterson, big-time gambler, strong voice. Big Jule, comic hood, straight role. Large dame chorus. 10 to 16 singers. Total cast, 36–50.

SCENES AND SETS: 2 acts, 17 scenes, 7 full stage

sets (including 2 drops), 1 partial stage set, 4 scene drops.

ACT I
Scene 1: Broadway.
Scene 2: Save-a-Soul Mission—Interior.
Scene 3: A Phone Booth.
Scene 4: The Hot Box.
Scene 5: Off Broadway.
Scene 6: Exterior of the Mission.
Scene 7: Off Broadway.
Scene 8: Havana, Cuba.
Scene 9: Outside El Café Cubaño.
Scene 10: Exterior of Mission.

ACT II
Scene 1: The Hot Box.
Scene 2: The West Forties.
Scene 3: The Crap Game.
Scene 4: Off Broadway.
Scene 5: Save-a-Soul Mission—Interior.
Scene 6: Near Times Square.
Scene 7: Broadway.

PERIOD AND COSTUMES: When gangsters were in fashion: double-breasted suits (pin stripes, wide lapels, etc.), wide ties, Salvation Army uniforms, Cuban calypso outfits, red checkered daisy halter and bikini "Bushel and Peck" costumes. "Take Back Your Mink" strip costumes, police uniforms, various New York fashions of times (rehearsal clothes, tourists, blindmen, sight-seeing tour salesman, etc.).

CHOREOGRAPHY: Choreographed opening: "The Beat of Times Square," nightclub girly numbers, jazz calypso, light chorus strip, "Crap Shooters' Ballet," production finale.

LIGHTING AND SPECIAL EFFECTS: Some dramatic lighting required, cross-fades, lighted flying-down-to-Cuba sign, lights of Times Square on set, smoke in El Café Cubaño (optional).

NOTES: *Guys and Dolls* is a near-perfect musical.

GYPSY

Jule Styne (Music),
Arthur Laurents (Book),
Stephen Sondheim (Lyrics)
Opened May 21, 1959
702 Performances

BASED ON: Memoirs of Gypsy Rose Lee

AGENT: Tams-Witmark

PUBLISHED TEXT: Random House, 1960; *Theatre Arts*, June, 1962.

RECORDINGS: COL OL-5420
COL OS-2017
WB(S)1480 (F)

DIGEST OF PLOT: Rose, a domineering stage mother, moves her two daughters to the big city to break into vaudeville. Needing an agent, she cons candy salesman Herbie into the job. She builds an act around her star daughter June. The years pass and the now young ladies are still doing a kid act. Herbie talks Orpheum Circuit booker Mr. Goldstone into taking on the act. Despite the obvious influences of the familiar act, the new one succeeds. Herbie wants Rose to marry him and let the girls have a life of their own. When Rose laughs at his suggestion, Herbie threatens to walk out, but as in times before she cons him into staying. A major producer is interested in June's acting ability and wants her to leave the act. When Rose refuses, June runs away to form her own dancing act with chorus boy Tulsa. Defeated and shaken, Rose is about to give up, but her dreams of having a star for a daughter will not permit. Louise is designated to become "the biggest star in show business." For plain Louise, Mama has chosen a blonde wig and charts a new act, this time with all girls. In addition to the limitations of the act, vaudeville is dying, and bookings are few and far between. Unknowingly, Herbie books the act into a fourth-rate burlesque house. Rose realizes that they have hit bottom and agrees to this final booking only because they need the money. She tells Herbie that she will marry him and Louise that she will finally get her wanted schooling. Just as the booking is about to end, the star stripper is arrested and a replacement can't be found. The unrelenting Rose at last sees a chance for her daughter in a star's spotlight. Herbie runs out in disgust and Louise reluctantly readies herself to fulfill her mother's wish. Louise brings to the burlesque stage the freshness of youth and a winning style that soon elevates her to

Aging strippers prove "You Gotta Have a Gimmick" in Gypsy.

a top name. Rose, however, persists in interfering with the now Gypsy Rose Lee to the point that Gypsy must have her barred from the theatre. Rose wonders why her daughters and Herbie have walked out on her, but answers her own questions in the confession that she was really doing it for herself.

MUSICAL NUMBERS: "May We Entertain You," "Some People," Traveling, "SMALL WORLD," "Baby June and Her Newsboys," "Mr. Goldstone, I Love You," "Little Lamb," "YOU'LL NEVER GET AWAY FROM ME," "Dainty June and Her Farmboys," "If Momma Was Married," "All I Need Is the Girl," "EVERYTHING'S COMING UP ROSES," "Madame Rose's Toreadorables," "TOGETHER, WHEREVER WE GO," "You Gotta Have a Gimmick," "LET ME ENTERTAIN YOU," "Rose's Turn."

INSTRUMENTATION: Violins A (2), B, viola, cello, bass, flute (pic, clar, alto sax), flute (pic, clar, bass clar, tenor sax, bass sax) oboe (Eng. horn, clar, tenor sax), clar (bass clar, bassoon, bari sax), horn, trumpets I–II, III, trombone I, II, III percussion I–II, piano-conductor.

CASTING: 45 parts, including 8–12 children who can sing and dance and a host of animals (lamb, monkey, dogs, cats, birds), 9 principals. Rose, stage mother, powerful voice, carries show. Baby June and Baby Louise, girls 7 or 8 who sing and dance well. Herbie, nice guy, intently helpful, sings. Louise, accomplished actress, sings well. June, teen-ager, sings and dances. Tulsa, tap dancer, sings. Tessie Tura, Mazeppa, and Electra, comedy strippers, bumps and grinds, sing. Large singing, dancing, and showgirl chorus. Total cast, 40–60.

SCENES AND SETS: 2 acts, 17 scenes, 11 full stage sets, 3 front pieces (a car, an American eagle with flags, and a barn with flags), 2 drops, front curtain representing the grand drape of three famous burlesque theatres. Original production used 1 large turntable.

ACT I
Scene 1: Uncle Jocko's Kiddie Show, Seattle.
Scene 2: Pop's Kitchen, Seattle.
Scene 3: On the Road.
Scene 4: Backstage of a Vaudeville House, Los Angeles.
Scene 5: Vaudeville Stage, Various Places in U.S.
Scene 6: Two Hotel Rooms in Akron.
Scene 7: Chinese Restaurant, New York.
Scene 8: Grantziger's Palace, New York.
Scene 9: Grantziger's Gothic Office.
Scene 10: Theatre Alley, Buffalo.
Scene 11: Railroad Terminal, Omaha.

ACT II
Scene 1: Desert Country, Texas.
Scene 2: Backstage Dressing Rooms, Wichita.
Scene 3: Backstage Corridor.
Scene 4: Dressing Rooms and Before Stage Cur-
tains in Detroit, Philadelphia, and Minsky's, New York.
Scene 5: Minsky's, Dressing Room.
Scene 6: Bare Stage.

PERIOD AND COSTUMES: Early 1920's to early 1930's: kids talent costumes, knickers, vests, funny hats, women's suits, dresses, and coats of the period. Men's suits and overcoats. Cow costume. Ermine coat, page jackets, light pants, top hats, pajamas and other nightclothes, white armed services costumes, Uncle Sam outfit, stripper costumes, g-strings, etc., briefly decorated girls forming Christmas tree, Spanish madam costumes, sophisticated strip dress, long white gloves, leather coat, spats.

CHOREOGRAPHY: Tap, vaude song-and-dance routines, strip, bumps and grinds.

LIGHTING AND SPECIAL EFFECTS: Flexible lighting essential, seed lights on set, fireworks and smoke.

NOTES: *Gypsy* is a highly tasteful, almost family-type show, which, unless heavy-handedly done, could never become offensive. It is a brilliant work —one that demands a superior overall cast and tour de force Rose.

HAIR

Galt MacDermot (Music),
Gerome Ragni, James Rado (Book, Lyrics)

Opened April 29, 1968

BASED ON: Original

AGENT: Apply directly to producer Michael Butler, The New Hair Company

PUBLISHED TEXT: Pocket Books, 1969 (P)

RECORDINGS: RCA LSO 1150
RCA LSO 1143 (Pre-Broad-way Cast)

DIGEST OF PLOT: Following extensive tribal mood-setting, signaling a time of change and introduction by shock, the action focuses on the plight of Claude's personal generation gap. Claude is a hippie with unsympathetic parents who are disgusted with him. They want him to get a job or join the Army. Uncle Sam obliges by serving Claude with his draft notice. The Tribe is so informed and many suggestions are offered to beat the rap. Berger, a dropout and dominating male Tribe member, leads the impromptu anti-establishment demonstration, following which Sheila arrives. She plays up to Berger, who can't be bothered. Claude wants Sheila in the worst way but receives the same cold shoulder Berger is handing out. Later at the "Be-In," Berger and Sheila host a draft card burning. Claude is last to burn. He puts his card in the flame, but withdraws it at the last minute. He has resigned to the draft. The Tribe decides there must be a proper sendoff. Amid the fes-

"I Got Life" number from the American tribal-love rock musical Hair.

tivities Berger tries to persuade Sheila to share Claude's last night by promising himself as her reward. Sheila nixes the barter, but that night Berger steers Claude and Sheila together. For a while she plays along, but breaks down to confess Berger's deal. However, Claude takes the initiative and casts his own spell over her, converting her to his own way of thinking. At the train station Claude has lost his long hair and appears neatly dressed in uniform. Sheila arrives just in time for the farewell. Ignoring Berger, she stands proudly as Claude is summoned to step forward and join in the ranks.

MUSICAL NUMBERS: "AQUARIUS," "Donna," "Hashish," "Sodomy," "Colored Spade," "Manchester England," "Ain't Got No," "I Believe in Love," "AIR," "initials," "I GOT LIFE," "Going Down," "HAIR," "My Conviction," "EASY TO BE HARD," "Hung," "Don't Put It Down," "Frank Mills," "Hare Krishna," "Where Do I Go?," "Electric Blues," "Black Boys," "White Boys," "Walking in Space," "Abie Baby," "Prisoners in Niggertown," "What a Piece of Work Is Man," "GOOD MORNING STARSHINE," "The Bed," "The Flesh Failures."

INSTRUMENTATION: Bass, woodwinds (reeds), trumpets (2), percussion (2), guitar, conductor-electric piano.

CASTING: 25 parts, 10 principals, although nearly every cast member has at least one featured part. All cast members sing, dance, and take part in choreographed movement. Balanced cast of Negroes and whites essential to original concept of show. Major portions of dialogue are carried by Berger, Claude, Sheila, Woof, Hud, Jeanie, Crissy, Mom, and Dad. Mom and Dad are only "over-30" cast members (could be youths with masks or makeup.) Total cast, 25–35.

SCENES AND SETS: Stripped stage. One raked playing area intimate to the audience; very easy access to audience and back. Totem poles (scaffolding decorated with the accoutrements of an affluent society), ramps and levels, tattered clothes, hangings, hippie decorations and posters. "Love" and other graffiti painted here and there.

PERIOD AND COSTUMES: The turned-on hippie generation: Indianlike buckskin jackets, loincloths, moccasins, pants, blankets, tribal masks possible, tee shirts, sweat shirts, old military uniforms, a single sequined gown in which three girls can fit, Afro fashions, wild flower-power shirts, pants and shifts, Indian bead headbands, Levis, bell bottoms, saris, and other Now fashions. Black leather outfits for band. White Indian linen, gold-embroidered gown.

CHOREOGRAPHY: Rock idiom; latest steps can be inserted to beat with no problem. The whole show is choreographed production; a three-ring circus with upstaging everywhere, including the audience. Each sequence overlaps the other to lead the viewer constantly about the production area, hardly ever allowing audience to catch up.

LIGHTING AND SPECIAL EFFECTS: Strobe lights, psychedelic colored lighting aimed among the audience, fireworks, tightly controlled lighting that often changes rapidly, moving light projections, sound-mixing equipment required, hand mikes. Projection of dark mysterious men, FBI, and CIA agents. Police puppets.

NOTES: Neither script nor score provides much production guidance in staging *Hair*. It must have been seen to duplicate. Its major achievement was direction, a masterful circuslike presentation with more concurrent actions than any single member of the audience could comprehend. *Hair* is perhaps best described as a complete assault on the senses with high-decibel music, flashing lights, cast members throughout the audience, and other gimmicks to create excitement and stimulation. Several rewrites were required during the run of the show to keep it current. Although it could be justified in many ways, the show's much celebrated nude scene served no purpose other than to generate publicity. Through the various transitions the ending and the part of Sheila were drastically rewritten to strengthen the show's anti-war theme. As rewritten there is no mention of a deal between Berger and Sheila. Nor does Claude have to win her over. In the revised version he simply goes off to war and is killed.

HALF A SIXPENCE

David Heneker (Music, Lyrics),
Beverly Cross (Book)
Opened April 25, 1965
511 Performances

BASED ON: *Kipps* by H. G. Wells

AGENT: Dramatic Publishing Company

PUBLISHED TEXT: Dramatic Publishing Co., 1967

RECORDINGS: RCA LOC(LSO) 1110

DIGEST OF PLOT: Orphan Arthur Kipps works as an apprentice at Shalford's Drapery Emporium from dawn to dusk. His fellow apprentices, Sid, the Socialist; Buggins, the pessimist; and Pearce, the dandy share their low wages and quarters above the shop. Sid's sister, Ann, and Kipps have been sweethearts ever since childhood. Since they rarely have a chance to meet, Kipps has a sixpence cut in half to serve as a love token in times of absence. The next day Kipps learns of a possible inheritance. He briefly dreams about having money, but his thoughts are shattered by Mr. Shalford, who demands Kipps attend evening classes designed to keep the working class off the streets. His instructor is beautiful socialite Helen Walsingham. The hopelessness of the love Kipps feels for her drives him to the nearest pub. The next day Ann is livid—he was out woodworking and drinking instead of keeping their date. As Ann leaves in a huff, Kipps receives official word that he has inherited a fortune. Helen and society soon begin to close in around him. In time Kipps proposes to Helen and she accepts. However, the formalities leading up to the occasion begin to wear on Kipps and he begins to realize that Ann is his real love. He promotes a quarrel with Helen and runs off to find a forgiving Ann. They are married, but Kipps still wants to make his way in society. He wants a mansion, but Ann wants only a little house. Compatibility is strained—at least until Kipps learns that his investments have gone bad. However, enough is left for a small bookshop and happiness for all.

MUSICAL NUMBERS: "All in the Cause of Economy," "Half a Sixpence," "Money to Burn," "A Proper Gentleman," "She's Too Far Above Me," "If the Rain's Got to Fall," "The Old Military Canal," "Long Ago," "Flash Bang Wallop," "I Know What I Am," "The Party's on the House."

INSTRUMENTATION: Violins I–II, cello, bass, reed I, II, III, IV, trumpet I, II, III, trombone I, II, guitar-banjo, percussion, piano-conductor.

CASTING: 23 parts, 13 principals. Arthur Kipps, winning actor who can sing, dance, and play the banjo (latter can be faked). Sid, Buggins, and Pearce, Kipps's singing and dancing buddies. Ann, Kipps's true love, legit voice. Helen, Kipps's other love, straight role, minor singing. Four shopgirls, sing and dance well. Others are straight roles with minor singing and dancing. Large singing and dancing chorus. Almost everyone dances at least a little. Total cast, 34–46.

SCENES AND SETS: 2 acts, 18 scenes, 9 full stage sets (including 3 drops), 4 scene drops. The original production used 1 large turntable.

Dick Kallman and the national company of Half a Sixpence *during "If the Rain's Got to Fall" number.*

ACT I
Scene 1: The Emporium.
Scene 2: The Promenade.
Scene 3: The Emporium.
Scene 4: "Hope and Anchor" Bar.
Scene 5: The Street.
Scene 6: The Classroom.
Scene 7: The Emporium.
Scene 8: The Promenade.
Scene 9: The Old Lighthouse.
Scene 10: Military Canal Regatta.

ACT II
Scene 1: Mrs. Botting's Solarium.
Scene 2: Kitchen.
Scene 3: Photographer's Studio.
Scene 4: Parlor of Rented House.
Scene 5: The Pier.
Scene 6: The Building Site.

Scene 7: The Promenade.
Scene 8: The Bookshop.

PERIOD AND COSTUMES: Folkestone, England, 1900: apprentice clothes, blazers, white pants, straw hats, morning suits, bowlers, black dresses with white trimming, society gowns and day dresses of the period, sailor dresses, maids' uniforms, knickerbockers, male evening clothes, barmaid, rough-looking costumes for bar patrons, wool caps, mufflers.

CHOREOGRAPHY: Opening ballet: a day's business at the Emporium; soft shoe, modern, promenade, couples number, tableau, modern, photograph number.

LIGHTING AND SPECIAL EFFECTS: Some dramatic and special lighting (day and night). Lamps on set, independent lighting on canal barge, party lighting.

Ethel Merman and the original cast of Happy Hunting *sing the title song.*

NOTES: *Half a Sixpence* is a dancer's show. A number called "The Party's on the House" used in the American version is not as good as the numbers "I'll Build a Palace (for My Girl)" or "I Only Want a Little House," which it replaced from the original English version. Loose construction—tight direction required.

HAPPY HUNTING

Harold Karr (Music),
Howard Lindsay, Russel Crouse (Book),
Matt Dubey (Lyrics)

Opened Dec. 6, 1956
408 Performances

BASED ON: Original

AGENT: Music Theatre

PUBLISHED TEXT: Random House, 1957

RECORDINGS: RCA LOC-1026

DIGEST OF PLOT: It's the wedding of the year. Grace Kelly of Philadelphia is soon to be Princess Grace of Monaco. Liz Livingstone, the darling outcast of Philadelphia's Main Line society, and her daughter, Beth, have come to Monaco, along with a regiment of reporters, tourists, and Main Liners to attend the wedding. Mrs. Sanford Stewart, Sr., the grande dame of the Main Line, and her son, Sandy, are also in the tiny principality. Ostensibly Sandy is there to check the faltering finances of the Hotel Riviera for the ownership syndicate that Sandy's law firm represents. Sandy and Beth meet outside the Palace gates while Liz is trying to run down their tardy invitations to the wedding. As it turns out, they were overlooked, but rather than admit the disappointment to Beth, Liz stages the theft of all her clothes and makes international headlines in her pajamas and jewels. However, Liz confesses the truth to Beth just before the hotel manager, Arturo, discovers the clothes stuffed in a linen closet. There has been a witness to the crime, the hotel's most honored guest, the Duke of Granada. He, of course, immediately recognizes Liz and is puzzled by her actions.

She gives him the story straight from the shoulder and in the next breath lines him up for a date with Beth. Meanwhile Sandy has discovered the hotel's red ink closely matches the credit extended the Duke over the last year. Arturo is proud to be one of the Duke's strongest supporters. Sandy isn't sympathetic to the problems of high-living royalty in exile and orders the Duke to pay up or get out. Liz is loaded and proposes a marriage for money between the Duke and Beth. The Duke accepts and the whole post-wedding crowd sails for the U.S.A. En route, Sandy, who is also Liz's lawyer, is directed to work out the marriage agreement with Arturo, who is now on the Duke's personal staff. By now the Duke is becoming more and more enchanted with Liz while Sandy is agonizingly dealing away his growing love for Beth (who toys with his predicament). Only after Beth's icy status rejection by Sandy's mother does she resolve to go through with her marriage to the Duke. Meanwhile the Duke confesses to Liz that the best part of the agreement will be his nearness to her. They kiss emotionally and Liz is ready to switch the signals, but she has already baited the press, and the Duke is forced to announce his engagement to Beth. Back in Philly Liz is throwing a party to introduce the Duke. Even the Main Liners who have snubbed Liz for years can't stay away from royalty. However, they seek to embarrass her with a hunt (the vehicle of Liz's previous outfall with society). But the plan backfires. Liz's showing convinces the Duke that she's really the woman for him. Just as well, too, for Beth has been secretly meeting Sandy, and they plan to elope. But when the Duke tells Liz he wants her, she believes he only wants her money and he storms out. However, they are reunited at the Hunt Ball where the Duke renounces his claim to the throne of Spain to announce his engagement to his delightful American commoner. Liz has really arrived.

MUSICAL NUMBERS: "Postage-stamp Principality," "Don't Tell Me," "It's Good to Be Here," "MUTUAL ADMIRATION SOCIETY," "For Love or Money," "Bikini Dance," "It's Like a Beautiful Woman," "Wedding-of-the-Year Blues," "Mr. Livingstone," "If'n," "This Is What I Call Love," "A NEW-FANGLED TANGO," "She's Just Another Girl," "The Game of Love," "Happy Hunting," "I'm a Funny Dame," "This Much I Know," "Just Another Guy," "Everyone Who's Who's Who."

INSTRUMENTATION: Violin A–C, B–D, viola, cello, bass, pic (flute, clar, alto sax), clar (alto sax, bass clar), tenor sax (flute, oboe, Eng. horn, clar), tenor sax (clar, flute), bari sax (bassoon, bass clar), trumpet I–II, III, trombone I, II, horn, percussion, guitar, piano-conductor.

CASTING: 32 parts, 6 principals, 3 featured roles. Liz, powerful singer/actress who carries show. Sandy and Beth, romantic leads who sing well and dance (Beth does dance solo). Duke of Granada, middle-aged, classy actor who sings. Arturo, character man. Maud, character woman. Mrs. Sanford Stewart, Sr.,

cold straight role. Featured reporters, sing 2 numbers. Separate singing and dancing choruses. Total cast, 40–60, plus 1 trained horse (equine or human).

SCENES AND SETS: 2 acts, 17 scenes, 9 full stage sets (original production used turntable), 3 scenic drops (1 transparent), gangplank set piece. (Several sets could be converted to drops or partial sets.)

ACT I
Scene 1: Outside the Palace Gates, Monaco.
Scene 2: Liz Livingstone's Suite, Hotel Riviera, Monaco.
Scene 3: Terrace of the Hotel Riviera.
Scene 4: Veranda of the Duke's Suite, Hotel Riviera.
Scene 5: The Quay.
Scene 6: The Ship's Bar.
Scene 7: Afterdeck of the Ship.
Scene 8: The Ship's Bar.
Scene 9: Afterdeck of the Ship.

ACT II
Scene 1: The Garden of Liz Livingstone's Estate, Near Philadelphia.
Scene 2: The Stables, Liz's Estate.
Scene 3: Summerhouse, Liz's Estate.
Scene 4: The Hunt Club.
Scene 5: Another Part of the Forest.
Scene 6: Liz's Boudoir.
Scene 7: A Corridor in the Hunt Club.
Scene 8: The Hunt Ball.

PERIOD AND COSTUMES: Mid 1950's: high-society dresses, suits. Everyday beat-up clothes for reporters, photographers, etc., uniforms for Monaco police sergeant, hotel staff, the Duke's servants and confidants, waiter, ship's officers and crew, bartender, stable groom. Duke's high style fashions. Casual deck clothes, negligees, robes and other casual clothes, evening clothes, boots, gaily colored hunt outfits, Goya period costumes for everyone attending Hunt Ball.

CHOREOGRAPHY: Solo beach ball dance, tango, modern ballet, ballroom steps, soft shoe.

LIGHTING AND SPECIAL EFFECTS: Thunderstorm, rain, rear-projected shadows of the hunt figures on horseback. Recorded offstage playback.

NOTES: This show is built around the marriage of Grace Kelly to the Prince of Monaco and is in that sense topical. However, even if fictional names were used it would have little effect on today's production. It was an added point of interest then, but now of little value. The subject has always been Liz Livingstone. The show could be updated or done as a period piece. Beth's beach ball dance solo is extraneous.

HELLO, DOLLY!

Jerry Herman (Music, Lyrics),
Michael Stewart (Book)

Ethel Merman–Russell Nype cast of Hello, Dolly! *as they appeared in "Put On Your Sunday Clothes."*

Opened Jan. 16, 1964
2,844 Performances

BASED ON: *The Matchmaker* by Thornton Wilder

AGENT: Tams-Witmark

PUBLISHED TEXT: D. B. S. Publications, 1968; Signet, 1968 (P)

RECORDINGS: RCA LOCD(LSOD)-1087
RCA LOCD(LSOD)-2007
(2d cast)

DIGEST OF PLOT: Yonkers hay-and-feed merchant Horace Vandergelder hires his matchmaker, Dolly Levi, to chaperone his niece to New York. He wants Emmengarde to forget Ambrose, an artistic suitor he considers undesirable. Under the guise of finding him a woman, Dolly plans that the rich and reluctant Horace shall be her own. Horace departs for New York to participate in the 14th Street parade and later to meet Dolly at Irene Molloy's hat shop where he intends to ask for Irene's hand in marriage. While the boss is away, his chief clerk, Cornelius, and assistant, Barnaby, decide to break away to kiss a girl in the big city. Learning of their intentions, Dolly coyly directs them to the hat shop. There, Irene and her assistant, Minnie, become interested in the two boys, who are passing themselves off as rich young playboys. Just as things are going well, Horace shows up. After a merry chase, he discovers the boys in their hiding places. He is infuriated to find any man with Irene Molloy, let alone his underlings, and storms from the shop. Dolly plans for everyone to be at the Harmonia Gardens restaurant that evening where she makes a triumphant entrance among old friends who respect her dearly. Horace loses his wallet during a ruckus he makes when he spots Emmengarde and Ambrose in the dance contest. It is found by the penniless Cornelius and Barnaby who have visions of imprisonment for not being able to pay. But Horace has touched off a riot and it's night court for all. From then on it's lover finding lover. Horace, of course, is last to admit his intentions. Finally, in the romantic words of a hay-and-feed merchant, he concedes by saying, "Dolly, you're a damned exasperating woman!"

MUSICAL NUMBERS: "I Put My Hand In," "It Takes a Woman," "Put On Your Sunday Clothes," "Ribbons Down My Back," "Motherhood," "Dancing," "Before the Parade Passes By," "Elegance," "The Waiters' Gallop," "HELLO, DOLLY!," "Come and Be My Butterfly," "It Only Takes a Moment," "So Long Dearie."

INSTRUMENTATION: Violin A (2), B–C, cello, bass, reed I (clar, alto sax, flute, pic), reed II (clar, alto sax, flute), reed III (clar, tenor sax, flute), reed IV (clar, bari sax, bass clar, bassoon), trumpets I–II, III, trombone I, II, percussion I–II, harp, guitar-banjo, piano-celeste, piano-conductor. (Reduced instrumentation available.)

CASTING: 14 parts, 7 principals. Dolly, engaging female arranger, accomplished character woman who also sings, minor dancing. Horace, strong-willed character man, sings. Ambrose, sings in one number. Cornelius and Barnaby, comics who sing and dance well. Irene Molloy, legit voice, minor dancing. Minnie Fay, dancer who sings. Large male dancing chorus. Large singing chorus of males and females who also do minor dance steps in company numbers. Total cast, 34–50.

SCENES AND SETS: 2 acts, 15 scenes, 7 full stage sets (including 2 drops), 2 partial stage sets (fly-ins), 1 single close traveler, 2 scene drops. The original production used a circular runway around the orchestra pit, which has become standard with the production. Three car train and fringe top carriage rolling set pieces.

ACT I
Scene 1: Along Fourth Avenue, New York City.
Scene 2: Grand Central Station.
Scene 3: A Street in Yonkers.
Scene 4: Vandergelder's Hay and Feed Store, Yonkers.
Scene 5: The Yonkers Depot.
Scene 6: Outside Mrs. Molloy's Hat Shop— Water Street, New York City.
Scene 7: Inside the Hat Shop.
Scene 8: A Quiet Street.
Scene 9: 14th Street.

ACT II
Scene 1: In Front of the Hoffman House on Fifth Avenue.
Scene 2: Outside the Harmonia Gardens Restaurant, on the Battery.
Scene 3: Inside the Harmonia Gardens Restaurant.
Scene 4: The Polka Contest.
Scene 5: The Courtroom on Centre Street.
Scene 6: The Hay and Feed Store, Yonkers.

PERIOD AND COSTUMES: Turn of the century: New York City and Yonkers. Bright, cartoon costumes of the dress and styles of the period. (Ruffled dresses, large hats, parasols, striped pants, vests, spats, waistcoats), shopkeeper smocks, horse costume, green waiter suits with white aprons, floor-length evening dresses, lodge uniform, tights, high-button shoes, parade costumes (police, sports club, dance-hall girls, opera Association etc.), male formal suit and evening cape, "Hello, Dolly" evening dress, sailor dress, traveling clothes for ensemble.

CHOREOGRAPHY: Strut, choreographed excitement, light modern, waltz, parade, "Elegance" walk, modern jazz, polka, "Put on Your Sunday Clothes" and "Hello, Dolly!" production number.

LIGHTING AND SPECIAL EFFECTS: Mostly general lighting—dramatic lighting can help in spots. Three-car train puffs smoke.

NOTES: *Hello, Dolly!,* to anyone viewing out-of-town tryouts, was to be almost a sure flop. However, director Gower Champion and his staff of musical doctors rewrote and restaged what became a modern miracle of musical theatre. Although no one can dispute the success of this fantastic show, it is not as good as its publicity. It would never have outrun *My Fair Lady* or even perhaps other long-run leaders had not the producer conceived several restagings to artificially stretch the production's life.

Carol Channing, the original Dolly.

HENRY, SWEET HENRY

Bob Merrill (Music, Lyrics),
Nunnally Johnson (Book)
Opened Oct. 23, 1967
80 Performances

BASED ON: *The World of Henry Orient* by Nora Johnson

AGENT: Samuel French, Inc.

PUBLISHED TEXT: Samuel French, Inc. 1969 (P)

RECORDINGS: ABCS-OC-4

DIGEST OF PLOT: Valerie Boyd is a love-starved daughter of a successful industrialist father and a social star mother. Val can have everything that money can buy, but that's all. Schoolmate Gil understands, and the two girls meet regularly at Central Park for various teen-age pranks. One day they spot avant-garde composer and aging philanderer Henry Orient. He is once again trying to seduce Stella, a husband-fearing romantic from Scarsdale. Val and Gil pester the couple until Stella runs off, leaving behind a frustrated Henry. They attend one of Henry's concerts where the age of man is musicalized by playing on human bodies instead of instruments. Later the girls decide that Henry is as hapless as they are. He shall be their hero. Val is excited by such creativity. She has found an idol to whom she can at least offer devotion. Val gets Gil to agree to a secret study of Henry's private and public life. During this time, Henry has managed to persuade Stella to a super-security rendezvous at his apartment. Meanwhile, Kafritz, an arrange-anything-for-a-price schoolmate, has sold Val and Gil as dates to two Knickerbocker Greys, students at a nearby boys' military school. But the girls have discovered Henry's address and are off to pursue their study. To protect their investment, the boys and Kafritz are in hot pursuit. Kafritz gets there first and tries to blackmail the girls. In jest they tell Kafritz that Val is a junkie in need of a fix. Annoyed by the girl's hostility, Kafritz tips the police that Henry runs a dope ring near the school. Inside, Henry is making headway for the first time in months. Outside, a good portion of New York City is descending on his unsuspecting doorstep. At that given signal the whistles and sirens go off, the crowds go wild, the police charge the believed dope ring hideout with guns drawn as Val and Gil are cheering their idol. Stella goes into shock. The cops shoot off all five locks and still manage to catch Henry *in flagrante*. The drug matter is straightened out, but Val has run away. Her mother decides to investigate this Henry Orient. When she does, the skillful Henry recognizes a new prey. Gil and Val arrive at Henry's apartment just as Val's mother is seen kissing Henry goodbye. Val is shattered and returns home to her father, who comforts her. Val discovers that she isn't the only love-starved person around the house. But there is new hope. The Knickerbocker Grey boys arrive for the forgotten Happening date. Gil persuades Val to come along for something real instead of a dream.

MUSICAL NUMBERS: "Academic Fugue," "In Some Little World," "Pillar to Post," "Here I Am," "I Wonder How It Is to Dance with a Boy," "Nobody Steps on Kafritz," "Henry, Sweet Henry," "Woman in Love," "The People Watchers," "Weary Near to Dyin'," "Poor Little Person," "I'm Blue Too," "To Be Artistic," "Forever," "Do You Ever Go to Boston."

INSTRUMENTATION: Violins, viola, cello I–II–III, bass, reeds I–V, horns I–II, trumpet I–II, III, trombone I–II, III, guitar, harp, percussion I–II, piano-conductor.

CASTING: 16 parts, 6 principals. Valerie, Marian (Gil), and Kafritz, teen-age girls who act, sing, and dance well. Henry Orient, rogue actor who sings. Stella, sexy character girl, minor singing. Mrs. Boyd, actress who sings. Strong choral work. Total cast, 35–55.

SCENES AND SETS: 2 acts, 5 scenes, 8 full stage sets, 6 partial stage sets.

ACT I
Scene 1: A Street in New York City.
Scene 2: Locker Room.
Scene 3: Central Park Zoo.
Scene 4: Two Bedrooms.
Scene 5: Concert Hall.
Scene 6: Val's Bedroom.
Scene 7: Telephone Booths.
Scene 8: Luncheonette.
Scene 9: Street Telephone Booth.
Scene 10: Orient's Apartment Building, Cutaway View and Surrounding Street Corner.

ACT II
Scene 1: Boyd's Living Room.
Scene 2: Washington Square.
Scene 3: Orient's Apartment.
Scene 4: Boyd's Living Room.
Scene 5: Exterior of School and Locker Room.
Scene 6: Cocktail Bar.
Scene 7: Exterior of Orient's Apartment.
Scene 8: Boyd's Living Room.
Scene 9: Orient's Bedroom.
Scene 10: Val's Bedroom.

PERIOD AND COSTUMES: The present: well-worn mink coat, girls' school uniforms, boys' military school uniforms, dresses, trench coats, suits, pajamas, disguises, hippie mod costume clothes, evening dresses, black dinner jackets, black gowns, black choir robes, white shorts, coolie hats, dressing robes, uniforms for policemen, policewoman, and usherette.

CHOREOGRAPHY: Modern, ballroom, "People Watchers" production number, waltz.

LIGHTING AND SPECIAL EFFECTS: Dramatic lighting helpful, but not essential. Shooting locks off door.

NOTES: Show has a bright, peppy score and one of the greatest first-act finales in musical theatre. The book construction on the other hand has some lumps. For tightening, suggest moving "Henry, Sweet Henry" number ahead to Scene 6 just before Val's mother enters; trim one chorus from most numbers; rewrite "Pillar to Post" to dialogue eliminating historical references and music; cut "To Be Artistic" number—make Henry's trap of Val's mother more sophisticated, and if second act could be reconstructed so that Val runs away to the hippie clan *after* she spots her mother at Henry's apartment, the whole show would hold together much tighter. Some material is topical and should be reviewed for possible updating.

HERE'S LOVE

Meredith Willson (Music, Book, Lyrics)
Opened Oct. 3, 1963
339 Performances

BASED ON: Movie, *Miracle on 34th Street*

AGENT: Music Theatre

PUBLISHED TEXT: Manuscript Only

RECORDINGS: COL KOL(KOS)-6000

DIGEST OF PLOT: Susan Walker's mother, Doris, is in charge of staging the Macy's Thanksgiving Day parade. Susan's life is one of stark reality. Doris is divorced and is determined that no fantasies will ever allow her child to fall into any such disillusionment as her former marriage. Faith, hope, and men are strictly taboo. When the parade Santa gets drunk, Mr. Kris Kringle, a jolly man with streaming natural white beard, pops up from nowhere. He is a big success in the parade and becomes Macy's store Santa. Meanwhile Susan has met Fred, a returning Marine vet and hopeful law student. He befriends Susan even though Doris believes it's a plot to get to her. Kris is a great Santa. He even tells mothers where to buy toys that Macy's doesn't sell. Mr. Macy is upset, but Doris sees a great promotional chance. Make Macy's a friendly store—the true Christmas spirit. The plan is a huge success, but in the process, Kris admits that he *is* the real Santa Claus. His strange behavior wins him an interview with the store's psychologist, Dr. Sawyer, who nearly goes mad trying to break down Kris's story and wants to have him committed. Susan and Kris have also become good friends. When she learns of Kris's plight, she asks Fred to help defend him. The move is seconded by Doris, who is discovering that Fred isn't like the other men she has known. At the sanity hearing Mr. Macy testifies that Kris is Santa Claus. So does the prosecuting attorney's little son. As a clincher Fred manages to get the U.S. Post Office to deliver all its "Dear Santa" letters to the courtroom. The judge sees his chance to jump from his political hook and accepts the U.S. Government recognition as proof of Kris's claim. Fred has won more than a hearing. He has won a prospective wife and daughter as well.

MUSICAL NUMBERS: "The Big Clown Balloons," "Arm in Arm," "You Don't Know," "The Plastic Alligator," "The Bugle," "Here's Love," "My Wish," "Pine Cones and Holly Berries," "Look, Little Girl," "Expect Things to Happen," "Love Come Take Me Again," "She Hadda Go Back," "That Man Over There," "My State," "Nothing in Common."

INSTRUMENTATION: Violins A–B–C, viola, cello I, II, bass, reed I (flute, clar, pic, alto sax, alto flute), reed II (clar, alto sax, flute, pic, E♭ clar), reed III (clar, tenor sax, oboe, Eng. horn), reed IV (clar, tenor sax, flute, pic), reed V (bass clar, bari sax, clar, alto sax), trumpet I–II, III, trombone I, II, III, horn, percussion, guitar, celeste, piano-conductor.

CASTING: 29 parts, plus 5 to 10 children, 9 principals. Mr. Kris Kringle, looks like Santa Claus, sings. Doris, mother and leading lady, sings well, minor dancing. Fred, leading man, good voice. Susan, talented youngster who sings, dances. Marvin, comic who sings 2 numbers. R. H. Macy, character man, sings. Others are mostly straight roles with some singing. Large dancing chorus, 7- to 14-member singing chorus. Total cast, 36–60.

SCENES AND SETS: 2 acts, 23 scenes, 6 full stage sets (including 6 drops), 6 partial stage sets, 5 scene drops, large sleigh set piece. Original drops were very simply done—pastel drops with simple suggestion of windows, trees, building outlines, etc.

ACT I
Scene 1: West 73rd Street, Thanksgiving Day.
Scene 2: Parade Assembly Area.
Scene 3: Along Central Park West.
Scene 4: 35th Street Roof.
Scene 5: Doris Walker's Apartment.
Scene 6: Briefing Room at Macy's.
Scene 7: Macy's Toy Department, Elevators, Escalator, and into Herald Sq.
Scene 8: Playground in Central Park.
Scene 9: Doris Walker's Office.
Scene 10: Fred Gaily's Apartment.
Scene 11: On the Way to Doris' Apartment.
Scene 12: Store Psychologist's Office at Macy's.
Scene 13: Macy's Toy Department.
Scene 14: The Party.
Scene 15: Macy's Toy Department.

ACT II
Several Weeks later, December 19th.
Scene 1: Judge Martin Group's Chambers.
Scene 2: In Isolation.
Scene 3: Fred's Apartment.
Scene 4: A Corridor in the New York Supreme Court.
Scene 5: The Courtroom.
Scene 6: The Courthouse Corridor.
Scene 7: The Courtroom.
Scene 8: Macy's Living Room Display. Christmas Eve.

PERIOD AND COSTUMES: The present: Thanksgiving Day to Christmas Eve. Santa Claus suits, Army and Marine uniforms, work dresses, overcoats, white parade uniforms with multiple costume accessories to change each into approximately 7 outfits (on the run), white boots, large fur plumes, drum major hats, toy soldier uniforms, white Santa costume, ice-skating outfits with muffs, Marine dress blues, judge robes, current style suits and dresses, mufflers, winter coats, sweaters, policeman, nurse, mailman, and Girl Scout uniforms.

CHOREOGRAPHY: Macy's Parade production number, hoedown steps, modern ballet, waltz, soft shoe steps.

LIGHTING AND SPECIAL EFFECTS: Mostly general lighting. Ten-minute version of Macy's Thanksgiving Day parade on stage requires many special effects to convey true spirit of the event. Lights on stage spelling out Macy's and bordering large display window.

Anthony Roberts and Wall Street widows sing "Step to the Rear" from How Now, Dow Jones?

NOTES: *Here's Love* is overburdened with extraneous material, mostly because of the musical numbers. Proper editing could result in a tight and powerful musical for production in late November or December. Suggest cutting the following numbers: "The Plastic Alligator," "She Hadda Go Back" plus scene that goes with it, and "My State."

HOW NOW, DOW JONES

Elmer Bernstein (Music),
Max Shulman (Book),
Carolyn Leigh (Lyrics)

Opened Dec. 7, 1967
201 Performances

BASED ON: Original

AGENT: Samuel French, Inc.

PUBLISHED TEXT: Samuel French, Inc., 1968 (P)

RECORDINGS: RCA LSO 1142

DIGEST OF PLOT: New York Stock Exchange tour guide Cynthia Pike has just explained the complicated world of high finance and joins friend Kate Montgomery (The Voice of Dow Jones). Kate bemoans the fact that her fiancé, Herbert, won't marry until the Dow Jones Industrial Average tops 1,000. When Cynthia leaves, Kate is joined by champion loser Charley Matson, who confesses that he is going to commit suicide after he drinks his lunch. They exchange their tales of woe and decide to have a fling together. The night-long romance restores hope, but Kate rejects Charley for a future of security instead of dreams. Meanwhile, brokerage firm-owner William Foster Wingate has come up with a plan to sell more stock and hires Charley to give his firm a little-man image. Charley is a winner with the rich-widow set and strikes it big at last. When the girls meet again, Cynthia confides that she has agreed to be Wingate's mistress but is dejected because it seems that he has forgotten about her. Kate explains her new problem—she's in love with Charley, engaged to Herbert, and expecting Charley's baby. When Kate learns that Charley has proposed to his childhood sweetheart, her impending motherhood leads her to panic. As "The Voice of Dow Jones" she announces that the Dow average has topped 1,000. Wingate realizes that Kate's report is fake but wonders why. Herbert and Cynthia provide the answers but the hoax is publicly discovered and the market bottom falls out. The truth is music to Charley, who thought Kate loved Herbert. He finds Kate and together with Cynthia they convince "A.K.," Wall Street's shrewdest and most closely watched tycoon, to buy. The market downslide is reversed and the future is bright—particularly for Charley and Kate.

MUSICAL NUMBERS: "A–B–C," "They Don't Make 'em Like That Anymore," "Live a Little," Crazy Night Ballet, "The Pleasure's About to Be Mine," "A Little Investigation," "Walk Away," "Goodbye, Failure, Goodbye," "Shakespeare Lied," "STEP TO THE REAR," "Big Trouble," "Credo," "One of Those Moments," "He's Here!," "Panic," "That's Good Enough for Me."

INSTRUMENTATION: Violins A, B, C, cello, bass, 1st flute (2d alto sax, clar), 1st clar (1st alto sax), tenor sax (clar), bari sax (bass clar), trumpets I–II, III, trombone I–II, III, harp, percussion I–II, guitar.

CASTING: 23 parts, 4 principals, 6 featured roles. Charley, good comic actor who sings well and dances. Kate, strong legit voice, acts well and dances. Cynthia, good comedienne with powerful singing voice, minor dance. Wingate, character man who sings. Widows (4–8) who sing and dance. Several legit chorus voices required for chorale and other numbers. Total cast, 36–50.

SCENES AND SETS: 2 acts, 18 scenes, 10 sets, several of which are partial but full stage revealed at all times. Sets consist of partial drops and set pieces, which are flying or sliding into place or removed as necessary. Each piece of scenery is a "building block." It's a continuous flowing change performed in full view of the audience.

ACT I
Scene 1: Financial District.
Scene 2: Childs Restaurant.
Scene 3: Wingate's Private Office.
Scene 4: Kate's Apartment.
Scene 5: Wall Street, Early Morning.
Scene 6: Wingate & Co., Brokers.
Scene 7: Kate's Apartment.
Scene 8: Mrs. Millhauser's Living Room.
Scene 9: Wingate's Private Office.
Scene 10: Wall Street.
Scene 11: Dow Jones Office.

ACT II
Scene 1: New York City.
Scene 2: Wingate's Private Office.
Scene 3: Mrs. Millhauser's Living Room.
Scene 4: Cynthia's Apartment.
Scene 5: Financial District.
Scene 6: Kate's Apartment.
Scene 7: Wingate & Co., Brokers.

PERIOD AND COSTUMES: The present: tourist casual clothes, guide uniform, office fashions, expensive suits, lion costume, dresses, lounging outfit, raincoats, sports jackets, etc.

CHOREOGRAPHY: Modern ballet, modern jazz, parades and patterns, choreographed "Panic," production numbers.

LIGHTING AND SPECIAL EFFECTS: Dramatic and area lighting required.

NOTES: A peppy show that is somewhat topical. Includes extraneous material that should be trimmed out of book. Suggest cutting numbers "They Don't Make 'em Like That Anymore" and "Shakespeare Lied."

HOW TO SUCCEED IN BUSINESS WITHOUT REALLY TRYING

Frank Loesser (Music, Lyrics),
Abe Burrows, Jack Weinstock, and Willie Gilbert (Book)

Opened Oct. 14, 1961
1,417 Performances

BASED ON: Book by Shepherd Mead

AGENT: Musical Theatre

PUBLISHED TEXT: Manuscript Only

RECORDINGS: RCA LOC(LSO)-1066
U.A.—4151
U.A.—5151

DIGEST OF PLOT: Window washer J. Pierrepont Finch decides to give up hard work to become a top corporate executive. His guide is a book that reveals the proven method to success without really doing anything. His target company is World Wide Wickets—small enough to go someplace, but big enough to get lost in office politics. Upon entrance, he crashes into the president, J. B. Biggley, who refers him to the personnel office. There he tells the manager, Bratt, that Biggley referred him for a job. He's in. His swift progress is observed by Rosemary, who is already planning to become Mrs. Finch. But it's the stockroom for Finch where he meets Bud Frump, Biggley's nephew. When the retiring stockroom manager is about to leave, he recommends Finch for the job. Bratt has a problem since Bud's mother is applying pressure for his advancement. Finch yields

Darryl Hickman as J. Pierpont Finch and his enemies at World Wide Wickets sing "I Believe in You," from How to Succeed in Business Without Really Trying.

to Bud and is promptly made a junior executive for his excellent thinking. Meanwhile J. B.'s all-body-and-no-brains mistress, Hedy LaRue, has landed and wants a job. It's now Saturday morning. Finch has staged a been-working-all-night clutter on a tip J. B. will be in to pick up his golf clubs. When J. B. arrives, Finch bravely makes mention of his workload when he'd really rather be watching his alma mater playing football. It turns out J. B. went to Old Ivy *too*. They sing the school's fight song, and Monday Finch has an office of his own, but one problem. Hedy didn't like the secretary pool and has been appointed his secretary. Finch sends Hedy to his boss, Gatch, who seizes the opportunity, and is soon transferred to Venezuela. Finch has replaced him. He really wanted the advertising department, but there's a new man to take that. At the party to welcome the advertising vice president, Finch gets him talking about his school—Old Ivy's arch rival. Now that Finch is V.P. in charge of advertising he must

finally do something. Bud manages to bait him with a campaign that already has been turned down by J. B. But Finch manages to sell the TV contest promotion by suggesting Hedy as the beautiful Treasure Girl. It's the night of the first telecast. To add a little drama, Finch has Hedy take an oath that she doesn't know where the treasure is hidden. It wasn't in the script and Hedy is off balance. She learned the hiding place the night before from J. B. and tells all —the treasure is hidden at all World Wide Wicket offices. Mob destruction of the company's buildings has wiped Finch out for sure—much to the satisfaction of his growing army of enemies. All but Rosemary have deserted him. Chairman of the Board Wally Womper has arrived to preside over Finch's trial and conviction to obscurity. Finch has decided to resign and return to window washing. However, Wally started as a window washer, too. J. Pierrepont Finch, Chairman of the Board—it has a nice ring. So does Hedy, the new Mrs. Womper. There will be a lot of changes around World Wide Wicket, but with this sound, new, aggressive management, profits are sure to soar!

MUSICAL NUMBERS: "How to Succeed," "Happy to Keep His Dinner Warm," "Coffee Break," "The Company Way," "Secretary I Not a Toy," "Been a Long Day," "Grand Old Ivy," "Paris Original," "Rosemary," "Cinderella, Darling," "Love from a Heart of Gold," "I BELIEVE IN YOU," "The Yo Ho Ho," "Brotherhood of Man."

INSTRUMENTATION: Violins A, B, C, cello, bass, flute (pic, B♭ clar, alto sax), oboe (Eng. horn, B♭ clar, alto sax), flute (B♭ clar, tenor sax), B♭ clar (sax), bass clar (bari sax), horn, B♭ trumpets I, II, trombones I, II, III, percussion I, II, harp. (Modified version available.)

CASTING: 19 parts, 6 principals. Finch, comedian/actor with split-second timing, sings and dances well. J. B. Biggley, mature straight man, good acting ability. Rosemary, all-American girl, sings well. Frump, nervous, clumsy, comic character man. Hedy, dumb, busty, status symbol, powerful voice helps. Smitty, character woman who sings well. Various other office types in good supporting roles. Chorus of 12–20 with accent on dancing, but must sing, too. Total cast, 30–46.

SCENES AND SETS: 2 acts, 24 scenes, 10 full stage sets, 3 partial stage sets, 2 scene drops, and 1 painted traveler (drop backgrounds are recommended for 5 of the full stage sets).

ACT I
Scene 1: Exterior of the World Wide Wicket Company.
Scene 2: Corridor.
Scene 3: Outer Office.
Scene 4: The Mail Room.
Scene 5: Biggley's Office.
Scene 6: Corridor.
Scene 7: The Elevator Landing.
Scene 8: The Outer Office.
Scene 9: Finch's First Office.
Scene 10: Plans and Systems Office.
Scene 11: Traveler (Corridor).
Scene 12: The Roof.
Scene 13: Elevator Landing.
Scene 14: Biggley's Office.

ACT II
Scene 1: The Outer Office.
Scene 2: Finch's New Advertising Office.
Scene 3: Biggley's Office.
Scene 4: Men's Washroom.
Scene 5: Board Room.
Scene 6: Television Show.
Scene 7: Wrecked Outer Office.
Scene 8: Elevator Landing.
Scene 9: Biggley's Office.
Scene 9A: Traveler.
Scene 10: The Outer Office.

COURTESY OF FEUER AND MARTIN

Original leads Rudy Vallee and Robert Morse do "Grand Old Ivy" fight song.

PERIOD AND COSTUMES: The present: latest office wear, 16 (or however many chorus girls + 2), identical Paris originals, executive suits (male chorus colorfully executed, principals in tasteful and distinguished fashions), World Wide Wickets blazers, gowns for bosomy Hedy, scrubwoman's rags, policeman's uniform, and TV "Treasure Chest" costumes.

CHOREOGRAPHY: Modern dance and other choreographed movement. Seven major production numbers.

LIGHTING AND SPECIAL EFFECTS: Lowering of principal on window washer's scaffold. Continuous lighting changes are vital to fast-paced production that the show requires.

NOTES: *How to Succeed* is a tightly constructed, fast-paced show. Direction must concur. Show is most successful when the majority of the audience is made up of office workers. Most of the music did not become popular apart from the show, but it's a great score. Show won the Pulitzer Prize for 1962.

I DO! I DO!

Harvey Schmidt (Music),
Tom Jones (Book, Lyrics)
Opened Dec. 5, 1966
584 Performances

BASED ON: *The Fourposter* by Jan de Hartog

Robert Preston and Mary Martin in scenes from I Do! I Do!

AGENT: Music Theatre

PUBLISHED TEXT: Manuscript Only

RECORDINGS: RCA LOC (LSO)-1128

DIGEST OF PLOT: Agnes and Michael are getting married. Their vows dutifully behind them, they enter their turn-of-the-century bedroom dominated by a large, carved oak, fourposter bed. Time passes swiftly following the tender embarrassments of the wedding night. Agnes is with child, Michael has pains and demands attention. It's a boy and all of a sudden life is so new. Soon there's a girl, too. Several years later Michael has become a successful author, and a dinner party is being given in his honor. He attempts to impose his superior attitude on their marriage, but Agnes is prepared to air his faults in return. Following the dinner, Michael admits to a little extramarital "research." Agnes is more mad than sad. She dons her go-to-hell hat and, while he is safely out of earshot, reaffirms her faith in herself. He returns to prevent her from leaving. All is forgiven. Maturity has set in, and soon the children are to be married. For the first time in 20 some years they are alone together. Agnes snowballs into depression. Michael is empty, too, and once again they discover how much they really need each other. It's time they were growing old and they do. They prepare to leave their large, empty house and trusting old bed. A bright, newly married young couple is to move in. Against Michael's wishes, Agnes leaves a tattered pillow upon which is em-broidered "God Is Love." Under it Michael leaves a bottle of champagne.

MUSICAL NUMBERS: "All the Dearly Beloved," "TOGETHER FOREVER," "I DO! I DO!," "Good Night," "I Love My Wife," "Something Has Happened," "MY CUP RUNNETH OVER," "Love Isn't Everything," "Nobody's Perfect," "A Well-Known Fact," "Flaming Agnes," "The Honeymoon Is Over," "Where Are the Snows?," "When the Kids Get Married," "The Father of the Bride," "What Is a Woman?," "Someone Needs Me," "Roll Up the Ribbons," "This House."

INSTRUMENTATION: Violin, viola, cello, bass, reed I (flute, pic, clar), reed II (flute, clar, bass clar), reed III (clar, oboe, Eng. horn), reed IV (clar, bassoon), trumpet I–II, trombone, horns I–II, percussion I–II, piano I–II, piano-conductor. (Duo-piano arrangement available when orchestration is not used.)

CASTING: He (Michael) and She (Agnes) are the entire show. Both must be versatile performers in all departments.

SCENES AND SETS: 2 acts, 1 set, a bedroom (including 1 marvelous revolving bed). Only 7 set pieces on the stage, plus 2 fly-ins (streamers and toys hung from battens).

PERIOD AND COSTUMES: The story covers 50 years of a marriage, beginning just before the turn of the century (1900): wedding dress, formal wear, housedresses, suits, dressing gowns, night-gowns, evening dress, special maternity dress, other house and evening wear from the various periods.

CHOREOGRAPHY: Small (barefoot) soft shoe and production numbers. With only two performers, almost entire show is choreographed.

LIGHTING AND SPECIAL EFFECTS: Continuously changing lighting and lighting effects are vital in creating rapidly changing moods and events.

NOTES: *I Do! I Do!* is extremely delicate and charming. Direction must be highly animated and slick to maintain interest.

IRMA LA DOUCE

Marguerite Monnot (Music),
Alexander Breffort (Book, Lyrics),
(English Book, Lyrics by Julian More, David Heneker, Monty Norman)
Opened Sept. 29, 1960
527 Performances

BASED ON: Original

AGENT: Tams-Witmark

PUBLISHED TEXT: Manuscript Only

RECORDINGS: COL OL-5560
COL OS-2029

DIGEST OF PLOT: Irma is one of Paris' most successful *poules* (tarts). She falls in love with Nestor, a penniless law student. She decides for the first time in her life she will have a *mec* (procuror). Nestor is jealous of Irma's customers and decides he must become her only buyer, so he disguises himself as Monsieur Oscar, a rich old fossil who asks only companionship, yet provides enough *grisbi* (money) to become her exclusive patron. Nestor soon becomes exhausted from his numerous jobs, studies, and lovemaking. Irma decides that Oscar is not getting his money's worth and seduces him more passionately than she ever has Nestor. This makes him more jealous than ever and he decides that Oscar must die. However, in bumping off his alias, Nestor is convicted of murder and sentenced to Devil's Island. When he learns Irma is with child he escapes on a raft and finally proves (by paying off the judge) that he and Oscar are one and the same. All this in time to witness the birth of his child on Christmas Eve.

MUSICAL NUMBERS: "Valse Milieu," "Sons of France," "The Bridge of Coulaincourt," "Our Language of Love," "She's Got the Lot," "Dis-Donc," "Le Grisbi Is le Root of le Evil in Man," "Wreck of a Mec," "That's a Crime," "From a Prison Cell," "Irma-la-Douce," "There Is Only One Paris for That," "The Freedom of the Seas," Arctic Ballet, "But," "Christmas Child."

INSTRUMENTATION: Bass, reed I (flute, pic), reed II (clar, bari sax), trombone I, II, percussion, guitar, accordion, piano-celeste.

CASTING: 21 parts, 9 principals. Irma, a dancer who sings and acts (the only female part in the show). Bob-le-Hotu, singing storyteller, character man. Nestor, romantic lead, good voice, little dancing, double role as older man with different voice and character. Other "mecs," gendarmes, prisoners, admirers; bar patrons are the all male chorous roles. They usually perform as a group, should include several good solo voices and a couple of lead dancers. Total cast, 21.

SCENES AND SETS: 2 acts, 23 scenes, 6 full stage sets, 4 partial stage sets, 1 scrim, 2 drops, 1 darkish sky drop.

ACT I
Scene 1: Outside the Bar-Des-Inquiets, Pigale.
Scene 2: Inside the Bar.
Scene 3: Irma's Room.
Scene 4: The Pont Coulaincourt (Hotel Rapid in Background).
Scene 5: Same.
Scene 6: Same.
Scene 7: Hotel Rapid.
Scene 8: The Bar.
Scene 9: Hotel Rapid.
Scene 10: Nestor and Irma's Room.
Scene 11: Same.
Scene 12: Narrow Street.
Scene 13: The Banks of the Seine
Scene 14: The Bar.

ACT II
Scene 1: A Law Court.
Scene 2: Prison Ship.
Scene 3: Street Outside Irma's House.
Scene 4: Devil's Island.
Scene 5: The Raft.
Scene 6: A Paris Street.
Scene 7: The Police Station.
Scene 8: The Street.
Scene 9: Irma's Room.

PERIOD AND COSTUMES: Old Paris, anytime: Irma wears black dress and black tights. Males wear French-flavored sweaters, shirts, slacks, caps, and coats. Black cutaway suit and bowler, tourist suits, overcoats, hats, prison uniforms, gendarme uniforms, judge robes, wig, and magistrate hat.

CHOREOGRAPHY: French-accented modern and modern ballet, traditional French steps and dance specialties, "Valse Milieu" (waltzlike).

LIGHTING AND SPECIAL EFFECTS: Dramatic lighting, special lighting effects, "electric" sparklers, searchlights and street lamps on stage. Smoke (optional).

NOTES: *Irma La Douce* can provide a pleasant diversion in a series of musicals or serve when a low-budget production is required.

IT'S A BIRD, IT'S A PLANE, IT'S SUPERMAN

Charles Strouse (Music),
David Newman, Robert Benton (Book),
Lee Adams (Lyrics)
Opened March 29, 1966
75 Performances

BASED ON: Comic strip, "Superman"

AGENT: Tams-Witmark

PUBLISHED TEXT: Manuscript Only

RECORDINGS: COL KOL-6570
COL KOS-2970

DIGEST OF PLOT: Superman is Metropolis' unrelenting guardian of right—thwarting evil at every turn. As he returns to his disguise as Clark Kent, mild-mannered reporter for *The Daily Planet,* he learns that gossip columnist Max Menken has launched an unmask-Superman campaign in an attempt to clear the way for his romantic interest in *Planet* reporter Lois Lane, who loves Superman. Lois is busy with Dr. Sedgwick, ten-time Nobel Prize loser, who is having dangerous problems with his new atomic reactor at M.I.T. He wants Lois to contact Superman for help. The indestructible Superman corrects the problem, much to the consternation of Sedgwick, who secretly wants revenge for being overlooked by the world. Max's secretary, Sydney, also suffers constant rejection from her overbearing boss and turns her attentions to Clark Kent. Meanwhile

Bob Holiday as Superman.

Lois has found she could fall for a human—Jim Morgan, Dr. Sedgwick's assistant. Max's plot to discover Superman's identity fails. Sedgwick's new plot, however, is progressing full-speed. He has managed to humiliate Superman in the eyes of the public and has his computer narrowing down all possible identity cover-ups. The computer tells him it is someone who works for *The Daily Planet* and he decides it's Max. Sedgwick has Max kidnaped by his Chinese henchmen. Once together they compare data and realize that Superman is really Clark Kent. Max and Sedgwick join forces to lure Superman to an abandoned powerhouse where Lois is held captive. Sedgwick tricks Superman with a psychological-hypnotic approach, which renders him powerless. A similar fate awaits Jim as he tries to save Lois. Sedgwick's Chinese henchmen turn out to be spies and award him the Mao Tse-tung Peace Prize and cut Max out of the picture. A helicopter is coming to pick them up before a missile attack is launched on Metropolis. Jim makes an attempt to prevent their departure and is shot. This evil jars Superman back to normal in time to clean up the place. Sedgwick makes a final attempt to escape with Lois as hostage, but Superman once more rescues her, and Sedgwick falls to his death. The police arrive, and Superman is on his way to single-handedly prevent the missile attack and reclaim his place in society.

MUSICAL NUMBERS: "Doing Good," "We Need Him," "It's Superman," "We Don't Matter at All," "Revenge," "The Woman for the Man," "YOU'VE GOT POSSIBILITIES," "What I've Always Wanted," "Everything's Easy When You Know How," "It's Super Nice," "So Long, Big Guy," "The Strongest Man in the World," "Ooh, Do You Love You!," "You've Got What I Need," "I'm Not Finished Yet," "Pow! Bam! Zonk!"

INSTRUMENTATION: Pic (flute, clar, alto sax), flute (clar), clar (tenor sax), clar (bass clar, tenor sax), clar (bari sax, bassoon), trumpets I–II, III, trombone I, II, III (tuba), bass, percussion I–II, organ-celeste.

CASTING: 34 parts, 6 principals, plus "Flying Lings" balancing act. Superman/Clark Kent, built to look the part, good actor who sings well. Max, plays good heavy, sings well and dances. Lois Lane, actress who sings. Sydney and Jim, singers who act well. Dr. Abner Sedgwick, good character man who sings and dances. Several musclebound bodies required. Singing-dancing chorus of 16. Total cast, 34–44.

SCENES AND SETS: 2 acts, 18 scenes, 1 basic "Metropolis" full stage set. All others fly in or move in on wagons as partial sets. The sky is always overhead for Superman to fly in or out of any situation. *Daily Planet* scrim and 1 sky drop.

ACT I
Scene 1: Outside the Chase-Metropolis Bank.
Scene 2: Offices of *The Daily Planet*.
Scene 3: A Telephone Booth.

Scene 4: Nuclear Reactor at M.I.T.
Scene 5: Offices, *Daily Planet*.
Scene 6: Dr. Sedgwick's Study.
Scene 7: The Screening Room.
Scene 8: Dr. Sedgwick's Home.
Scene 9: Offices, *Daily Planet*.
Scene 10: Atop City Hall Tower.
Scene 11: The M.I.T. Dedication Grounds.

ACT II
Scene 1: The Front Page.
Scene 2: Clark Kent's Apartment.
Scene 3: Street in Metropolis.
Scene 4: Dr. Sedgwick's Laboratory.
Scene 5: Meanwhile.
Scene 6: An Abandoned Power Station.
Scene 7: Power Station.

PERIOD AND COSTUMES: The present: Superman blue body suit with logo "S" and red cape. Human suits and dresses for office wear. Mod mini fashions, cheerleader dresses, coats, hats, sweaters. "Flying Lings" costumes. New and tattered "lead" suits. Various uniforms for football players, waitress, bank robbers, etc.

CHOREOGRAPHY: Opening "Superman overpowers 7 crooks," modern, rock, Flying Lings balancing and gymnast exhibition, production numbers, soft shoe, "Pow! Bam! Zonk!" fight sequence.

LIGHTING AND SPECIAL EFFECTS: Superman's flying rig, film on the origin of Superman (available from the leasing agent), fantastic feats of strength (helped by special rigging), explosion of city hall. Cork bullets bounce off Superman.

NOTES: *Superman* was produced in a fad period of "camp," tongue-in-cheek humor. It was a super idea in this era of pop art when original Superman comic books were selling for as much as $50 or more a copy. The show would have been more successful if it had stuck to this style, but it often slipped into a musical comedy cliché. This burden must be borne in today's production with the additional problem of the passing of "camp." However, the music, fun, and interest packed into this comic strip superhero make it worth the effort. The first act is rather sound, but the second falls apart. The major mistake is in trying to humanize Superman and making him out to be an oaf. Suggest cutting Act II, Scene 2 and strengthening Superman image in Act I finale and throughout second act. He can be tricked and stunned, but he can never be less than Superman. Also suggest cutting "You've Got What I Need" number. Good number, but it doesn't fit. Comic page (Act II, Scene 5) could be newspaper comic format rather than the three-level comic book set used on Broadway.

THE KING AND I

Richard Rodgers (Music),
Oscar Hammerstein II (Book, Lyrics)

COURTESY OF THE LYNN FARNOL GROUP, INC.

Yul Brynner, Gertrude Lawrence, and original cast of The King and I.

Opened March 29, 1951
1,246 Performances

BASED ON: *Anna and the King of Siam* by
Margaret Landon

AGENT: R & H

PUBLISHED TEXT: Modern Library #200

RECORDINGS: DEC-(7)9088
RCA LOC(LSO)-1092
CAP W(SW)-740(F)

DIGEST OF PLOT: The King of Siam employs
Anna, an English schoolteacher, to educate his household of children. He is an advanced and fair king
but deeply steeped in the traditions of his country.
Anna soon wins the hearts of the Siamese people,
but has decidedly more difficulty in her battle for
a private house away from the palace, which the
king had promised as part of the original bargain.
Conflicts develop between the cultures of East and
West and between the two strong-willed people who
admire each other very much. Progress on many
issues is bargained for and won by both. However,
when Anna talks the King out of beating Tuptim,
a runaway slave who loves another, he interprets it
as his loss of strength. Although personally a broken

and dying man, he knows his personal defeat has
bettered his country for its place in the changing
times of the world.

MUSICAL NUMBERS: "I WHISTLE A HAPPY
TUNE," "My Lord and Master," "HELLO, YOUNG
LOVERS," "MARCH OF THE SIAMESE CHIL-
DREN," "A Puzzlement," "The Royal Bangkok
Academy," "GETTING TO KNOW YOU," "We
Kiss in a Shadow," "Shall I Tell You What I Think
of You?," "Something Wonderful," "Western People
Funny," "I HAVE DREAMED," Ballet: "The Small
House of Uncle Thomas," "SHALL WE DANCE?"

INSTRUMENTATION: Violins A–B, C, D, cello,
viola, flute, oboe (Eng. horn), B♭ clar I, II, bassoon,
horns I, II, trumpets I–II, III, trombones I, II,
percussion, harp.

CASTING: 14 parts, plus Siamese princes and
princesses, royal dancers, wives, amazons, priests,
and slaves, 8 principals including 2 young boys.
Anna, accomplished actress, legit voice, 1 dance
number. King, accomplished actor, sings, 1 dance
number. Tuptim and Lun Tha, young romantic
interest, legit voices. Lady Thiang, legit voice.
Young Louis and Prince Chulalongkom, boys about
10 years old, straight roles. Sir Edward, dignitary,
straight role. Strong choral work. Total cast, 40–50.

SCENES AND SETS: 2 acts, 12 scenes, 6 intermediate scenes, 5 full stage sets including 2 drops, 1 partial stage set, 3 scene drops. The action passes in and around the King's palace, Bangkok, Siam.

ACT I

Scene 1: Deck of the Chow Phya Ship; A Palace Corridor.
Scene 2: King's Study in the Royal Palace.
Scene 3: The Palace Grounds.
Scene 4: The Schoolroom; The Palace Corridor.
Scene 5: Anna's Bedroom; The Palace Corridor.
Scene 6: The King's Study.

ACT II

Scene 1: The Schoolroom.
Scene 2: The Palace Grounds.
Scene 3: The Theatre Pavilion.
Scene 4: The King's Study; The Palace Grounds.
Scene 5: A Room in Anna's House; A Palace Corridor.
Scene 6: The King's Study.

PERIOD AND COSTUMES: 1860's: Bangkok, Siam. Large hoop skirts, silky-looking garb for the royal Siamese wives, children, palace guards, slaves, and the king. Ship's captain and sailor uniforms, diplomatic formal wear with sash and medals. Costumes and masks for Uncle Tom's Cabin characters (with heavy Siamese styling): Uncle Thomas, Topsy,

COURTESY OF THE LYNN FARNOL GROUP, INC.

"Shall We Dance?" Anna invites the King.

Little Eva, Eliza (no mask), King Simon of Lagree, Angel, Buddha, and bloodhounds.

CHOREOGRAPHY: March, ballet (Siamese styles

for "The Small House of Uncle Thomas"), two-step, waltz.

LIGHTING AND SPECIAL EFFECTS: Some dramatic lighting required. Cloth and prop weather effects in "Small House of Uncle Thomas" sequence.

NOTES: A classic of musical theatre made even more popular by its ease of production.

KISMET

Alexander Borodin (Music),
Charles Lederer, Luther Davis (Book),
Robert Wright, George Forrest (Lyrics)
Opened Dec. 3, 1953
583 Performances

BASED ON: *Kismet* by Edward Knoblock

AGENT: Music Theatre

PUBLISHED TEXT: Random House, 1954

RECORDINGS: COL OL 4850
                 COL OS 2060
                 RCA LOC(LSO)1112(R)
                 METRO (S) 526(F)

DIGEST OF PLOT: A poet happens upon a Baghdad mosque and accepts alms in the name of Hajj the beggar. A fortunate mistake in identity until the desert thief Jawan has him kidnaped for a curse placed upon him by the real Hajj. But the new Hajj talks his way out of torture and death and receives 100 gold pieces to find the dying Jawan's lost son. Meanwhile, the ruthless Wazir of Police has sent his wife, Lalume, to the land of Ababu to obtain a loan. The gold has been granted on the condition that the Wazir use his influence to arrange a high-ranking marriage for the three primitive Princesses of Ababu—to the exalted Caliph no less. The handsome Caliph, weary of the many royal females flocking to proclaim themselves worthy to wive, spots the poet's daughter, Marsinah, in the Bazaar of the Caravans. He follows her into a garden and assumes the role of a gardener. This is the girl of his dreams, and she can hardly contain her joy. But their meeting is brief for the Caliph must attend to affairs of state. The Wazir has his hands full with the Princesses and is in his usual tyrannical mood when Hajj is brought before him as a thief with too much gold. Once again he faces torture, but Jawan has been captured and proclaims he had given Hajj the gold to help find his son, who turns out to be the Wazir. After sentencing his father to death, the Wazir is about to return his attentions to Hajj when the Caliph enters to announce he has found his true love. All other applicants are to be rejected. Facing financial ruin, the Wazir turns to whatever powers Hajj might possess. He shall be made an Emir if the Caliph should change his mind. Hajj seizes the opportunity at freedom to run to the

Alfred Drake (Hajj) and Joan Diener (Lalume) in the Wazir's harem in the original production of Kismet.

garden and warn Marsinah to flee to Damascus. She had told her gardener she would wait there until moonrise, but reluctantly obeys her father. Moments later the Caliph arrives to find she has left. The Wazir's spies report this turn of events, and Hajj receives his reward in time to retrieve Marsinah and bring her to the Wazir's harem for protection. The Caliph calls on the Wazir to launch a search for his lost love. Meanwhile, Marsinah is explaining her own loss to her father. With tongue-in-cheek compassion, the Wazir offers the Caliph the choice of his own harem. There he spots Marsinah and, believing her to belong to the Wazir, is extremely distressed to find his love is a runaway slave. He defeatedly returns to his throne to declare once again his eligibility for marriage. By this time Hajj has put together the pieces and disrupts the demonstrations of the prospective brides by drowning the Wazir and unveiling the truth about Marsinah to the Caliph.

MUSICAL NUMBERS: "Sands of Time," "Rhymes Have I," "Fate," "Bazaar of the Caravans," "Not Since Nineveh," "BAUBLES, BANGLES, AND BEADS," "STRANGER IN PARADISE," "He's in Love!," "Gesticulate," "Night of My Nights," "Was I Wazir?," "Rahadlakum," "AND THIS IS MY BELOVED," "The Olive Tree," "Ceremonial of the Caliph's Diwan," Presentation of Princesses."

INSTRUMENTATION: Violins A–C, B–D, viola, cello, bass, clar I, II, bass clar, flute, oboe, bassoon, horns, trumpet I–II, III, trombone I, II, tuba, percussion, harp, piano-conductor.

CASTING: 38 parts, 7 principals, plus 6 featured female dancers. Poet (Hajj), masterful and cunning actor who sings well. Marsinah, his daughter and the Caliph, young romantic interest, legit voices. Wazir of Police, a strong comic character man who can play a likable evil part, sings. Lalume, voluptuous, sexy, powerful restrained voice. Three Princesses of Ababu, wild lead dancers. Three featured dance specialties (belly and cymbal ceremonial dance, Hindu temple dance, belly dance). Strong choral work. Total cast, 38–50.

SCENES AND SETS: 2 acts, 14 scenes, 7 full stage sets (including 3–7 drops), 2 partial stage sets, 4 scene drops, 1 scrim.

ACT I
(From Dawn to Dusk)
Scene 1: On the Steps of the Mosque.
Scene 2: A Tent Just Outside the City.
Scene 3: The Bazaar of Caravans.
Scene 4: A Side Street.
Scene 5: A Garden.
Scene 6: A Street Near the Bazaar.
Scene 7: The Throne Room of His Exalted Excellency, the Wazir of Police.

ACT II
(From Dusk to Dawn)
Scene 1: Along the Route of the Caliph's Procession.
Scene 2: The Garden.
Scene 3: Anteroom to the Wazir's Harem.
Scene 4: Rooftop Pavilion in the Wazir's Palace.
Scene 5: Corridor in Wazir's Palace.
Scene 6: Anteroom to Wazir's Harem.
Scene 7: The Ceremonial Hall of the Caliph's Palace.

PERIOD AND COSTUMES: A day in ancient Baghdad: high priest robes, beggar's rags, pantaloons, harem outfits (halters, veils, beaded panties, beads around legs), black Wazir and police uniforms, Arabian robes, paneled skirts, head- and footgear, princely robes, a robber's finery, striking and brief costumes for featured dancers, swords, feathers, plumes, palace guard uniforms.

CHOREOGRAPHY: Whirling dervish, Arabian-flavored modern dance, jungle modern, native dances of the ancient East, shimmy, belly dance, few bumps and grinds.

LIGHTING AND SPECIAL EFFECTS: Some dramatic lighting required. Torches. Drowning of Wazir in a pool onstage.

NOTES: *Kismet* is the best example of writing lyrics for existing classical musical themes. The result is excitingly modern and a unique balance of an outstanding number of interesting songs and varied dance numbers.

KISS ME KATE

Cole Porter (Music, Lyrics),
Sam and Bella Spewack (Book)
Opened Dec. 30, 1948
1,077 Performances

BASED ON: Original

AGENT: Tams-Witmark

PUBLISHED TEXT: Knopf, 1953; *Theatre Arts,* January, 1955

RECORDINGS: COL OL-4140
COL OS-2300
MGM-3077(F)

DIGEST OF PLOT: Divorced husband-and-wife team Fred Gram and Lili Vanessa are reunited for Fred's production of Shakespeare's *Taming of the Shrew.* Just as the old romance begins to bloom again, Lili receives misdirected flowers and a note intended for Fred's latest love interest. In venting her anger, she becomes an infuriated Kate onstage. Fred turns her over his knee and renders punishment befitting her childish actions. Meanwhile, Bill, a losing gambler and member of the cast, has signed Fred's name to a $10,000 I.O.U. During intermission, two hoods show up to collect; Fred convinces them that he will be unable to pay if Lili departs from the show as threatened. Fearing for her life, Lili is persuaded to stay, but calls Harrison Howell, her new fiancé and man-about-Washington, for help. Suddenly, the heat is called off by a change of underworld management, and Lili is free to leave. Instead, she returns to Fred and the show, singing the intent of her love in the words of Kate.

MUSICAL NUMBERS: "ANOTHER OP'NIN', ANOTHER SHOW," "Why Can't You Behave," "WUNDERBAR," "SO IN LOVE," "We Open in Venice," "Tom, Dick, or Harry," "I've Come to Wive It Wealthily in Padua," "I HATE MEN," "Were Thine That Special Face," "I Sing of Love," "Kiss Me Kate," "TOO DARN HOT," "Where Is the Life that Late I Led," "Always True to You (in My Fashion)," "Bianca," "Brush Up Your Shakespeare," "I Am Ashamed that Women Are So Simple."

INSTRUMENTATION: Violins A, B, C, viola, cello, bass, alto sax (clar), alto sax (clar, bass clar), sax (clar, flute, oboe, Eng. horn), sax (clar, bass clar), horn, trumpets I–II, III, trombone, percussion, harp, piano (celeste), guitar (mandolin doubles violin B).

CASTING: 23 parts, 7 principals. Separate singing and dancing ensembles. Leads Fred and Lili, accomplished actors with excellent, strong singing voices, minor dancing. Lois, comedienne who sings. Bill, light character man, dances and sings. Harrison, straight comedy role. 2 hoods, underworld comics who sing, do light soft shoe. Stage Doorman, tap dancer, sings "Too Darn Hot." Total cast, 40–50.

SCENES AND SETS: 2 acts, 16 scenes, 8 full stage sets including 3 drops. (Could be done with 2 fewer sets by adding an extra drop for "Exterior Church"), 2 scene drops, 1 curtain, scrim helpful (replacing 1 scene drop).

ACT I
Scene 1: Ford Theatre, Baltimore.
Scene 2: The Corridor Backstage.
Scene 3: Fred and Lili's Dressing Rooms.
Scene 4: Padua.
Scene 5: Street Scene, Padua.
Scene 6: Backstage.
Scene 7: Fred and Lili's Dressing Rooms.
Scene 8: Exterior Church.

Alfred Drake surrounded by the original cast of Kiss Me, Kate.

ACT II
Scene 1: Theatre Alley.
Scene 2: Before the Curtain.
Scene 3: Petruchio's House.
Scene 4: The Corridor Backstage.
Scene 5: Fred and Lili's Dressing Rooms.
Scene 6: The Corridor Backstage.
Scene 7: Backstage.
Scene 8: Baptista's Home.

PERIOD AND COSTUMES: Ford Theatre, Baltimore, not long ago: rich-looking dressing gowns, modern suits and dresses, shirts and pants. Shakespearean costumes for *Taming of the Shrew* (medieval dresses, headdresses, tights, tunics, feather caps, etc.), gangster suits and guns, overcoats, and uniforms for a doctor, nurses, cab driver, messengers, and truck driver.

CHOREOGRAPHY: Modern, tap, soft shoe, ballet, tarantella.

LIGHTING AND SPECIAL EFFECTS: General lighting, whip handling.

NOTES: Although the show is original, it "borrows" from Shakespeare's *Taming of the Shrew*. Tight construction, good score, and funny lines have made this show a standard of musical theatre.

LI'L ABNER

Gene de Paul (Music),
Johnny Mercer (Lyrics),
Norman Panama and Melvin Frank (Book)

Opened Nov. 15, 1956
693 Performances

BASED ON: Characters Created by Al Capp

AGENT: Tams-Witmark

PUBLISHED TEXT: Manuscript Only

RECORDINGS: COL OL-5150
COL OL-5460(F)
COL OS-2021(F)

DIGEST OF PLOT: *Li'l Abner* is Dogpatch U.S.A. come to life onstage. It characterizes virtually all its most important comic-strip figures and probably its most important event, the marriage of Daisy Mae to Li'l Abner. Along the way, Dogpatch is proclaimed the most unnecessary town in the country and proposed as a site for nuclear tests. To save the town, Mammy Yokum reveals her secret Yokumberry tonic, which makes musclemen out of weaklings. It saves the town but involves its people in a Washington fiasco when Mammy wants to *give* the rights of the tonic to the Government. In an attempt to nab the priceless formula for himself, General Bullmoose enters his protégée, Appassionata Von Climax, in the annual Sadie Hawkins Day race. To ensure that she will catch Li'l Abner for her husband —and joint ownership—he hires Evil Eye Fleagle. However, the plan is foiled by the simple uprighteousness of the community. Li'l Abner claims Daisy Mae for himself, and Marryin' Sam performs the joyful event on the spot—after due homage to the town's only other hero, Jubilation T. Cornpone.

MUSICAL NUMBERS: "A Typical Day," "If I Had My Druthers," "Jubilation T. Cornpone," "Rag Offen the Bush," "Namely You," "Unnecessary," "What's Good for General Bullmoose," "The Country's in the Very Best of Hands," "Sadie Hawkins Day," Ballet, "Oh Happy Day," "I'm Past My Prime," "Love in a Home," "Progress Is the Root of All Evil," "Put 'Em Back," "The Matrimonial Stomp."

INSTRUMENTATION: Violins A–C, B–D, viola, cello, bass, clar (alto sax, flute, pic), clar (alto sax, bass clar), clar (sax, flute), clar (sax, oboe, Eng. horn), clar (bari sax, bassoon), trumpets I–II, III, trombone I, II, III, percussion, guitar (banjo), piano.

CASTING: 29 parts, 10 principals. All principals —Marryin' Sam, Earthquake McGoon, Daisy Mae, Pappy and Mammy Yokum, Li'l Abner, Sen. Jack S. Phogbound, General Bullmoose, Appassionata Von Climax, Evil Eye Fleagle—look (or can be made to look) like the comic-strip characters. All must sing well with the exception of Mammy and Pappy, Appassionata, and Fleagle, which are straight roles. Separate large singing and dancing ensembles. 5 or 6 musclebound males required. Total cast, 36–60.

SCENES AND SETS: 2 acts, 20 scenes, 7 full stage sets (including 4 drops), 1 partial stage set, 2 scene drops.

ACT I
Scene 1: Dogpatch, U.S.A.
Scene 2: The Yokum Cabin.
Scene 3: The Fishing Hole.
Scene 4: Cornpone Square.
Scene 5: Dogpatch Road.
Scene 6: Cornpone Square.
Scene 7: Washington, D.C., Sequence:
  A. Government Laboratory.
  B. President's Office.
Scene 8: General Bullmoose's Office.
Scene 9: Dogpatch Road.
Scene 10: Dogpatch.
Scene 11: Dogpatch Road.
Scene 12: Dogpatch.

ACT II
Scene 1: Government Testing Laboratory, Washington.
Scene 2: The Yokum Cabin.
Scene 3: General Bullmoose's Office.
Scene 4: Corridor in Bullmoose Mansion.
Scene 5: Ballroom in Bullmoose Mansion.
Scene 6: Corridor in Bullmoose Mansion.
Scene 7: The Government Testing Laboratory.
Scene 8: Cornpone Square.

PERIOD AND COSTUMES: Modern backwoods Dogpatch U.S.A.: bright Dogpatch rag skirts and overalls, Daisy Mae mini, Marryin' Sam's black waistcoat suit, Mammy's outfit, Appassionata's skintight dresses and fur wraps, burlap rags for the Scraggs, McGoon's outfit, Phogbound's white suit, Bullmoose's formal suits, secretaries' office clothes (short and busty), Fleagle's green zoot suit and chain, laboratory smocks, briefs for musclemen, Colonel uniform, evening gowns, and formal wear.

CHOREOGRAPHY: Modern (knee slappin', hand clappin', foot stompin' exuberance), "Sadie Hawkins Day" modern ballet, street or light soft shoe, the "Matrimonial" stomp.

LIGHTING AND SPECIAL EFFECTS: Some dramatic lighting. Special lighting when Fleagle puts on his Whammy.

NOTES: *Li'l Abner* is a dancer's show. Much of the effect and success of this show lies in duplicating the comic-strip style in sets, makeup, costuming, and characterization.

LITTLE MARY SUNSHINE

Rick Besoyan (Music, Book, and Lyrics)

Opened Nov. 18, 1959
1,143 Performances

BASED ON: Original

AGENT: Metromedia

PUBLISHED TEXT: *Theatre Arts,* December, 1961

RECORDINGS: CAP (S)WAO 1240

DIGEST OF PLOT: Captain Jim's forest rangers billet at Little Mary's Colorado Inn, which she has built on land purchased from the government with money she made by selling cookies. Their mission is to seek out reported hostile Indian activity in the Kadota tribe. This is puzzling to Little Mary since Chief Brown Bear (who has raised Little Mary since finding her in the woods), a senile guide named Fleet Foot, and Chief's renegade son, Yellow Feather, are the only surviving members of the tribe. Also staying at the inn are a bevy of young ladies from Eastchester Finishing School and the opera star, Mme. Ernestine von Liebedich. A more pressing problem is Little Mary's inability to pay the mortgage on her inn. She stands to lose everything. Captain Jim decides to handle the dangerous mission by himself with Fleet Foot as his guide, but orders Corporal Billy

Dom De Luise (*Billy*) *and Sonja Savig* (*Nancy*) *in* Little Mary Sunshine.

Jester to back him up with the troops if he doesn't return by 9 o'clock. By this time all the forest rangers and young ladies have fallen in love except Little Mary's frivolous maid, Nancy, and jealous Billy who've had their ins and outs on the subject of love several times before. As Captain Jim is leaving to track down Yellow Feather, he professes his undying love for Little Mary. Just after he leaves Little Mary spots Yellow Feather and begins to fear for her dear Captain. To break the tension, Little Mary hosts a merry party. General Oscar Fairfax (ret.) arrives and dallies with the young ladies until he learns they are all engaged to forest rangers. He discovers Mme.

Ernestine and renews an old romance. Billy is off to Point Look-Out to be made the honorary son of Chief Brown Bear. Nancy is getting into her Mata Hari disguise to follow Billy into the woods as it's now past 9. Captain Jim, Billy, and Nancy narrowly miss capturing Yellow Feather in the woods, and he sneaks back to capture Little Mary at the inn. Captain Jim arrives in the nick of time to save her and tame Yellow Feather in a savage battle. General Oscar then announces that Chief Brown Bear's legal battle to regain the lands of the Kadota Indians has been won. Little Mary's inn is saved. Everyone is in love, even Billy and Nancy, and all is right with the world.

MUSICAL NUMBERS: "The Forest Rangers," "Little Mary Sunshine," "Look for a Sky of Blue," "You're the Fairest Flower," "In Izzenschnooken on the Lovely Essenzook Zee," "Playing Croquet and Swinging," "How Do You Do?," "Tell a Handsome Stranger," "Once in a Blue Moon," "Colorado Love Call," "Every Little Nothing," "What Has Happened?," "Such a Merry Party," "Say, Uncle," "Me, a Big Heap Indian," "Naughty, Naughty Nancy," "Mata Hari," "Do You Ever Dream of Vienna?," Shell Game, "Coo Coo."

INSTRUMENTATION: Violins I–II, viola, cello, bass, flute, oboe, clar I, II, bassoon, trumpet I–II, trombone, horn I–II, percussion, harp. (Duo-piano arrangement available.)

CASTING: 19 parts, 7 principals, 2 support roles, and a chorus of no more than 14 or 16. Little Mary, Captain Jim, and Mme. Ernestine, legit voices. Billy and Nancy, comic team who sing and dance. Uncle Oscar, 1 patter song. Other principals, straight-comic roles. Chorus emphasis on singing. Total cast, 19–27.

SCENES AND SETS: 2 acts, 11 scenes, 2 sets, and 2 drops. Swings hang from the grid at the proscenium arch to enable girls to swing out over orchestra pit.

ACT I
A Summer Afternoon
Scene 1: In Front of the Colorado Inn.
Scene 2: The Garden.
Scene 3: The Inn.
Scene 4: The Primrose Path.
Scene 5: The Inn.

ACT II
That Evening
Scene 1: The Inn.
Scene 2: Point Look-Out.
Scene 3: In Front of Chief Brown Bear's Teepee.
Scene 4: Cora's Bedroom.
Scene 5: The Primrose Path.
Scene 6: Point Look-Out.
Scene 7: The Inn.

PERIOD AND COSTUMES: Early 20th Century at the Colorado Inn, high in the Rocky Mountains. Indian buckskins and headdress, forest ranger uniforms (similar to Canadian Mounties), opera style dresses, maid uniform, formal suit with sash, and very proper nightgowns and floor-length dresses for the young ladies.

CHOREOGRAPHY: March patterns, soft shoe, Indian dance (comedy), and choreographed movements, pantomiming and overacting typical of operetta days.

LIGHTING AND SPECIAL EFFECTS: General day and night lighting. Snowfall in the second-act finale.

NOTES: *Little Mary Sunshine* is a satire of early 20th-Century operetta days. Every song, line, and movement is recalled from the works of Strauss, Friml, Herbert, and others. The plot and melodies seem the same yet somehow different. The direction and everything about the production *must* work within this mood and framework. The acting style borders on the ridiculous, yet is played completely straight with forthrightness and honor.

MAGGIE FLYNN

Hugo Peretti, Luigi Creatore, George David Weiss (Book, Music, Lyrics)
Opened Oct. 23, 1968
82 Performances

BASED ON: Original Idea by John Flaxman

AGENT: Samuel French, Inc.

PUBLISHED TEXT: Samuel French, Inc., 1968 (P)

RECORDINGS: RCA LSOD-2009

DIGEST OF PLOT: Maggie Flynn, deserted almost seven years ago by her Irish rogue husband, Phineas, runs an orphanage for offspring of runaway slaves. The Civil War rages in the South, and there is talk of a draft law to combat the lack of enlistments. This makes Maggie's fund-raising for Negro children none too easy but she has been cajoling men for a long time now and manages to scrape through the winter and spring. She is out walking the children when a circus parade comes to town. Something about the featured clown is strangely familiar. Maggie follows him to his tent to discover her soon-to-be-pronounced-legally dead husband. She has plans to marry a respectable gentleman, Colonel John Farraday, and wants Phineas to give her a divorce. Phineas doesn't like the idea, but agrees. To help raise money, Maggie has rented the basement of the orphanage to two strangers who later turn out to be Southern spies. Meanwhile Phineas has accidently walked in on Farraday's proposal to Maggie during a visit to bring the children balloons and merriment. Farraday leaves, but Phineas is caught in a quarantine when several of the children come down with the measles. The predicament is delicious for Phineas, but awkward for Maggie and Farraday. During

the period of isolation, Phineas easily conquers the children and manages to warm Maggie a little to the old flame. When the quarantine is lifted, he successfully helps raise money for the home. Maggie's romance is confused, but she won't be hurt again. She asks Phineas to sign the divorce agreement. Reluctantly he does so; however, there is still the Charity Ball that Phineas has arranged. There they are dancing in their old glory. Phineas is about to sweep Maggie off her feet when the ball is called to a halt because of a riot over the new conscription draft law and reported Confederate plot. Phineas sees Maggie safely back to the home where they learn the mission of the basement tenants. Farraday's men have made the same discovery independently. Maggie and the children are put in jail for harboring Confederate spies. Phineas tries to intercede but is renounced and permitted only a short visit with the brood. The General, however, grants Maggie a pardon when the prisoners admit she had no part in their plan. But the anti-draft crowd has turned violent and put the torch to the Negro orphanage. Phineas finds them roaming the streets just in time to prevent bloodshed. They band together to escape the angry mob and rejoin Phineas' circus, leaving Farraday to his Army career.

MUSICAL NUMBERS: "Never Gonna Make Me Fight," "It's a Nice Cold Morning," "I Wouldn't Have You Any Other Way," "Learn How to Laugh," "Maggie Flynn," "THE THANK YOU SONG," "Look Around Your Little World," "I Won't Let It Happen Again," "How About a Ball?," "Pitter Patter," "Why Can't I Walk Away," "The Game of War," "MR. CLOWN," The Riot, "Don't You Think It's Very Nice?"

INSTRUMENTATION: Violins A–B–C, cello, bass, reed I, II, III, IV, V, trumpets I, II, III, trombone I, II, horns I, II, percussion I, II, guitar, conductor.

CASTING: 45 parts, 11 principals, plus 9 Negro children of various ages. Maggie, strong actress/singer who dances. Phineas, versatile actor/singer who dances. Farraday, singer who can act. O'Brien and Donnelly, character men who sing. Timmy, acts and sings. 6 featured parts, act and sing. Separate singing and dancing choruses. Choral work. Total cast, 40–60.

SCENES AND SETS: Prologue, 2 acts, 17 scenes, 12 full stage sets, portable circus cages. The mechanical settings of the original were restricted by a large elevator that brought the basement of the orphanage from the basement of the theatre. As a result, two large military recruitment poster units remained onstage in most scenes.

ACT I
Prologue: Streets of New York City, 1863.
Scene 1: Dormitory and Façade of Meagan Orphan Home.
Scene 2: Barlow's Saloon.
Scene 3: Christopher Street.

Jack Cassidy, Shirley Jones, and children sing "Mr. Clown" from Maggie Flynn.

Scene 4: Dressing Tent.
Scene 5: Parlor and Façade of Orphanage.
Scene 6: Kitchen of Orphanage and Street.
Scene 7: Kitchen of Orphanage.
Scene 8: Solarium of Vanderhoff Mansion.
Scene 9: Union Army Headquarters and the Kitchen.

ACT II
Scene 1: Barlow's Saloon and a Street.
Scene 2: Veranda of Vanderhoff Mansion.
Scene 3: Basement of the Orphanage.
Scene 4: The Parlor.
Scene 5: A Jail.
Scene 6: Jail Office.
Scene 7: Various New York Streets.
Scene 8: Kitchen and Front of Orphanage.

PERIOD AND COSTUMES: New York 1863: military uniforms for several ranks and regiments, suits, dresses, high-button shoes, band and circus costumes, tattoo tights, clown suit, children's pajamas, playclothes, winter coats, laborer's clothes, rich widow hooped dresses, old-woman disguise, ball gowns, dress suits and uniforms, tattered versions of earlier costumes as riot and destruction rage on, tart dresses, bums' clothes, and clown costume accessories.

CHOREOGRAPHY: Marching patterns, modern, waltz, soft shoe, polka, "Mr. Clown" production number, choreographed riot.

LIGHTING AND SPECIAL EFFECTS: Dramatic lighting required, lights on set, burning of the orphanage, riot effects, smoke.

NOTES: The critics must have been in a bad mood the night they reviewed *Maggie Flynn*. Perhaps they were against the spectacle, or perhaps the awkwardness of the sets bothered them. Whatever the reason, nonprofessionals can correct this error. However, it is good to remember that it is a big show with a large mouthful of plot exposition that requires firm and fast-paced direction. Construction can be improved by a more workable set arrangement. Some cutting might be advisable. The events and places in *Maggie Flynn* are historical, the characters are not.

Maggie and children returning to orphanage after some entertaining fund-raising.

MAME

Jerry Herman (Music, Lyrics)
Jerome Lawrence, Robert E. Lee (Book)
Opened May 24, 1966
1,508 Performances

BASED ON: *Auntie Mame* by Patrick Dennis, and Play by Lawrence & Lee

AGENT: Tams-Witmark

PUBLISHED TEXT: Random House, 1967

RECORDINGS: COL KOL-6600
COL KOS-3000

DIGEST OF PLOT: Agnes Gooch brings young Patrick Dennis from a farm in Des Moines to his only living relative, Mame Dennis. This notorious Auntie Mame is a swinger; a fad-following, high-living friend to everyone. Knowledge, love, and the stock market are her dearest possessions. She is overjoyed with Patrick. Unfortunately her authority over him is shared with Dwight Babcock, a trustee for the Knickerbocker Bank. They clash on schooling, but the will spells out a conservative education. He wins, but Mame is busy opening exciting windows for Patrick behind Babcock's back. Babcock catches Pat-

rick enrolled in Ralph Devine's Laboratory of Life and packs him away to boarding school. To add to her problems, the stock market has crashed and Mame must attempt the only thing in the world for which she is unsuited—work. She upstages her actress-friend, Vera Charles, and is fired. Jobs come easy, but go just as fast. Mame is so broke the servants have paid the bills with their rainy day money. Suddenly Santa Claus appears in the person of Beauregard Jackson Picket Burnside. It's obvious that he and Mame are a born pair. The proposal comes fast, but Mame must meet his Southern relatives. As a prospective Yankee in the family, her reception is not the warmest. Especially from Sally Cato, who has been engaged to Beau since grammar school. Sally gets Mame to agree to a hunt designed to make a fool of her. But the plot backfires. Mame captures the fox alive and wins the respect of all. She and Beau are married and depart for an around-the-world honeymoon. Patrick is now in college and is pursuing love interests of his own. Several years into the honeymoon Beau slips from the Matterhorn and is killed. Mame returns to her old friends and is persuaded to write her memoirs. During her absence Patrick has joined Junior Babcock's circle of friends and is engaged to Gloria Upson. Mame is invited to the country to meet the family, plus their novelty-store taste and public prejudices. The Upsons have everything planned, including a buy-up of the unrestricted land next to theirs on which the kids will build a house and thereby keep away the riff-raff. Mame is stunned and asks Patrick how he can put up with such bigotry. Unkind words are aired, and both are hurt. However, Mame has designed an engagement party of her own. The Upsons and Babcock arrive and the event is typical Mame. Her friends drop in, leaving the guests aghast. Pregnant Agnes shows up and admits she's not married. Mame uses the shocked silence to announce that she has purchased the country homesite to establish the Burnside Memorial Home for Single Mothers. The guests storm out. Their poor behavior is enough for Patrick to realize his mistakes. He and Mame are reunited. Decorator Pegeen Ryan, who has been putting the final touches on Mame's apartment during the progress of the party, has caught Patrick's eye. As Mame had suspected, they make a perfect couple and at curtain she's off to India with Stephen, their 10-year-old son, to help him open the windows of the world.

MUSICAL NUMBERS: "St. Bridget," "It's Today," "OPEN A NEW WINDOW," "The Man in the Moon," "My Best Girl," "We Need a Little Christmas," "The Fox Hunt," "MAME," "Bosom Buddies," "Gooch's Song," "That's How Young I Feel," "If He Walked into My Life."

INSTRUMENTATION: Violins I (2), II, viola, cello bass, reed I (pic, flute, clar, alto sax), reed II (flute, clar, bass clar, alto sax), reed III (oboe, Eng. horn, clar, tenor sax), reed IV (clar, bari sax), reed V (clar, tenor sax), trumpets I–II, III, trombone I,

Janis Paige in the "Mame" number.

II, III, percussion, harp, guitar/banjo, piano-celeste. (Minimum instrumentation available.)

CASTING: 30 parts, 15 principals. Mame, accomplished actress, good strong voice, dances well. Patrick age 10, large part, sings. Ito, Chinese servant boy, sings 1 number. Babcock, good character man. Vera, character actress, sings, dances. Agnes, comedienne, sings. Adult Patrick, handsome, legit voice. Beau, accomplished actor who sings well. Devine, Woolsey, Sally Cato, Babcock, Jr., Mr. & Mrs. Upson, Gloria, and Pegeen Ryan, all straight roles. Strong choral work. Large separate singing and dancing ensembles. Total cast, 40–56.

SCENES AND SETS: 2 acts, 16 scenes, 4 full stage sets, including 3 drops, 2 partial stage sets, 1 large crescent-shaped moon. (Mame's Apartment, one of the full stage sets, must flow on- and offstage during one number. The decor of room must change frequently as Mame's fads dictate (done with interchangeable panels in set). It's a two-floor apartment complete with spiral staircase.

ACT I
Scene 1: Somewhere in New York, 1928.
Scene 2: Mame's Apartment.
Scene 3: Hallway of Mame's Apartment.
Scene 4: Mame's Bedroom.
Scene 5: Mame's Living Room (and All Around New York).
Scene 6: Mame's Apartment.
Scene 7: Shubert Theatre, New Haven.
Scene 8: Salon Pour Messieurs.

Scene 9: Mame's Apartment.
Scene 10: Peckerwood.

ACT II
Scene 1: Prep School, College (and Singapore).
Scene 2: Mame's Apartment.
Scene 3: Mame's Apartment (6 Months Later).
Scene 4: Upson Farm.
Scene 5: Mame's Apartment.
Scene 6: Mame's Apartment, 1946.

PERIOD AND COSTUMES: New York City, 1928–1946: winter coats, mufflers. Female bellbottom pantsuits, gold pajamas, flapper dresses, other late 1920's evening and party wear, Patrick's short pants suit, suits, waiter uniforms, Greek Orthodox bishop's habit, Texan outfit, Ito's houseboy uniform, bathrobes, 1930's dresses, fashion helmets, smocks, "Man in Moon" costumes (tights, filmy dresses, tunics, headpieces), topcoats, day dresses, long pants for Patrick, Southern belle dresses, riding habits (red coats, white pants, top hats, parasols), Mame's riding habit, tourist costumes accenting countries visited, college sweaters, slacks. Fur-trimmed coat, maternity clothes, dinner jackets, evening dresses, barbecue sports clothes.

CHOREOGRAPHY: Charleston, modern, production numbers, fox-hunt ballet, light soft shoe.

LIGHTING AND SPECIAL EFFECTS: Dramatic lighting required. Day and night exteriors. Lights of New York on set.

NOTES: The *Auntie Mame* classic profits little in the musical version; but it's a great work to begin with. The construction is loose in many spots, and the musical numbers are often the reason for the drag. *Mame* is one of the rare Broadway productions that suffered because of its sets and production flow. Improvement in this area and proper editing could add tremendously to the success of a local production.

MAN OF LA MANCHA

Mitch Leigh (Music),
Dale Wasserman (Book),
Joe Darion (Lyrics)
Opened Nov. 22, 1965
2,329 Performances

BASED ON: Original based on the life and major works of Miguel de Cervantes.

AGENT: Tams-Witmark

PUBLISHED TEXT: Random House, 1966

RECORDINGS: KAPP (S)-4505
DEC DXSA 7203 (two-record set of British production.)

DIGEST OF PLOT: Tax collector-soldier-author Miguel de Cervantes and his man, Sancho, are cast into the prison common room by the Spanish Inquisition because they foreclosed on a church delinquent in its taxes. The thieves and robbers are quick to descend upon them and ravish their possessions. Cervantes concedes all but a carefully wrapped package of papers that he begs of the prisoners he should be allowed to win back by convincing them it's of value only to himself. The prisoners agree and assist him in dramatizing the fantasies of Cervantes' classic character, Don Quixote. As the knight-errant he tilts at windmills and champions an unwilling slut named Aldonza. To Quixote's "touched" mind she is the fair maiden Dulcinea, and through his kind words and attention she begins to believe in a better way of life. Together with Sancho they band together to rout the muleteers' attempt to torment Aldonza. For his valor Quixote persuades the lord of the castle (the innkeeper) to knight him, following which the muleteers catch Aldonza alone and brutally assault her.

Set for Man of La Mancha.

Quixote's family has sent the daughter's fiancé, Dr. Carrasco, to bring him back to his senses and his home. Posing as the Knight of Mirrors, he succeeds. Reality is so inhumane that the old man is soon near death. Aldonza has found his home to beg forgiveness for her ingratitude. As Don Quixote, he has brought beauty and warmth to her life for the first time. The old man rallies to Quixote's idealism, but his frail body succumbs in his last moment of triumph. Moved by his story, the prisoners vote that the tale of Don Quixote shall live. They return the manuscript just as Cervantes is called before the Inquisition.

MUSICAL NUMBERS: "Man of La Mancha (I, Don Quixote)," "It's All the Same," "Dulcinea,"

Don Quixote and Sancho ride to adventure in Man of La Mancha.

"I'm Only Thinking of Him," "I Really Like Him," "Little Bird, Little Bird," "Barber's Song," "Golden Helmet of Mambrino," "To Each His Dulcinea," "THE QUEST (THE IMPOSSIBLE DREAM)," The Combat, "The Dubbing," "The Abduction," Moorish Dance, "Aldonza," "The Knight of Mirrors," "A Little Gossip," "The Psalm."

INSTRUMENTATION: String bass, flute I, II, pic I, II, oboe, clar I, bassoon (clar II), horns I–II, trumpets I–II, trombone I, II (tenor trombone, bass with F attachment), Spanish guitars I–II, timpani, percussion I–II, piano-conductor.

CASTING: 19 parts, 8 principals, but virtually every character has an important supporting part. Don Quixote (Cervantes), strenuous dual role for a top actor and powerful singer. Aldonza, accomplished actress, powerful voice. Sancho, comic char-acter man, sings. Padre, legit tenor voice. Innkeeper, Dr. Carrasco, and Captain of Inquisition, straight roles. Barber, comic singer. Antonia, legit voice. Muleteers, male dancers. A guitarist. Remainder of company provides strong choral work. Total cast, 19–25.

SCENES AND SETS: 1 act (full-length, but with-out intermission), continuous action, 1 set—a com-mon room of a stone prison—an almost full-stage-size raked level extending over the orchestra pit (or-chestra is onstage). 2 stairways into pit for down-stage entrances and exits. A large staircase from the back wall raises and lowers on huge heavy-duty chains from a level of about 15 to 20 feet.

PERIOD AND COSTUMES: A prison in Seville, Spain, at the end of the 16th Century: prisoners' togs. Steel-gray velvet suit for Quixote with shabby armor. Two stylized horse heads. Sancho's pantaloons, blouse, and leather vest. Aldonza, net blouse, tights, tattered skirt, leather tunic. Padre's habit, knight uniforms, rough muleteer outfits (leather, rough textiles, knee pants, heavy boots), Moorish dancer costume (halter and harem pants), nightcap and gown, Spanish matron dresses, terrorizing uniforms for the soldiers of the Inquisition. Mirrored knight uniforms and mirror shields.

CHOREOGRAPHY: Stationary clog dance (horses), modern, combat ballet, apache, Moorish dance (belly dancer).

LIGHTING AND SPECIAL EFFECTS: Highly dramatic lighting required. Mirrored shields (must be worked correctly for proper dramatic effect and to avoid blinding audience).

NOTES: A highly stylized and engrossing production. Show is tightly constructed and 15 to 20 minutes longer than a normal musical. Absolutely no room for directional or playing errors. Production must be extremely well rehearsed, so plan for longer rehearsal period. One of the most powerful musicals available—does what numerous other plays and operas failed to do—bring the story of Don Quixote successfully to the stage. Originally performed without an intermission, though one added late in run.

ME AND JULIET

Richard Rodgers (Music),
Oscar Hammerstein II (Book, Lyrics)
Opened May 28, 1953
358 Performances

BASED ON: Original

AGENT: R & H

PUBLISHED TEXT: Random House, 1953; Modern Library #200

RECORDINGS: RCA LOC(LSO)-1098

DIGEST OF PLOT: Chorus girl Jeanie and possessive playboy-electrician Bob have begun a romance during pre-Broadway road tryouts. Assistant stage manager Larry also loves Jeanie, but is resigned to her love for Bob. It's painful for him to train her as an understudy. As he does so, however, Jeanie realizes that he is more her type of man. Bob senses Jeanie's new tenderness to Larry and warns he will kill him should he try to beat his time. Stage manager Max also warns Larry not to get mixed up with a girl under his management. As Max cites his cardinal rule, he offers other possibilities; for example, Betty Loraine, the girl from the

Original cast of Me and Juliet.

COURTESY OF THE LYNN FARNOL GROUP, INC.

show across the street whom Max has been dating. When the producer hires Betty as a replacement, Max sticks to his rule and turns on the ice. But Larry isn't successful. He and Jeanie fall hard and are secretly married. Betty can't break Max, but succeeds in making him jealous by her actions on-stage. But it's Jeanie's actions offstage that are being watched from the electrical bridge. When Bob sees the newly married lovers embrace, he almost destroys the Act I finale. Ruby, the company manager, is temporarily successful in hiding Larry and Jeanie from Bob, who stations himself at the bar across the street to stalk the theatre's only exit doors. Later he comes back and breaks into the locked office where they are hiding. There is a brawl in which Larry, Jeanie, Max, Betty, and Ruby all try to subdue Bob, who is eventually knocked cold. Max learns that he has been assigned to a new show and is free again to pursue his love for Betty. Larry returns backstage to call the final cues. When Bob awakens, Ruby tells him that Larry and Jeanie are married, and Bob resigns himself to the fact. Larry has found new confidence in himself and whips the cast through a post-curtain rehearsal reprising the major songs.

MUSICAL NUMBERS: "A Very Special Day," "That's the Way It Happens," Dance Impromptu, "Overture to 'Me and Juliet,'" "Opening of 'Me and Juliet,'" "MARRIAGE TYPE LOVE," "KEEP IT GAY," "The Big, Black Giant," "NO OTHER LOVE," Dance, "It's Me," "First Act Finale of 'Me and Juliet,'" "Intermission Talk," "It Feels Good," "Sequence in Second Act of 'Me and Juliet,'" "We Deserve Each Other," "I'm Your Girl," "Second Act Finale of 'Me and Juliet.'"

INSTRUMENTATION: Violins A, B, C, viola, cello, bass, reed I (flute, pic, clar, bari sax), reed II (oboe, Eng. horn, clar, tenor sax), reed III (clar, flute, alto sax), reed IV (clar, flute, bass clar), reed V (bassoon, clar, tenor sax, bass sax), horns, trumpet I–II, III, trombone I–II, III, drums, harp, conductor, piano.

CASTING: 30 parts, 14 principals. Featured performances spread fairly evenly over the principal characters. Jeanie (chorus singer), Larry (assistant stage manager), George (2nd assistant stage manager), Dario (conductor), Lily (singing lead), Jim (dancing lead), Susie (dancing lead), Charlie (featured acting lead), Bob (electrician), Betty (dancer who gets a break), Buzz (lead dancer), Ruby (company manager), Herbie (vendor). Everyone sings, most dance. Virtually the whole production staff is in the show. Medium-size separate singing and dancing ensembles. Total cast, 30–40.

SCENES AND SETS: 2 acts, 16 scenes, 5 full stage sets (1 is almost a bare stage), 2 partial stage sets, 2 scene drops (1 scrim). Action also takes place in orchestra pit at the conductor's stand. Action also on a light bridge that raises and lowers over center stage. The entire action takes place in and around the theatre in which *Me and Juliet* is currently playing.

ACT I
Scene 1: Backstage.
Scene 2: The Orchestra Pit.
Scene 3: Scene 1 of *Me and Juliet*.
Scene 4: The Light Bridge.
Scene 5: The Bare Stage.
Scene 6: The Alley.
Scene 7: Betty's Dressing Room.
Scene 8: The Light Bridge.
Scene 9: Act I Finale of *Me and Juliet*.

ACT II
Scene 1: The Lobby.
Scene 2: The Bar, Across the Street.
Scene 3: Act II Sequence of *Me and Juliet*.
Scene 4: Theatre Manager's Office.
Scene 5: The Orchestra Pit.
Scene 6: Act II Finale of *Me and Juliet*.
Scene 7: Backstage.

PERIOD AND COSTUMES: The present, a theatre: rehearsal clothes, stagehand work clothes, smocks, dinner jacket, costumes for the *Me and Juliet* production (tights, Shakespearean dresses and tunics, Carmen dress, etc.), dungarees, lounge clothes, nightclub flower girl costume.

CHOREOGRAPHY: Modern ballet, waltz, jazz steps.

LIGHTING AND SPECIAL EFFECTS: Lighting is part of the set.

NOTES: *Me and Juliet* is a musical of curious and instructive construction. It fairly accurately portrays a company of actors in a given Broadway musical beyond the glamour of being a star, which has been so stereotyped in films. New York audiences found it a little too basic, and it did not enjoy a long run. (The original cast was also miserably miscast, thus hastening its demise.) However, for high-school students who haven't yet learned what it's really all about, this show (with proper cutting and updating) can be interesting and highly rewarding. The music for the "Keep it Gay" number was reworked for *Cinderella*, first presented on TV March 31, 1957. The music for "No Other Love" is taken from a major theme in Rodgers' film score *Victory at Sea*. Production people in show could be the persons who are actually performing the backstage functions.

MILK AND HONEY

Jerry Herman (Music, Lyrics),
Don Appell (Book)
Opened Oct. 10, 1961
543 Performances

BASED ON: Original

AGENT: Tams-Witmark

Molly Picon in the Independence Day hora from Milk and Honey.

PUBLISHED TEXT: Manuscript Only

RECORDINGS: RCA LOC(LSO)-1065

DIGEST OF PLOT: American Phil Arkin is visiting his married daughter in Jerusalem. He meets Ruth Stein, a tourist on a group tour with other widows from America. During the Israeli Independence Day celebration they keep running into each other, and their friendship grows rapidly. This bothers Phil because he is already married, even though he and his wife have separated many years ago. In spite of Phil's feelings, his daughter, Barbara, likes Ruth and invites her to come with them to their farm in Negev. Phil and Ruth are captivated by the young spirit of the land. Love blossoms, and they run off together. The planned stay is ended, but Phil asks Ruth to stay. He reveals plans to build a house. When he tells Barbara, she admits that things have gone further than she expected. She advises Phil to tell Ruth about his marriage. Reluctantly he does so. During the night Ruth runs off to rejoin her tour. The next morning Phil tries to find her through the tour leader, Clara Weiss, but is unsuccessful. When they find each other, Ruth offers to stay, but Phil knows there is only one solution. They leave on separate planes. Phil to Paris to seek a divorce from his wife and Ruth home to the U.S., confident that he will be successful.

MUSICAL NUMBERS: "Shepherd's Song," "SHALOM," "Independence Day Hora," "Milk and Honey," "There's No Reason in the World," "Chin Up, Ladies," "That Was Yesterday," "Let's Not Waste a Moment," "The Wedding," "Like a Young Man," "I Will Follow You," "Hymn to Hymie," "As Simple as That."

INSTRUMENTATION: Violin A, B, viola, cello, bass, reed I (flute, pic), reed II (flute, clar), reed III (oboe, Eng. horn), reed IV (clar, E♭ clar), reed V (clar, bass clar), bassoon, horns I–II, trumpets I–II, III, trombone I (euphonium), II, harp, percussion I–II, piano-celeste.

CASTING: 27 parts, 9 principals. Ruth, good voice, minor dancing. Phil, legit voice. Clara, character woman, comedienne, sings well. Visiting husband-seekers (ladies), mostly comic roles, sing, minor dancing. David, accomplished dancer who sings well. Adi, comedian, sings and dances. One small boy. A cow, goats, and several sheep. Total cast, 30–46.

SCENES AND SETS: 2 acts, 12 scenes, 8 full stage sets (3 are simple fly-ins), 1 partial stage set (airplane gangway), 2 scene drops, 1 painted cyclorama. (Original production used projected sky patterns very effectively.)

ACT I
Scene 1: A Street in Jerusalem.
Scene 2: Another Street—That Night.
Scene 3: A Desert Moshav.
Scene 4: David's House. A Week Later.
Scene 5: The Barn.
Scene 6: A Hill Overlooking the Valley.
Scene 7: The Wedding.

ACT II
Scene 1: Another Part of the Moshav. Next Morning.
Scene 2: The Café Hotok, Tel Aviv. Same Night.
Scene 3: A Street in Jerusalem. That Night.
Scene 4: Outside Adi's House. A Day Later.
Scene 5: The Airport. Tel Aviv.

PERIOD AND COSTUMES: Israel, early 1960's: traveling dresses, playclothes, shepherds' clothes. Porter, policeman, and guide uniforms. Male suits and work khakis. Festival costumes and sandals, evening clothes. Cantors' habits, wedding dress, cloaks, fezzes. Female work briefs (sun suits). Soldier uniforms. Also Arabs, waiters, tradesmen, and farmers.

CHOREOGRAPHY: Hora and other Jewish folk steps, modern ballet, dance using 15-foot lengths of irrigation pipe.

LIGHTING AND SPECIAL EFFECTS: Dramatic lighting used in original production. Onstage lights on festival set.

NOTES: *Milk and Honey* was Jerry Herman's first Broadway musical and foretold of the spirited music that later emerged in *Hello, Dolly!, Mame,* and *Dear World*. Much of the humor in this work is in Yiddish and is most appreciated by a predominantly Jewish audience.

MOST HAPPY FELLA, THE

Frank Loesser (Music, Book, Lyrics)

Opened May 3, 1956

678 Performances

BASED ON: *They Knew What They Wanted* by Sidney Howard

AGENT: Music Theatre

PUBLISHED TEXT: *Theatre Arts,* October, 1958

RECORDINGS: COL OL-5118
COL OS-2330
COL O3L-240 (Complete show)

DIGEST OF PLOT: Tony, a Napa valley grape grower, falls in love with a waitress while on business in San Francisco. He leaves a valuable tie pin as a tip with a request that the girl write him. She does, and through a series of letters the relationship gets serious. He is a much older man, and when Rosabella requests his picture, Tony sends one of his young, handsome foreman, Joe. Joe had planned to move on, but when he hears that Tony is planning to marry, he stays around. The day of Rosabella's arrival is planned as a big wedding-day celebration. Tony, realizing that the game is up, drives his pickup truck off the mountainside. Rosabella is delivered to the scene of the festivities by the postman. She spots Joe and believes him to be Tony. Joe sets her straight just as the broken body of Tony is brought into the yard. Rosabella marries Tony anyway, thinking he is going to die. Out of disappointment and spite, she runs off with Joe for the wedding night. Tony improves, and Rosabella falls in love with him while nursing him back to health. It seems that all is well, but it turns out that Rosabella is pregnant. Tony learns that it was Joe and sets out in a rage to kill him. Joe, unaware of any of the new events, has already left town. When Tony finds this out he calms down. He tells Rosabella about his accident and finds understanding in hers. There'll be a big wedding celebration after all.

MUSICAL NUMBERS: "Ooh, My Feet," "I Know How It Is," "Seven Million Crumbs," "The Letter," "Somebody Somewhere," "The Most Happy Fella," "STANDING ON THE CORNER," "JOEY, JOEY, JOEY," "Soon You Gonna Leave Me, Joe," "Rosabella," "Abbondanza," "Plenty Bambini," "Sposalizio," "Special Delivery!," "Benvenuta," "Aren't You Glad?," "Don't Cry," "Fresno Beauties," "Love and Kindness," "Happy to Make Your Acquaintance," "I Don't Like This Dame," "BIG 'D,'" "How Beautiful the Days," "Young People," "Warm All Over," "Old People," "I Like Everybody," "I Love Him," "Like a Woman Loves a Man," "My Heart Is So Full of You," "Hoedown," "Mama, Mama," "Goodbye, Darlin'," "Song of a Summer Night," "Please Let Me Tell You," "Tony's Thoughts," "She's Gonna Come Home with Me," "I Made a Fist."

INSTRUMENTATION: Violin I, II, viola, cello, bass I–II, flute (pic, alto flute), oboe (Eng. horn),

Robert Weede and original cast of Most Happy Fella *singing title song.*

clar (soprano sax, flute), clar (bass clar), bassoon, trumpet I–II, trombone I, II (bass trombone), horns I–II, III, harp, accordion, percussion I–II. (Duo-piano arrangement available.)

CASTING: 24 parts, 9 principals. Tony, accomplished actor, excellent voice. Rosabella, legit voice, acting ability, minor dancing. Cleo, comedienne, good voice, dancing ability. Herman, comic, sings, dances. Joe, handsome, strong baritone voice. Giuseppe, Pasquale, Ciccio, Italian trio, comedy supporting team. Strong choral work, 42 musical sequences in all. Large separate singing and dancing chorus. Total cast, 35–55.

SCENES AND SETS: 3 acts (can be done in 2 by merging Acts I and most of II), 11 scenes, 6 full stage sets including 2 drops, party decorations fly in.

ACT I
Scene 1: A Restaurant in San Francisco; January, 1927.

Scene 2: Main Street, Napa, Calif. In April.
Scene 3: Tony's Barn. A Few Weeks Later.
Scene 4: Tony's Front Yard.

ACT II
Scene 1: The Vineyards in May.
Scene 2: Later in May.
Scene 3: The Vineyards in June.
Scene 4: The Barn.
Scene 5: The Vineyards in July.

ACT III
Scene 1: The Barn an Hour Later.
Scene 2: Napa Station. A Little Later.

PERIOD AND COSTUMES: 1927, Napa, in the heart of the California vineyard country: waitress and postman uniforms, streetwear of the period, work clothes, chef hats and aprons, priest habit, Western party dresses.

COURTESY OF MUSIC THEATRE INTERNATIONAL

Jo Sullivan and Susan Johnson in opening scene from Most Happy Fella.

CHOREOGRAPHY: Modern, folk and square-dance steps, styled tarantella, waltz, production numbers: "Most Happy Fella," "Sposalizio," "Big 'D,' " and "Hoedown."

LIGHTING AND SPECIAL EFFECTS: Some dramatic lighting required. Party lights onstage.

NOTES: *The Most Happy Fella* is one of the most ambitious undertakings available for any group. Demanding singing roles. Highly dramatic. Twice the average number of musical entries. A fantastic show, but demands extra planning, production time, and an extra special effort.

MR. PRESIDENT

Irving Berlin (Music, Lyrics),
Howard Lindsay, Russel Crouse (Book)
Opened Oct. 20, 1962
265 Performances

BASED ON: Original

AGENT: Music Theatre

PUBLISHED TEXT: Manuscript Only

RECORDINGS: COL KOL-5870

DIGEST OF PLOT: *Mr. President* deals with the family life of a President of the United States with two swinging children to keep out of trouble and a wife to keep happy for the last four months of his presidential term. During this period he is to make a goodwill trip to Russia. Because of problems within the family he privately decides to call it off. He confides the decision to his wife, Nell, who later tells daughter Leslie when she complains about making the trip. While partying that evening, Leslie lets this slip to her boy friend, Youssein. The next morning the Russian embassy announces to the press that the President has called off his trip and turns the matter into a propaganda bonanza. Angered, the President denies his family's happiness and revises his decision. The Afro-Asian tour is going well. However, just as the presidential plane is about to land in Moscow, Steve learns that the Russians have been angered by some of his speeches and deny him permission to land. He directs the plane to land anyway, but only a handful of Soviet ground workers pay him any heed. He explains that he is not interested in political speechmaking or diplomatic games. He only wants American and Russian people to get to know each other better. It is a personal triumph for Steve but a disaster for his party back home. The other party has won the election by a landslide with the bulk of the blame placed on the presidential blunder. Steve and Nell return to private life with their children, who are equally happy to leave behind the pressures of Washington. Leslie finds her true love in the Secret Service agent who had protected her life, and son Larry finds less need for fast women and cars. An opportunity presents itself for Steve to be appointed to fill an unexpired term in the Senate, but he learns there are political strings attached and refuses. The new President learns of Steve's self-sacrifice and appoints him to an important international conference in which Steve will once more serve his country.

MUSICAL NUMBERS: "Let's Go Back to the Waltz," "In Our Hide-Away," "The First Lady," "Meat and Potatoes," "I've Got to Be Around," "The Secret Service," "It Gets Lonely in the White House," "Is He the Only Man in the World?," "They Love Me," "Pigtails and Freckles," "Don't Be Afraid of Romance," "Laugh It Up," "Empty Pockets Filled with Love," "Glad to Be Home," "You Need a Hobby," "The Washington Twist," "The Only Dance I Know," "I'm Gonna Get Him," "THIS IS A GREAT COUNTRY."

INSTRUMENTATION: Violin A, B, viola, cello, bass, pic (flute, alto sax, clar), clar (alto sax), clar (tenor sax), clar (tenor sax, bass clar), trumpet I–II, III, trombone I, II, harp, percussion, guitar.

CASTING: 32 parts, 6 principals, 1 featured belly dancer. Steve, actor who sings and dances. Nell, good character woman for light comic role, sings and dances. Leslie, cute young actress who sings and dances. Pat, actor with good voice, minor dance. Youssein, mostly straight role, sings 1 number. Dual singing and dancing chorus. Total cast, 35–50.

The First Lady on a huge elephant during a goodwill tour.

Robert Ryan, Nanette Fabray, Jerry Strickler, and Anita Gillette—the first family in
Mr. President.

SCENES AND SETS: 2 acts, 22 scenes. Original
set consisted of 1 center turntable with permanent
curved wall units in which 88 electromagnets were
mounted. Most scenes were made up of a series of
set or prop pieces magnetized to this background.
These pieces included a revolving sign, presidential
seal, doorways, windows, paintings, borders, drapes,
bed canopy. There was also a tent fly-in, super-
market exterior and a large aluminum grate curtain.
Many sets are partial stage with tight area lighting.

ACT I

Prologue
Scene 1: Oval Room, White House.
Scene 2: Private Sitting Room.
Scene 3: Lawn Party in Chevy Chase.
Scene 4: President's Bedroom.

Scene 5: President's Office.
Scene 6: The Trip.
Scene 7: President's Plane.
Scene 8: Street in Middle East.
Scene 9: Youssein's Apartment.
Scene 10. President's Plane.
Scene 11: Airfield.
Scene 12: Television Studios.
Scene 13: Private Sitting Room.
Scene 14: Office in White House.
Scene 15: President's Office.

ACT II
Scene 1: Street in Mansfield.
Scene 2: Living Room of the Henderson Home.
Scene 3: Anteroom in White House.
Scene 4: Judging Pavilion of the Tioga County
   Fair.

Scene 5: Midway of the Fair.
Scene 6: Another Part of Fair.
Scene 7: Living Room, Henderson Home.

PERIOD AND COSTUMES: The present (1962): high society and formal wear from several nations, teen-age evening gowns, business suits, casual wear, work clothes, heavy winter coats, belly dancer costume, native costumes representing an around-the-world tour, 1 huge pink elephant costume.

CHOREOGRAPHY: Twist, waltz, modern, belly dance, swing, ballroom.

LIGHTING AND SPECIAL EFFECTS: Dramatic lighting required. Visual effects, snow.

NOTES: Show is somewhat topical and needs to be updated in both words and music. It presents an interesting side to the presidency in a loose construction, which could be tightened by cutting extraneous songs and material.

THE MUSIC MAN

Meredith Willson (Music, Book, Lyrics)
Opened Dec. 19, 1957
1,375 Performances

BASED ON: Original story by Meredith Willson and Franklin Lacey

AGENT: Music Theatre

PUBLISHED TEXT: G. P. Putnam's Sons, 1958

RECORDINGS: CAP SW-8-0990
W.B. (S)-1459(F)

DIGEST OF PLOT: Professor Harold Hill has developed a reputation among traveling salesmen—all bad. In order to sell his band instruments and uniforms he promises to form a local student band. After he's paid off it's a fast freight and no band. He is active once again in River City, Iowa. To focus attention on the need for a boys' band he attacks the town's new pool hall as a sign of depravity creeping into the community. His argument is convincing, but it turns out the pool hall is owned by Mayor Shinn who orders the school board to check out Harold's credentials. When they approach him he turns them into a barbershop quartet and disappears. An old friend has warned him about Marian, the town librarian and music teacher. To Harold this is an old problem, but his advances are met with a brick wall. Later at the Fourth of July celebration Harold takes advantage of a disrupting prank to move in and sell his band idea. The Mayor continues to push for proper credentials, but Harold is slippery. Marian's research pays off, but she withholds the evidence when she discovers Harold is helping her problem-child brother, Winthrop. With the exception of the Mayor, the town is now under Harold's firm control. Even Marian is coming around. The band instruments have arrived, but it takes a little longer for the uniforms and instruction books. Future band members have been busily working on Harold's "Think System" of musicianship, and Harold has just met Marian at the footbridge. She confesses that she's known he was a fake since the third day he was in town. Now it's Harold who

Forrest Tucker as Prof. Harold Hill in the opening scene of The Music Man.

is off balance. The uniforms arrive but so does Charlie Cowell, Harold's archenemy, the anvil salesman. Marian tries to prevent Charlie from getting to the Mayor, but is unsuccessful. She wants to warn Harold, but Charlie reaches him first. He still has time to run, but can't. He's hooked on Marian. The angry town, hearing that he's a fake, drags Harold to the ice cream social where everyone has gathered. Mob talk is ugly, but Marian speaks out in his defense. She's a good salesman herself, but there's a clincher. The band arrives in assorted unaltered uniforms. Harold is handed a baton. "Think, men, think" is his command. At the drop of his arm comes the "Minuet in G" as it has never been "played" before. But each struggling note is music to each parent's ears. Harold has his band at last and a truly loving librarian besides.

MUSICAL NUMBERS: "Rock Island," "Iowa Stubborn," "TROUBLE," "Piano Lesson," "GOODNIGHT MY SOMEONE," "SEVENTY-SIX TROMBONES," "Sincere," "The Sadder-But-Wiser Girl," "Pickalittle," "GOODNIGHT LADIES," "Marian the Librarian," "My White Knight," "Wells Fargo Wagon," "It's You," "Shipoopi," "LIDA ROSE," "Will I Ever Tell You," "Gary, Indiana," "TILL THERE WAS YOU."

INSTRUMENTATION: Violins A–B–C, cello, bass, flute (pic), clar (oboe, Eng. horn), clar (E♭ clar, soprano sax), clar (flute, bass clar), bass sax (clar, bassoon), trumpet I–II, III, trombone I, II, III, percussion, piano-conductor. (Reduced version available.)

CASTING: 29 parts, 14 principals, including 2 children, and an authentic barbershop quartet. 6 to 10 children. Harold Hill, disarming, articulate actor, sings and dances. Marian, accomplished actress, legit voice, minor dancing. Marcellus, comic who sings and dances. Mayor Shinn, straight character role. Zenetta and Tommy, young lovers, dancers who sing. Mrs. Shinn and 5 women, busybodies who sing. Mrs. Paroo, character woman who sings. Winthrop, small boy with speaking impediment, sings and acts. Amaryllis, 10-year-old girl, sings, helps if she plays the piano. A horse. Large singing and dancing ensembles. Total cast, 40–60.

SCENES AND SETS: 2 acts, 16 scenes, 7 full stage sets (including 4 drops), 1 fly-in (hotel), 2 scene drops, 1 painted traveler. Locomotive orchestra drop optional.

ACT I
Scene 1: Railway Coach.
Scene 2: Town Square, River City, Ia.
Scene 3: The Paroos' House.
Scene 4: Madison Gymnasium.
Scene 5: Exterior of Madison Library.
Scene 6: Interior of Madison Library.
Scene 7: A Street.
Scene 8: The Paroos' Porch.
Scene 9: Town Square.

ACT II
Scene 1: Madison Gymnasium.
Scene 2: Hotel Porch.
Scene 3: The Paroos' Porch.
Scene 4: The Footbridge.
Scene 5: A Street.
Scene 6: Madison Park.
Scene 7: River City High School Assembly Room.

PERIOD AND COSTUMES: River City, Iowa, July 4, 1912: loud traveling salesmen suits and straw hats. Suit coat that reverses to band uniform jacket. Hat converts to plumed band cap. Conductor uniform, band uniforms, housedresses and aprons, tiered dresses, parasols, knickers, suits, spats, etc., for townspeople, go-to-meetin' clothes for same. July 4th costumes, Indians, Grecian draperies, girls' basketball bloomers, constable outfit.

CHOREOGRAPHY: Modern, soft shoe, square dance, waltz, "Shipoopi," "Seventy-Six Trombones," and "Marian the Librarian" production numbers.

LIGHTING AND SPECIAL EFFECTS: Some dramatic lighting required (day and night exteriors). CO_2 steam for opening locomotive effect if used. Moving lights behind Pullman car interior.

NOTES: A major creative achievement and detailed presentation of early 20th-Century America. A tightly constructed musical, as well, with a steady run of hit songs.

MY FAIR LADY

Frederick Loewe (Music),
Alan Jay Lerner (Book, Lyrics)
Opened March 15, 1956
2,717 Performances

BASED ON: *Pygmalion* by G. B. Shaw

AGENT: Tams-Witmark

PUBLISHED TEXT: Coward-McCann, 1956; Signet, 1958 (P)

RECORDINGS: COL OL-5090
COL OS-2015
COL KOL-8000
COL KOS-2600

DIGEST OF PLOT: Col. Pickering has arrived in London to seek out a colleague in speech research, Professor Henry Higgins. They meet by chance near Covent Garden where Higgins is taking notes on British dialects, primarily of a Cockney flower girl named Eliza Doolittle. Higgins remarks that he could make her into a lady simply by improving her diction. The next day she arrives at Higgins' home offering to buy such lessons. Higgins is intrigued by

Caroline Dixon and the National Company of My Fair Lady *doing "Wouldn't It Be Loverly."*

the idea. Pickering makes it a wager and agrees to pay expenses. The painstaking lessons begin. Eliza's father finds out that she is now living in Higgins' house. He goes there in what turns out to be a touch for money. Higgins, fascinated by his earthy philosophy, gladly buys him off. Progress is slow and despair awaits at every turn. Then there's a breakthrough. The hours of tyrannical grueling work have paid off. Eliza is triumphant in correct pronunciation. It's time for a test in public. Higgins selects his mother's box at Ascot. It's the day of the big opening race. Society is in full bloom. Eliza is doing well in conversation (limited as her subjects are) with Mrs. Eynsford-Hill and her son, Freddy. She has achieved a proper reserve, but when Freddy places a wager for her, she is undone. In the excitement of the finish, she emits some very unladylike words. Freddy thinks she is marvelous and pursues her affections. But it's more unending hours of training by Higgins

in preparation for the Embassy Ball. The event has arrived. Higgins has chosen a stunning gown and is forced to admit that it looks more beautiful on Eliza than he would have imagined. They're off to the ball where she is acclaimed a princess. Once home everyone praises Higgins for his achievement. He is extremely pleased with himself and recounts the whole experience for his fans. Eliza feels *she* has played some part in his success and in anger runs out of the house and into Freddy's arms. During the period of Eliza's training Higgins has referred all his troublesome speaking engagements to her father who has now become so rich and respectable he is being forced to marry his wife. Higgins is disturbed that Eliza has run off and seeks advice from his mother. A confused Eliza is already there for some female comfort. Again they have words and Eliza runs out, threatening to marry Freddy. Mrs. Higgins is inclined to impart a few words about love and women. For once Henry is inclined to listen. On the way home he curses her ingratitude, but admits that he, too, is lonely. He plays some cylinder recordings of her early progress. Suddenly the voice is live. Eliza has returned for better or for worse.

Jane Powell as Eliza and Fran Stevens as Mrs. Higgins.

MUSICAL NUMBERS: "Why Can't the English?," "WOULDN'T IT BE LOVERLY," "WITH A LITTLE BIT OF LUCK," "I'm an Ordinary Man," "Just You Wait," "THE RAIN IN SPAIN," "I COULD HAVE DANCED ALL NIGHT," "Ascot Gavotte," "ON THE STREET WHERE YOU LIVE," "The Embassy Waltz," "You Did It," "Show Me," "GET ME TO THE CHURCH ON TIME," "A Hymn to Him," "Without You," "I'VE GROWN ACCUSTOMED TO HER FACE."

INSTRUMENTATION: Violins A, B, viola, cello, bass, flute (pic), oboe (Eng. horn), clar I, II, bassoon, horns I–II, trumpets I–II, III, trombone I, II, tuba, harp, percussion, piano-conductor. (Reduced instrumentation available.)

CASTING: 42 parts, 7 principals. 2 quartets, large singing chorus and dance specialties. Eliza, accomplished actress, legit voice, minor dancing. Higgins, outstanding actor, sings. Freddy, legit voice. Alfred P. Doolittle, strong character man, dances, sings. Pickering, mostly straight role, minor singing. Mrs. Pearce and Mrs. Higgins, straight roles. 3 buskers, male dancers. Servants, mixed quartet. 4 cockneys, male quartet. Large singing and dancing chorus. Total cast 40–60.

SCENES AND SETS: 2 acts, 18 scenes, 9 full stage sets (including 4 drops), 1 partial stage set (Higgins' doorway), 4 scene drops. If done as original, 5 sets back up one another (3 on a pair of portable "Y" units, 2 on another), which are mounted on double turntables.

ACT I
Scene 1: Outside Covent Garden. A Cold March Night.
Scene 2: A Tenement Section—Tottenham Court Road.
Scene 3: Higgins' Study.
Scene 4: Tenement Section.
Scene 5: Higgins' Study.
Scene 6: Outside Ascot.
Scene 7: Ascot.
Scene 8: Outside Higgins' House, Wimpole Street.
Scene 9: Higgins' Study.
Scene 10: Transylvania Embassy.
Scene 11: The Ballroom of the Embassy.

ACT II
Scene 1: Higgins' Study.
Scene 2: Outside Higgins' House.
Scene 3: Flower Market of Covent Garden.
Scene 4: Upstairs Hall of Higgins' House.
Scene 5: The Garden Behind Mrs. Higgins' House.
Scene 6: Outside Higgins' House.
Scene 7: Higgins' Study.

PERIOD AND COSTUMES: London, 1912: formal evening wear, capes, cloaks. Flower girl dress and hat, durable tweeds and other typically English dress of the poor and working class. Servant, chauffeur, and footman uniforms. Ascot suits and gowns, ball gowns, formal morning suits, silk dressing gowns, sweaters, tiered dresses, floor-length pleated skirt, feather boas, parasols, etc.

CHOREOGRAPHY: Soft shoe, waltz, strut, production numbers.

LIGHTING AND SPECIAL EFFECTS: Opportunity for many outstanding lighting setups, but none absolutely required. Smudge-pot fire, recorded voice effects.

NOTES: *My Fair Lady* is probably the most perfect musical written to date. Almost every line, song, and dance advances the plot. It remains engrossing, endearing, and thoroughly enjoyable after several viewings. It has a large reputation to live up to, and no group should attempt this masterpiece unless they intend to do it right. If you can do only one expensive show in ten years make it *My Fair Lady*. If you don't intend to provide full sets, full costumes, and first-class cooperation and financing, postpone the show to a future year.

NEW GIRL IN TOWN

Bob Merrill (Music, Lyrics),
George Abbott (Book)

Opened May 14, 1957
431 Performances

BASED ON: *Anna Christie* by Eugene O'Neill

AGENT: Music Theatre

PUBLISHED TEXT: Random House, 1958

RECORDINGS: RCA LOC(LSO)-1106

DIGEST OF PLOT: Chris Christopherson, an old, hard-drinking Swedish barge captain, gets word that his daughter, Anna, is coming to visit him. He hasn't seen her since she was 5 and is expecting the innocent young girl he remembers. Anna arrives and is greeted by Marthy, Chris's common-law wife. She confesses her life is quite different from what Chris has imagined. Recently the "house" where she was working was raided. The resulting jail sentence has ruined Anna's health. She is hoping Chris will put her up until she regains her strength. Chris welcomes her with open arms and reformed manner. Chris is different from what Anna expected, and she hides her hurt from him. His respectable airs even force him to evict Marthy. Chris takes Anna on his next barge run to Boston. On the return trip they rescue three shipwrecked sailors, including Mat Burke, a defiant, worldly ox of a seaman. After she repulses his initial passes, they become fast friends. Anna is proud of her new-found dignity. The change is healthful and brings elegance to her character. On land the romance continues. One reward is tickets to society's Check Apron Ball where Anna is the standout in the crowd. Marthy has taken all she can and begins drinking. She becomes loud, and when Mat tries to quiet her down, Marthy tells him the truth about Anna's past. Anna tries to convince Mat that she has changed, but his disillusionment will no longer permit him to accept their love. He joins a ship sailing for China to try and forget her. Anna has picked up the pieces before and she does so again. She becomes a farmer in Staten Island and finds compassion in Henry, a produce shop owner. Marthy repents and swears off drinking. It's a year later, Marthy is beating a drum for the Seamen's Home, and Mat is back in port. Chris tries to keep him away from Anna who is visiting, but the meeting is inevitable. Mat has come to find her and find her he does. She is in her potato-picking rags, yet a beautiful sight to Mat. Time has healed and Anna is as lovely as that first night on the barge.

MUSICAL NUMBERS: "Roll Yer Socks Up," "Anna Lilla," "Sunshine Girl," "On the Farm," "Flings," "It's Good to Be Alive," "LOOK AT 'ER," "Yer My Friend, Aintcha?," "Did You Close Your Eyes?," "At the Check Apron Ball," "There Ain't No Flies on Me," "Ven I Valse," "If That Was Love," Ballet, "Chess and Checkers."

INSTRUMENTATION: Violins A–B, viola, cello, bass, clar (flute, pic), flute (pic, clar), oboe (Eng. horn), bass clar (clar, flute), clar (bari sax, bassoon), trumpet I–II, III, trombone I–II, horn, guitar, percussion, piano-conductor.

CASTING: 30 parts, 10 principals. Anna, accomplished dancer-actress who sings. Mat, actor with powerful legit voice, minor dancing. Chris, old character man, sings, dances. Marthy, character woman, sings, dances. Other principals are small roles that require singing, dancing, and acting talent. Good medium-sized dancing and singing ensembles. Total cast, 35–40. (2 or 3 children optional.)

SCENES AND SETS: 2 acts, 16 scenes, 4 full stage sets (including 4 drops), 1 partial stage set, 1 fence fly-in of multi-colored doors, 4 drop scenes.

ACT I
Scene 1: The Waterfront.
Scene 2: Street with Fence.
Scene 3: Johnny-the-Priest's Saloon.
Scene 4: A Street in the Warehouse District.
Scene 5: Chris's Barge.
Scene 6: A Street Near the Waterfront.
Scene 7: The Waterfront.
Scene 8: Street with Fence.
Scene 9: Chris's Room.
Scene 10: A Street.
Scene 11: The Ball (The Brewery Decorated).

ACT II
Scene 1: Same as Act I, Scene 11.
Scene 2: In the Street, Outside the Brewery.
Scene 3: A Street in the Warehouse District.
Scene 4: Chris's Room.
Scene 5: The Waterfront.

PERIOD AND COSTUMES: Shortly after turn of the century (1900): New York City waterfront. Waterfront sailor and dock worker garb. Prostitute finery of the times (high-button shoes, low-cut blouses, bright and striped skirts hitting slightly below the knee). Bulky sweaters, sea captain uniform. Society floor-length bustled dresses, large hats, loud striped and checked suits. Black overcoat, dungarees, broad-striped shirts, old farm clothes, society girl Seamen's Home uniforms.

CHOREOGRAPHY: Modern, soft shoe, ballroom spins, waltz, "Check Apron Ball" production number.

LIGHTING AND SPECIAL EFFECTS: Dramatic lighting required. Fog, foghorns, and other waterfront effects.

NOTES: Despite a lack of publicity, this is a good musical that stands well on its own.

NO STRINGS

Richard Rodgers (Music, Lyrics),
Samuel Taylor (Book)
Opened March 15, 1962
580 Performances

Diahann Carroll and Richard Kiley in Richard Rodger's offbeat production of No Strings.

BASED ON: Original

AGENT: R & H

PUBLISHED TEXT: Random House, 1962

RECORDINGS: CAP (S)O 1695

DIGEST OF PLOT: David is a successful, one-novel author bumming around Europe in search of material for his second work—or so he tells himself. At a friend's photography studio in Paris he meets fellow American Barbara, a top fashion model. They become attracted to each other. As they stroll to Barbara's apartment, they are like young university students discovering a new philosophy of life. In an abrupt turn, Barbara cautions David not to see her again and bids him goodbye. The reason is Louis de Pourtal, her wealthy patron who awaits inside. Louis outlines the evening's gaiety as Barbara dresses. She hears little as her thoughts keep returning to David. In the meantime, David has been drawn to Nice by Mike Robinson and his hard-living traveling companion, Comfort O'Connell. He is relieved by the diversion, but later back in Paris is upset to discover Barbara with Louis. He manages to get Barbara alone, confesses his love, and demands she stop seeing Louis. He has no right to make such demands, and she lets him know it. David flees in anger and disappointment. Later that evening David goes to Barbara's apartment and finds her alone. Their inner feelings concur and they are inseparable. They travel to Honfleur where Barbara hopes to inspire David to begin work on his next book. The romance flourishes, but progress on the novel is nil. David's thoughts are of the parties in Deauville. When Barbara pushes the issue he takes off to join friends. Barbara returns to Louis in Paris. During his fling at Deauville, David realizes the rut his life is in. He returns to Paris, finds Barbara, and pleads for another try. She persuades him to return to the U.S. and write. He wants her to return with him, but her life is in Paris. As they part, David promises to make good on her hopes for him and return to her with reason to be accepted.

MUSICAL NUMBERS: "THE SWEETEST SOUNDS," "How Sad," "Loads of Love," "The Man Who Has Everything," "Be My Host," "La La La," "You Don't Tell Me," "Love Makes the World Go," "Nobody Told Me," "Look No Further," "Maine," "An Orthodox Fool," "Eager Beaver," "NO STRINGS."

COURTESY OF THE LYNN FARNOL GROUP, INC.

Bernice Massi as Comfort O'Connell leads "Eager Beaver" number in No Strings. *Note trumpet player over Richard Kiley's shoulder at right of photo.*

INSTRUMENTATION: Bass pic (flute, alto flute, clar, tenor sax), flute (clar, bass clar, bassoon, bari sax), pic (flute, oboe, clar, alto sax), flute (clar, bass clar, alto sax), (2) flute (clar, alto sax), flute (clar, bass clar, tenor sax), clar (bass clar, bassoon, bari sax), trumpet I–IV, I–III, trombone I, II, III (bass trombone), drums, percussion, guitar, harp, piano, conductor. (Small orchestration available.)

CASTING: 12 parts, 8 principals. Barbara, exceptional singer, good actress (written for a Negro although no reference is made to race). David, actor with legit voice. Jeanette, typical French maid, petite, sings. Luc, straight role. Louis, handsome, stately actor who sings. Comfort, character girl, sexy, good strong voice. Other principals sing. No female dancers, but 10–15 "mannequins." 6 male dancers. No singing chorus. Total cast, 35–45.

SCENES AND SETS: Prologue, 2 acts, 10 scenes, written for rolling set pieces that tilt from one side to the other. 5 locations, requiring 9 separate sets. The action takes place in Paris, Monte Carlo, Honfleur, Deauville, and St. Tropez. Continuous action.

ACT I

Prologue
Scene 1: Paris, Enormous Photographic Studio.
Scene 2: A Paris Street. (Scenery moves up and down to represent changing parts of Paris.)
Scene 3: Barbara's Apartment.
Scene 4: Monte Carlo Auto Races.

ACT II
Scene 1: Honfleur—at the Edge of the Sea on the Normandy Coast.
Scene 2: House in Honfleur.
Scene 3: Deauville Casino.
Scene 4: A Beach Near St. Tropez.
Scene 5: Luc's Photographic Studio in Paris.
Scene 6: A Street in Paris.

PERIOD AND COSTUMES: Paris and about France, the present: suits, coats, dresses, slacks, sweaters, body stockings (all very stylish in the most advanced designs). Leotards, sleeveless turtlenecks, white shirt for Jeanette, various high-fashion dresses and gowns being modeled. Housecoat. Evening dresses, negligee, comfortable old clothes, beach wear, bolero tops and tight pants, bikinis.

CHOREOGRAPHY: Tableaux of various modeling scenes, modern, ballroom steps, fan-dance steps, ballet.

LIGHTING AND SPECIAL EFFECTS: Dramatic lighting required. Photographic studio set consists almost entirely of special illuminated lighting units. Auto racing effects.

NOTES: The orchestra is onstage, and at times featured musicians rove about the action, playing their parts. In an attempt to soften the ending, one of the best numbers in the show, "Yankee Go Home," was cut. It still may appear in some scores for the show. It definitely does appear in the copy of the score Rodgers donated to the Library of Congress.

OKLAHOMA!

Richard Rodgers (Music),
Oscar Hammerstein II (Book, Lyrics)
Opened March 31, 1943
2,212 Performances
BASED ON: *Green Grow the Lilacs* by Lynn Riggs

AGENT: R & H

PUBLISHED TEXT: Random House, 1943; Modern Library #200

RECORDINGS: DEC (7)9017
CAP (S)WAO 595(F)

Original cast of Oklahoma! *Principals around surrey are l. to r., Lee Dixon (Will), Celeste Holm (Ado Annie), Alfred Drake (Curly), Joan Roberts (Laurey), Howard Da Silva (Jud), Betty Garde (Aunt Eller), and Joseph Buloff (Ali Hakim, kneeling).*

DIGEST OF PLOT: Curly arrives at Aunt Eller's farm to court his gal, Laurey. She feels that he's taking her too much for granted and tries to give the impression there are other men in her life. There is one—the repulsive hired hand, Jud Fry, who has an obsession about her. When Curly asks Laurey to drive with him to the Box Social, Jud bursts in and says that he is taking her. Laurey is angry because Curly says the fancy surrey with the fringe on top he had described was just a myth. Laurey doesn't answer. Jud interprets this as Laurey's desire to go with him, and Curly finds the situation a little hard to believe. The tense mood is broken by the return of Will Parker from Kansas City. He's won $50— the amount Ado Annie's pa had set for a fitting dowry. Annie, however, is currently involved with a smooth-talkin' peddler, Ali Hakim. When Hakim finds out she is marriage-minded, he is anxious to return her to Will. The problem is how. Meanwhile, Curly tells Laurey that folks *expect* her to go to the Social with *him*. This only makes matters worse. Alone, Laurey conjures up a dream about the Social

that turns into a nightmare. She is awakened by Jud, who tells her that it is time to leave. Fearing that the harm to Curly prophesied in the dream might come true, she agrees to ride with Jud. At the Social, the charity bidding for the box lunches, and the girl who prepared it, is brisk. Ado Annie reveals that only hers and Laurey's remain. Ali uses the occasion to unload Annie back on Will. But Jud is prepared to spend his whole savings on Laurey's basket. To meet the challenge, Curly sells his horse, saddle, and gun before he is top bidder. Later, during the dance, Jud manages to get Laurey alone. He tells her that she really loves him and he knows it. When Laurey spurns him, Jud makes threats. She stands up to him and tells him he's fired, and Jud runs off. Afraid for her life, Laurey calls Curly. She admits she was only trying to make him jealous. Curly asks her to marry him and she agrees. Three weeks later, the afternoon of the wedding, Jud returns to the farm and tries to kill Curly. In the struggle, Jud falls on his own knife and is fatally wounded. Once again, it's Aunt Eller who reverses the mood that permits the couple to begin their life together without guilt.

MUSICAL NUMBERS: "OH, WHAT A BEAUTIFUL MORNIN'," "THE SURREY WITH THE FRINGE ON TOP," "Kansas City," "I CAIN'T SAY NO," "Many a New Day," "It's a Scandal, It's an Outrage!," "PEOPLE WILL SAY (We're in Love)," "Poor Jud (Is Dead)," "Lonely Room," "OUT OF MY DREAMS," "The Farmer and the Cowman," "ALL ER NOTHIN'," "OKLAHOMA!."

INSTRUMENTATION: Violin A (2), B (2), viola, cello, bass, flute (pic), oboe (Eng. horn), clar I (bass clar), II, horns I–II, trumpet I–II, trombone, percussion, guitar, harp, piano-conductor.

CASTING: 22 parts, 10 principals. Aunt Eller, character woman, sings. Curly and Laurey, romantic leads, legit voices, good acting ability, minor dancing. Will, comic actor who dances well and sings. Jud, character man with rich, deep voice. Ado Annie, comedienne who sings well and dances. Carnes, Cord Elam, Ali Hakim, mostly straight roles with singing. Large separate singing and dancing ensembles. Total cast, 35–50.

SCENES AND SETS: 2 acts, 6 scenes, 4 full stage sets, 2 large partial stage sets (the smokehouse and the Skidmores' kitchen porch), 1 sky drop, ground row of rolling fields, rustic fence, white picket fence, 1 surrey with fringe on top.

ACT I
Scene 1: The Front of Laurey's Farmhouse.
Scene 2: The Smokehouse.
Scene 3: A Grove on Laurey's Farm.

ACT II
Scene 1: The Skidmore Ranch.
Scene 2: Skidmores' Kitchen Porch.
Scene 3: The Back of Laurey's Farmhouse.

PERIOD AND COSTUMES: Just after the turn of the century (1900): Indian territory (now Oklahoma). Floor-length summer housedresses, bright fringe-trimmed cowboy outfits, regular ranch hand outfits, cowboy boots, gun belts, etc. Loud striped and plaid suits. Jud's dirty farming clothes. Go-to-meetin' clothes for entire cast.

CHOREOGRAPHY: Modern ballet built on Western themes, couples numbers, hoedown square dancing, Oriental steps, two-step, ragtime, soft shoe, waltz.

LIGHTING AND SPECIAL EFFECTS: General outdoor lighting (day and night). Party lights on corral set for barn dance. Dramatic lighting on smokehouse. Smoke (optional).

"The Farmer and the Cowman" number as performed by the 1949 National Company.

COURTESY OF THE LYNN FARNOL GROUP, INC.

PHOTO BY RANK STRAND ELECTRIC, LONDON

Oliver! set design by Sean Kenny.

NOTES: *Oklahoma!* marked the beginning of modern musical theatre. In the beginning there wasn't the sophistication there is today, particularly in the book element. It could probably stand some updating and a slicker production to frame the almost complete score of hit songs.

OLIVER!

Lionel Bart (Music, Book, Lyrics)

Opened Jan. 6, 1963

775 Performances

BASED ON: Adapted from *Oliver Twist* by Charles Dickens

AGENT: Tams-Witmark

PUBLISHED TEXT: Manuscript Only

RECORDINGS: RCA LOCD(LSOD)-2004

DIGEST OF PLOT: Orphan Oliver Twist is considered a pest and ingrate at the boys' workhouse run by Widow Corney. She has Mr. Bumble offer the boy for sale. Oliver is sold to Mr. Sowerberry, the undertaker, by whom he is grossly mistreated. He runs away and is befriended by the Artful Dodger, ringleader of a group of young pickpockets. The boys have been organized by petty crook Fagin, who provides instruction and food in return for the wallets, watches, and other loot the boys manage to lift. Oliver is receiving his training when Nancy and Bet arrive to prepare the evening meal. They have a grand time and it's easy for the impressionable Oliver to see that life is better in the underworld than the oppressions of the world he has known. Eager to try his hand, Oliver joins the boys for next day's petty thieving. However, he is captured by the police. Oliver is cleared by the rich victim and is escorted to his home for a better chance at life. At the "Three Cripples" tavern Nancy and Fagin report Oliver's capture to overlord Bill Sykes. Bill treats them roughly for letting the boy fall into the hands of the authorities, thus jeopardizing the whole operation. They must get Oliver back. Meanwhile, Oliver is marveling at his new-found fortune. When Oliver is dispatched on an errand, Nancy is waiting to snatch him off to Fagin's. Both know that Bill has murder on his mind, which neither wants. Regretting her part, Nancy arranges to return the boy near London Bridge. Bill gets wind of the idea and tracks them down. Nancy is fatally beaten. Bill grabs Oliver, but the noise has attracted the police. A pistol shot rings out and Bill, too, is dead. Oliver is returned to his benefactor. Fagin has escaped detection, but the boys have scattered; his hideout and money are gone. There is little else for him to do but go straight —or is there?

MUSICAL NUMBERS: "Food, Glorious Food," "Oliver!," "I Shall Scream," "Boy for Sale," "That's Your Funeral," "WHERE IS LOVE?," "CONSIDER YOURSELF," "You've Got to Pick a Pocket or Two," "It's a Fine Life," "I'd Do Anything," "Be Back Soon," "Oom-Pah-Pah," "My Name," "AS LONG AS HE NEEDS ME," "WHO WILL BUY?," "Reviewing the Situation."

INSTRUMENTATION: Violin I, II, viola, cello, bass, flute (pic), oboe (Eng. horn), clar (bass clar), bassoon, horns I–II, trumpets I–II, trombone I, II, percussion, piano-conductor. (Also available with reduced combo instrumentation.)

CASTING: 16 parts, plus 13 small boys and a singing chorus of 16 to 20, 7 principals. Oliver, boy 8–12 years old, sings well, clear innocent voice, minor dancing. Nancy, outstanding actress with powerful legit voice, minor dancing. Fagin, winning character man, sings, moves well. Dodger, boy 10–15 who sings and dances, charming actor. Mr. Bumble and Mrs. Corney, comedy couple, sing well. Bill Sykes, deep, powerful voice. The Sowerberrys, sing. Bet, young girl who sings and dances. Other principals mostly straight roles, but also sing. Total cast, 35–45.

SCENES AND SETS: 2 acts, 12 scenes, unit set built around large center turntable augmented with fly-ins: coffins for undertaker's shop, ½-depth sketched drop of London's skyline, solid beam panels to form Fagin's "Thieves' Kitchen," window units, pub sign, and London Bridge complete with light towers.

Time: About 1850

ACT I
Scene 1: The Workhouse.
Scene 2: The Workhouse Parlor Street.
Scene 3: The Undertaker's.
Scene 4: The Undertaker's.
Scene 5: Paddington Green.
Scene 6: The Thieves' Kitchen.

ACT II
Scene 1: The "Three Cripples."
Scene 2: The Brownlows'.
Scene 3: The Thieves' Kitchen.
Scene 4: The Workhouse.
Scene 5: The Brownlows'.
Scene 6: London Bridge.

PERIOD AND COSTUMES: London, 1850's: workhouse uniforms (pants with tie at waist, shirt, and vest). Uniform of the Beadle. Male and female clothes of the lower class, pauper's dress, black undertaker's suit, 2 black dresses, the richness of Fagin's rags, dark red dress for Nancy, purple dress for Bet, tattered coat, vest, pants, shirt, and battered top hat for Dodger, similar for his pickpocket gang. Suit, coat, and hat for Bill Sykes. Fancy dresses, men's suits, cloaks, etc., of London's upper class.

CHOREOGRAPHY: Parading about, light soft shoe, light modern.

LIGHTING AND SPECIAL EFFECTS: Dramatic lighting required. Smoke-filled tavern, fire pots on-stage.

NOTES: A masterful adaptation of a classic. A highly dramatic show that demands a number of capable young boy actors, which can be a major drawback for presenting this show. Suggest knowing who these actors will be before scheduling the show.

ON A CLEAR DAY YOU CAN SEE FOREVER

Burton Lane (Music),
Alan Jay Lerner (Book, Lyrics)
Opened Oct. 17, 1965
280 Performances

BASED ON: Original

AGENT: Tams-Witmark

PUBLISHED TEXT: Random House, 1966

RECORDINGS: RCA LOCD(LSOD)-2006

DIGEST OF PLOT: Dr. Mark Bruckner discovers that Daisy Gamble has keen extrasensory powers. He promises her that he will help her curb her uncontrollable desire for cigarettes if she will consent to be a subject in a research project. During hypnosis, Daisy reverts to a prior life in the 18th Century as Melinda Wells. Mark is almost as enchanted with his discovery as Daisy is with pleasing Mark. She rejoices with her stodgy boy friend Warren and friends. At the next session Mark returns her to Melinda and an 18th-Century love conflict between Sir Hubert Insdale and Edward Moncrief. Mark too is rapidly falling in love with Melinda. He is convinced that he has stumbled upon a true psychic phenomenon and publishes a report on his findings. Mark is ridiculed by his colleagues, but the report establishes the existence of an Edward Moncrief during the period being relived by Daisy. One day as Daisy arrives early for her appointment she turns on Mark's tape recorder and discovers his love for Melinda. He is only using her as a go-between to his love! Daisy runs out resolved to become normal again. Her encounter with Warren and his preoccupation with the structures of a "normal" life are anything but reassuring. Mark learns of Daisy's discovery and tracks her down to ask her to appear with him before the medical board investigating the matter. She turns him down, but he promises to use his extrasensory control over her to summon her to the meeting. Whatever the means, Daisy is greeted the next day by an awaiting Mark who by now has modernized his love by a couple hundred years.

MUSICAL NUMBERS: "Hurry! It's Lovely Up Here," "Ring Out the Bells," "I'll Not Marry," "ON A CLEAR DAY," "On the S.S. Bernard Cohn," "At the Hellrakers'," "Don't Tamper with My Sister," "She Wasn't You," "Melinda," "When I'm Being Born Again," "WHAT DID I HAVE THAT I DON'T HAVE," "Wait 'Til We're Sixty-Five," "COME BACK TO ME."

INSTRUMENTATION: Violins A–C (2), B–D, viola, cello, bass, flute (pic, clar), flute (pic), clar, clar (bass clar), oboe (Eng. horn), horn I, II, trumpet I–II, III, trombone I, II, percussion I–II, piano, celeste, harpsichord, piano-conductor.

CASTING: 23 parts, 9 principals. Daisy (Melinda), accomplished actress with good voice, who also dances. Mark, good actor who sings. Warren, comic who plays it straight, sings. Kriakos, small character part, sings. Edward, actor who sings, minor dance steps. Servants, Muriel, Preston, and Millard, small supporting singing-dancing roles. Total cast, 45–55.

SCENES AND SETS: 2 acts, 11 scenes, 5 full stage sets, 1 backdrop. Scrim and 18th-Century set pieces part of modern "Dr. Mark Bruckner's" office set (or behind large venetian blinds as in original production).

ACT I
Scene 1: Bruckner Clinic, New York.
Scene 2: Solarium of Clinic.
Scene 3: Dr. Bruckner's Office.
Scene 4: Rooftop of Daisy's Apartment.
Scene 5: Dr. Bruckner's Office.
Scene 6: Dr. Bruckner's Office.

ACT II
Scene 1: The Solarium.
Scene 2: Dr. Bruckner's Office.
Scene 3: Rooftop of Daisy's Apartment.
Scene 4: Dr. Bruckner's Office.
Scene 5: Municipal Airport.

PERIOD AND COSTUMES: The present and 18th Century: suits, dresses, sportswear. Eighteenth-Century ball gowns, servant uniforms, dresses, tights, shirts, and court uniforms.

CHOREOGRAPHY: Modern, Greek steps, ballet, toe.

LIGHTING AND SPECIAL EFFECTS: Some dramatic lighting required.

NOTES: *On a Clear Day* started as a collaboration between two musical theatre greats—Alan Jay Lerner and Richard Rodgers. Burton Lane entered the project when Rodgers resigned because of incompatibility. From the outcome it looks as if Rodgers was right. The show's construction is extremely weak. Scenes are contrived for songs that are just stuck in. Suggest possible salvation of good numbers and mystique of ESP plot by eliminating "On the S.S. Bernard Cohn" (cute number, but simply a drag to show), "When I'm Being Born Again" (out of characterization and useless to construction), and possibly "Wait 'Til We're Sixty-Five."

ONCE UPON A MATTRESS

Mary Rodgers (Music),
Jay Thompson, Marshall Barer, Dean Fuller (Book),
Marshall Barer (Lyrics)
Opened May 11, 1959
470 Performances

BASED ON: Fairy tale, "The Princess and the Pea"

AGENT: Music Theatre

PUBLISHED TEXT: *Theatre Arts,* July, 1960

RECORDINGS: KAPP 4507
KAPP 5507

DIGEST OF PLOT: King Sextimus has been cursed speechless "until the Mouse devours the Hawk." The oppressive Queen Agravain has taken over the Kingdom and decreed that no one in the kingdom shall marry until her son, Dauntless the Drab, is married to a true princess of royal blood. It soon appears that Agravain intends to continue domination over her son by rejecting all comers. Young lovers of the court are distressed at the bleak outlook. The problem is immediate for Sir Harry and Lady Larkin. She has announced that they will soon be three—marriage or no marriage. Sir Harry departs to distant lands to find a true princess. He returns with Winifred the Woebegone. The entrance is a memorable one. Winifred swims the moat and comes over the castle wall dripping wet. The Queen is shocked. The test must be more severe. There must be no chance that Winifred will pass. She rushes to confer with her Wizard to make plans for such a test. But Dauntless is delighted; his pleasure is noted by the Minstrel, the Jesters, and the King who set out to discover the construction of this special test and how to foil it. The Queen decides it's to be a secret sensitivity test. Winifred will lie atop 20 of the softest mattresses under which is placed a pea. If she is a true princess, she will not sleep. To make sure she will sleep the Queen proclaims merrymaking of the most exhaustive sort. Much to the

Queen's disdain, Winifred reigns as the champion weight lifter, drinker, and dancer. Sir Harry and Lady Larkin are distraught that the Queen will once again have her way and plan to elope to Normandy. But after witnessing Winifred's one-woman exhibition, Dauntless is sure he's to be wed. The King agrees and gives his son a lecture on the facts of life—in pantomime. Meanwhile, the Minstrel and Jester are trying to flatter the Wizard into revealing the test. At that moment Winifred is being tucked in by the Queen who has added hypnotic mirrors, poppy incense, and spiked warm milk as an extra measure. The next morning the Queen jubilantly announces that Winifred has failed her test. But no sooner has she revealed the test than Winifred staggers into the room. She hasn't slept a wink all night. Furious, the Queen tries to force Winifred to leave, but Dauntless steps in to put his mother in her place. "The Mouse has devoured the Hawk," and the King makes it clear that he is once more in charge. Lovers are reunited and no one need leave the kingdom. The Minstrel reveals the assorted armor and weapons he had placed in the bed as Winifred snores peacefully stretched out on the breakfast table.

MUSICAL NUMBERS: "Many Moons Ago," "An Opening for a Princess," "In a Little While," "Shy," "The Minstrel, The Jester, and I," "Sensitivity," "Swamps of Home," "Normandy," "Spanish Panic," "Song of Love," "Quiet," "Happily Ever After," "Man-to-Man Talk," "Very Soft Shoes," "Yesterday I Loved You," "Lullaby."

INSTRUMENTATION: Violins A–B–C, viola, cello I–II, III, bass, flute (pic), clar (oboe), clar, bass clar, trumpet I–II, III, trombone I, II, III, horn, percussion, harp, guitar, piano-conductor.

CASTING: 27 parts, 9 principals. Princess Winifred, a comedienne who sings and dances. Prince Dauntless, comic actor who sings, minor dancing. The Queen, character woman who sings. The King, accomplished pantomimist, does not speak. Sir Harry and Lady Larkin, lovers in trouble, legit voices. Minstrel, singing guitar player. Jester, accomplished dancer. Wizard, character man. Large singing and dancing chorus. Strong choral work. Total cast, 27–37.

SCENES AND SETS: Prologue, 2 acts, 17 scenes, 9 full stage sets, 3 drop scenes, 1 large flight of steps. A bed with 20 mattresses. Original sets for this show were mostly yardgoods. Brightly colored "soft scenery," i.e. banners, streamers, cloth panels, drapes, etc. All drops were made up of several panels rather than one piece of material.

ACT I
Prologue
Scene 1: Throne Room.
Scene 2: The Yellow Gallery.
Scene 3: Courtyard.
Scene 4: A Corridor.
Scene 5: Winifred's Dressing Chamber.
Scene 6: The Grey Gallery.

Scene 7: On the Greensward.
Scene 8: The Yellow Gallery.
Scene 9: Great Hall.

ACT II
Scene 1: Castle.
Scene 2: Winifred's Dressing Chamber.
Scene 3: A Corridor.
Scene 4: Wizard's Chamber.
Scene 5: The Grey Gallery.
Scene 6: The Bedchamber.
Scene 7: A Corridor.
Scene 8: Breakfast Hall.

PERIOD AND COSTUMES: A Castle, many moons ago: medieval court dress (tunics, robes, dresses, wimples, cone veil headpieces, tights, crowns, special footwear, fur-trimmed robes). Nightgown, costume for the "Nightingale of Samarkand" (pink leotard and tights, plumes, feathers, etc.).

CHOREOGRAPHY: Parade, modern, soft shoe, "Spanish Panic" (modern jazz), soft shoe rhythm numbers.

LIGHTING AND SPECIAL EFFECTS: Dramatic lighting required. Flash pot, Wizard's bubbling, frothing cauldron.

NOTES: *Mattress* is a lighthearted fun musical, written for tight quarters and ease of production.

PAINT YOUR WAGON

Frederick Loewe (Music),
Alan Jay Lerner (Book, Lyrics)
Opened Nov. 12, 1951
289 Performances

BASED ON: Original

AGENT: Tams-Witmark

PUBLISHED TEXT: Coward-McCann, Inc., 1952; *Theatre Arts,* November, 1952

RECORDINGS: RCA LOC(LSO)-1006

DIGEST OF PLOT: Ben Rumson and his blossoming daughter, Jennifer, have discovered gold at Rumson Creek. A fast fortune is to be made and the rush is on. Soon there is a rowdy camp and the lonely miners are no longer looking at Jennifer as a little girl. Ben wants to send Jennifer back East to school to protect her from the fast pace of the gold-hungry town. But it's too late, she has fallen in love with Julio, a handsome young Mexican miner. Jacob, a Mormon, chances upon the town with his two wives. The miners convince him that it's not fair to have "two of somethin' they got none of." The second wife must be auctioned off. Ben is the highest bidder and welcomes the obedient Elizabeth to his cabin. Jennifer disapproves of his wanton desires. Disgusted, she goes East to school until Julio can afford to send for her. The boom town fandango girls arrive as the first permanent buildings go up. However, Rumson Creek is like hundreds of other bust towns—a little gold, but hardly enough to sustain an economy. Soon Ben owns all the town. More of its population is departing every day. Months later Jennifer returns in search of Julio, who has long since struck out for a more promising claim. Jennifer is determined to wait for his return, so Ben settles down to try farming. Jacob has prospered on the soil as one of the town's few remaining citizens, but Ben is haunted by his lifelong quest for the big strike. One day the beaten Julio returns on his way home to Mexico. He and Jennifer are reunited. Ben knows Julio will go no further. Ben is free to grab his pack and head for his next golden dream.

MUSICAL NUMBERS: "I'm on My Way," "Rumson," "What's Goin' On Here?," "I Talk to the Trees," "THEY CALL THE WIND MARIA," "I Still See Elisa," "How Can I Wait?," "Trio," "In Between," "Whoop-Ti-Ay!," "Carino Mio," "There's a Coach Comin' In," "Hand Me Down that Can o' Beans," "Another Autumn," "Movin'," "All for Him," "WAND'RIN STAR," "Strike!"

INSTRUMENTATION: Violin A–B (3), viola, cello, bass, flute, oboe, clar I–II, tenor sax, trumpets I–II, III, trombone I, II, percussion, guitar-banjo, piano-conductor.

CASTING: 33 parts, 12 principals. Jennifer, actress who sings and moves well. Ben, character man who sings. Julio, actor who sings and dances. Jacob, Sarah, and Elizabeth Woodling, straight roles. Suzanne, French dancer. Walt, Pete, Salem, Steve, Jake, miners, good-sized parts, sing and dance. Fandango girls, sing and dance. Large male singing chorus. Total cast, 40–55.

SCENES AND SETS: 2 acts, 17 scenes, 6 full stage sets, 1 partial stage set, 1 blue sky drop, 3 scene drops (including 1 scrim), stagecoach, and wagon.

ACT I
Scene 1: A Hilltop in Northern California. A Spring Evening, 1853.
Scene 2: Outside Salem's Store, Rumson. Evening, Four Months Later.
Scene 3: Outside Rumson's Cabin. Evening, Two Months Later.
Scene 4: Rumson's Cabin, Immediately Following.
Scene 5: A Hill Near Rumson Town, Two Nights Later.
Scene 6: Dutchie's Saloon, the Following Sunday.
Scene 7: Outside Rumson's Cabin, Later That Night.
Scene 8: Julio's Cabin, Later That Night.
Scene 9: The Diggin's, the Next Morning.
Scene 10: The Square, Immediately Following.

ACT II
Scene 1: Jake's Palace, October, 1855.
Scene 2: The Diggin's, Two Months Later.

Scene 3: Rumson's Cabin, Two Days Later.
Scene 4: A Street in Rumson, the Next Night.
Scene 5: Jake's Palace, That Night.
Scene 6: A Hill Near Rumson, the Following Dawn.
Scene 7: Rumson Square, the Following Spring.

PERIOD AND COSTUMES: California gold rush days, 1853 to 1856: gold miners' togs (bright plaid shirts, overalls, boots, hats), dude outfit, gingham dresses, Mexican outfit, long black coat, wide-brim hat, black dresses, fandango dresses, dress of a girl straight from finishing school.

CHOREOGRAPHY: Modern ballet with Western accent, minuet-influenced impromptu square dance, dance specialty, rope dance, can-can.

LIGHTING AND SPECIAL EFFECTS: Some dramatic lighting. Stars. Flexible lighting equipment required.

NOTES: *Paint Your Wagon* suffers from a ponderous and not too exciting book. The score is good, however. More than cutting is required. Something new must be added to make it more than just an average evening. Like the gold, the good qualities of the show just peter out.

PAJAMA GAME, THE

Richard Adler, Jerry Ross (Music, Lyrics), George Abbott, Richard Bissell (Book)
Opened May 13, 1954
1,063 Performances

BASED ON: *7½ Cents* by Richard Bissell

AGENT: Music Theatre

PUBLISHED TEXT: Random House, 1954; *Theatre Arts,* September, 1955

RECORDINGS: COL OL-4840
COL OL-5210(F)

DIGEST OF PLOT: The workers at Mr. Hasler's Sleep-Tite pajama factory are pushing for a 7½-cent raise. The new superintendent, Sid Sorokin, is trying to get the plant into peak production. In the process he falls in love with Babe Williams, a member of the union's grievance committee. Vernon Hines, the plant's jealous time-study man, is similarly inclined towards Gladys, Mr. Hasler's secretary. The romance between Babe and Sid has built concurrently with union ferment over wage demands. Events surrounding the company picnic give evidence wedding bells are in the air. But the union has decided on a slowdown. When Sid manages to get things speeded up, Babe short circuits the machines in her department. It's a blatant act that forces Sid to fire her. In an attempt to reconcile their differences and head off a strike, Sid takes Gladys out and gets her drunk in

Janis Paige and cast of The Pajama Game *singing "Once a Year Day."*

order to get the key to Mr. Hasler's private files. Meanwhile, a strike vote is affirmed at a union meeting. Babe sees Sid out with Gladys and is even more inflamed. Sid's research pays off. He calls the union delegation to his office and asks them to hold off the union rally until they hear from him. Babe sees that he is trying to get to the bottom of things and agrees to cancel a previous date in order to meet Sid after the rally. Sid has found that Hasler had added the 7½-cent raise to costs six months before. When he confronts Hasler, he agrees to a settlement. Everyone is reunited and Hasler throws an employee relations party where the latest styles of pajamas are modeled.

MUSICAL NUMBERS: "The Pajama Game," "Racing with the Clock," "A New Town Is a Blue Town," "I'm Not at All in Love," "I'll Never Be Jealous Again," "HEY THERE," "Her Is," "Sleep-Tite," "Once a Year Day," "Small Talk," "There Once Was a Man," "STEAM HEAT," "Think of the Time I Save," "HERNANDO'S HIDEAWAY," Jealousy Ballet, "7½ Cents."

INSTRUMENTATION: Violins A–C, B–D, viola, cello, bass, alto sax (pic, flute, clar), alto sax (clar), tenor sax (clar, Eng. horn), tenor sax (clar), bari sax (clar, bass clar, bassoon), trumpet I–II, III, trombone I, II, III, guitar, percussion, piano-conductor.

CASTING: 17 parts, 8 principals, plus 2 featured dancers. Babe, accomplished actress, good powerful voice, minor dancing. Sid, leading man, powerful baritone voice. Hines, character man who sings and dances. Gladys, comedienne and accomplished dancer who sings. Prez, comic character man who sings, minor dancing. Mabel, actress who sings and dances. Large separate singing and dancing ensembles. Total cast, 38–44.

SCENES AND SETS: 2 acts, 18 scenes, 5 full stage sets, 5 scene drops (can be done with 4 easily), 1 grand drape of union hall (regular auditorium drape with flag bunting).

ACT I
Scene 1: Pajama Factory.
Scene 2: Same.
Scene 3: A Hallway in the Factory.
Scene 4: The Office—Styled About 1910.
Scene 5: Wooded Path on Way to Picnic.
Scene 6: Picnic Grounds.
Scene 7: Picnic Path.
Scene 8: Kitchen of Babe's House.
Scene 9: The Factory.
Scene 10: The Shop.

ACT II
Scene 1: Eagle Hall.
Scene 2: Kitchen of Babe's House.
Scene 3: Hall in Factory.
Scene 4: The Office.
Scene 5: Hernando's Hideaway.
Scene 6: The Office.
Scene 7: A Street Near the Park.
Scene 8: Hernando's Hideaway.

PERIOD AND COSTUMES: Midwest factory town, 1950's: female work dresses, slacks. Suits, work clothes, smocks. Black lace negligee ensemble, sweaters, slacks. Picnic sportswear, bathing suits, bathrobe, sailor uniform, safari khakis, pirate costumes, Spanish lover costume, 3 black "Steam Heat" suits with derbies, evening wear, pajamas for entire cast.

CHOREOGRAPHY: Modern, modern ballet, tap, soft shoe, jazz.

LIGHTING AND SPECIAL EFFECTS: Some dramatic lighting required. Match-lighting effect during "Hernando's Hideaway." Knife-throwing effects (knives spring out of sets as if thrown).

NOTES: Easily staged set-drop-set-drop production sequence, which could be updated to tighten the production flow. Several drops could be eliminated by revolving sets.

PAL JOEY

Richard Rodgers (Music),
John O'Hara (Book),
Lorenz Hart (Lyrics)
Opened Dec. 25, 1940
374 Performances

BASED ON: Original

AGENT: Tams-Witmark

PUBLISHED TEXT: Random House, 1952

RECORDINGS: CAP S-310
COL OL-4364
CAP W (S)-912(F)

DIGEST OF PLOT: Joey Evans talks his way into an M.C. job at Mike's Bar. Not that Mike believed Joey's fabricated claims to success, he just needed a

new face to enliven his third-rate Chicago night spot. When Joey isn't out for Joey, he's after girls, but none of the girls in the line gives him a tumble. He finds a more gullible admirer, Linda English, standing in front of a pet shop. Later she comes to the club to catch his act. Joey joins her, but Mike soon ushers him to the table of a big spender, Vera Simpson, Chicago's Mrs. Society. When Vera questions the truth of his billing Joey insults her into walking out. Mike fires him, but Joey bets his salary that she'll be back within two days. Joey baits her with a sarcastic phone call. She shows up after hours and literally steals the "show." Joey is now her "beauty," complete with tailored suits, pin money, and a plush apartment. Mike's is to be converted to Chez Joey in honor of the new owner. Joey's newly acquired manager, Ludlow Lowell, and dancer Gladys Bumps plan a shakedown for Vera and her obnoxious lover.

COURTESY OF THE LYNN FARNOL GROUP, INC.

Gene Kelley and Vivienne Segal in original 1940 production of Pal Joey.

However, Linda overhears the plot and relays the information to Vera, who employs her friend the police commissioner to shortstop the blackmail attempt. Joey is now too hot a risk. The club is his, but it's "so long, beauty." Linda is faithfully waiting for the rebound. Joey has developed a fondness for Linda but tells her that he has a big offer in New York. As she reluctantly leaves him behind, he spots a shapely new conquest with no strings attached.

MUSICAL NUMBERS: "You Mustn't Kick It Around," "I COULD WRITE A BOOK," "Chicago," "That Terrific Rainbow," "What Is a Man?," "Happy Hunting Horn," "BEWITCHED, BOTHERED, AND BEWILDERED," "Pal Joey," Joey Looks into the Future Ballet, "The Flower Garden of My Heart," "Zip," "Plant You Now, Dig You Later," "In Our Little Den," "Do It the Hard Way," "Take Him."

INSTRUMENTATION: Violin A, B, C, cello, bass, clar (alto sax, flute, pic), clar (alto sax, oboe, Eng. horn), clar (tenor sax, bass clar, basset horn), clar (tenor sax, flute, pic), clar (tenor sax, bassoon), horn, trumpets I–II, III, trombone, percussion, piano-conductor.

CASTING: 25 parts, 8 principals. Joey, conniving big-shot role, sings and dances. Mike, straight role. Gladys, dumb blonde who dances and sings. Linda, naive girl who gets burned, good voice. Vera, patronizing, middle-aged socialite, good actress, good voice. Melba, comedienne, singer (does strip without taking anything off). Ludlow Lowell, character man who does a good heavy, straight role. Louis, featured tenor. Featured dancers in 2 numbers. Total cast, 35–40.

SCENES AND SETS: 2 acts, 12 scenes. 2 full stage sets, Mike's South Side Night Club, which converts to Chez Joey Night Club during act break (could be one set with lush overdrapings), 2 partial sets (tailor shop and Joey's apartment), 2 insert sets (phone booth and Vera's boudoir), and skeleton Pet Shop fly-in, plus gaily colored abstract dance drop.

ACT I
Scene 1: Mike's South Side Night Club.
Scene 2: The Pet Shop.
Scene 3: Mike's Night Club.
Scene 4: (a) A Phone Booth.
　　　(b) Vera's Boudoir.
Scene 5: Mike's Night Club.
Scene 6: The Tailor Shop.
Scene 7: Ballet.

ACT II
Scene 1: Chez Joey.
Scene 2: Joey's Apartment.
Scene 3: Chez Joey.
Scene 4: Joey's Apartment.
Scene 5: The Pet Shop.

PERIOD AND COSTUMES: Chicago, late 1930's or updated to present: bartender's shirt and apron, suits, casual clothes, dancers' work clothes. Overcoats, tuxedo, nightclub wardrobe, "Happy Hunting" costumes, society gown and jewels, male evening dress. Flower garden showgirl briefs for a sunflower, violet, lily, heather, American Beauty rose, and lilac. Female lounging negligee, tailored suits, smocks, dresses, and various uniforms.

CHOREOGRAPHY: Modern, ballet, featured striptease, soft shoe, tango steps, showgirl production number.

LIGHTING AND SPECIAL EFFECTS: Dramatic lighting required.

NOTES: The lackluster book of *Pal Joey* is balanced somewhat by the score. The movie version added to this asset by inserting the following numbers from other shows: "There's a Small Hotel," "The Lady Is a Tramp" (a very tight insertion), and "Funny Valentine." The first and last were used to replace club numbers in the stage score.

PETER PAN

Mark Charlap, Jule Styne (Music),
James M. Barrie (Book),
Carolyn Leigh, Betty Comden, Adolph Green (Lyrics)
Opened Oct. 20, 1954
149 Performances

BASED ON: Play by James M. Barrie

AGENT: Samuel French

PUBLISHED TEXT: Manuscript Only

RECORDINGS: RCA LOC(LSO)-1019

DIGEST OF PLOT: Mr. and Mrs. Darling have just made sure their children John, Peter, Michael, and Wendy are fast asleep. However, the four are awakened by Peter Pan, who spins tales of Neverland where children don't grow up. Peter can teach them to fly, too. He does, and they're off to Peter's island of Lost Boys, pirates, Indians, and giant animals. Meanwhile, Captain Hook and his pirate henchmen have discovered the underground home used by Peter and the boys, but have been frightened off by Tiger Lily and her band of Henny Penny Indians. Wendy is slightly injured on her arrival when jealous Tinker Bell gets the boys to shoot at her with their bows and arrows, but soon recovers to become their mother. The pirates sneak a poison cake into their midst, but Wendy takes it away in motherly fashion. Hook retreats to formulate a new plan. In the process the pirates capture Tiger Lily, but Peter tricks them into releasing her. The pirates get Peter, but Tiger Lily returns to drive them off. Peter and the Indians are now allies. They camp above the underground home to guard it. The adventure has been fun, but Michael and John are homesick and want to return to the nursery. The Lost Boys also want to return for a chance to grow up. When Wendy agrees, Peter's pride is hurt. He will stay behind and let Tinker Bell lead the way back. But the pirates have attacked the guarding Indians. They pull a clever deception to make Peter and his boys believe the routed Indians had won. As each boy squeezes through the secret tree-stump entrance he is hauled away to the pirate ship. The dirty deed done, Hook poisons Peter's medicine. To save the stubborn Peter, Tink returns to drink the contents of the glass and is revived only by a special petition to the children of the world to believe in fairies. Peter rounds up the Indians for an assault on Hook's ship where the boys are being prepared to walk the plank. Peter has brought along the crocodile who long ago tasted of Hook's hand and now wants the rest. Peter sta-

Peter Pan (Mary Martin) closes in on Captain Hook (Cyril Ritchard) as the Lost Boys look on.

tions himself in a dark cabin and eliminates two pirates. When it appears there is a monstrous killer aboard, Hook sends the boys into the darkness to take his measure. Peter frees them. They hide as Hook turns for vengeance on Wendy for causing bad luck on the ship, but Peter discards his disguise for the final duel, which ends with Hook in the crocodile's mouth. The return to the nursery is a joyous event for Mr. and Mrs. Darling, their children, and the Lost Boys, who are immediately adopted. Many years later Peter returns to enchant Wendy's daughter, Jane, and once more begin an adventure to Neverland.

MUSICAL NUMBERS: "Tender Shepherd," "I've Got to Crow," "Neverland," "I'm Flying," "Pirate Song," "A Princely Scheme," "Indians!," "Wendy," "Another Princely Scheme," "Neverland Waltz," "I

Won't Grow Up," "Mysterious Lady," "Ugg-a-Wugg," "The Pow-Wow Polka," "Distant Melody," "To the Ship," "Hook's Waltz," "The Battle."

INSTRUMENTATION: Violins A (2), A–B, A–B–C, viola, cello, bass, flute I, II, oboe, clar I, II, bassoon, trumpets I–II, III, trombone, horn, harp, percussion, piano-conductor.

CASTING: 25 parts, 8 principals. Peter Pan, young actress who sings. Wendy, John, and Michael, mostly straight roles, minor singing. Captain Hook (Mr. Darling), strong character man who sings and dances. Smee, straight role, minor singing. Tiger Lily, dancer who sings. Nana, dog. Liza, dancer. Various animals, Indians, and pirates. Total cast, 40–50.

SCENES AND SETS: 3 acts, 9 scenes, 4 full

stage sets, 1 blue sky drop, 1 scene drop, cloud scrim, small house that is built piece by piece on-stage.

ACT I
Scene 1: Nursery of the Darling Residence.
Scene 2: Flight to Neverland.

ACT II
Scene 1: Neverland.
Scene 2: Path Through Woods.
Scene 2: Neverland Home Underground.

ACT III
Scene 1: Pirate Ship.
Scene 2: Path Through the Woods.
Scene 3: Nursery of the Darling Residence.
Scene 4: Nursery Many Years Later.

PERIOD AND COSTUMES: Victorian London and Neverland: upper-class English house clothes and evening clothes for Mr. and Mrs. Darling. Nightgowns and sleepers for children. Peter, green tights, tunic, and cap plus flying girdle. Children, flying girdles. Animal costumes for a dog, lion, bird, kangaroo, ostrich, and crocodile. Several tree costumes. Pirate and Indian costumes. Captain Hook's red coat, breeches, boots, and hook. Full dancing dress.

CHOREOGRAPHY: Children play dancing, aerial ballet, pirate march, Indian dance, tango and tarantella steps, waltz ballet solo, "Pow-Wow Polka," waltz.

LIGHTING AND SPECIAL EFFECTS: Controlled lighting (keep lighting as low as possible to avoid showing fly wires). Flying rigs for Peter, Wendy, Michael, John, and Liza. Portable smoke machine. Tinker Bell is represented by a small flickering spot of light, required in several scenes.

NOTES: Traditionally the part of Peter Pan is played by a female. This stems from the early 1900's when any female costume that allowed her figure to be discernible to the audience was considered to be highly risqué. What is now a children's show was at one time a daring adult attraction. This custom was carried over to the musical version.

PLAIN AND FANCY

Albert Hague (Music),
Joseph Stein, Will Glickman (Book),
Arnold B. Horwitt (Lyrics)
Opened Jan. 27, 1955
461 Performances

BASED ON: Original

AGENT: Samuel French

PUBLISHED TEXT: Random House, 1955; *Theatre Arts,* July, 1956

RECORDINGS: CAP W 603

DIGEST OF PLOT: Dan King and his girl, Ruth Winters, are lost in the heart of Amish Pennsylvania in search of Bird-in-Hand. Dan has inherited property there and has agreed to sell the land to Papa Yoder for a wedding gift to his daughter, Katie, and her intended, Ezra. When they finally arrive, preparations for the wedding are in full swing. Sophisticated Ruth marvels at their naivité but longs for New York. Hilda Miller, a spunky Amish maiden, falls for Dan and misinterprets his kind words as words of love. The Amish men are teasing Ezra about marrying Katie. His only retort is, "Why not?" But Ezra's brother Peter, banished from the community for fighting, has returned. He and Katie were childhood sweethearts, and the feelings are very much alive. Dan tries to intercede for the lovers, but stubborn Papa Yoder reminds him that he is a guest in a different way of life. Taunted by Ezra, Peter raises his hand against his own brother. Just as he does, the barn on Dan's property is struck by lightning and burns to the ground. Papa declares that Peter's evil actions are responsible and Peter is "shunned," even by a frightened and confused Katie. In true Amish tradition, the barn is rebuilt. Peter manages to get Katie alone, but to no avail. Ruth is having the same kind of luck in the Amish kitchens and retreats to her trusty bottle of Scotch. When Ezra asks what she's drinking, she covers up by answering "vegetable juice." Ezra requests a sample and in short order is completely plowed. He decides he's to have a bachelor fling at the Lancaster carnival and departs. Hilda finds out that Dan doesn't love her and also wants to see the outside world. At the carnival, Ezra gets into a brawl and is almost killed by a knife-wielding roustabout. But Peter has followed him. He steps in to break it up and returns his still-soused brother to the wedding gathering. Ezra, too, is now disgraced, but Dan is successful in obtaining Papa's consent to a marriage between Katie and Peter with Dan's farm thrown in free as a wedding present. The experience has brought Dan and Ruth closer together as they return to New York.

MUSICAL NUMBERS: "You Can't Miss It," "It Wonders Me," "Plenty of Pennsylvania," "YOUNG AND FOOLISH," "Why Not Katie?," "By Lantern Light," "It's a Helluva Way to Run a Love Affair," "This Is All Very New to Me," "Plain We Live," "The Shunning," "How Do You Raise a Barn?," "Follow Your Heart," "City Mouse, Country Mouse," "I'll Show Him!," Carnival Ballet, "Take Your Time and Take Your Pick."

INSTRUMENTATION: Violin A–C (2), B–D (2), viola, cello, bass, reed I, II, III, IV, V, horn, trumpet I, II, III, trombone I, II, harp, percussion, conductor.

CASTING: 30 parts, 9 principals, a few children. Dan, straight role, minor singing in 1 number. Ruth, comedienne, sings. Hilda, comic actress with legit

A revival production of Plain and Fancy.

voice who also dances. Peter and Katie, young love interest, legit voices. Papa Yoder, character man and good, deep singing voice. Emma, character woman who sings. Large separate singing and dancing ensembles. Total cast 35–50.

SCENES AND SETS: 2 acts, 17 scenes, 7 full stage sets (including 4 drops), 2 partial stage sets, 2 scene drops. One sports car or set piece car. Amish carriage.

ACT I
Scene 1: A Section of Road Outside Lancaster.
Scene 2: Another Part of the Road.
Scene 3: The Yoder Barnyard.
Scene 4: The Yoder Parlor.
Scene 5: Side Porch of the Yoder Home.
Scene 6: Barnyard on the River Farm.
Scene 7: A Bedroom in the Yoder Home.
Scene 8: The Yoder Barnyard.
Scene 9: In the Yoder Barn.

ACT II
Scene 1: The River Farm.
Scene 2: Kitchen of the Yoder Home.
Scene 3: Back Porch of the Yoder Home.
Scene 4: Bedroom of the Yoder Home.
Scene 5: A Section of Road.
Scene 6: A Carnival Grounds.
Scene 7: Side Porch of the Yoder House.
Scene 8: The Yoder Barnyard.

PERIOD AND COSTUMES: Bird-in-Hand, a town in the Amish country of Pennsylvania, the present: Amish suits, wide-brim hats, vests, work aprons, long dresses, plain kitchen aprons, Amish bonnets, modern suits for Dan, Ruth's modern fashions and undergarments. Officer's uniform. Carnival costumes (girlie, Swami, sailor uniform, clown, barkers, mambo).

CHOREOGRAPHY: Modern, modern ballet, ballet, dance specialties (Little Egypt).

LIGHTING AND SPECIAL EFFECTS: Mostly general lighting. Dramatic lighting on first-act finale, but not difficult. Working water pump on stage, lighting, barn burning, barn raised on stage in three minutes (accomplished by floor anchor platform, interlocking wood framing, trusses raised from ground from offstage and anchored by fly wires, roof [audience side only], which snaps into place and holds trusses in place).

NOTES: A delightful show that drives home some basic principles that society has largely cast aside. The book is funny, but sometimes ponderous. Some cutting should be considered. Tight production flow is essential.

PORGY AND BESS

George Gershwin (Music),
DuBose Heyward (Book),
DuBose Heyward, Ira Gershwin (Lyrics)

Opened Oct. 10, 1935
124 Performances

BASED ON: *Porgy* by Dorothy and DuBose Heyward

AGENT: Tams-Witmark

PUBLISHED TEXT: Manuscript Only

RECORDINGS: DEC (S)-9024
COL OL-5401(F)
COL OS-2016(F)

DIGEST OF PLOT: Porgy is a penniless, crippled beggar eking out an existence in Catfish Row along the Charleston fishing docks. Bess is a woman who can't afford morals. She has found security in Crown, a powerful wharf hand capable of taking what he wants. He is also a man of temper. It is provoked, and Crown kills one of the men of the once-proud

Catfish Row set from the original 1935 production of Porgy and Bess.

ghetto. He escapes, and the police seek Bess for questioning. Well acquainted with their methods, Bess takes refuge with Porgy—and in time she comes to prefer his warm affections and need for love to the brute force of Crown. Porgy has never been happier, and the women of Catfish Row have slowly come to accept Bess as his woman. On a picnic at Kittiwash Island Bess is successful in dodging the fancy promises of dandy Sportin' Life, but is accosted by Crown. She tells him she is now Porgy's woman and later manages to escape. Crown can't comprehend her love for the cripple, but returns to Catfish Row during a storm to kill Porgy. However, after a bitter battle of strength it is Crown who is dead. Porgy is taken away by the police and Bess is once more alone. Sportin' Life has returned to tempt her with the pleasures of New York, and, believing Porgy a victim of white justice, she falls under his spell to go with him. But Porgy is released and returns in search of Bess. Reluctantly, the neighbors tell him of her departure to New York with Sportin' Life. Porgy is disappointed but unshaken. He will go after her in his goat cart. His determination is strong as his ghetto friends bid him goodbye and good luck. He is on his way!

MUSICAL NUMBERS: "SUMMERTIME," "A WOMAN IS A SOMETIME THING," "The Wake," "My Man's Gone Now," "I GOT PLENTY OF NOTHIN'," "BESS, YOU IS MY WOMAN NOW," "Morning," "I Can't Sit Down," "IT AIN'T NEC-ESSARILY SO," "I Ain't Got No Shame," "What You Want with Bess?," "I Loves You, Porgy," "A Red-Headed Woman," "Clara, Clara," "There's a Boat that's Leavin' Soon for New York," "Oh, Where's My Bess?," "I'm on My Way."

INSTRUMENTATION: Violin I (2), II, viola, cello, bass, flute (pic), oboe (Eng. horn), clar I (alto sax), clar II (alto sax), bass clar (tenor sax), trumpets I–II, trombone I, II, percussion, piano, piano-conductor.

CASTING: 23 parts, 8 principals, 4–6 children. Porgy, cripple, actor with powerful voice. Bess, broad range actress/singer. Crown, powerfully built bass singer, good actor. Sportin' Life, clever dandy who does soft shoe steps and sings, light character part. Clara, sings "Summertime," featured soloist. Serena, Maria, Lily, featured soloists. Jim, Jake, featured character singers. All legit voices for detailed choral work. Total cast, 45–60.

SCENES AND SETS: 3 acts, 7 scenes, 3 full stage sets (one is fly-in—Serena's room could be partial stage set).

ACT I
Scene 1: Catfish Row, Charleston, S.C.
Scene 2: Serena's Room.

ACT II
Scene 1: Catfish Row
Scene 2: A Palmetto Jungle

Scene 3: Catfish Row
Scene 4: Serena's Room

ACT III
Scene 1: Catfish Row

PERIOD AND COSTUMES: 1935, Charlestown, S.C., waterfront ghetto: shabby shirts, dresses, headbands, hats, overalls. Dandy suit, spats, gloves, and derby for Sportin' Life. Sunday-go-to-meetin' clothes for picnic, band uniforms, parasols, etc.

CHOREOGRAPHY: Production numbers, soft shoe steps, ballet type of movement, Negro folk dance movement, no formal dance numbers as such.

LIGHTING AND SPECIAL EFFECTS: Dramatic lighting required. Storm effects.

NOTES: Unfortunately this classic is not available to all groups. The copyright owners must okay each applicant. Permission for production has been almost exclusively restricted to professional companies.

PROMISES, PROMISES

Burt Bacharach (Music),
Hal David (Lyrics),
Neil Simon (Book)
Opened Dec. 1, 1968

BASED ON: Film, "The Apartment"

AGENT: Tams-Witmark

PUBLISHED TEXT: Random House, 1969

RECORDINGS: UAS-9902

DIGEST OF PLOT: Chuck Baxter is an ambitious clerk with a conveniently located bachelor apartment. Married executives in need of temporary quarters to entertain certain friends are quick to spot the intelligence of a young man in their organization who can supply such facilities. Chuck's own love life revolves around a lovely executive dining-room hostess, Fran Kubelik. Fran is friendly, but her love interest is clearly someone else. Chuck's rapid advancements come to the attention of personnel manager Sheldrake. Just when Chuck is convinced the jig is up, Sheldrake reveals that he, too, has a friend. Chuck is handed two pro basketball tickets in exchange for his apartment keys. Chuck waits for Fran and asks her to attend the game with him. She agrees to meet Chuck after brushing off another suitor. The suitor turns out to be her negligent married boy friend, Mr. Sheldrake. Fran's determination not to get burned again is no match for Sheldrake's persuasion—leaving Chuck with two unused tickets. At the company Christmas party Sheldrake's secretary gets high and tells Fran about his many other conquests. Chuck runs into Fran and tries to lift her rather

Basic plexiglass, steel, foil-covered Promises, Promises *set during Christmas office party.*

shaken confidence by asking her opinion of his new "executive model" hat. In the process she offers him the use of her compact. Chuck is shattered as it's the same unmistakable compact once left in his apartment by Sheldrake's "friend." Prior to leaving to spend the Christmas holidays with his family, Sheldrake has met Fran at Chuck's apartment. She confronts him with his parade of amours, but he insists that she is different. But when Sheldrake gives her $100 instead of a Christmas gift, Fran begins to draw a much different picture of herself. When Sheldrake leaves, she downs a bottle of sleeping pills. Meanwhile Chuck is tempering his own hurt with booze and a barfly named Marge. He's got Marge properly primed and back to his room only to find Fran in an unusually deep sleep. Chuck bolts for Dr. Dreyfuss' apartment across the hall, shoving Marge out in the process. Dreyfuss is aware of the activities in Chuck's apartment and attributes them to the owner. He moves in to save Fran's life and continues to chide Chuck for such reckless, promiscuous behavior. While getting well, Fran's eyes are opened to Chuck's warmth and adoration. Things are going great until Fran's musclebound brother arrives on a tip from some of Chuck's ex-keymates. Chuck is quickly flattened. Meanwhile Sheldrake's secretary

has quit and told all to his wife. Sheldrake has no longer to fear his marriage and decides to make everything up to Fran by asking her to marry him. When Chuck learns this he quits the rapid-rise trail and prepares to leave town. He'd have made it, too, if Sheldrake hadn't been turned down for a more lovable guy.

MUSICAL NUMBERS: "Half as Big as Life," "Upstairs," "You'll Think of Someone," "Our Little Secret," "She Likes Basketball," "KNOWING WHEN TO LEAVE," "Where Can You Take a Girl?," "Wanting Things," "Turkey Lurkey Time," "A Fact Can Be a Beautiful Thing," "Whoever You Are," "A Young Pretty Girl Like You," "I'LL NEVER FALL IN LOVE AGAIN," "PROMISES, PROMISES."

INSTRUMENTATION: 3 violins I–II, cello, bass (fender bass), flute (pic, clar, alto sax), clar (bass clar, tenor sax), clar (tenor sax), clar (bari sax), horn, trumpets I–II (flugelhorn), III, trombone I, II, percussion I–II, guitars I–II (elec guitar, bass guitar), piano (elec piano), piano-conductor. Note: Orchestra voices, violin I–II, cello, horn, trombone II parts optional.

Jerry Orbach in crowded Grapes of Roth bar.

CASTING: 25 parts, 9 principals, plus 3 featured female dancers and 4 female voices in orchestra pit. Chuck, a warm, friendly comic actor with strong singing voice. Fran Kubelik, winning smile, cute rather than glamorous, powerful broad-range singing voice, good diction. Sheldrake, the heavy, good actor who sings. Dobitch, Kirkeby, Eichelberger, and Vanderhof, light character men who sing in quartet. Dr. Dreyfuss, exceptional character comic, sings 1 number with Chuck. Marge MacDougall, good character woman, minor singing. Vivien, Miss Polansky, and Miss Wong, featured dancers who sing "Turkey Lurkey Time." Total cast 36–46.

SCENES AND SETS: 2 acts, 14 scenes, 4 full stage sets, 4 partial sets (one has pivoting signs that change from Consolidated Life Office to Madison Square Garden identification), 3 major "glass and steel" fly-ins.

ACT I
Scene 1: Offices of Consolidated Life. Second Avenue Bar.
Scene 2: Chuck's Apartment House.
Scene 3: Medical Office.
Scene 4: Mr. Sheldrake's Office.
Scene 5: Lobby.
Scene 6: Lum Ding's Restaurant and Madison Square Garden.
Scene 7: Lobby, Executive Dining Room. Executive Sun Deck.
Scene 8: At the Elevator.
Scene 9: 19th-Floor Christmas Party.

ACT II
Scene 1: Clancy's Lounge.

Scene 2: Chuck's Apartment.
Scene 3: Offices of Consolidated Life.
Scene 4: Lum Ding's Restaurant and Street.
Scene 5: Chuck's Apartment.

A. Larry Haines (Doc) and Jerry Orbach (Chuck) cheer up Jill O'Hara (Fran) following her overdose of sleeping pills.

PERIOD AND COSTUMES: The present: latest in office clothes, expensive-looking suits for executives, mini dresses, coats, evening wear, casual shirts and slacks, overcoats, hats, caps, etc., derby, owl-feathered coat, and uniforms for bartender, nurses, doctor, nightclub hostess, waiter, and laborer.

CHOREOGRAPHY: Modern and featured female dance trio.

LIGHTING AND SPECIAL EFFECTS: Dramatic and area lighting required for numerous cross-fades and lighting of partial sets.

NOTES: As the film "The Apartment," this show won the Academy Award. As *Promises, Promises,* the show is twice as funny, with construction much tighter (despite the insertion of musical numbers), and an all-around winning musical.

PURLIE

Gary Geld (Music),
Peter Udell (Lyrics),
Ossie Davis, Philip Rose, Peter Udell (Book)
Opened March 15, 1970

BASED ON: *Purlie Victorious* by Ossie Davis

AGENT: Samuel French, Inc.

PUBLISHED TEXT: Samuel French, Inc., 1971 (P)

RECORDINGS: Ampex-A40101

DIGEST OF PLOT: Ol' Cap'n Cotchipee is dead. His glorious funeral shakes the halls of Big Bethel, the church he sought to destroy. The man on the pulpit is Purlie Victorious, a new kind of preacher man, who sings the praises of life rather than the uncertainties of life in the hereafter. But it wasn't long ago when Purlie arrived with Lutiebelle and a scheme to deceive the Ol' Cap'n into giving him money that rightfully belonged to his mother—money that would buy Big Bethel. Ol' Cap'n is holding the inheritance due to a long-lost cousin. Purlie has searched the country for a look-alike that would fool the Ol' Cap'n. When the girl Lutiebelle realizes the danger in the plan she tries to run away; it's her love of Purlie, not money or any church, that brought her here. But Purlie and Aunt Missy, wife of Purlie's brother Gitlow, persuade her to go through with the hoax. Gitlow and Purlie arrange a little softening up by naming Ol' Cap'n the "Great White Father of the Year." Lutiebelle manages to fool him but signs the wrong name to the receipt for the money. The game is up. Back at Gitlow's shack the failure and frustration are rehashed. Gitlow enters and reveals that Ol' Cap'n gave him money to get Lutiebelle up to the big house. Soon thereafter she comes running in decrying the advances of the dirty old man. Purlie is outraged and charges up the hill to defend her honor. Lutiebelle and Aunt Missy stay up all night worrying. When Purlie returns, they demand a blow-by-blow description. He obliges with elaborate detail of his strengths and power, but he soon admits not a word is true. However, enraged by the attempted fraud and Lutiebelle's rejection, Ol' Cap'n has ordered his folk-song-writing son, Charlie, to buy Old Bethel for burning. Charlie buys, but has Purlie's name recorded on the deed. When the Ol' Cap'n finds out, he drops dead. So here is Purlie dedicating Big Bethel with the funeral of the man who made it both necessary and possible for such a festive occasion.

MUSICAL NUMBERS: "WALK HIM UP THE STAIRS," "New-Fangled Preacher Man," "Skinnin' a Cat," "Purlie," "The Harder They Fall," Charlie's Songs, "Big Fish, Little Fish," "I GOT LOVE," "Great White Father," "Down Home," "First Thing Monday Mornin'," "He Can Do It," "The World Is Comin' to a Start."

INSTRUMENTATION: Violin I, II, viola, cello (all strings amplified), pic I (C flute, alto flute, clar, alto sax, tambourine), II (same), flute I (alto flute, clar, tenor sax, tambourine), II (same), bass (clar, bari sax, flute, tambourine), trumpet I (flugelhorn, tambourine), II (same), III (jazz, flugelhorn, tambourine), trombone I (bass, tenor), II (bass, tenor), jazz guitar I (elec, acoustic, classical), II (elec, acoustic, banjo), organ, drums, percussion.

Purlie! *principals (l. to r.): Sherman Hemsley (Gitlow), Melba Moore (Lutiebelle),*
Novella Nelson (Missy), and Cleavon Little (Purlie).

CASTING: 7 parts, 5 principals, 2 featured roles, featured female lead singer, powerful legit voice. Purlie, engaging actor who carries show, sings and dances. Lutiebelle, singer who acts and dances. Ol' Cap'n, character man who sings and son Charlie, folk singer who acts (playing guitar helps) are only 2 white members of cast. Missy, actress who sings and dances. Gitlow, character man who sings. Several good voices required for extensive choral work. Total cast, 32–42.

SCENES AND SETS: Prologue, 2 acts, 8 scenes, epilogue (similar to prologue), 3 full stage sets, 1 drop.

Prologue: Big Bethel, a Country Church in South Georgia, Not Too Long Ago.

ACT I Some Time Before Prologue.
Scene 1: A Shack on the Plantation.
Scene 2: Outside Ol' Cap'n's Commissary.

Scene 3: Same.
Scene 4: The Shack.

ACT II
Scene 1: On the Plantation, 4 A.M.
Scene 2: The Shack, Just Before Dawn.

Epilogue: Time and Place as in the Prologue.

PERIOD AND COSTUMES: Not long ago (1970): black preacher's suit, vest, hat, dresses, and coat for Lutiebelle, patched housedresses and work-clothes, white Kentucky colonel long coat suit, choir robes, misc. suits, dresses, and go-to-meetin' clothes.

CHOREOGRAPHY: Modern, modern jazz, swing.

LIGHTING AND SPECIAL EFFECTS: Mostly general lighting.

NOTES: Although there have been several Negro musicals (*Cabin in the Sky, Simply Heavenly, Carmen Jones, Golden Boy, Hallelujah, Baby!*, and *Porgy and Bess*), *Purlie* showed the first real signs of a Broadway musical's ability to attract a predominantly Negro audience. It's a great show with an exceptional score. Broad-minded white audiences appreciate the show too. The one major weak spot is when Ol' Cap'n "drops dead standing up," which spoils one of the best numbers in the show as audience watches to see if he will move a muscle. Suggest having him drop dead and hauled off.

REDHEAD

Albert Hague (Music),
Herbert and Dorothy Fields, Sidney Sheldon, David Shaw (Book),
Dorothy Fields (Lyrics)

Opened Feb. 5, 1959
455 Performances

BASED ON: Original

AGENT: Music Theatre

PUBLISHED TEXT: Manuscript Only

RECORDINGS: RCA LOC (LSO)-1104

DIGEST OF PLOT: Essie Whimple sculptures figures for the Simpson Sisters' Wax Museum, run by her aunts, Maude and Sarah. They are preparing to unveil a new sketch in horror, the yet-unsolved strangulation of beautiful actress Ruth LaRue. The murder has captured the interest of the press and all of London. The event is being attended by Inspector White of Scotland Yard; producer of Ruth's show, Howard Cavanaugh; and the show's comedian, George Poppett. Another cast member, strongman Tom Baxter, breaks in after the unveiling to request the exhibit be destroyed. Tom is the man of Essie's recurring visions, and she is dumbfounded. He is repulsed by her crudeness, but she manages to gain some ground by agreeing to remove the exhibit. Later, to make sure Tom's exit from her life is not permanent, Essie fakes an attempt on her life and tells Tom she believes it to be the same person who killed Ruth. Tom and George offer their protection and get Howard to put her in his show so they can keep a close eye on her. Tom's close friend, Sir Charles Willingham, drops by the theatre, and the audience immediately recognizes his unmistakable red hair and beard as those of Ruth's murderer as witnessed in the prologue. Sir Charles was engaged to Ruth and wants to question Essie to learn how good a look she had at her alleged attacker. Tom stalls Sir Charles because he is anxious for his first date with Essie. The evening is a complete delight, but Essie now has to keep her part of the bargain by sculpturing the head of Ruth's killer. She confesses the deception to her aunts and George. They help try to conjure up a vision of the murderer. During the proceedings, the image of Sir Charles appears. Essie can now prepare the likeness for Tom. However, the next evening Sir Charles is in the front

box, Essie sees him and renders the show a shambles. When Tom asks why, she names Sir Charles as the guilty party. Tom is furious and gets Essie to admit her charade and vision of Sir Charles. Their romance is washed up. After the show Sir Charles corners Essie and tries to take her to his apartment for a chat. However, on the way she takes up with some tarts and eventually lands in jail. Her aunts and George visit her. George has a plan to force Sir Charles's hand. Essie manages to escape to put the plan into effect. The move almost costs her life because the real killer is George made up to look like Sir Charles. However, Tom arrives in time to save both Essie and their love.

MUSICAL NUMBERS: "The Simpson Sisters," "The Right Finger of My Left Hand," "Just for Once," "Merely Marvelous," "The Uncle Sam Rag" Dance, "Erbie Fitch's Twitch," "She's Not Enough Woman for Me," "Behave Yourself," "LOOK WHO'S IN LOVE," "My Girl Is Just Enough Woman for Me," "Essie's Vision," "Two Faces in the Dark," "I'm Back in Circulation," "We Loves Ya, Jimey," Pickpocket Tango, "I'll Try."

INSTRUMENTATION: Violin A–B–C, viola, cello, bass, flute (pic, clar, alto sax), clar (alto sax), clar (oboe, Eng. horn, tenor sax), clar (flute, tenor sax), bari sax (bass clar, bassoon), trumpet I–II, III, trombone I, II, horn, guitar, harp, percussion, piano-conductor.

CASTING: 16 parts, 7 principals. Essie, excellent dancer who sings. Tom, actor with good voice, minor dancing. George, character song-and-dance man. Maude and Sarah Simpson, character women who sing. Inspector White, character man, straight role. Jailer, featured dancer. Separate singing and dancing ensembles. Several good dancers required. Strong choral work. Total cast, 35–45.

SCENES AND SETS: Prologue, 2 acts, 16 scenes, 5 full stage sets, 1 partial stage set, 3 scene drops.

ACT I
Prologue: A Theatre Dressing Room.
Scene 1: Outside the Simpson Sisters' Waxworks.
Scene 2: The Interior of the Waxworks.
Scene 3: Essie's Workshop.
Scene 4: A Street.
Scene 5: Stage of the Odeon Theatre.
Scene 6: Corridor, Backstage.
Scene 7: Tom's Apartment.
Scene 8: Outside the Museum.
Scene 9: Backstage of the Odeon Theatre.
Scene 10: Stage of the Odeon Theatre.

ACT II
Scene 1: Tom's Apartment.
Scene 2: A Street.
Scene 3: The Green Dragon Pub.
Scene 4: The Jail Cell.
Scene 5: Corridor, Backstage.
Scene 6: The Museum.

PERIOD AND COSTUMES: London, 1890's: costumes for several historical people for use on effigies (wax figures) at the wax museum. Tiered bustled dresses, cutaway suits, spats, bobby uniform, sexy strapless gown, parasols, men's umbrellas, dress of lower class (dresses and men's wear), red and white costumes for "Uncle Sam Rag" (1 suit, chorus girl dresses) black leotards, tights, high-button shoes, special tops, black suits, fancy shirts, vests, and coats.

CHOREOGRAPHY: Modern, parade (ragtime), soft shoe, modern ballet, "Pickpocket Tango" (bordering on an apache).

LIGHTING AND SPECIAL EFFECTS: Mysterious, dramatic lighting required for several effects. Makeup for the killer is critical.

NOTES: One of the few mystery musicals and a good one. A dancers' show, but some dance sequences should be trimmed. Ending, after murderer is unmasked, is weak. Perhaps long chase contributes to this situation. Good chance to improve construction by rewriting.

RIVERWIND

John Jennings (Book, Music, Lyrics)
Opened Dec. 12, 1962
443 Performances

BASED ON: Original

AGENT: Music Theatre

PUBLISHED TEXT: Manuscript Only

RECORDINGS: LON AM 48001
LON AMS 78001

DIGEST OF PLOT: Riverwind is a broken-down resort on Indiana's Wabash River run by Leona Farrell and her wide-eyed daughter, Jenny. The hired boy, John, is bashful about his love for Jenny, and she is distraught about his lack of attention. Annual guests Burt and Virginia are kookie lovers with an understanding about being unmarried. New guests are Dr. Fred Sumner and his too-long-married wife, Louise. They spent their wedding night here 17 years ago and Louise wants to see if a visit can rekindle their love. Their unhappiness is easily apparent. To Fred, Riverwind is just some rundown river cabins, until he spots Jenny. In pursuing his interest in her he discovers himself describing Jenny as he did Louise those many years ago. Spurred by competition, John finds the words to express his love to Jenny. The spirit of people finding themselves spreads to Burt and Virginia. He asks her to marry him, an event for which Virginia has waited seven years—but she turns him down in favor of the current licenseless faith in each other. The next morning the Sumners have resolved the void between them. In a way, Louise's plan has worked. Only her

method has failed. And when it did, Leona's philosophy and Riverwind were there to fill the gap.

MUSICAL NUMBERS: "I Cannot Tell Her So," "I Want a Surprise," "Riverwind," "American Family Plan," "The Wishing Song," "Pardon Me While I Dance," "Sew the Buttons On," "Almost, but Not Quite," "A Woman Must Think of These Things," "I Love Your Laughing Face," "A Woman Must Never Grow Old," "I'd Forgotten How Beautiful She Could Be."

INSTRUMENTATION: Bass, percussion, piano-conductor.

CASTING: 7 parts, 7 principals. All have good-sized parts and should sing well. Virginia and Burt have some comic sense to their roles. Total cast, 7.

SCENES AND SETS: 2 acts, 8 scenes. Realistic unit set—2 or 3 rustic cabins on stilts. Sumner cabin opens up to reveal interior (perhaps rolls forward); there is also an area of river bank (with log) for fishing scene.

ACT I
Scene 1: Riverwind Tourist Resort.
Scene 2: Same.
Scene 3: Same.
Scene 4: Sumner Cabin.

ACT II
Scene 1: Riverwind Tourist Resort.
Scene 2: Same.
Scene 3: Picnic Area.
Scene 4: Sumner Cabin.

PERIOD AND COSTUMES: The present along Indiana's Wabash River: housedresses, traveling clothes, recreation slacks, shorts and cutoffs, bathrobes, lounging lingerie outfit, work clothes, fishing hat.

CHOREOGRAPHY: None.

LIGHTING AND SPECIAL EFFECTS: Outdoor and indoor general lighting. Some night lighting required.

NOTES: A good show for small budgets and/or small stages.

THE ROAR OF THE GREASEPAINT—THE SMELL OF THE CROWD

Leslie Bricusse and Anthony Newley (Book, Music, Lyrics)
Opened May 16, 1965
232 Performances

BASED ON: Original

AGENT: Tams-Witmark

PUBLISHED TEXT: Manuscript Only

RECORDINGS: RCA LOC (LSO)-1109

DIGEST OF PLOT: Sir is the wealthy establishment, and Cockey is his foil. They have gathered once again to play the game. Sir commands that Cockey must always lose, even if the rules must be changed to keep him in his place. Cockey plays the game again and again without success. With each defeat he is required to write a new restrictive rule in his book of life. Cockey tries to revolt, but Sir throws up a smoke screen of hope and dreams. When finally Cockey refuses to play anymore, he is goaded into giving it one more try—this time for the Girl of his dreams. It looks as if Cockey will win, but Sir moves in and captures the Girl with his wealth. Cockey turns his frustrations to heaven and prays. Whom can he turn to? But now Cockey has a new attitude. If you can't beat them, help them beat others. The task is easy when a Negro wants to play the game. Cockey is now as vindictive as Sir. Cockey is reinforced by his new confidence and wins the game for the first time. Having tasted of power, he challenges Sir's authority to make the rules and proposes a few of his own. Sir realizes that neither can now win the game alone and suggests that they meet the future with mutual understanding and respect.

MUSICAL NUMBERS: "The Beautiful Land," "A WONDERFUL DAY LIKE TODAY," "It Isn't Enough" "Things to Remember," "Put It in the Book," "This Dream," "Where Would You Be Without Me?," "Look at That Face," "My First Love Song," "THE JOKER," "WHO CAN I TURN TO (WHEN NOBODY NEEDS ME)," "A Funny Funeral," "That's What It Is to Be Young," "What a Man!," "FEELING GOOD," "Nothing Can Stop Me Now!," "My Way," "Sweet Beginning."

INSTRUMENTATION: Violin A (2), B, cello I–II, bass, flute (pic, clar, alto flute), flute (clar), clar (bass clar, tenor sax), clar (bassoon), horns I–II, trumpets I–II, trombone (euphonium), percussion, harp, guitar-banjo, piano-conductor.

CASTING: 6 parts, 2 principals. All-girl chorus of 15. Cockey, character man, legit voice, minor dancing. Sir, character man, sings, minor dancing. Sir and Cockey carry the show. The Kid, sings. The Girl, attractive, sings. The Negro, deep bass voice. The Bully, big, straight bit part. Total cast, 21–26.

SCENES AND SETS: 2 acts, continuous action. Unit set, raised platforms, including large center game board and playing areas on each side. Large book set piece.

PERIOD AND COSTUMES: Victorian-style rags (burlesque styled) for the aristocrat and the little man of the working class. Urchins wear nondescript pants, shirts, and some jackets.

CHOREOGRAPHY: Modern steps, parade, soft shoe, burlesque duo.

LIGHTING AND SPECIAL EFFECTS: General lighting will do, with some flexibility. Game board that lights up (optional) and large (7 ft. diameter) moon behind thin drop or scrim.

NOTES: Show is done in naive pantomime styling that author Anthony Newley introduced in *Stop the World—I Want to Get Off*.

1776

Sherman Edwards (Music, Lyrics),
Peter Stone (Book)
Opened March 18, 1969

BASED ON: Original Conception by Sherman Edwards

AGENT: Music Theatre

PUBLISHED TEXT: Viking Press, 1970

RECORDINGS: COL BOS 3310

DIGEST OF PLOT: It's another sultry day in Philadelphia—Washington's army needs money, the flies are murder, and John Adams keeps harping on Independency. Members of the Continental Congress are sick of his words, and Ben Franklin knows it. He persuades John to let someone else, perhaps from the South, introduce the measure. Franklin has asked the gullible Richard Henry Lee to stop by and permits him to think of such a solution. Lee is off to his state legislature to be so directed. Lee finally returns and wastes no time in bringing the motion to the floor. Opponents quickly move to have the measure postponed. Adams, for once, convinces the congress that the matter should at least be discussed. The narrow vote is against defeat. The opposition counters with a motion that any vote on independency be unanimous, and the motion carries. It is decided the best way to present the measure would be in the form of a declaration. But who will write it? Everyone in the committee tries to dodge the job. They have agreed that Thomas Jefferson should pen it, but he wants to spend some time with his young wife, Martha, from whom he has been away too long. Adams arranges for her to be brought to Philadelphia, and work on the document progresses vigorously. The Independency Committee is called to investigate the wenching, drinking, and "French disease" reported in Washington's army and settle other grim matters the General keeps bringing before the Congress. In their absence, the conservatives have their day by pleading the case against independency and loyalty to the most powerful crown in the world. However, when Adams, Franklin, and the others return from the front, they are fired with the ability to win. The spirit is infectious. It paves the way for debate on the Declaration. There are changes and compromises, but nothing of serious consequence. That is, until Edward Rutledge threatens to lead the South against the measure if the freeing of slaves is

The 2nd Continental Congress tells John Adams (William Daniels) "Sit Down, John," in 1776.

permitted to remain in the proposal. Adams puts up a heated argument, but Franklin, the founder of America's first antislavery society, suggests they agree to the deletion in order to give birth to the nation. A game of carefully waged politics wins the last few remaining holdouts. American liberty is born as each member signs his name to the Declaration of Independence.

MUSICAL NUMBERS: "Sit Down, John," "Piddle, Twiddle, and Resolve," "Till Then," "The Lees of Old Virginia," "But, Mr. Adams," "Yours, Yours, Yours," "He Plays the Violin," "Cool, Cool, Considerate Men," "Momma Look Sharp," "The Egg," "Molasses to Rum," "Is Anybody There?"

INSTRUMENTATION: Violin, viola (2), cello (2), bass, flute (piccolo), clar (flute), oboe (Eng. horn, clar), bassoon (clar), horns I–II, trumpet, trombone I, II, III (tuba), harp, harpsichord, percussion. (Smaller orchestration available.)

CASTING: 25 parts, 6 principals, but congressmen are onstage most of the time with heavy supporting roles. All sing. John Adams, accomplished actor who sings, minor waltz ability. Benjamin Franklin, jovial character actor who sings, minor waltz and strut. Thomas Jefferson, actor, minor singing. Abigail Adams and Martha Jefferson, legit voices. Richard Henry Lee, comic, powerful singing voice. Courier, sings 1 number. Total cast, 25.

SCENES AND SETS: 1 act, 7 scenes. A single setting representing the Chamber and an anteroom of the Continental Congress; a mall, High Street, and Thomas Jefferson's room in Philadelphia; and certain reaches of John Adam's mind. Originally performed without intermission.

Scene 1: The Chamber of the Continental Congress.
Scene 2: The Mall.
Scene 3: The Chamber.
Scene 4: Jefferson's Room Above High Street.
Scene 5: The Chamber.
Scene 6: Congressional Anteroom.
Scene 7: The Chamber.

PERIOD AND COSTUMES: May, June, and July, 1776: the dress—long coat suits vary from the "liberal greens, golds, brocades, and laces of the conservative Southerns to the conservative browns, blacks, mean cloth, and plain linen of the radical New Englanders."

CHOREOGRAPHY: Minor prancing, kicking, and modified soft shoe steps—not really dancing—brief waltz.

LIGHTING AND SPECIAL EFFECTS: Dramatic lighting, but set up one time, need not be flexible.

NOTES: A revelation to all but the most avid history buffs. Dramatizes brilliantly how close the United States came to not being born, and the tremendous impact of the compromises of 1776. A masterpiece of construction, historically accurate and highly entertaining.

David Ford as John Hancock and Howard Da Silva as Benjamin Franklin signing the Declaration of Independence.

SHE LOVES ME

Jerry Bock (Music),
Joe Masteroff (Book),
Sheldon Harnick (Lyrics)
Opened April 23, 1963
302 Performances

BASED ON: *Parfumerie,* by Miklos Laszlo

AGENT: Tams-Witmark

PUBLISHED TEXT: Dodd, Mead & Co., 1964

RECORDINGS: MGM (S)4118 (OC-2)

DIGEST OF PLOT: Zoltan Maraczek runs a plush perfumery in the accepted autocratic manner of high-class European shops. His regimented clerks, headed by Georg Nowack, are highly proper and most efficient. Their private lives, however, are a different story. Sipos is a middle-aged family man; Laszlo an ambitious delivery boy who wants to become a clerk; Kodaly a rogue; and Ilona a girl with the knack for the wrong men, currently Kodaly. Even Georg, who dines with the Maraczeks, is driven to placing a lonely-hearts ad. When Amelia Balash applies for a clerk's job she is at first rejected, but quickly sells some merchandise to prove her worth. She and Georg are constantly at each other with petty bickering. Suddenly Maraczek is on him, too, and without reason, the standing dinner invitation is withdrawn. Georg's only real progress is with his new-found letter-writing romance. On the night they are finally to meet, Maraczek orders the shop decorated for Christmas. Amelia reveals to Ilona that she can't stay because she must meet a "Dear Friend" to whom she's been writing. When she tells Georg, they fight. Maraczek demands that Georg stay, but rather than do so he resigns. A detective arrives to reveal the lover Maraczek has suspected his wife has been keeping. His suspicions confirmed, he shoots himself. At the rendezvous cafe, Georg, with Sipos along for moral support, discovers that his mystery lover is really Amelia. But rather than admit he is the "Dear Friend," he tells her that he has come to celebrate his freedom from Maraczek. She is left believing that her eagerly awaited friend saw her and was disappointed. Laszlo has managed to cover up Maraczek's "accident" and wins a clerkship as his reward. Georg is summoned to Maraczek's hospital bed to learn that he was suspected, but his wife's lover was really Kodaly. He rehires Georg to fire Kodaly and to visit Miss Balash, who is suddenly sick. When they meet they recognize their love for each other, but Georg remains silent. The last hectic weeks of Christmas shopping quickly pass, and Christmas Eve arrives with the relief only retail clerks can appreciate. Following the shop's champagne celebration, Georg admits his love for her. In return, she confesses her tremendous attraction to him. But she has a dinner date with "Dear Friend." He has finally agreed to meet in person for Christmas Eve dinner. Georg begins to quote from her "Dear Friend" letters. Amelia is dumbfounded and heartened as she mentally puts the pieces together and jubilantly jumps into his arms.

MUSICAL NUMBERS: "Good Morning, Good Day," "Sounds While Selling," "Thank You, Madam," "Days Gone By," "No More Candy," "Three Letters," "Tonight at Eight," "I Don't Know His Name," "Perspective," "Goodbye, Georg," "Will He Like Me?," "Ilona," "I Resolve," "A Romantic

Jack Cassidy and Barbara Baxley in She Loves Me.

Atmosphere," "Tango Tragique," "Dear Friend," "Try Me," "Where's My Shoe?," "Ice Cream," "SHE LOVES ME," "A Trip to the Library," "Grand Knowing You," "Twelve Days to Christmas."

INSTRUMENTATION: Violins (3), viola, cello, bass, flute (pic, alto flute), oboe (Eng. horn), B♭ clar, clar (bass clar), bassoon, horns I–II, III, trumpet (flugelhorn), trombone (euphonium), harp, accordion-celeste, percussion, piano-conductor.

CASTING: 28 parts, 9 principals. 1 stage violinist (this could be faked). No singing or dancing chorus. All principals sing well, most with legitimate voices, accents. All others in cast sing, too. Arpad, 15-year-old delivery boy. Sipos, Miss Ritter, Kodaly, clerks with personal problems. Maraczek, strict store owner. Georg and Amelia, leads who find romance. Waiter, comic character man. Total cast, 24–36.

SCENES AND SETS: 2 acts, continuous action (equivalent of 10 scenes), unit set includes revolving exterior and interior of Maraczek's exclusive perfumery, workroom at the perfumery, and the Café Imperiale. Also, Maraczek's hospital room, Amelia's bedroom, Maraczek's office, and a park scene drop.

PERIOD AND COSTUMES: A city in Europe, 1930's: checked, double-breasted suits, working dresses, white blazer smocks for clerks, winter coats, overcoats, evening dresses, pajamas, and robes. Uniforms for a waiter, busboy, gypsy violinist, delivery boy, and nurse.

CHOREOGRAPHY: The musical numbers, especially during shop scenes, flow with not quite dance movements. No formal dance numbers, except a brief tango.

LIGHTING AND SPECIAL EFFECTS: Dramatic lighting suggested. Street lamp on set. Various other lights illuminating the store interior. Christmas decorations. Falling leaves and snow.

NOTES: *She Loves Me* is unusual in form. It is more delightful than overpowering and an excellent use of the musical theatre form. For some reason it isn't done nearly as much as it should be.

SHOW BOAT

Jerome Kern (Music),
Oscar Hammerstein II (Book, Lyrics)
Opened Dec. 27, 1927
575 Performances

BASED ON: Novel by Edna Ferber

AGENT: R & H

PUBLISHED TEXT: Cimino, 1970 (T. B. Harms Co., 1927, Copyright Renewed)

RECORDINGS: COL OL-4058 (R)
OL-5820 (R)
OS-2220 (R)
METRO (S)-527 (F)

DIGEST OF PLOT: Captain Andy's show boat is tying up at the Natchez, Miss. levee, and the ballyhooing has begun. It's "just one big happy family" until deckhand Pete notices Queenie, a Negro woman, wearing a gold pin he has given to the *Cotton Blossom's* leading actress, Julie LaVerne. When Pete confronts her with this outrage, she admits the gift because her husband Steve would object to her accepting. When Pete becomes forceful, Steve moves in to knock him cold. For revenge Pete tells the sheriff that Julie is really half Negro and "illegally" married to a white man in the eyes of Southern justice. Cast members Frank and Ellie warn Steve of Pete's actions. He pricks Julie's finger and sucks her blood so the others can swear that he, too, has Negro blood. They voluntarily leave the show boat, but now Captain Andy is without stars. His daughter, Magnolia (Nola), like a sister to Julie, is dazed by the sudden turn of events and wants to leave with her. But Julie persuades her to stay and take over her roles. And Frank has discovered dashing Gaylord Ravenal (who previously captured Nola's heart on the levee) to become the leading man. The rivertown crowds are thrilled by the new romantic leads, mainly because they are really in love. Before long, Gaylord and Magnolia are married, even though she has learned that he is really a riverboat gambler. Several years later at the Chicago World's Fair, Gaylord is enjoying a hot streak and the world is marvelous, but by 1904 it's been ten rocky years of hot and

Show Boat *"Cotton Blossom" as she appeared in 1946 revival with Colette Lyons, Buddy Ebsen, Ralph Dumke, and Ethel Owens heading the cast.*

cold compulsive gambling. Now there is a daughter, Kim. Frank and Ellie are a successful vaudeville team and find Nola just as she learns that Gaylord, despite his love for wife and daughter, is vacating their lives so they will not be dragged down with him. Frank takes her to audition before the manager of the Trocadero, where Julie, now an alcoholic, is the featured singer. Unbeknownst to Nola, Julie hears her audition and walks out on the show so Nola will be hired. As fate would have it, Captain Andy is there to see the debut of a new theatrical star. It's 1927 and Captain Andy has arranged a family re-union aboard the *Cotton Blossom*. The era has changed, but the reunited love burns strong—no bitterness, "just one big happy family."

MUSICAL NUMBERS: "Cotton Blossom," "Oh! That Show Boat," "Who Cares If My Boat Goes Upstream?," "ONLY MAKE BELIEVE," "OL' MAN RIVER," "CAN'T HELP LOVIN' DAT MAN," "LIFE UPON THE WICKED STAGE," "Ballyhoo," "Olio Dance," "YOU ARE LOVE," "At the Fair," Dance, "WHY DO I LOVE YOU?," "In Dahomey," "BILL," "Goodbye, My Lady Love," Cake Walk, "AFTER THE BALL," "Nobody Else But Me," Dancing in the '20's.

INSTRUMENTATION: Violins (4) A–B–C–D, viola, cello, bass, flute, oboe, clar I–II, trumpet I–II, trombone, horn I–II, bassoon, banjo-guitar, percussion, piano, conductor.

CASTING: 35 parts, 9 principals. Captain Andy, engaging character actor, minor singing and dancing. Gaylord Ravenal, handsome leading man, legit voice. Magnolia, strong actress with legit voice, plays or fakes piano. Queenie, Negro character woman, powerful legit voice. Joe, powerful Negro bass, sings "Ol' Man River." Julie, actress who sings. Parthy, straight role. Frank and Ellie, song-and-dance team, light acting required. Strong choral work. Several children helpful. Total cast of Negroes and whites, 40–60.

SCENES AND SETS: 2 acts, 15 scenes, 4 full stage sets, 2 partial stage sets, 4 scene drops. The major set problem for this show is the 3-level *Cotton Blossom* side-wheeler, river boat that must "float" on- and offstage.

ACT I
Scene 1: The Levee at Natchez on the Mississippi. 1880's.
Scene 2: Kitchen Pantry of the *Cotton Blossom*.
Scene 3. Auditorium and Stage of the *Cotton Blossom*.

Scene 4: Greenville, in Front of Box Office.
Scene 5: Auditorium and Stage During Third Act of "The Parson's Bride."
Scene 6: The Top Deck.
Scene 7: The Levee at Natchez.

ACT II
Scene 1: Midway Plaisance, Chicago World's Fair, 1893.
Scene 2: A Room on Ontario Street, 1904.
Scene 3: Trocadero Music Hall Rehearsal Room.
Scene 4: St. Agatha's Convent.
Scene 5: Trocadero Music Hall, New Year's Eve, 1905.
Scene 6: Stern of the *Cotton Blossom,* 1927.
Scene 7: Top Deck of the *Cotton Blossom.*
Scene 8: The Levee at Natchez.

PERIOD AND COSTUMES: 1880's to 1927: colorful summer finery of the period, work clothes, captain uniform, dresses, aprons, backwoods overalls, dandy long-coat suit and high hat, villain outfit and cape, parson's frock, frilly dresses and wigs, 1890's bathing beauty outfits, Dahomey native briefs, Fatima cooch outfit, midway costumes, evening gowns and suits, waiters, rehearsal clothes, 1920's fashions.

CHOREOGRAPHY: Parade, soft shoe, ballet, cake walk, Charleston, hootchy-kootchy, song-and-dance number, Dahomey "savage" dance.

LIGHTING AND SPECIAL EFFECTS: Dramatic lighting required. Constantly aging characters pose a special makeup problem.

NOTES: *Show Boat* is the *Gone with the Wind* of musical theatre. The longest-enduring classic that played an incredible 15 years before *Oklahoma!* The book is powerful, but tends to drag if not guided by sure-handed, fast-paced direction. Oscar Hammerstein II was always careful to point out that the lyrics for "Bill" were written by P. G. Wodehouse. The current script available for production is the 1946 revival version, which eliminates 1 scene and 3 minor musical numbers. There is still some extraneous material, most notably Frank's dance at the end of ACT I, Scene 5, and the Dahomey song and dance sequence.

SILK STOCKINGS

Cole Porter (Music, Lyrics),
George S. Kaufman, Leueen MacGrath, Abe Burrows (Book)
Opened Feb. 24, 1955
478 Performances

BASED ON: *Ninotchka* by Melchior Lengyel

AGENT: Tams-Witmark

PUBLISHED TEXT: Manuscript Only

RECORDINGS: RCA LOC(LSO)-1102

DIGEST OF PLOT: Theatrical agent Steve Canfield has persuaded noted Russian composer Peter Ilyitch Boroff to stay in Paris beyond the one performance granted by the Commissar of Art. Canfield's plan is to get him to score a film starring another of his clients, the temperamental Janice Dayton. The Russian Commissar sends three agents, Ivanov, Brankov, and Bibinski, to "bring" Boroff back home. Canfield produces papers showing that Boroff has a French father and diverts the matter into the French courts. While the three agents are becoming fond of freedom and the pleasures of Paris, the Commissar of Arts has been replaced. The new Commissar Markovitch dispatches another agent to bring the Russian delegation home, a gorgeous, worker-minded female named Ninotchka. At their first confrontation Canfield is overwhelmed and makes bold advances. Ninotchka is interested only in her mission and whatever intelligence she can pick up. Janice Dayton arrives with her spectacular entourage. Boroff is at her heels, but Janice wants no part of him—until Canfield convinces her that he is the key to publicity for her new movie. Janice's arrival and show-biz closeness to Steve has triggered an emotion that even the best-programmed Russian woman cannot ignore—Ninotchka is jealous. She discards her worker's uniform for some feminine clothes. She and Steve have a wonderful night. Over the next several weeks there is a whirlwind romance, and Steve is preparing to propose. However, Janice has twisted Boroff and the entire production crew around her little finger. When the Russians see what has been done to the great Boroff's music, they suspect a master plot to destroy Russian culture. Ninotchka and Steve argue over the significance of the matter and she leads Boroff and the others back behind the Iron Curtain. Back home, they are severely downgraded for the loose handling of the affair. It's several weeks later. Ninotchka is holding a party for the Paris group and other underground pleasure-seekers. Boroff has written a snappy new song—very anti-Russian. Canfield has managed to enter the country and gets to Ninotchka. However, Commissar Markovitch raids the party, and Siberia looms for everyone. However, Canfield convinces Markovitch that fame and fortune await in America. Together they plan for Markovitch's best friend, the Commissar of Air, to supply the plane for the whole group to defect to the free world.

MUSICAL NUMBERS: "Too Bad," "Paris Loves Lovers," "Stereophonic Sound," "It's a Chemical Reaction, That's All," "ALL OF YOU," "Satin and Silk," "WITHOUT LOVE," "Hail, Bibinski," "As On Through the Seasons We Sail," "Josephine," "Siberia," "Silk Stockings," "The Red Blues."

INSTRUMENTATION: Violins A–C (2), B–D (guitar), viola, cello, bass, clar (alto sax, bass clar), clar (alto sax, flute, pic), clar (tenor sax, bass sax, bass clar), clar (bari sax, alto sax, bass clar, oboe, Eng. horn), horn, trumpets I–II, III, trombone I, II, III, harp, percussion, piano-conductor.

CASTING: 33 parts, 9 principals. Ivanov, Brankov, Bibinski, comic Russians who don't want to go home, sing. Boroff, escaped composer, straight role. Steve, American leading man, sings. Vera, experienced dancer. Commissar Markovitch, comedy character man. Ninotchka, lead, sings and dances. Janice Dayton, movie actress (à la blonde bombshell), sings and dances. Total cast, 30–46.

SCENES AND SETS: 2 acts, 13 scenes, 8 full stage sets (including 2 drops), 3 scene drops.

ACT I
Scene 1: Hotel Lobby, Paris.
Scene 2: Commissar's Office, Russia.
Scene 3: Hotel Royal Suite, Paris.
Scene 4: Hotel Lobby, Paris.
Scene 5: Canfield's Hotel Sitting Room, Paris.
Scene 6: Commissariat Offices, Russia.
Scene 7: Couturiere's Shop, Paris.
Scene 8: Hotel Royal Suite, Paris.

ACT II
Scene 1: Bookstalls on Left Bank, Paris.
Scene 2: Exterior of French Movie Studio.
Scene 3: Movie Studio, France.
Scene 4: Hotel Lobby, Paris.
Scene 5: Ninotchka's Apartment, Russia.

PERIOD AND COSTUMES: Paris and Moscow, not long ago: uniforms for hotel doorman, Russian commissar, guards, and Olympics contestants. Typical clothes for hotel manager, flower girl, choreographer, reporters, saleslady, bookstall man, French comrades, movie director and assistant. Dresses, tights, dancers' tutus, sweat suits, Russian and Western fashions, evening wear, 2 chorus line changes, sweaters, overcoats, leather coat.

CHOREOGRAPHY: Modern, production numbers, ballet, toe.

LIGHTING AND SPECIAL EFFECTS: Some dramatic lighting required. Lights of Paris on set.

NOTES: The show's topical nature remains current at this writing. Most dated is the "Stereophonic Sound" number, which is the most out-of-place song in the show in any case. If deleted it would not be missed and its omission would strengthen the construction.

SKYSCRAPER

James Van Heusen (Music),
Peter Stone (Book),
Sammy Cahn (Lyrics)
Opened Nov. 13, 1954
248 Performances

BASED ON: *Dream Girl* by Elmer Rice

AGENT: Samuel French

PUBLISHED TEXT: Samuel French, 1967 (P)

RECORDINGS: CAP VAS 2422

DIGEST OF PLOT: Chronic daydreamer Georgina Allerton refuses to sell her brownstone home and antique shop to make way for a new skyscraper. She floats from one dream to another, avoiding the realities of progress. She hasn't halted construction, however. The building is going up around her in the hope that she will eventually give in. The developer Bert Bushman keeps making better offers, now up to $150,000, but Georgina stands firm. Bert's architect brother Tim is no longer connected with the project (his design has been rejected), but he is interested in Georgina. He asks her out, but she believes him part of the enemy Bushman. Nonetheless, Tim starts appearing in her daydreams. Bert raises his offer to $165,000. Georgina's assistant in the Litterbug Antique Shop, Roger Summerhill, needs money to promote his film festival. He plots with Bert to help get Georgina to sell. Tim, in the meantime, finally corners Georgina for a date following which he takes her atop the new building's steel skeleton. He gives her some insight as to progress and a candid view of himself. She is won to both. The next day, Roger, unable to get Georgina to sell in any other way, asks her to run away with him. But Tim comes in and tells Georgina she is more concerned over losing her safe dream world than the brownstone. She goes into a dream, but Tim is now a part of her and in the dream too. He turns the dream against her and snaps her back to reality. They are married and spend their wedding night in the brownstone. She sells the house to Bushman with the condition that Tim's design be used. Tomorrow they will leave it to progress.

MUSICAL NUMBERS: "Occasional Flight of Fancy," "Run for Your Life," "Local 403," "Opposites," "Just the Crust," "Everybody Has a Right to Be Wrong," "Wrong!," "The Auction," "The Gaiety," "More Than One Way," "Don't Worry," "I'll Only Miss Her When I Think of Her," "Spare That Building."

INSTRUMENTATION: Violins A, B, C, cello, guitar, flute (2d alto sax, clar), 1st alto sax (1st clar), tenor sax (clar), tenor sax (bass clar, clar), trumpets I–II, III, trombone I, II, III, bass drums, harp.

CASTING: 18 parts, 4 principals. Georgina, actress who sings, minor dancing. Bert, character man who sings. Tim, actor with good voice. Roger, comic character man who sings. Total cast, 40–50.

SCENES AND SETS: 2 acts, 25 scenes (several very brief), unit set of tower steelwork plus several fly-ins. 1 second-level scene rolls on framework from offstage wings. Drop-size photographic mural of New York skyline. The entire action takes place yesterday in New York City, in and around a large skyscraper and a small brownstone.

Julie Harris as Georgina (background) converses with her family in their breakfast nook.

ACT I
Scene 1: Georgina's Bedroom—Allerton Kitchen.
Scene 2: Construction Site.
Scene 3: Bushman Building—Construction Shack.
Scene 4: The Construction Site.
Scene 5: Skyscraper—Ground Level.
Scene 6: The Site—as Before.
Scene 7: Construction Shack.
Scene 8: Construction Site.
Scene 9: The Litterbug.
Scene 10: Construction Site.
Scene 11: The Litterbug.
Scene 12: The Construction Site.
Scene 13: Two Phone Booths.
Scene 14: Knickerbocker Auction Galleries.
Scene 15: Two Phone Booths.
Scene 16: Georgina's Bedroom.

ACT II
Scene 1: Gaiety Delicatessen.
Scene 2: Limbo.
Scene 3: Film Festival.
Scene 4: Construction Site.

Scene 5: Skyscraper—on Top of Unfinished Structure.
Scene 6: Construction Site.
Scene 7: Litterbug.
Scene 8: The Skyscraper—a Dream.
Scene 9: The Allerton Bedroom—Georgina's Bedroom.

PERIOD AND COSTUMES: The present: office work clothes, modern fashions, suits, construction clothes, hardhats, casual wear, dream costumes— Arabian Nights, doctors, dueling musketeers, mad scientists, etc. Uniforms for policeman, cab driver, waiter, auctioneer, jazz musician.

CHOREOGRAPHY: Modern, modern ballet, odd-ball dream sequences, choreographed auction.

LIGHTING AND SPECIAL EFFECTS: Dramatic lighting required. Original production used brief film clip, which is easily cut. Smoke pots.

NOTES: *Skyscraper* is a formula musical spectacular with a lot of extraneous material. Tightening the book and trimming the length of some bits could whip the show into an enjoyable change-of-pace evening. Not a great show by any means, but strikes a happy note for kooks and anti-eye pollution supporters.

SONG OF NORWAY

Robert Wright, George Forrest (Music, Lyrics), Milton Lazarus (Book)
Opened Aug. 4, 1944
860 Performances

BASED ON: Play by Homer Curran

AGENT: Tams-Witmark

PUBLISHED TEXT: Manuscript Only

RECORDINGS: Decca 9019

DIGEST OF PLOT: Based on the life and music of Edvard Grieg, *Song of Norway* paints a vivid picture of the customs and legends that surround one of the world's finest composers. Historical and ro-

mantic, the story progresses from Grieg's promise to compose music for his friend's poem entitled "The Song of Norway" until he finishes the work—known to the world as Grieg's Concerto in A Minor. The plot argument is built by a charming Countess who diverts Grieg to more frivolous ways, but still manages to inspire him to write his immortal "Peer Gynt Suite."

MUSICAL NUMBERS: "The Legend," "HILL OF DREAMS," "FREDDY AND HIS FIDDLE," "NOW," "Strange Music," "Midsummer's Eve," "March of the Trollgers," "Hymn of Betrothal," "Papillon," "Bon Vivant," "THREE LOVES," "Down Your Tea," "Nordraak's Farewell," "Waltz Eternal," "PEER GYNT," "I Love You," "At Christmastime," "THE SONG OF NORWAY."

INSTRUMENTATION: Violin I (2), II, viola, cello, bass, flute I–II, oboe, clar I–II, bass clar, bassoon, horns I–II, III, trumpets I–II, trombones I–II, harp, percussion, piano, solo piano, piano-conductor.

CASTING: 31 parts (4 to 6 children), 13 principals, including 5 featured ballet dancers. Edvard Grieg, baritone. Rikard Nordraak, tenor, poet and friend. Nina, lyric soprano, high C, two-octave range,

Members of the Ballet Russe de Monte Carlo troupe as they appeared with Lawrence Brooks (Edvard Grieg) and Helena Bliss (Nina) in Song of Norway.

WISCONSIN CENTER FOR THEATRE RESEARCH

Grieg's bride-to-be. Father Nordraak, straight role. Father Grieg, tenor. Mother Grieg, soprano. Count Peppi le Louys, light baritone, 1 number only. Countess Louisa Giovanni, dramatic soprano, beautiful with good acting ability. Friends and townsfolk. Legitimate voices required, operetta style. Strong choral work. Full corps de ballet. Total cast, 40–56.

SCENES AND SETS: 2 acts, 7 scenes, 6 sets, including 3 drops.

ACT I
Scene 1: Troldhaugen (Hill of the Trolls)—Just Outside the Town of Bergen, Norway. Midsummer's Eve—in the 1860's.
Scene 2: A Square on the Outskirts of Bergen.

ACT II
Scene 1: Copenhagen—Reception Room of the Royal Conservatory. One Year Later.
Scene 2: Rome—Tito's Chocolate Shop. One Year Later.
Scene 3: Rome—Ballroom of Villa Pincio.
Scene 4: Troldhaugen—Interior of the Grieg Home. Sometime Later.
Scene 5: The Song of Norway.

PERIOD AND COSTUMES: 19th Century: formal and society wear, colorful peasant costumes. Blousy shirts and knickerlike britches for casual male dress. Women principals in hoop skirts throughout.

CHOREOGRAPHY: Folk dancing, ballet, polka steps, and waltz.

LIGHTING AND SPECIAL EFFECTS: Bright exteriors. Dramatic colored lighting during some ballet and musical sequences.

NOTES: The operetta style of this work can seem labored to modern audiences; however, it could be a fine production for groups known for outstanding choral achievement.

SOUND OF MUSIC, THE

Richard Rodgers (Music),
Howard Lindsay, Russel Crouse (Book),
Oscar Hammerstein II (Lyrics)
Opened Nov. 16, 1959
1,443 Performances

BASED ON: *The Trapp Family Singers* by Maria Augusta Trapp

AGENT: R & H

PUBLISHED TEXT: Random House, 1960; Bantam, 1967 (P)

RECORDINGS: COL KOL-5450
COL LOS-2020
RCA LOCD(LSOD)-2005
(F)

DIGEST OF PLOT: Maria is a postulant in Austria's Nonnenberg Abbey. Her spirit and faith are strong, but the Mother Abbess has concluded that Maria is not quite ready for the religious life. She sends Maria to become the temporary governess for the seven children of Captain von Trapp, a recent widower and retired officer of the Austrian Navy. Maria arrives to find him running his home like a ship. She is quick to change things and introduce the children to the great pleasures of their youth, particularly singing. She easily wins the adoration of the children, even the eldest, Liesl, who is feeling the pains of first love for a boy named Rolf. The Captain returns from a trip to Vienna with his wealthy fiancée, Elsa Schraeder, and friend, Max Detweiler, a theatrical promoter. Elsa persuades the Captain to give a party. At the party Maria realizes that she loves the Captain. She feels this is a sin for a postulant and runs away to return to the Abbey. There the Mother Abbess helps Maria understand that love of a man is holy and that she must accept God's direction even if it is against her own plan. Maria returns to the von Trapp villa to discover an argument between the Captain, Elsa, and Max over cooperation with the Nazis in what seems an imminent invasion. In the process, the engagement is called off. Soon thereafter the Captain and Maria recognize their love. They are married two weeks later at the Abbey. Returning from the honeymoon, the Captain is angered by Max who has entered the children in the Kaltzberg Music Festival. He also learns that the Nazis have taken over and have commissioned him into their Navy. Maria delays for time by proving the family must sing at the festival. On performance night, the Nazis announce the Captain must leave the stage to enter service to Hitler. Max manages to stall for more time while the family escapes to hiding in the Abbey. The Abbey is searched. Young Rolf, now a Nazi youth leader, spots them, but his love for Liesl compels him to say that no one is in the garden. The family bids farewell to the nuns and climbs the mountains to Switzerland and freedom.

MUSICAL NUMBERS: "Preludium," "THE SOUND OF MUSIC," "MARIA," "MY FAVORITE THINGS," "DO RE MI," "You Are Sixteen," "The Lonely Goatherd," "How Can Love Survive?," "So Long, Farewell," "CLIMB EVERY MOUNTAIN," "No Way to Stop It," "Ordinary Couple," processional, "Edelweiss."

INSTRUMENTATION: Violin I (2), II (2), viola, cello, bass, flute I–II (pic), oboe (Eng. horn), clar I–II, bassoon, horn I–II, trumpet I–II, III, trombone I, II, tuba, harp, guitar, percussion, conductor, piano.

CASTING: 23 parts, 15 principals (including 7 children, 2 boys, 5 girls). Maria, winning actress, legit voice, dances. Mother Abbess, legit voice. Captain von Trapp, accomplished actor who sings, minor dancing. Children, must sing, dance, and act well. Rolf, young actor, straight role, sings. Elsa Schraeder, sings. Max, good character man. Large combined

COURTESY OF THE LYNN FARNOL GROUP, INC.

Mary Martin (Maria) and Theodore Bikel (Captain) in wedding scene from The Sound of Music.

singing and dancing chorus. Strong choral work. Total cast, 45–55.

SCENES AND SETS: 2 acts, 19 scenes, 7 full stage sets, 4 scene drops. Large 3-level revolving von Trapp house interior backs up the terrace set.

ACT I
Scene 1: Nonnenberg Abbey.
Scene 2: Mountainside Near the Abbey.
Scene 3: The Office of the Mother Abbess.
Scene 4: A Corridor in the Abbey.
Scene 5: The Living Room of the Trapp Villa.
Scene 6: Outside the Trapp Villa.
Scene 7: Maria's Bedroom.
Scene 8: The Terrace of the Trapp Villa.
Scene 9: A Hallway in the Trapp Villa.
Scene 10: The Living Room.
Scene 11: A Corridor in the Abbey.
Scene 12: The Office of the Mother Abbess.

ACT II
Scene 1: The Terrace.
Scene 2: A Corridor in the Abbey.
Scene 3: The Office of the Mother Abbess.
Scene 4: A Cloister Overlooking the Chapel.
Scene 5: The Living Room.
Scene 6: The Concert Hall.
Scene 7: The Garden of Nonnenberg Abbey.

PERIOD AND COSTUMES: Austria, early 1938: decorated Austrian folk costumes, nuns' and novices' habits, assorted Austrian and Nazi military uniforms, casual and society dress of the time, formal evening wear.

COURTESY OF THE LYNN FARNOL GROUP, INC.

Maria teaches the children how to sing "Do Re Mi."

CHOREOGRAPHY: Austrian folk dance, waltz, love duet, and processional.

LIGHTING AND SPECIAL EFFECTS: Not all sets should be full size. Tight control on lighting is extremely important to an attractive production.

NOTES: *The Sound of Music* was one of the few musicals to be faithfully reproduced in the film version, and became the most successful movie ever made. It was also the last show on which Rodgers and Hammerstein collaborated. "Edelweiss" was written by Hammerstein in his hospital bed—the last song he wrote. He never saw the show.

SOUTH PACIFIC

Richard Rodgers (Music),
Oscar Hammerstein II, Joshua Logan (Book),
Oscar Hammerstein II (Lyrics)
Opened April 7, 1949
1,925 Performances

BASED ON: *Tales of the South Pacific* by James A. Michener

AGENT: R & H

PUBLISHED TEXT: Random House, 1949; Modern Library #200

RECORDINGS: COL OL-4180
COL OS-2040
RCA LOC(LSO)-1032(F)

DIGEST OF PLOT: Emile de Becque, a middle-aged French planter farming a South Pacific island during World War II, is entertaining a young, vibrant American nurse, Nellie Forbush, at his country home. There is love, but Nellie is reluctant over the age difference. The island is also the base for Seabees and Bloody Mary, friend to the American serviceman who provides anything for a price. Her competition is Luther Billis, a fast-buck operator. To compete, however, he must get to Bali Ha'i, an off-limits island of treasure and girls. His only hope is Lt. Joseph Cable, a newly arrived officer who can obtain a launch for transport to the island. Cable's mission is a dangerous one. He seeks to set up a spy outpost on a Japanese-held island and has come to persuade Emile to go with him. The planter once lived on the island and knows it well. When Emile turns him down, Cable remembers Mary's haunting description of Bali Ha'i. On the island Mary takes him to Liat, a lovely young Polynesian girl, who turns out to be Mary's daughter. It's a marvelous night, but Cable can stay no longer. Back on the main island, Nellie is attending a party at Emile's. She is ready to give up her concern over their ages when she discovers Emile has been married to a Polynesian woman. Her immediate feeling is disappointment. Later when Emile learns she has asked for a transfer, he is bitter. He comes across Mary asking Cable to marry Liat. But Cable's prejudice, too, prevents him from joining his love. Emile has lost his reason for not going with Cable and agrees to make the mission. Through their efforts the Japanese are forced to evacuate the area, but the success costs Cable his life. Nellie has realized that nothing matters but her love for Emile. Not knowing if he will ever return, she returns to his house to care for his two children. The Allies move in to mop up the Japanese territory and Emile is rescued and returned to Nellie and his family.

MUSICAL NUMBERS: "Dîtes-Moi Pourquoi," "A Cockeyed Optimist," "Twin Soliloquies," "SOME ENCHANTED EVENING," "Bloody Mary Is the Girl I Love," "THERE IS NOTHING LIKE A DAME," "BALI HA'I," "I'M GONNA WASH THAT MAN RIGHT OUTA MY HAIR," "I'M IN LOVE WITH A WONDERFUL GUY," "YOUNGER THAN SPRINGTIME," Soft Shoe Dance, "HAPPY TALK," "HONEY BUN," "You've Got to Be Taught," "This Nearly Was Mine."

INSTRUMENTATION: Violin A, B, C, D, viola, cello, bass, flute (pic), oboe (Eng. horn), clar I–II, trumpet I–II, III, trombone I, II, bassoon, horn I–II, III, tuba, harp, drums, conductor, piano.

CASTING: 35 parts, 8 principals. Ensign Nellie Forbush, attractive young nurse, legit voice. Emile de Becque, French planter about 50, legit voice. Bloody Mary, Americanized native witch, age unknown, strong voice helps. Luther Billis, con man, character man, need not sing. Joseph Cable, handsome young tenor, legit voice. A small boy and girl who sing. Officers, natives, nurses, and enlisted men. Total cast, 45–60.

SCENES AND SETS: 2 acts, 24 scenes, 5 full stage sets (2 are front and back of camp show

Ezio Pinza (Emile) and Mary Martin (Nellie) ponder "Some Enchanted Evening" in South Pacific.

proscenium arch), 2 scene drops (1 is a 2-piece scrim traveler), 4 partial stage sets.

ACT I
Scene 1: Emile de Becque's Plantation Home on an Island in the South Pacific.
Scene 2: Beach Where Seabees, Sailors and Marines Lounge.
Scene 3: Edge of a Palm Grove Near Beach, Bali Ha'i in Background.
Scene 4: Company Street.
Scene 5: Inside Island Commander's Office.
Scene 6: Company Street.
Scene 7: The Beach.
Scene 8: Brackett's Office.
Scene 9: Bali Ha'i.
Scene 10: Interior of Native Hut.
Scene 11: Bali Ha'i.
Scene 12: Emile's Terrace.

ACT II
Scene 1: G.I. Stage During Performance of "The Thanksgiving Follies."
Scene 2: In Back of the Stage.
Scene 3: G.I. Stage.
Scene 4: Behind Stage.
Scene 5: Black (Sounds of Airplanes).
Scene 6: Radio Shack.
Scene 7: Group of Pilots Around a Radio Set.
Scene 8: Radio Shack.
Scene 9: Company Street.
Scene 10: The Beach.
Scene 11: Company Street.
Scene 12: Emile's Terrace.

COURTESY OF THE LYNN FARNOL GROUP, INC.

Mary Martin in "Honey Bun" number.

PERIOD AND COSTUMES: South Sea islands during World War II: military uniforms, Army, Navy, and Marine (male and female), swim suits, native costumes (grass skirts, loincloths, wild wigs, etc.), white suits, evening wear.

CHOREOGRAPHY: Native, brief waltz, soft shoe, and production numbers.

LIGHTING AND SPECIAL EFFECTS: Colorful tropical lighting essential for the exterior settings and the magical island of Bali Ha'i.

NOTES: A standard of musical theatre that has been overdone in some areas. Show won Pulitzer Prize for 1950.

STOP THE WORLD— I WANT TO GET OFF

Leslie Bricusse, Anthony Newley (Music, Book, Lyrics)
Opened Oct. 3, 1962
555 Performances

BASED ON: Original

AGENT: Tams-Witmark

PUBLISHED TEXT: Manuscript Only

RECORDINGS: London 58001

DIGEST OF PLOT: Littlechap, an unsuspecting male, finds himself a father before his time. He agreed to marry Evie because it offered him certain business advantages. Now he succeeds in his position, but finds himself trapped in the responsibility of a premature family. He turns to the women of the world, but finds only empty fulfillment. In the twilight of his years he finally discovers that he has wasted his life looking for something that was before him all the time—his wife's true love.

MUSICAL NUMBERS: "The A.B.C. Song," "I Want to Be Rich," "Typically English," "A Special Announcement," "Lumbered," "Welcome to Sludgepool," "GONNA BUILD A MOUNTAIN," "Glorious Russian," "Meilinki Neilchick," "Family Fugue," "Typische Deutsche," "Nag! Nag! Nag!," "All American," "ONCE IN A LIFETIME," "Mumbo Jumbo," "Welcome to Sunvale," "Someone Nice Like You," "WHAT KIND OF FOOL AM I?"

INSTRUMENTATION: Bass, flute (pic, clar, tenor sax), flute (clar, alto sax), clar (bass clar, tenor sax), clar (alto sax, bari sax), bassoon, horn, trumpets I–II, trombone I, II, percussion, piano-conductor.

CASTING: 4 parts, 2 principals. Littlechap, good voice. His wife, Evie, and continental lady friends (played by the same girl), good voice. Both main characters should be accomplished pantomimists. Their twin daughters, sing, minor dance. 9- to 15-member girl chorus who sing and dance. Total cast, 13–21.

SCENES AND SETS: Unit set, resembles inside of European circus tent arena with 3- or 4-level risers around the circumference. In the center is a draped arch entrance with small traveler. Continuous action.

PERIOD AND COSTUMES: Anytime: tights, baggy pants, and frilled collars were used in the original production, but costumes could be almost anything.

CHOREOGRAPHY: Movement to lyrics only. Pantomime styling.

LIGHTING AND SPECIAL EFFECTS: Dramatic lighting required. Projected treadmill, shadow effects, and other lighting effects.

NOTES: A unique approach to musical theatre that once again proves the universality of the basic art form. However, the styling of *Stop the World* tends to wear a little thin. Some cutting would probably be in order. Takes a superb direction job to put over well.

SWEET CHARITY

Cy Coleman (Music),
Neil Simon (Book),
Dorothy Fields (Lyrics)
Opened Jan. 29, 1966
608 Performances

BASED ON: *Nights of Cabiria* by Federico Fellini

AGENT: Tams-Witmark

PUBLISHED TEXT: Random House, 1966

RECORDINGS: COL KOL-6500
KOS-2900

DIGEST OF PLOT: Charity Hope Valentine wants so desperately to be loved that she is eager to cater to her man's every whim. The only problem is she falls for every louse in the book. Charlie has just pushed her in the lake and absconded with their furniture money. It's back to the Fandango Ballroom where Charity works as a taxi dancer. She vows to the girls that there'll never be another man. On the way home Charity is caught in an argument between film star Vittorio Vidal and his hastily departing girl friend, Ursula. To spite her, Vittorio asks Charity to spend the evening with him at the Pompeii Club, a society discothèque. Later at Vittorio's apartment things are going well, but Ursula crashes the occasion, and Charity retreats to the closet while the screen lovers patch up their differences. The Fandango girls are heartened by Charity's latest escapade and vow to better themselves. Charity decides to broaden her cultural knowledge at the "Y" lecture series where she meets Oscar Lindquist; they are trapped in an elevator and Charity helps bring Oscar through an attack of claustrophobia. By the time they are freed, they've missed the lecture. So they take in Oscar's Church-of-the-Month club. On their next date at Coney Island it is Oscar who comes to Charity's aid. All along, Charity has concealed her occupation, but she has wired Oscar to meet her at Barney's Chile Hacienda to reveal the awful truth. He already knows, but asks to marry her anyway. The gang at the Fandango give Charity a big going away celebration. However, it turns out that Oscar has another phobia—marriage. Charity is left high and dry as she finds herself in the lake once more —only this time by accident and this time it didn't cost her any money. She decides that things are improving and sets out to live *hopefully* ever after.

MUSICAL NUMBERS: "You Should See Yourself," "The Rescue," "BIG SPENDER," "Charity's Soliloquy," "Rich Man's Frug," "IF MY FRIENDS COULD SEE ME NOW," "Too Many Tomorrows," "There's Gotta Be Something Better Than This," "I'm the Bravest Individual," "Rhythm of Life," "Baby, Dream Your Dream," "Sweet Charity," "Where Am I Going?," "I'm a Brass Band," "I Love to Cry at Weddings."

INSTRUMENTATION: Violin I–II (3), cello, bass, pic (flute, alto flute, clar, alto sax), oboe (clar, tenor sax), flute (clar, bass clar, tenor sax), bassoon (clar, bass clar, bari sax), trumpets I–II (flugelhorns), III, IV, trombone I, II, III, percussion I, II, chordavox (optional piano), guitar I (elec guitar), II (bass guitar, elec guitar), piano-conductor.

CASTING: 30 parts, 7 principals. Charity, accomplished dancer-actress who sings, carries the show. Helene and Nickie, Charity's sidekicks, comic roles, good actresses who sing and dance. Vittorio Vidal, actor who does accent well, sings 1 number. Oscar, good actor for timid role, sings. Big Daddy Johann Sebastian Brubeck, great, swinging character man who sings. Herman, featured tenor. Total cast, 36–40.

SCENES AND SETS: 2 acts, 19 scenes, 8 full stage sets, 2 partial stage sets (1 is a ferris wheel gondola that flies). Throughout the show subtitles are flashed to the audience via lights (as in the original production) or signboards.

ACT I
Prologue
Scene 1: The Park.
Scene 2: Hostess Room.
Scene 3: Fandango Ballroom.
Scene 4: New York Street.
Scene 5: Pompeii Club.
Scene 6: Vittorio Vidal's Apartment.
Scene 7: Hostess Room.
Scene 8: 92nd Street "Y."

ACT II
Scene 1: 92nd Street "Y."
Scene 2: Rhythm of Life Church.
Scene 3: Going Crosstown.
Scene 4: Charity's Apartment.
Scene 5: Coney Island.
Scene 6: Fandango Ballroom.
Scene 7: Times Square.
Scene 8: Barney's Chile Hacienda.
Scene 9: "I'm a Bass Band."
Scene 10: Fandango Ballroom.
Scene 11: The Park.

PERIOD AND COSTUMES: New York City, the present: Charity's basic black mini dress. Gangster suit. Uniforms for ice cream vendor, football players, policemen, doorman, waiter, servant, and good fairy. Gaudy dance-hall hostess dresses. Tuxedos, evening clothes, high-fashion dresses. Mod minis and way-out men's styles. Beatnik sweatshirts, cut-off pants, sandals, complete with psychedelic decorative trimmings. Raincoats and work clothes.

CHOREOGRAPHY: Modern jazz, frug, monkey, other rock fads, soft shoe, ballroom, parade.

LIGHTING AND SPECIAL EFFECTS: Dramatic lighting required. Working elevator that gets stuck between floors. In the Broadway production the subtitles were electric. They could be "seed lights" or painted signs.

Arthur Godfrey as Uncle Sid in Take Me Along.

NOTES: *Sweet Charity* was in tune with plotless films that were popular during the same period. In a way the show is a good cartoon of some very tragic people. As a musical it is loosely constructed, but still manages to come off as a fun evening. It is a dancers' show.

TAKE ME ALONG

Bob Merrill (Music, Lyrics),
Joseph Stein, Robert Russell (Book)
Opened Oct. 22, 1959
448 Performances

BASED ON: *Ah, Wilderness* by Eugene O'Neill

AGENT: Tams-Witmark

PUBLISHED TEXT: Manuscript Only

RECORDINGS: RCA LOC(LSO)-1050

DIGEST OF PLOT: Nat Miller is publisher of the highly reserved Centerville, Connecticut, newspaper. His wife, Essie, his sister Lily, and the rest of Nat's family are the envy of the community. Richard is the possible exception. He has been caught reading passionate poetry to his girl, Muriel Macomber. Sid Davis (Essie's brother) arrives from Watertown, concealing the fact that he's been fired for telling off his boss while drinking. He is welcomed into the Miller household just as Muriel's father storms in to demand that Richard be punished for his "erotic" actions. Nat takes issue with Macomber's narrow-mindedness and throws him out. Sid convinces Lily that he's reformed and proposes to her. She accepts on the condition that he stay sober during the Fourth of July picnic. It's a great holiday in Centerville for everyone—except Richard, who receives a letter from Muriel stating she no longer loves him. A friend, Wint, tries to tempt Richard into drowning his sorrows with booze and wild women, but he is not sure. However, when Nat and Sid stagger home late, falling-down drunk, his illusions of romantic faithfulness are shattered along with the last hopes of Lily. Richard runs off to join Wint at the Pleasant Beach House and gets drunk. Back at the house Sid is pleading with Lily for one more chance, but her hurt has calloused all hope. Sid's only comfort is the returning Richard, who needs the understanding Sid knows so well. Muriel finally gets word to Richard that she was forced to write her note and that her love commands they meet secretly on the beach. As Sid watches Richard's happiness at the news he realizes that he is unworthy of Lily—that he, too, must make the sacrifice that will make their love binding. Sid phones his former boss, apologizes, and is reinstated. He prepares to return alone and prove himself. But at the trolley, Lily is waiting with bags packed to make the venture into a new life—a joint one.

MUSICAL NUMBERS: "The Parade," "Oh, Please," "I Would Die," "Sid, Ol' Kid," "Staying Young," "I Get Embarrassed," "We're Home," "TAKE ME ALONG," "For Sweet Charity," "Pleasant Beach House," "That's How It Starts," "The Beardsley Ballet," "Promise Me a Rose," "Little Green Snake," "Nine O'Clock," "But Yours."

INSTRUMENTATION: Violin A–C (2), viola, cello, bass, alto sax (clar, flute, pic), alto sax (clar), tenor sax (clar), bari sax (clar), horns I–II, trumpets I–II, trombone, percussion, harp, piano-conductor.

CASTING: 20 parts, 8 principals. Nat Miller, sturdy actor, voice helps. Essie Miller, good voice. Lily, good, robust character woman, legit voice. Richard Miller, young romantic interest, sings and dances. Muriel, good voice, featured in ballet. Sid (a no-account brother-in-law), character actor, singing not essential. Wint, dancer. Mr. Macomber, straight role. Three younger Miller children, townsfolk, salesmen, and girlies. Singing and dancing chorus. Total cast, 36–50.

SCENES AND SETS: 2 acts, 13 scenes, 4 full stage sets (including 2 drops), 1 partial stage set, 2 scene drops. (The Miller home is a cutaway of a 2-story house.) Trolley car for Sid's entrance.

ACT I
Scene 1: The Miller Home.
Scene 2: The Macomber Home.
Scene 3: The Car Barn.
Scene 4: The Miller Home.
Scene 5: A Street.
Scene 6: The Picnic Grounds.
Scene 7: The Miller Home.

ACT II
Scene 1: Bar Room of the Pleasant Beach House.
Scene 2: The Miller Home.
Scene 3: Richard's Bedroom.
Scene 4: The Beach.
Scene 5: The Miller Home.
Scene 6: The Car Barn.

PERIOD AND COSTUMES: Centerville, Connecticut, 1910: Sunday-best suits, floor-length dresses, many hats, spats, vests, and cloaks. Casual picnic dress, brief chorus-girl outfits. Conductor, band, and fireman uniforms. Gaudy "wild women" dresses. White frilly dress for Muriel, black stylized Beardsley ballet costumes. (Salome, dwarf, executioners, Herod, Richard and Muriel, sand girls, Lysistrata girls, Camille, clowns, women ringmasters, one-girl horses and Oscar Wilde).

CHOREOGRAPHY: Production numbers, soft shoe, ballet, and rowdy modern at the picnic.

LIGHTING AND SPECIAL EFFECTS: Fourth of July effects and external day and night lighting.

NOTES: The reviews for Take Me Along tended to compare it with the classic Ah, Wilderness! and questioned if it was a valid addition to theatre. Certainly if a group had just done Ah, Wilderness!, they wouldn't want to do Take Me Along. Anyone else should judge the show on its own merits. The show ties in nicely with the 4th of July.

TENDERLOIN

Jerry Bock (Music),
George Abbott, Jerome Weidman (Book),
Sheldon Harnick (Lyrics)
Opened March 17, 1960
216 Performances

BASED ON: Novel by Samuel Hopkins Adams

AGENT: Tams-Witmark

PUBLISHED TEXT: Random House, 1960

RECORDINGS: CAP WAO-1492

DIGEST OF PLOT: New York's meat-cutting district, the Tenderloin, becomes the target of a reformer. At first little heed is paid Reverend Brock. As he strengthens his position, his parishioners feel he should preach on the glory of God instead of voicing the wrath of the Tenderloin. In a daring incognito visit to Clark's, one of the more noted dens of sin, Brock uncovers names of responsible officers on the take. He uses his information to the ultimate destruction of the vice center. Even though he is successful in his mission, he is forced by his congregation to move on.

MUSICAL NUMBERS: "Bless This Land," "Little Old New York," "Dr. Brock," "Artificial Flowers,"

"What's in It for You?," "Reform," "Tommy, Tommy," "The Picture of Happiness," Dance, "Dear Friend," "The Army of the Just," "How the Money Changes Hands," "Good Clean Fun," "My Miss Mary," "My Gentle Young Johnny," "The Trial," "The Tenderloin Celebration."

INSTRUMENTATION: Violins (3), viola, cello, bass, alto sax (clar, flute, pic), Eb clar (Bb clar, bass clar, flute, alto flute), tenor sax (clar, flute, oboe, Eng. horn), bari sax (clar, bass clar, bassoon), horns I–II, trumpets I–II, trombone I, II, percussion, harp, guitar-banjo, piano-organ-celeste.

CASTING: 27 parts, 8 principals, featured dance duo. Reverend Brock, strong actor, legitimate voice not required. Tommy, actor, good baritone voice. Nita, strong voice desirable. Laura, sweet voice, good actress. Gertie and Margie, character broads who dance, lookers. Purdy and Lt. Schmidt, straight roles. Separate singing and dancing choruses—both work hard. Total cast, 40–60.

SCENES AND SETS: 2 acts, 24 scenes, 10 sets, 5 full stage, 2 partial sets, 1 scrim, 1 scenic drop, plus insert pieces. Scenes must change rapidly to help pick up the slack in the story line.

COURTESY OF HAROLD PRINCE

Maurice Evans as he appeared as Reverend Brock in Tenderloin.

ACT I
Scene 1: Limbo—Dark Stage.
Scene 2: Street Outside the Church.
Scene 3: Parish House.
Scene 4: Street in Front of 19th Precinct.

Scene 5: 19th Precinct Police Station.
Scene 6: Precinct Street.
Scene 7: Laura Crosbie's Fifth Avenue House.
Scene 8: Street in Front of Clark's.
Scene 9: Clark's, Popular Tenderloin Haunt.
Scene 10: Street in Front of Clark's.
Scene 11: A Beach.
Scene 12: Street in Front of Clark's.
Scene 13: Clark's, 11:00 P.M., in Full Swing.

ACT II
Scene 1: Central Park.
Scene 2: A Street.
Scene 3: Clark's.
Scene 4: The Trial.
Scene 5: Clark's.
Scene 6: Parish House.
Scene 7: Precinct Street.
Scene 8: The Courtroom.
Scene 9: A Street.
Scene 10: Parish House.
Epilogue.

PERIOD AND COSTUMES: New York, late 19th Century: suits, dresses, and beachwear of the time. Gaudy dresses and loud suits for the Tenderloin rounders.

CHOREOGRAPHY: Singing production numbers, suggestive modern dance, minor soft shoe.

LIGHTING AND SPECIAL EFFECTS: Tight lighting on opening. Multiple lighting setup for day, night, interiors, and exteriors. Original cast used special horse-riding effect in Central Park scene (horse bodies on wheels hidden behind wall surrounding the riding track).

NOTES: The show has a cumbersome book, but could be a good change-of-pace show for little-theatre groups with the right cutting and staging.

THE THREEPENNY OPERA

Kurt Weill (Music),
Bertolt Brecht with translation by Marc Blitzstein (Book, Lyrics)
Opened April 13, 1933 and March 10, 1954
12 Performances in 1933,
2,611 from 1954

BASED ON: *The Beggar's Opera* by John Gay

AGENT: Tams-Witmark

PUBLISHED TEXT: Grove Press, 1964 (Translation by Demond Vessy and Eric Bentley)

RECORDINGS: MGM E 3121

DIGEST OF PLOT: Mr. and Mrs. J. J. Peachum run a shop devising diguises for beggars to make their looks more pathetic and passersby more gener-

The beggar's disguise shop of Mr. and Mrs. J. J. Peachum as it appeared in the original 1933 production of The Threepenny Opera.

ous. Polly, their daughter, reportedly has been seen with Macheath (Mack the Knife), undisputed king of London's Soho underworld district. They strive to stop such meetings, but Polly and Mack are wed. The guest of honor is none other than the Commissioner of Police, Tiger Brown, an old Army buddy and important confidant in Mack's underworld dealings. In an attempt to dissolve the marriage, Mrs. Peachum hires Mack's old flame, Jenny, to betray him to the police. Tiger Brown gets a "leave-town" message to Macheath through Polly. Before Mack leaves he instructs Polly in the workings of his gang and puts her in charge. One of his major assets in hiding is Lucy Brown, daughter of Tiger and mistress of Newgate Prison. They fall in love and are bound to each other. At the bordello in Wapping, Jenny and Macheath are briefly reunited prior to his incarceration by the constable she has brought along. His capture and jailing at Newgate bring him all the closer to Lucy. During a visit by Polly he is forced to choose between his two wives and picks Lucy, who in turn manages to engineer

Macheath's escape. But he is recaptured and doomed to hang on Queen Victoria's Coronation Day. On the fateful day Peachum is preparing the beggars for their best take in years, but prior to taking up their stations they pass by Macheath's gallows to pay their last respects. Jenny is there with a final torch song. As Macheath is prepared for hanging, an old rogue friend, posing as a messenger from the Queen, arrives to announce a full pardon, so that her Coronation will not be marred. Once more Macheath is free to pursue his passion for life.

MUSICAL NUMBERS: "BALLAD OF MACK THE KNIFE," "Morning Anthem," "Instead-of Song," "The Bide-a-Wee in Soho," "Wedding Song," "Army Song," "Love Song," "Ballad of Dependency," "The World Is Mean," "Polly's Song," "Pirate Jenny," "Tango Ballad," "Ballad of the Easy Life," "Barbara Song," "Jealousy Duet," "How to Survive," "Useless Song," "Solomon Song," "Call from the Grave," "Death Message," "The Mounted Messenger."

INSTRUMENTATION: Clar (alto sax), clar (tenor sax), trumpets I–II, trombone, percussion, piano (harmonium-celeste), guitar (banjo, Hawaiian guitar), piano-conductor.

CASTING: 23 parts, 8 principals. Streetsinger, singer who narrates. Mr. and Mrs. Peachum, character actors who sing. Macheath (Mack the Knife), actor who sings, minor dancing. Polly Peachum, actress who sings. Jenny, torch singer, minor acting. Brown, straight role. Lucy, actress who sings. Beggars, henchmen, constables, etc. Total cast, 21–35.

SCENES AND SETS: Prologue, 3 acts, 8 scenes, 2 interludes, 5 full stage sets, 1 scene drop.

ACT I

Prologue: A Street.
Scene 1: Peachum's Beggars' Outfit Shop.
Scene 2: An Empty Stable.
Scene 3: Peachum's Shop.

ACT II
Scene 1: The Stable.
Interlude: A Street.
Scene 2: A Brothel in Wapping.
Scene 3: Newgate Prison.

ACT III
Scene 1: Peachum's Shop.
Interlude: A Street.
Scene 2: Newgate Prison Death Cell.

PERIOD AND COSTUMES: 19th Century London: wretched beggar costumes and makeup, dark suits, print dresses with tie belts, torch singer's costume, dress suits, top hats, cloaks, garish harlot dresses, Polly's wedding dress, hats, coats, prison uniform, constable uniform.

CHOREOGRAPHY: Negligible, one minor dance with harlots at Wapping.

LIGHTING AND SPECIAL EFFECTS: Dramatic and eerie lighting enhance the production. Stable is transformed into plush room for wedding. Hurdy-gurdy.

NOTES: Show is highly stylized; typically Brecht. A number of signboards are used to precisely identify each scene. Songs are used to "illuminate" the character or scene rather than being part of the show's construction (even though some songs do advance the plot).

THE UNSINKABLE MOLLY BROWN

Meredith Willson (Music, Lyrics),
Richard Morris (Book)
Opened Nov. 3, 1960
533 Performances

BASED ON: Original

AGENT: Music Theatre

PUBLISHED TEXT: Putnam, 1961; *Theatre Arts*, February, 1963

RECORDINGS: CAP W(SW)-2152
MGM (S)-4232ST(F)

DIGEST OF PLOT: Molly Brown rises from a ragamuffin in a tumbledown shanty to become an international heroine. Upon leaving her Irish father's side she storms the Colorado countryside in search of money and success. In her travels she meets and later marries Leadville Johnny Brown who soon discovers one of the largest silver mines in the United States. Now rich, Molly tries to besiege the Denver social register. Set back in her attempts, she decides that she and Johnny need the cultures of Europe. In Europe, Molly thrives on her cultural opportunities. However, Johnny feels out of place and dreams only of the pleasures of Colorado. Eventually even his unbounding love for his wife is not enough to keep him in Europe and he persuades Molly that they must return home. Molly accepts but invites several of her royal friends to come socialize with her in Denver. Her dreams of leadership of the Denver 400 soon fade as her royal coming-out party is turned into a donnybrook by some of Johnny's friends. Ultimately defeated, Molly returns to Europe, leaving Johnny behind. After achieving social boredom in a lonely year with royal society, she sails for home on the ill-fated *Titanic*. When the ship is destroyed at sea, Molly leads a lifeboat of survivors to safety—a superhuman feat inspired by her longing to return home to Johnny. Her heroism wins the admiration of the society that had spurned her.

MUSICAL NUMBERS: "I AIN'T DOWN YET," "Belly Up to the Bar, Boys," Dance, "I've A'ready Started In," "I'll Never Say No," "My Own Brass Bed," "The Denver Police," "Beautiful People of Denver," "Are You Sure?," "Happy Birthday, Mrs. J. J. Brown," "Bon Jour," "If I Knew," "Chick-a-pen," "Keep A-Hoppin'," Leadville Johnny Brown (Soliloquy), "Up Where the People Are," "Dolce Far Niente," "Colorado, My Home."

INSTRUMENTATION: Violin, cello, bass, clar (E♭ clar double-lined for B♭), pic (flute, alto flute), clar, clar (bass clar), bari sax (clar), trumpet I–II, III, trombone I, II, horns I, II, III, percussion, piano-conductor.

CASTING: 38 parts, 6 principals, 3 featured male dancers. Molly, carries show with tour de force performance, sings and dances. Johnny, good baritone voice a must, minor dance. Shamus Tobin and Christmas Morgan, hard-drinking character men who sing and dance. Prince DeLong, charming actor, good voice helps. Princess DeLong, Grand Duchess, other royalty, Robert, Monsignor Ryan, 3

COURTESY OF DRAMATICS MAGAZINE

Harve Presnell and Tammy Grimes (Johnny and Molly, center) as old miner pals turn Molly's royal coming-out party into a free-for-all, in The Unsinkable Molly Brown.

Tobin brothers, good-sized supporting roles with some song and dance. Mrs. McGlone, straight heavy role. Total cast, 40–60.

SCENES AND SETS: 2 acts, 20 scenes, 11 full stage sets, 3 scene drops.

ACT I
Scene 1: Exterior of the Tobin Shack, Hannibal, Mo. Turn of Century.
Scene 2: Road by the Tobin Shack.
Scene 3: The Saddle Rock Saloon, Leadville, Colorado.
Scene 4: Street in Front of the Saddle Rock.
Scene 5: Johnny's Log Cabin.
Scene 6: The Same.

Scene 7: Pennsylvania Avenue, Denver, Col.
Scene 8: Terrace of Mrs. McGlone's Denver Mansion.
Scene 9: Pennsylvania Avenue.
Scene 10: Red Parlor of the Browns' Denver Mansion.

Act II
Scene 1: The Browns' Paris Salon.
Scene 2: Upper Hallway of the Browns' Denver Mansion.
Scene 3: The Red Parlor.
Scene 4: Same.
Scene 5: Street in Front of the Saddle Rock.
Scene 6: A Monte Carlo Club—1912.
Scene 7: Outside the Club.

Scene 8: The Mid-Atlantic. Shortly After 2:30 A.M., April 15, 1912.
Scene 9: Upper Hallway, Brown Home.
Scene 10: The Rockies.

COURTESY OF DRAMATICS MAGAZINE

Molly and Johnny dream of the riches the money from his silver strike will buy.

PERIOD AND COSTUMES: The turn of the century to 1912: backwoods rag dress, overalls, shirts, boots, miners' shirts and overalls, gaudy prostitute dresses, society day and evening dress (both U.S. and European), formal wear, priests' cassocks, sheriff, butler, bartender, servant, page, maitre d', and sailor uniforms.

CHOREOGRAPHY: Barroom hoedown. Denver police (close-up, fast clog number), modern ballet, knock-down, drag-out brawl.

LIGHTING AND SPECIAL EFFECTS: Dramatic lighting required. Sinking of *Titanic*. Lifeboat tossing on the ocean waves.

NOTES: *Molly Brown* is a spirited show with the right Molly. Second act tends to drag. Tight direction required throughout.

WALKING HAPPY

James Van Heusen (Music),
Roger O. Hirson, Ketti Frings (Book),
Sammy Cahn (Lyrics)
Opened Nov. 26, 1966
161 Performances

BASED ON: *Hobson's Choice* by Harold Brighouse

AGENT: Samuel French

PUBLISHED TEXT: Samuel French 1967 (P)

RECORDINGS: CAP-VAS 2631

DIGEST OF PLOT: Maggie Hobson realizes that her father intends marriage for her two younger sisters, but plans for her to stay on to run his boot shop and cook his meals—leaving him free to sit in the Moonrakers pub. Not to be trod upon, the commanding Maggie tells her timid master bootmaker, Will Mossop, that they will be married and open their own boot shop. Her sisters, Alice and Vicki, take over the shop. Hobson would like to get them married off, but is confounded by their choice of husbands—the sons of George Beenstock, grain merchant and head of the temperance league. He's a constant thorn to Hobson and his drinking friends. Maggie finds out Will is already engaged but manages to convince the sibling girl that he would be better off with her. Her tact is different with Mrs. Hepworth, a wealthy customer whom Maggie gets to finance the new shop. Will is also finding it easy to adjust. He hangs out his shop sign and begins striking out on his own. He is even becoming attracted to Maggie. Meanwhile Hobson has agreed to let the other daughters marry, but is aghast to learn that Beenstock wants a dowry of £250 each. The girls turn to Maggie for help. Maggie has a plan and it works to perfection. They are all together at the new shop celebrating their victory and Maggie and Will's marriage when Hobson arrives. He wants Maggie and Will to come back, but is more concerned about the lawsuits Maggie's plan has brought him. She, of course, has all the solutions waiting, and the business is quickly culminated—making Will a full partner in Hobson's. Will and Maggie are suddenly alone on their wedding night. Maggie can no longer tell Will what to do—realizing that marriage is an *equal* partnership. She tries to leave, ever so reluctantly. Will will have none of it. He tells her she got him into this thing, he likes it, and that she had better get used to the kind of man she wished all along he could be.

MUSICAL NUMBERS: "Think of Something Else," "Where Was I?," "How D'ya Talk to a Girl?," "Clog and Grog," "If I Be Your Best Chance," "A Joyful Thing," "What Makes It Happen?," "Use Your Noggin," "You're Right, You're Right," "I'll Make a Man of the Man," "WALKING HAPPY," "I Don't Think I'm in Love," "Such a Sociable Sort," "It Might as Well Be Her," "People Who Are Nice."

INSTRUMENTATION: Violin, viola, cello, bass, pic, flute, oboe, clar, bass sax, horns, trumpet I–II, trombone I, II, III, percussion, guitar, harp.

CASTING: 23 parts, 4 principals, 6 supporting roles. Hobson, character actor who sings. Beenstock, actor who sings. Will, dancing actor who sings. Maggie, good domineering actress, legit voice. Tubby, character man, sings. Vicki and Alice, sing, minor dance. Total cast, 30–45.

SCENES AND SETS: 2 acts, 17 scenes, 5 full stage sets, 2 partial stage sets, 1 elevator platform from orchestra pit to stage level.

ACT I
Scene 1: Moonrakers Pub.
Scene 2: Hobson's Bootery.
Scene 3: Cellar of Bootery.
Scene 4: Moonrakers.
Scene 5: The Park.
Scene 6: Exterior Street—Poor Section of Salford.
Scene 7: An Alley.
Scene 8: Hobson's Bootery.

ACT II
Scene 1: Mrs. Hepworth's Sitting Room.
Scene 2: A Cellar.
Scene 3: Flat Iron Market.
Scene 4: Will and Maggie's Cellar.
Scene 5: Exterior of Moonrakers.
Scene 6: Exterior of Beenstock's Corn Warehouse.
Scene 7: Hobson's Bootery.
Scene 8: Beenstock's Grain Elevator.
Scene 9: Mossop Bootery.

PERIOD AND COSTUMES: 1880: suits, vests, hats, dresses, high-button shoes and boots, peasant versions of similar clothes, footman uniform, Joker-like devil costumes (in shades of purple and black), 2 snake costumes, pajamas.

CHOREOGRAPHY: Modern ballet, clog dance (tap with wood sole shoes), soft shoe solo that builds to "Walking Happy" production number, barrel dance.

LIGHTING AND SPECIAL EFFECTS: General lighting would do for all except devil scene (strobe light was used for this in original, but not necessary), flash paper and other effects for devil scenes.

NOTES: *Walking Happy* was another of the rare shows to suffer a cumbersome set. The three major sets were all on the same slow-moving turntable, causing constant drag that the show's book cannot stand. The show merely dramatizes Hobson's Choice ("In any given situation, the necessity to accept whatever is offered or go without. Where to elect is but one. 'Tis Hobson's choice—take that or none."—Thomas Ward, England's Reformation, 1638). That premise doesn't provide 2 1/2 hours of entertainment, and the score, although quite serviceable, could use more numbers of the magnitude of the title song. Tightening and cutting, a workable set, and good direction, plus an exceptional Will Mossop could add up to a memorable evening.

WEST SIDE STORY

Leonard Berstein (Music),
Arthur Laurents (Book),
Stephen Sondheim (Lyrics)
Opened Sept. 26, 1957
732 Performances

BASED ON: Conception of Jerome Robbins

AGENT: Music Theatre

PUBLISHED TEXT: Random House, 1958; *Theatre Arts,* October, 1959; Dell, 1965 (P)

RECORDINGS: COL OL-5230
COL OL-2001
COL OL-5670(F)
COL OL-2070(F)

DIGEST OF PLOT: Tensions are rising between the American-born Jets and Puerto Rican Sharks, street gangs. Jets leader Riff has arranged to challenge for a rumble. He tries to talk Tony, co-founder of the Jets, into attending a drugstore war council with him. Tony has matured beyond gang activities but agrees to attend the dance at the gym where the first confrontation will take place. There he falls in love with Maria, the sister of Sharks leader Bernardo. Tony and Maria are completely oblivious as the rival couples vent their hatreds in dance. Later Tony leaves Maria at her fire escape with the promise to meet her the following afternoon at the dress shop where she and Bernardo's girl friend Anita work. Meanwhile, the war council has convened at Doc's drugstore to decide the time, place, and weapons for the rumble. Tony comes to the meeting to make sure it will be a fair fight. The gangs agree it will be hand-to-hand combat between the best man of each gang. Tony and Maria meet the next afternoon to confirm their impossible love in a mock wedding ceremony. Maria asks him to call off the fight between the gangs. Tony goes to the rumble, where Bernardo accuses him of cutting in on Chino, second in command of the Sharks, who is to be engaged to Maria. Suddenly switchblades are drawn. Riff and Bernardo are stalking each other. Tony tries to break it up, but is restrained. Riff is distracted and is stabbed with Bernardo's knife. Everyone is stunned as Tony removes the blade from the dead Riff and stabs Bernardo in blind revenge. The unwanted terrors erupt into a full-fledged gang war until the police arrive. Maria awaits Tony believing all is well until Chino breaks in and screams that her lover has killed her brother. He grabs a gun and leaves to hunt Tony. Tony has entered Maria's room through the window and tries to explain to the agonized Maria. They have been drained of everything but their love. They cling to each other for the strength to run away together. Anita interrupts to break the news. Maria stalls her until Tony slips out the fire escape to meet Maria later at Doc's. Anita realizes that Tony has been there and chides Maria for letting him near her. Maria confesses her undeniable love and prays to salvage something from the disastrous turn of events. The police arrive to question Maria, and Anita reluctantly agrees to convey the reason for Maria's delay. When she arrives at Doc's she is savagely tormented by the members of the Jets. Out of spite she tells them that Chino has shot Maria rather than let her go to Tony. Doc relays the message to Tony who bolts from his basement hiding place to find her. Maria is on her way to him, but Chino's gun has found its mark, and Tony dies in her arms. This final senseless killing reaches the souls of all the gang members. Rather than let the police touch Tony's body, they join together to carry it to the waiting ambulance.

MUSICAL NUMBERS: Prologue (Dance), "Jet Song," "Something's Coming," The Dance at the Gym, "MARIA," "TONIGHT," "America," "Cool," "One Hand, One Heart," "The Rumble," "I FEEL PRETTY," "Somewhere," "Gee, Officer Krupke," "A Boy Like That," "I Have a Love," the Taunting.

Larry Kert (Tony) *and Leila Martin* (Maria) *in the national company of* West Side Story.

INSTRUMENTATION: Violin I, II, cello, bass, pic (flute, alto sax, clar), E♭ clar (B♭ clar), bass clar (tenor sax, clar, oboe, Eng. horn), clar (flute, pic, bass sax), bassoon, trumpet I–II, III, trombone I–II, percussion, guitar, piano, piano-conductor. (Modified version available.)

CASTING: 39 parts, 6 principals, 9 strong supporting roles. All principals except Tony, Maria, and adults are accomplished dancers (some could be just singers and fake in the background). All principals also sing and act. Adults, all straight roles.

Tony and Maria, good singer-actors who do minor dancing. Total cast, 39–50.

SCENES AND SETS: Prologue, 2 acts, 15 scenes, 5 full stage sets (including 4 drops), 4 partial stage sets, 1 fence of doors fly in, 2 scene drops, one batten of unfurling 3″-wide ribbons (optional). The action takes place on the West Side of New York City during the last days of summer.

ACT I
Prologue: The Months Before.
5:00 P.M. The Street.
5:30 P.M. A Backyard.
6:00 P.M. The Bridal Shop.
10:00 P.M. The Gym.
11:00 P.M. A Back Alley.
Midnight. The Drugstore.
The Next Day
5:30 P.M. The Bridal Shop.
6:00 to 9:00 P.M. The Neighborhood.
9:00 P.M. Under the Highway.

ACT II
9:15 P.M. The Bedroom.
10:00 P.M. Another Alley.
11:30 P.M. The Bedroom.
11:40 P.M. The Drugstore.
11:50 P.M. The Cellar.
Midnight. The Street.

PERIOD AND COSTUMES: The present (1955): dungarees, muscle shirts, monogrammed jackets (Jets and Sharks) hats, sneakers, nonconformist suits, Spanish-influenced ruffled dresses, mini dresses, wedding veil, formal wear, nightgown, police uniform.

CHOREOGRAPHY: Modern,   modern   ballet, blues, jazz, march, comedy patter number, rumble and ballet version of same.

LIGHTING AND SPECIAL EFFECTS: Dramatic lighting required. Police raid effects.

NOTES: The original idea for this masterpiece was conceived early in 1949. It was to be an up-to-date version of *Romeo and Juliet,* with the lovers played by a Jewish girl and an Italian Catholic boy living on the Lower East Side of Manhattan. Work on the then titled "East Side Story" was abandoned soon after its conception. Late in 1954 work was resumed, which resulted in *West Side Story.*

It is probably the only musical for which the dances were "written" first. It obviously requires several exceptional dancers. This can be accomplished by advanced dance rehearsals. Prior dance training is preferred, although several groups with proper drive have done great productions. A great choreographer is essential.

WHERE'S CHARLEY?

Frank Loesser (Music, Lyrics),
George Abbott (Book)

The "New Ashmolean Marching Society and Students' Conservatory Band" scene from Where's Charley?

Opened Oct. 11, 1948
792 Performances

BASED ON: *Charley's Aunt* by Brandon Thomas

AGENT: Music Theatre

PUBLISHED TEXT: Manuscript Only

RECORDINGS: Monmouth-Evergreen S7029 (Reissue of British original cast recording. American cast was never recorded.)

DIGEST OF PLOT: Soon-to-be-graduated Jack Chesney and his roommate at Oxford, Charley Wykeham, have arranged a luncheon with their intendeds, Kitty Verdun and Amy Spettigue. Charley's aunt, the recently widowed Donna Lucia d'Alvadorez whom Charley has never seen, is arriving from Brazil to be introduced and chaperone the gathering. The girls arrive, but leave when they dis- cover Donna Lucia has not yet arrived. Unexpectedly, Jack's father, Sir Francis, arrives to disclose the family's finances are a bit shaky. Jack asks his father to lunch as an entree to the wealthy Donna Lucia. When the boys learn that she will be delayed, Jack persuades Charley to use his female theatrical costume to pose as his own aunt. None too soon, as the girls return and are taken with Charley's disguised version of his aunt. Mr. Spettigue, Amy's uncle and Kitty's guardian, prematurely returns from a business engagement to find the girls missing. He traces them to the boys' quarters, but the disguised Charley turns him away. However, Spettigue returns and is invited to stay—there's no other choice. Only his manners prevent him from loathing the costumed Charley—that is, until he learns that Donna Lucia is a millionairess. Jack finds a moment to get Kitty alone and proposes. Soon confounded by the elusive Donna Lucia, Spettigue threatens to leave and take the girls to Scotland. Charley convinces him that his aunt is overwhelmed by his attentions and makes a mad dash for his aunt's wardrobe. Once again, disguised Charley meets Sir Francis, who proposes. Charley turns him down and proceeds to lead

Spettigue a merry chase. Relieved at his rejection, Sir Francis encounters a delightful old friend, the real Donna Lucia. She realizes something is up, but plays along by posing as a Mrs. Beverly-Smythe. It's teatime. Donna Lucia uses the occasion to put the pressure on her imposter, but Charley muddles through gallantly. Charley is forced to show up for his graduation picture. By now Amy is questioning his lack of attention. He reassures her of his love and asks her to trust him for just a few more hours while he helps his aunt clear the way with Spettigue. Amy tells Charley that his aunt must meet her and Kitty at the ladies' dressing room soon because the old man has promised trouble if he doesn't get prompt action. It's a wild time for Charley until he learns the girls want Donna Lucia to get Spettigue's permission to marry Jack and Charley in writing. To do so Charley agrees to announce Donna's proposal to Spettigue that evening at the Red Rose Cotillion in return for the letter of consent. Spettigue finally notices the amazing family resemblance between Donna and Charley. He demands to see Donna—then Charley—then Donna—then Charley, but Jack accidently steps on Donna's skirt, and as Charley dashes off, his lower disguise remains. Spettigue is irate and demands his letter back. However, the real Donna Lucia steps forward and grabs the letter announcing that it has been delivered as addressed—to Donna Lucia d'Alvadorez. The weddings will take place. Perhaps even a third, as Donna Lucia and Sir Francis embrace.

MUSICAL NUMBERS: "The Years Before Us," "Better Get Out of Here," "THE NEW ASHMOLEAN MARCHING SOCIETY AND STUDENTS' CONSERVATORY BAND," "MY DARLING, MY DARLING," "Make a Miracle," "Serenade with Asides," "Lovelier Than Ever," "The Woman in His Room," "Pernambuco," "Where's Charley?," "ONCE IN LOVE WITH AMY," "The Gossips," "At the Red Rose Cotillion."

INSTRUMENTATION: Violin A, B, C, viola, cello, bass, flute (pic), clar I, II, III, bassoon, trumpet I–II, III, trombone, horn, percussion, piano-conductor.

CASTING: 16 parts, 7 principals. Charley, comic actor who sings and dances, carries show. Jack, good singer who acts, minor dance. Amy, actress who sings and dances. Kitty, good singer who acts. Sir Francis, mostly straight role, minor singing, 1 number. Mr. Spettigue, good character man who sings (or talks) 1 number. Donna Lucia, trained voice, good actress. Separate singing and dancing choruses. Total cast, 40–55.

SCENES AND SETS: 2 acts, 9 scenes, 4 full stage sets, 3 scene drops.

ACT I
Scene 1: A Room at Oxford University.
Scene 2: A Street.
Scene 3: The Garden.
Scene 4: Where the Nuts Come From!

ACT II
Scene 1: The Garden.
Scene 2: A Street.
Scene 3: Where the Ladies Go.
Scene 4: A Garden Path.
Scene 5: The Ballroom.

PERIOD AND COSTUMES: 1892: day and evening dresses and suits, Charley's Aunt disguise, uniforms for band, manservant and maid, Spanish-influenced South American work and dress clothes (stylized), graduation robes, Spanish-influenced dresses for Donna Lucia, stringed corsets and assorted female undergarments.

CHOREOGRAPHY: Dance solos, tap, couples numbers, modern ballet, one tells story of Donna Lucia's arrival in Brazil, parade.

LIGHTING AND SPECIAL EFFECTS: Mostly general lighting.

NOTES: *Charley's Aunt* has long been a classic of true burlesque comedy. The musical version sticks close to the play and manages to add several hit songs. Some of Charley's dance solos could be cut or trimmed, as these were largely inserted to display the dancing talents of the star who played the title role.

WILDCAT

Cy Coleman (Music),
N. Richard Nash (Book),
Carolyn Leigh (Lyrics)
Opened Dec. 16, 1960
168 Performances

BASED ON: Original

AGENT: Tams-Witmark

PUBLISHED TEXT: Manuscript Only

RECORDINGS: RCA LOC-1060

DIGEST OF PLOT: Wildcat "Wildy" Jackson and sister Janie land in oil-rich Centavo City with dreams of a big strike—and little else in the way of capital or know-how. By accident she meets Joe Dynamite, the most successful crew foreman in the territory. He is off-balanced by her rugged charm and agrees to be her foreman if she can prove ownership to her claimed land and hire a crew. All Wildy needs now is the land and crew. She finds ten acres owned by a wiry, woman-hating old hermit prospector named Sookie. She takes his measure and corrals a crew at the same time. When she presents the package to Joe he claims there isn't a chance of oil on the property and furthermore he has had enough of Wildy's dreams and lies. Meanwhile, Joe's sidekick, Hank, has fallen for the lame Janie and discovers she's the real reason Wildy wants to strike oil. Wildy tries a more direct, all-woman approach but is still rejected. Infuriated she tells the sheriff that Joe is a wanted man and later manages to get him released into her custody. The search for black gold is under way. That is, until Joe learns that it was Wildy who tipped off the sheriff. Joe's anger is not to be restrained. He tells the crew they are digging a dry well. Wildy is left stranded. In desperation she throws Joe's dynamite into the well. Fortunately he returns just in time to clear her from the blast area. Joe confesses his love just as the explosion goes off bringing a Texas-size gusher.

MUSICAL NUMBERS: "I Hear," "HEY LOOK ME OVER," "Wildcat," "You've Come Home," "That's What I Want for Janie," "What Takes My Fancy," "You're a Liar," "One Day We Dance," "GIVE A LITTLE WHISTLE AND I'LL BE THERE," "Tall Hope," "Tippy Tippy Toes," "El Sombrero," "Corduroy Road."

INSTRUMENTATION: Violin (3) A, B, C, D, cello A, B, C, bass, alto sax (clar, bass clar, pic, flute, alto flute), alto sax (Eb clar, Bb clar, bass clar, flute, pic, bass sax), tenor sax (clar, flute, pic), tenor sax (clar, oboe, Eng. horn), bari sax (clar, flute, pic, bassoon), horn, trumpets I-II, III, trombone I, II, III, percussion I-II, guitar-banjo (mandolin), piano-conductor.

CASTING: 19 parts, 9 principals. Wildcat, comedienne lead who carries show, sings and dances. Joe, actor with powerful singing voice. Sookie, young comic character actor to do old man part, sings and dances. Countess, straight role. Janie, mostly straight role, but sings 2 duets. Sheriff Sam, straight role. Hank, Matt, Corky, Oney, Tatoo, Cisco, crew members who sing and dance. Seperate singing and dancing choruses (15 dancers, 8 singers). Strong choral work. Total cast, 35-50.

SCENES AND SETS: 2 acts, 19 scenes, 4 full stage sets, 3 drops, 1 partial stage set, Joe Dynamite's wagon, Stutz-Bearcat-type auto, working oil derrick. Centavo City, a boarder town.

ACT I
Scene 1: A Street.
Scene 2: A Prairie.
Scene 3: A Street.
Scene 4: The Plaza.
Scene 5: Countess' Sitting Room.
Scene 6: Sookie's House.
Scene 7: The Prairie.
Scene 8: The Street.
Scene 9: The Plaza.
Scene 10: The Jail.
Scene 11: Sookie's Hill.

ACT II
Scene 1: Countess' Sitting Room.
Scene 2: On Way to the Fiesta.
Scene 3: The Plaza.
Scene 4: The Street.

Scene 5: Sookie's House.
Scene 6: Sookie's Hill.
Scene 7: Outside Miguel's Cantina.
Scene 8: Sookie's Hill.

PERIOD AND COSTUMES: 1912: blue jeans, flannel shirts, vests, dresses, suits, ponchos, sombreros, fandango dresses, evening dresses, female disguises, dusty coverall and shirt for Sookie, ornate belts, drillers' safety shoes.

CHOREOGRAPHY: Opening parade, modern, "El Sombrero" stylized number, soft shoe.

LIGHTING AND SPECIAL EFFECTS: Some dramatic lighting required. Shooting effects, oil well brings in gusher (black confetti).

NOTES: Show closed prematurely when star Lucille Ball was forced to withdraw because of illness. Story lacks depth, but can produce an enjoyable evening with the right female lead. Strong dancers' show.

WISH YOU WERE HERE

Harold Rome (Music, Lyrics),
Arthur Kober, Joshua Logan (Book)
Opened June 25, 1952
598 Performances

BASED ON: *Having a Wonderful Time* by Arthur Kober

AGENT: Music Theatre

PUBLISHED TEXT: Manuscript Only

RECORDINGS: RCA LOC-1108

DIGEST OF PLOT: Teddy Stern joins friend Fay Fromkin at Camp Karefree for two weeks of fun and relaxation—to forget about her approaching marriage to rich and helpful Herman Fabricant. Anti-Herman Fay removes Teddy's engagement ring and introduces her friends—and special friend, Itchy Flexner, the camp social director. Pinky Harris, the camp's most successful playboy, does the honors himself, but Teddy's thoughts are of her engagement. Meanwhile, the camp's new athletic director, Harry "Muscles" Green, arrives. Fay is impressed and changes partners. Back at the waiter's locker room, camp owner Lou Kandel is laying down the law. Mix and mingle with the unattached girls or get fined. Chick Miller can afford neither. He's saving all his money for his college tuition. Later, Chick persuades Teddy to be his partner so he won't get fined. When they discover that they both want to avoid a lasting relationship, they make a deal to just have fun together. Days later Muscles has instituted so many strenuous activities that every one is too pooped for the social events. To retaliate, Itchy devises a restful "By Candlelight Evening" with Fay as Queen. There's too much candlelight and the social hall burns. Itchy is demoted to boatboy, and Muscles is named director of activities. By now Chick and Teddy are hopelessly in love. Chick proposes, and Teddy reveals the truth. Chick is hurt and angered. Even though Teddy loves him she feels indebted to Herman and feels Chick could be more understanding. At this turn of events, Teddy decides to enter Pinky's poolside bathing beauty contest, but when Pinky forceably kisses Teddy, Chick knocks him into the pool—and the battle is on. To make matters worse Kandel falls in the pool trying to bail Pinky out. Chick grabs the girl who's been throwing herself at him and heads for the woods. Teddy is in tears, but Pinky is comforting her. That night at a lakeside campfire cookout everybody patches up their differences. A thunderstorm breaks out and Pinky manages to get Teddy to his cabin to pick up her prize for winning the bathing suit competition. His seduction is skilled, but Teddy passes out. Herman returns the next morning amid wild goings on. With the thunderstorm, not all the boys made it back to the boys' side nor the girls to the girls' side. Even though he learns Teddy spent the night in Pinky's bed, the marriage is still on. But Muscles got his sleep and is ready for the big basketball game. Teddy and Itchy bolster each other for unhappy events—Itchy, the game against Muscles; and Teddy's leaving Chick behind. When Itchy makes a mess of Muscles' big game, he flattens him. Just the move Fay needed to switch back to Itchy. Chick watches Teddy drive off with Herman, only to return a few minutes later devoid of her ring.

MUSICAL NUMBERS: "Camp Karefree," "There's Nothing Nicer Than People," "Social Director," "Shopping Around," "Bright College Days," "Mix and Mingle," "Could Be," "Tripping the Light Fantastic," "WHERE DID THE NIGHT GO?," "Certain Individuals," "They Won't Know Me," "Summer Afternoon," "Don Jose," "Everybody Love Everybody," "WISH YOU WERE HERE," "Relax," "Flattery."

INSTRUMENTATION: Violin A, B, C, viola, cello, bass, alto sax (flute, pic, clar), alto sax (clar, bari sax, bass clar), tenor sax (oboe, clar, Eng. horn), tenor sax (clar, flute), bari sax (alto sax, bass clar), trumpet I–II, III, trombone I, II, horn, percussion, harp, piano-conductor.

CASTING: 25 parts, 8 principals. Teddy and Chick, romantic leads who act, sing, and dance. Fay, semi-comic blonde bombshell who sings and dances. Itchy, comic character man, good dancer who sings. Muscles, weight lifter type able to act a light heavy, no singing or dancing. Herman Fabricant and Lou Kandel, character parts. Three male dancing partners for Fay. Several good chorus dancers. Strong choral work for separate singing chorus. Good swimmers and divers required if pool is used. Total cast, 47–60.

SCENES AND SETS: 2 acts, 15 scenes, 7 full stage sets, 3 fly-in partial stage sets with 2 scenic drops. Camp Karefree, a summer camp for adults, "where friendships are formed to last a whole life-time through," is located in the heart of Vacationland. It could be the Berkshires, the Adirondacks, the Poconos, the White Mountains—or even the Catskills.

ACT I
Scene 1: Outside Teddy's Cabin.
Scene 2: Locker Room.
Scene 3: Porch of Social Hall.
Scene 4: Social Hall.
Scene 5: Path Through the Woods.
Scene 6: Athletic Field.
Scene 7: Path Through the Woods.
Scene 8: Eagle Rock.
Scene 9: The Boat House.
Scene 10: The Lake Front.

ACT II
Scene 1: The Campfire.
Scene 2: Path Through the Woods.
Scene 3: Pinky's Cabin.
Scene 4: Porch of Social Hall.
Scene 5: Basketball Court.

PERIOD AND COSTUMES: Present (see Notes): casual traveling clothes, waiter uniforms, assorted bathing suits, leopard-skin swimming trunks, bikinis, etc., summer evening dresses and dinner jackets, blue jeans, slacks, Oriental dressing gown, play suits, sweat suits, pajamas, sweaters, Queen Candlelight gown, red Dan Cupid diaper, wings, and quiver of arrows, bathing beauty suits and sashes, sombrero, blanket, bathrobes, raincoats, Paris "original" evening gown.

CHOREOGRAPHY: Pantomime, male dance team to back up Fay, modern, "whistle dance," waltz, Charleston, lindy, rumba, fast boogie, slow boogie (if show is updated, lastest dance fads can be inserted, but would require a major musical adjustment), acrobatics, swimming and diving exhibition, stop-action freezes, rhythm number (be-bop), basketball game dance.

LIGHTING AND SPECIAL EFFECTS: Rear projection silhouettes, burning social hall in distance, campfire, P.A. system on stage, continuous rainstorm (hose sprinkling against windows). Some indoor, but mostly day and night dramatic lighting required throughout. Twinkling stars and moonlight.

NOTES: Wish You Were Here substituted a spectacular production for big-name stars and could be a major undertaking if done as the original. The authors, realizing this problem, have written an alternate ending to the first act eliminating the need for an onstage swimming pool. They have also provided ideas for simplifying other sets. The topical book is somewhat dated and should probably be done as a period piece to show the Now generation what it was like when young singles enjoyed camp activities and a less sophisticated way of getting to know one another. Most of the musical numbers are too long and reprised too often. One way every group could do this show as the Broadway production is by building

The backyard scene from Wonderful Town *in which another drama of Greenwich Village of the 1930's unfolds.*

the temporary pool in the orchestra pit or front stage area and using a miked orchestra onstage.

WONDERFUL TOWN

Leonard Bernstein (Music),
Joseph Fields, Jerome Chodorov (Book),
Betty Comden, Adolph Green (Lyrics)

Opened Feb. 25, 1953
559 Performances

BASED ON: *My Sister Eileen* by Joseph Fields, Jerome Chodorov and stories by Ruth McKenney

AGENT: Tams-Witmark

PUBLISHED TEXT: Random House, 1953

RECORDINGS: DEC (7)-9010

DIGEST OF PLOT: Two Ohio girls, Ruth and Eileen Sherwood, arrive in New York City to seek fame and fortune. Landing in the heart of Greenwich Village, they meet Appopolous, a persuasive land-lord-artist, who talks them into renting a one-room basement apartment. Upon payment of their first month's rent, they rapidly discover a rash of curious characters and events surrounding their less-than-private quarters. Eileen quickly assembles friends who she hopes will help her theatrical aspirations and her sister to become a noted writer. On her own, Ruth meets Bob Baker, a magazine editor who becomes interested in her work, but cools when she insults him. In an attempt to prove herself, she jumps at an assignment to cover the landing of the Brazilian Navy, which one of Eileen's boy friends tells her about in order to get Eileen alone. The language barrier makes interviewing the cadets difficult, but she finds that they have a mutual understanding in the "conga." Mass "conga" lines dancing through the streets of New York get out of hand, and in the mixup Eileen lands in jail. The publicity proves to be just what the girls needed. Ruth's coverage of the story makes her a success, and the now-famous Eileen becomes a singer-actress in demand.

MUSICAL NUMBERS: "Christopher Street," "OHIO," "Conquering New York," "One Hundred Easy Ways," "What a Waste," "Never Felt This Way Before," "Pass the Football," "Conversation Piece," "A Quiet Girl," "Conga," "My Darlin' Eileen," "Swing!," "IT'S LOVE," "Wrong Note Rag."

INSTRUMENTATION: Violins A–C (2), B–D, viola, cello, bass, clar (alto sax), clar (tenor sax), clar (bass clar, tenor sax), clar (bari sax), trumpets I–II, III, trombone I, II, percussion, piano.

CASTING: 36 parts, 8 principals. Ruth, comic actress who sings and does conga. Eileen, perky, cute, and charming actress with excellent voice that blends with Ruth's. Baker, actor who sings, no dance. Appopolous, good character man. Wreck, muscle man who sings. Frank, deadpan actor, bumbles, straight role. Chick Clark, shady operator, and Lonigan, neighborhood cop, straight roles. Five policemen, blending voices for "My Darlin' Eileen" number. Separate singing and dancing choruses, 16 each. Total cast, 40–56.

SCENES AND SETS: 2 acts, 13 scenes, 5 full stage sets, 2 partial stage sets, 1 scene drop.

ACT I
Scene 1: Christopher Street.
Scene 2: The Studio.
Scene 3: The Street.
Scene 4: Baker's Office.
Scene 5: The Street.
Scene 6: The Backyard.
Scene 7: The Navy Yard.
Scene 8: The Backyard.

ACT II
Scene 1: The Jail.
Scene 2: The Street.
Scene 3: The Studio.
Scene 4: Street in Front of Vortex.
Scene 5: The Vortex.

PERIOD AND COSTUMES: 1935, New York's Greenwich Village: guide uniform, Bohemian dress for painters, sculptors, actors, etc., tourists in natty Midwestern suits and dresses. Gaudy satin dress. Police uniforms, nightgowns, zoot suit, editor's vested suits, sweat suit, Ruth's job interview dress, admiral and shore patrol uniforms. Ice cream jacket, white or light cream suit for Frank, tux, light-up sign dress for Ruth, evening wear, and entertainer dresses.

CHOREOGRAPHY: Modern, conga, Irish jig, modern dance, swing, pantomime sequences, 1 riot.

LIGHTING AND SPECIAL EFFECTS: Mostly general lighting, but some dramatic lighting required. Scrim helps on Ruth's story. Explosions—scenery should shake if possible. Onstage lighting for Vortex sign. Ruth's light-up dress essential.

NOTES: *Wonderful Town* has tight construction, good songs, and comedy. None of the production aspects is difficult. If cutting is required, the most vulnerable sections are Ruth's story vignettes and Wreck's "Pass the Football" number. Leonard Bernstein once commented that the "Conversation Piece" number was his favorite musical theatre composition.

YOU'RE A GOOD MAN, CHARLIE BROWN

Clark Gesner (Music, Lyrics),
John Gordon (Book)
Opened March 7, 1967
1,597 Performances

BASED ON: Comic Strip "Peanuts" by Charles M. Schultz

AGENT: Tams-Witmark

PUBLISHED TEXT: Random House, 1967

RECORDINGS: MGM-S1E9

DIGEST OF PLOT: *Charlie Brown* is more revue than book musical but is tied together by the same characters doing the various sketches, all center around Charlie Brown. First Charlie is introduced as the well-meaning, hard-luck optimist. In short order Charlie is before domineering Doctor Lucy for five cents worth of psychiatric help. Then it's on to blanket-loving Linus and lovable Snoopy. Unshaken by his many failures, Charlie Brown once more attempts to fly a kite. It's flying high at last, but look out for that kite-eating tree! Crunch! Homework, too, is a battle for each of the characters and each solves it in his own inimitable style. The baseball game is there—Charlie loses again—and Lucy educating her brother Linus in little-known facts—all wrong. Lucy also gets her usual putdown from Schroeder, and Snoopy makes a grand event of receiving his supper. During the final sketch all the characters reflect on happiness. The show is simply the "Peanuts" comic strip come to life.

MUSICAL NUMBERS: "You're a Good Man, Charlie Brown," "Schroeder," "Snoopy," "My Blanket and Me," "The Kite," "Dr. Lucy," "Book Report," "The Red Baron," "T.E.A.M. (The Baseball Game)," "Glee Club Rehearsal," "Little-Known Facts," "Suppertime," "Happiness."

INSTRUMENTATION: Violin I (2), II, viola, cello, bass, flute (pic), clar, clar (alto sax), bass clar (tenor sax), trumpets I–II, trombone I, II, percussion I–II, piano.

One of the many New York companies of You're a Good Man, Charlie Brown.

CASTING: 6 parts, all principals. Linus, Charlie Brown, Peppermint Patty, Schroeder, Snoopy, and Lucy, all sing and act. Physical appearance matched with characterizations of comic-strip counterparts, if possible. Total cast, 6.

SCENES AND SETS: Colorful drops and legs, doghouse, and "several oversized, brightly painted objects, simple geometric shapes." (See Notes below.)

PERIOD AND COSTUMES: The present world of 5-year-old children—costumes are realization of comic-strip models, except long pants for the boys. Lucy's red dress and Patty's polka-dotted one. Snoopy, white sweater and black trousers, plus hat, World War I flying helmet and goggles, scarf.

CHOREOGRAPHY: None.

LIGHTING AND SPECIAL EFFECTS: General lighting.

NOTES: A light, happy event that offers primarily a good feeling. Suggest making set more cartoonish than in original production.

YOUR OWN THING

Hal Hester, Danny Apolinar (Music, Lyrics), Donald Driver (Book)

Opened Jan. 13, 1968
935 Performances

BASED ON: *Twelfth Night* by Shakespeare

AGENT: Tams-Witmark

PUBLISHED TEXT: Dell, 1969 (P)

RECORDINGS: RCA LSO-1148

DIGEST OF PLOT: A shipwreck separates twins Viola and Sebastian. Viola arrives in Illyria (New York City). She finds the glass-and-steel skyscrapers distasteful and unfriendly in her search for work. Finally, with the aid of Budda, she learns that the Apocalypse, a hot boys' rock group, needs a replacement singer. She passes herself off as a boy to Orson, the group's manager. Sebastian has been hospitalized from injuries in the wreck, but is now trying to find his way in this overpowering Illyria. Budda has the same words of advice, and Orson has another twin to interview. He has just dispatched Viola (now Charlie) to deliver a love letter to Olivia, a discothèque owner who'd rather Orson focused his attentions elsewhere. Olivia finds Charlie interesting and tries to seduce "him." Viola, of course, is very stand-offish. Thinking Sebastian and Viola are the same person, Orson sends "Charlie" (Sebastian) on his way with another letter. Olivia also thinks the

The Apocalypse pan a patronizing Olivia.

courier is the same Charlie, but finds this one far more receptive. Orson is a prolific letter writer, and Viola sees the futility of his efforts. She counsels him

Original cast of Your Own Thing *as Viola tries out for the Apocalypse.*

about love, barely hiding her own growing feelings about him. Orson is caught in the magnetic atmosphere of love, but is disturbed by the attraction he feels for this "boy." Meanwhile, Olivia has found Sebastian a most agreeable lover. When Orson admits his love to "Charlie," Viola begins to wonder about this man she loves. The mistaken identity is also giving Olivia and Sebastian problems. Finally Viola sets the record straight by removing her shirt to prove she is 100 percent woman. Orson is both relieved and ecstatic, but Olivia is aghast. She *knew* Charlie wasn't a girl. Sebastian enters, and there's a happy reunion between brother and sister. Her confusion alleviated, Olivia turns her charms to the younger but eager Sebastian.

MUSICAL NUMBERS: "No One's Perfect, Dear," "The Flowers," "I'm Me!," "Baby! Baby!," "Come Away, Death," "I'm on My Way to the Top," "Let It Be," "She Never Told Her Love," "Be Gentle," "What Do I Know?," "The Now Generation," "The Middle Years," "When You're Young and in Love,"

"Hunca Munca," "Don't Leave Me," "Do Your Own Thing."

INSTRUMENTATION: Flute (clar, alto sax), clar (alto sax, bari sax), trumpets I–II, trombone I, II (bass trombone or tenor with bass attachment), percussion, elec guitar, elec bass guitar (fender bass), elec organ (organ-conductor). Can be played with just elec organ, elec guitar, elec bass guitar, and percussion only.

CASTING: 10 parts, 7 principals. Viola, sings and dances. Sebastian, sings, some dance. Danny, John, and Michael, zany actors, good rock singers and should be good dancers. Orson, good voice. Olivia, seductive actress with powerful voice. Nurse, comedienne. Total cast, 9.

SCENES AND SETS: 2 acts, unit set calling for 4 rear projection screens, plus 1 front scene projector. Slides and film are projected on what otherwise is an all-white set. Continuous action.

PERIOD AND COSTUMES: The Now generation: unisex outfits for twins Sebastian and Viola plus wigs or long hair styled for look alikeness. Wild mod costume clothes for three-member Apocalypse rock group. Orson, mod suits. Olivia, slinky hostess gowns. Purser and nurse uniforms. Casual stage manager's shirt and pants. White cowboy suits.

CHOREOGRAPHY: Rock-discothèque-type movement, tableaux, and Viola solos.

LIGHTING AND SPECIAL EFFECTS: Tight dramatic lighting is essential. Projections, rear and front, comprise the entire set interest and must be cued exactly to help show from dragging. Famous-character voice tape also must synchronize. Over 400 slides were used in original. Basic slides and voice tape are available from leasing agent in various formats. Some 35-mm slides must be shot by each producing group. Some dummies used.

NOTES: *Your Own Thing* is one of the most refreshing rock-based musicals available. It has class and a score that embraces all age groups. Its imaginative production format is not difficult, yet highly effective and impressive.

ZORBA

John Kander (Music),
Joseph Stein (Book),
Fred Ebb (Lyrics)
Opened Nov. 17, 1968
305 Performances

BASED ON: *Zorba the Greek* by Nikos Kazantzakis

AGENT: Metromedia

PUBLISHED TEXT: Random House, 1969

RECORDINGS: CAP SO 118

DIGEST OF PLOT: A modern-day Greek bouzouki circle decides they will act out the story of Zorba, the street philosopher whose one goal is to live life as if it will end tomorrow. The stage is set back to 1924 and the Piraeus café. Here Zorba meets Nikos, a scholarly young man who has inherited an abandoned mine in Crete, which he's about to reopen.

The bouzouki circle in Zorba.

COURTESY OF HAROLD PRINCE

Zorba's winning ways soon makes it a joint venture. In Crete the village is looking forward to the promise of renewed mining activity. After a brief search for lodgings, they decide on the villa of Mme. Hortense, an aging French chanteuse with fond memories—and an eye for Zorba. Of course, Zorba is anxious to oblige her. The next day Zorba quickly sizes up the mine and spells out the need for equipment and supplies. Nikos dispatches Zorba to the mainland to secure them, but before he can leave Hortense tries to persuade him to bring back a ring so they can be married. It isn't long before Zorba writes that he has spent all Nikos' money on a belly dancer and will be delayed. Hortense sees Nikos reading Zorba's letter and asks what message he has included for her. Not even knowing if Zorba will return (and since Hortense will hear of nothing else), Nikos finally announces that Zorba is bringing the ring. While Zorba is gone, Nikos decides to return the attentions of a young widow. Their love-making is observed by Pavli, whose own romantic appeals to the widow have been coldly rejected. Rather than face reality, the boy kills himself. Finally Zorba returns with some supplies and expresses regret over the loss of the money. Nikos' only compassion is that he has managed to engage Zorba in his absence. That evening the mine is blessed, but as the widow attempts to enter the church she is stabbed by a member of Pavli's family. The next day the mine is opened only to reveal it's a hopeless venture. Nikos is disgusted with Zorba's friendliness to the people who killed the widow, but Zorba explains that death is only part of life. In their frustration they receive word that Hortense is very sick and rush to her deathbed to bring her some last-minute joy. Infuriated by the village hags who ravage her possessions, they dance away their anger and emptiness. With nothing to keep them in Crete, Nikos heads for Athens, and Zorba the way his toes are pointing.

MUSICAL NUMBERS: "Life Is," "The First Time," "The Top of the Hill," "No Boom Boom," "Vive la Difference," "The Butterfly," "Goodbye, Canavaro," Belly Dance, "Grandpapa," "Only Love," "The Bend of the Road," Bells, "Y'assou," "Why Can't I Speak?," Mine Celebration, "The Crow," "Happy Birthday," "I Am Free."

INSTRUMENTATION: Violin I–II, viola, cello, oboe (Eng. horn), bassoon, flute (pic), B♭ clar, bass, trumpet I, II, III (trombone II), trombone I, French horn, bouzouki (or mandolin I), bouzouki (or mandolin II), guitar, accordion, percussion, elec harpsichord (or piano). (Three ethnic parts included above.)

CASTING: 39 parts, 5 principals. Zorba, engaging actor who sings and dances, carries show. Hortense, actress who sings and dances. Leader, powerful dramatic singer. Nikos, actor who sings and dances. Widow, actress who sings. Separate singing and dancing choruses. Total cast, 28–39.

SCENES AND SETS: 2 acts, 19 scenes, basic platform unit set with 4 sets of fly-in units, portable house interior and wall units, 2 partial sets.

ACT I
Scene 1: Bouzouki Circle.
Scene 2: Café Piraeus.
Scene 3: Village Square.
Scene 4: Hortense's Garden.
Scene 4a: Vive la.
Scene 5: Hortense's Bedroom.
Scene 6: The Mine.
Scene 7: "Butterfly"—"Not Too Fast."
Scene 8: Hortense's Garden.
Scene 9: Khania.
Scene 9a: "After Love."
Scene 10: Widow's House.

ACT II
Scene 1: Village Square.
Scene 2: Hortense's Garden.
Scene 3: Road.
Scene 4: Road.
Scene 5: Village Square.
Scene 6: Mine.
Scene 7: Hortense's Bedroom.

COURTESY OF HAROLD PRINCE

Herschel Bernardi (Zorba) leads the mine celebration dance.

Scene 8: Street.
Scene 9: Bouzouki Circle.

PERIOD AND COSTUMES: Present and 1924: modern Greek suits, dresses, sweaters, etc. 1924 double-breasted suits, overcoats, peasant and miners' clothes, black dresses, boots, fancy dresses for Hortense, admiral hats, safari coat, belly dancer's ensemble, hag hooded robes and masks, poncho, sheep-fur-lined vest.

CHOREOGRAPHY: Bouzouki, modern ballet with Greek folk dance overtones, belly dance.

LIGHTING AND SPECIAL EFFECTS: Dramatic and area lighting required. Mine explosion.

NOTES: *Zorba* borders on symbolism and is often difficult for less-sophisticated audiences to follow. A good show for groups that like to avoid formula musicals.

Little Me *principals (l. to r.) Sid Caesar, Peter Turgeon, Nancy Andrews, and Adnia Rice.*

COMPREHENSIVE LIST OF MUSICALS GENERALLY AVAILABLE

The following list of musicals includes every musical that was being offered by a major rights leasing agent as of January 1, 1971. Each listing indicates the title, authors, and leasing agents. To obtain perusal copies of the script or additional information, write the agent listing the particular shows in which you are interested. Also indicate production dates, number of performances, seating capacity, admission price, and complete address including school or organization being represented.

A given musical available from more than one leasing agent will often mean that the ability to lease is somewhat restricted. Some agents are able to grant only professional or semi-professional rights, whereas the other agent listed is free only to grant amateur performance rights. Following is a list of major agents who license rights to musicals and their complete address as of publication. Next to each is an abbreviation used to designate the agent throughout the list of musicals.

Anchorage Press (AP)
Cloverlot
Anchorage, Ky. 40223

Century Library, Inc. (CL)
225 West 44th Street
New York, N.Y. 10036

Dramatic Publishing Co. (D)
86 E. Randolph Street
Chicago, Ill. 60601

Dramatists Play Service, Inc. (DPS)
440 Park Avenue South
New York, N.Y. 10016

Metromedia On Stage (MM)
1700 Broadway
New York, N.Y. 10019

Music Theatre International (MTI)
119 West 57th Street
New York, N.Y. 10019

Rodgers and Hammerstein
Library (RH)
598 Madison Avenue
New York, N.Y. 10022

Samuel French, Inc. (SF)
25 West 45th Street
New York, N.Y. 10036

G. Schirmer (S)
609 Fifth Avenue
New York, N.Y. 10017

Tams-Witmark Music Library,
Inc. (TW)
757 Third Avenue
New York, N.Y. 10017

*

ADVENTURES OF MARCO POLO (SF)
Clay Warnick, Mel Pahl: Music
William Friedberg, Neil Simon: Book
Edward Eager: Lyrics

* *ALLEGRO* (RH)
Richard Rodgers: Music
Oscar Hammerstein II: Book, Lyrics

ALL IN LOVE (MTI)
Based on Richard Sheridan's *The Rivals*
Jacques Urbont: Music
Bruce Geller: Book, Lyrics

AMERICA'S SWEETHEART (TW)
Richard Rodgers: Music
Herbert Fields: Book
Lorenz Hart: Lyrics

———

* Musicals featured in Section I.

AMOROUS FLEA, THE (DPS)
Based on Molière's *School for Wives*
Bruce Montgomery: Music, Lyrics
Jerry Devine: Book

* *ANNIE GET YOUR GUN* (RH)
Irving Berlin: Music, Lyrics
Herbert and Dorothy Fields: Book

* *ANYONE CAN WHISTLE* (MTI)
Stephen Sondheim: Music, Lyrics
Arthur Laurents: Book

* *ANYTHING GOES* (TW)
Cole Porter: Music, Lyrics
Guy Bolton, P. G. Wodehouse, Howard Lindsay, and Russel Crouse: Book

* *APPLAUSE* (TW)
Charles Strouse: Music
Betty Comden, Adolph Green: Book
Lee Adams: Lyrics

* *APPLE TREE, THE* (MTI)
Based on stories by Mark Twain, Frank R. Stockton, and Jules Feiffer
Additional book material by Jerome Coopersmith
Jerry Bock: Music
Sheldon Harnick: Lyrics

AROUND THE WORLD IN EIGHTY DAYS (D)
Based on Jules Verne novel
Gilbert Leibinger: Music
Peter Gurney: Book, Lyrics

AROUND THE WORLD IN 80 DAYS (TW)
Sammy Fain and Victor Young: Music
Sig Herzig: Book
Harold Adamson: Lyrics

ASK ANY GIRL (D)
Mark Bucci: Music
Winifred Wolfe: Book
David Rogers: Lyrics

BABES IN ARMS (RH)
Richard Rodgers, Lorenz Hart: Book, Music, Lyrics
Further adapted by George Oppenheimer

* *BAKER STREET* (TW)
From stories by Sir Arthur Conan Doyle
Marian Grudeff, Raymond Jessel: Music, Lyrics
Jerome Coopersmith: Book

BAREFOOT BOY WITH CHEEK (D)
Sidney Lippman: Music
Max Shulman: Book
Sylvia Dee: Lyrics

* *BELLS ARE RINGING* (TW)
Jule Styne: Music
Betty Comden, Adolph Green: Book, Lyrics

* *BEN FRANKLIN IN PARIS* (SF)
Mark Sandrich, Jr.: Music
Sidney Michaels: Book, Lyrics

BEST FOOT FORWARD (TW)
Hugh Martin, Ralph Blane: Music, Lyrics
John Cecil Holm: Book

BEST OF BROADWAY (*Revue*) (D)
Created by Broadway composers, lyricists, and comedy skit writers.

BIBLE SALESMAN, THE (SF)
(See *DOUBLE ENTRY*)

BILLION DOLLAR BABY (TW)
Morton Gould: Music
Betty Comden, Adolph Green: Book, Lyrics

* *BLOOMER GIRL* (TW)
Based on play by Dan Lilith James
Harold Arlen: Music
Sig Herzig and Fred Saidy: Book
E. Y. Harburg: Lyrics

BODY BEAUTIFUL, THE (SF)
Jerry Bock: Music
Joseph Stein, Will Glickman: Book
Sheldon Harnick: Lyrics

* *BOY FRIEND, THE* (MTI)
Sandy Wilson: Music, Book, Lyrics

BOYS FROM SYRACUSE, THE (RH)
Based on Shakespeare's *A Comedy of Errors*
Richard Rodgers: Music
George Abbott: Book
Lorenz Hart: Lyrics

* *BRIGADOON* (TW)
Frederick Loewe: Music
Alan Jay Lerner: Book, Lyrics

* *BYE BYE BIRDIE* (TW)
Charles Strouse: Music
Michael Stewart: Book
Lee Adams: Lyrics

BY HEX (DPS)
Based on idea by Richard Gehman
Howard Blankman: Music, Lyrics
John Rengier: Book
Additional lyrics by Richard Gehman, John Rengier

BY THE BEAUTIFUL SEA (MTI)
Arthur Schwartz: Music
Herbert and Dorothy Fields: Book
Dorothy Fields: Lyrics

* *CABARET* (TW)
Based on play by John Van Druten and stories by Christopher Isherwood
John Kander: Music
Jose Masteroff: Book
Fred Ebb: Lyrics

* *CALAMITY JANE* (TW)
Sammy Fain: Music
Paul Francis Webster: Lyrics
Charles K. Freeman: Screenplay adaptation
(Screenplay by James O'Hanlon)

The original Broadway cast of A Tree Grows in Brooklyn.

* *CALL ME MADAM* (MTI)
Irving Berlin: Music, Lyrics
Howard Lindsay, Russel Crouse: Book

* *CAMELOT* (TW)
Based on T. H. White's *The Once and Future King*
Frederick Loewe: Music
Alan Jay Lerner: Book, Lyrics

* *CAN-CAN* (TW)
Cole Porter: Music, Lyrics
Abe Burrows: Book

* *CANTERBURY TALES* (MTI)
Based on translation from Geoffrey Chaucer by Nevill Coghill
Richard Hill, John Hawkins: Music
Martin Starkie, Nevill Coghill: Book
Nevill Coghill: Lyrics

CARMEN JONES (RH)
Based on Georges Bizet's *Carmen*
Oscar Hammerstein II: Book, Lyrics

* *CARNIVAL!* (TW)
Based on material by Helen Deutsch
Bob Merrill: Music, Lyrics
Michael Stewart: Book

* *CAROUSEL* (RH)
Based on Ferenc Molnar's *Liliom*
Richard Rodgers: Music
Oscar Hammerstein II: Book, Lyrics

CATCH COLT, THE (DPS)
Mary O'Hara: Book, Music

* *CELEBRATION* (MTI)
Harvey Schmidt: Music
Tom Jones: Words

CHAIN OF JADE (SF)
Musical version of Dan Totheroh's *The Stolen Prince*
By David Rogers and Mark Bucci

CHEAPER BY THE DOZEN (D)
Based on book by Frank Gilbreth and Ernestine Gilbreth Carey
David Rogers and Mark Bucci Score

CINDERELLA (RH)
Richard Rodgers: Music
Oscar Hammerstein II: Book, Lyrics

CINDY (TW)
Based on idea by Johnny Brandon and Stuart Wiener

Johnny Brandon: Music, Lyrics
Joe Sauter, Mike Sawyer: Book

* *COMPANY*
Stephen Sondheim: Music, Lyrics
George Furth: Book

COMPLAINING ANGEL, THE   (SF)
Natalie E. White, J. D. Tumpane, Sr. M. Francis,
  PC, A. J. Hope, CSC, D. Birder: Music, Lyrics
Natalie E. White: Book

CONNECTICUT YANKEE, A   (TW)
Richard Rodgers: Music
Herbert Fields: Book
Lorenz Hart: Lyrics

CRADLE WILL ROCK, THE   (TW)
By Marc Blitzstein

CUMBERLAND FAIR   (S)
Alec Wilder: Music
Arnold Sundgaard: Libretto

CURLEY McDIMPLE   (SF)
By Mary Boylan, Robert Dahdah

* *DAMES AT SEA*   (SF)
Jim Wise: Music
George Hainsohn, Robin Miller: Book, Lyrics

* *DAMN YANKEES*   (MTI)
Based on *The Year the Yankees Lost the Pennant*
  by Douglass Wallop
Richard Adler, Jerry Ross: Music, Lyrics
George Abbott, Douglass Wallop: Book

DEAREST ENEMY   (TW)
Richard Rodgers: Music
Herbert Fields: Book
Lorenz Hart: Lyrics

* *DESTRY RIDES AGAIN*   (TW)
Based on story by Max Brand
Harold Rome: Music, Lyrics
Leonard Gershe: Book

* *DO I HEAR A WALTZ?*   (RH)
Richard Rodgers: Music
Arthur Laurents: Book
Stephen Sondheim: Lyrics

DONNYBROOK!   (SF)
Based on novel by Maurice Walsh
Johnny Burke: Music, Lyrics
Robert E. McEnroe: Book

* *DO RE MI*   (TW)
Jule Styne: Music
Garson Kanin: Book
Betty Comden, Adolph Green: Lyrics

DOUBLE ENTRY   (SF)
Two one-act musicals, *The Oldest Trick in the
  World* and *The Bible Salesman*

DOWN IN THE VALLEY   (S)
Kurt Weill: Music
Arnold Sundgaard: Libretto

DRACULA, BABY   (D)
Claire Strauch: Music
Bruce Ronald, John Jakes: Book
John Jakes: Lyrics

DRAT! THE CAT!   (SF)
Milton Schafer: Music
Ira Levin: Book, Lyrics

DU BARRY WAS A LADY   (TW)
Cole Porter: Music, Lyrics
Herbert Fields, B. G. DeSylva: Book

EDUCATION OF H*Y*M*A*N*
  K*A*P*L*A*N, THE   (D)
Paul Nassau, Oscar Brand: Music, Lyrics
Benjamin Bernard Zavin: Book

* *ERNEST IN LOVE*   (MTI)
Lee Pockriss: Music
Anne Croswell: Book, Lyrics

FADE OUT–FADE IN   (TW)
Jule Styne: Music
Betty Comden, Adolph Green: Book, Lyrics

* *FAMILY AFFAIR, A*   (MTI)
John Kander: Music
James and William Goldman: Book
James Goldman and John Kander: Lyrics

* *FANNY*   (TW)
Based on the trilogy by Marcel Pagnol
Harold Rome: Music, Lyrics
S. N. Behrman, Joshua Logan: Book

FANNY, THE FRIVOLOUS FLAPPER   (SF)
Charles George: Music, Book, Lyrics

* *FANTASTICKS, THE*   (MTI)
Harvey Schmidt: Music
Tom Jones: Book, Lyrics

* *FIDDLER ON THE ROOF*   (MTI)
Based on Sholem Aleichem stories by special per-
  mission of Arnold Perl
Jerry Bock: Music
Joseph Stein: Book
Sheldon Harnick: Lyrics

FIFTY MILLION FRENCHMEN   (TW)
Cole Porter: Music, Lyrics
Herbert Fields: Book

* *FINIAN'S RAINBOW*   (TW)
Burton Lane: Music
E. Y. Harburg, Fred Saidy: Book
E. Y. Harburg: Lyrics

* *FIORELLO!*   (TW)
Jerry Bock: Music
Jerome Weidman, George Abbott: Book
Sheldon Harnick: Lyrics

FIRST IMPRESSIONS   (SF)
Adapted from Jane Austen's *Pride and Prejudice*
  and play by Helen Jerome

COURTESY OF THE LYNN FARNOL GROUP, INC.

Ray Bolger (with gun) during the "Slaughter on Tenth Avenue" ballet sequence of the 1936 Rodgers and Hart musical On Your Toes.

Robert Goldman, Glenn Paxton, George Weiss:
   Music, Lyrics
Abe Burrows: Book

* *FLOWER DRUM SONG*   (RH)
Richard Rodgers: Music
Oscar Hammerstein II, Joseph Fields: Book
Oscar Hammerstein II: Lyrics

FUNNY FACE   (TW)
George Gershwin: Music
Fred Thompson, Paul Gerard Smith: Book
Ira Gershwin: Lyrics

* *FUNNY GIRL*   (TW)
Jule Styne: Music
Isobel Lennart: Book
Bob Merrill: Lyrics

* *FUNNY THING HAPPENED ON THE WAY TO THE FORUM, A*   (MTI)
Stephen Sondheim: Music, Lyrics
Burt Shevelove, Larry Gelbart: Book

* *GENTLEMEN PREFER BLONDES*   (MTI)
Jule Styne: Music
Joseph Fields, Anita Loos: Book
Leo Robin: Lyrics

* *GEORGE M*   (TW)
George M. Cohan: Music, Lyrics
Michael Stewart, John and Fran Pascal: Book
Mary Cohan: Lyrics and musical revisions

GIDGET GOES HAWAIIAN   (D)
Based on novel by Frederick Kohner
By Anne Coulter Martens, Liz Martens

GIFT OF THE MAGI   (TW)
Based on the O'Henry story
Richard Adler: Music, Lyrics
Wilson Lehr: Book

GIRL CRAZY   (TW)
George Gershwin: Music
Guy Bolton, Jack McGowan: Book
Ira Gershwin: Lyrics

* *GOLDEN APPLE, THE*   (TW)
Jerome Moross: Music
John Latouche: Book

* *GOLDEN BOY*   (SF)
William Gibson, Clifford Odets: Book
Charles Strouse: Music
Lee Adams: Lyrics

GOLDEN RAINBOW   (MM)
Based on play by Arnold Shulman
Walter Marks: Music, Lyrics
Ernest Kinoy: Book

* *GOLDILOCKS*   (SF)
Leroy Anderson: Music
Jean and Walter Kerr: Book
Jean and Walter Kerr, Joan Ford: Lyrics

GOOD MORNING, DEARIE   (TW)
Jerome Kern: Music
Anne Caldwell: Book

GOOD NEWS   (SF)
Ray Henderson: Music   (TW *)
Laurence Schwab, B. G. DeSylva: Book
B. G. DeSylva, Lew Brown: Lyrics

GREAT SCOT!   (DPS)
Based on escapades of young Robert Burns
Don McAfee: Music
Mark Conradt, Gregory Dawson: Book
Nancy Leeds: Lyrics

GREENWILLOW   (MTI)
Based on novel by B. J. Chute
Frank Loesser: Music, Lyrics
Lesser Samuels, Frank Loesser: Book

* *GUYS AND DOLLS*   (MTI)
Based on story and characters by Damon Runyon
Frank Loesser: Music, Lyrics
Jo Swerling, Abe Burrows: Book

* *GYPSY*   (TW)
Based on memoirs of Gypsy Rose Lee
Jule Styne: Music
Arthur Laurents: Book
Stephen Sondheim: Lyrics

* *HAIR*   (Apply New York producer Michael Butler)
Galt MacDermot: Music
Gerome Ragni, James Rado: Book, Lyrics

* *HALF A SIXPENCE*   (D)
David Heneker: Music, Lyrics
Beverley Cross: Book

HALLELUJAH, BABY!   (MTI)
Jule Styne: Music
Arthur Laurents: Book
Betty Comden, Adolph Green: Lyrics

HANNAH   (SF)
Fred Silver: Music
Helen Kromer: Book, Lyrics

HAPPIEST GIRL IN THE WORLD   (TW)
Jacques Offenbach: Music
Fred Saidy, Henry Myers: Book
E. Y. Harburg: Lyrics

* *HAPPY HUNTING*   (MTI)
Harold Karr: Music
Howard Lindsay, Russel Crouse: Book
Matt Dubey: Lyrics

HAPPY TIME, THE   (D)
John Kander: Music
N. Richard Nash: Book
Fred Ebb: Lyrics

HAZEL FLAGG   (TW)
Jule Styne: Music
Bob Hilliard: Lyrics
Ben Hecht: Book

HEIDI   (SF)
TV adaptation from Johanna Spyri's book
Clay Warnick: Music
William Friedberg, Neil Simon: Book

* *HELLO, DOLLY!*   (TW)
Based on *The Matchmaker* by Thornton Wilder
Jerry Herman: Music, Lyrics
Michael Stewart: Book

* *HENRY, SWEET HENRY*   (SF)
Based on *The World of Henry Orient* by Nora Johnson
Bob Merrill: Music, Lyrics
Nunnally Johnson: Book

* *HERE'S LOVE!*   (MTI)
Based on *Miracle on 34th Street*
Story by Valentine Davies, screenplay by George Seaton
Meredith Willson: Book, Music, Lyrics

HIGH-BUTTON SHOES   (TW)
Jule Styne: Music
Stephen Longstreet: Book
Sammy Cahn: Lyrics

HIGH SPIRITS   (TW)
Based on *Blythe Spirit* by Noel Coward
Hugh Martin, Timothy Gray: Music, Book, Lyrics

HIT THE DECK   (TW)
Vincent Youmans: Music
Herbert Fields: Book
Leo Robin, Clifford Grey: Lyrics

---

* Professional groups only.

HOW NOW, DOW JONES   (SF)
Elmer Bernstein: Music
Max Shulman: Book
Carolyn Leigh: Lyrics

HOW TO SUCCEED IN BUSINESS WITHOUT REALLY TRYING   (MTI)
Based on novel by Shepherd Mead
Frank Loesser: Music, Lyrics
Abe Burrows, Jack Weinstock, Willie Gilbert: Book

I CAN GET IT FOR YOU WHOLESALE (TW)
Harold Rome: Music, Lyrics
Jerome Weidman: Book

I DREAM OF JEANIE   (TW)
Based on spirit and songs of Stephen Foster
Myles Standish: Book

I DO! I DO!   (MTI)
Based on *The Fourposter* by Jan de Hartog
Harvey Schmidt: Music
Tom Jones: Book, Lyrics

ILLYA DARLING   (TW)
Based on film "Never on Sunday"
Manos Hadjidakis: Music
Jules Dassin: Book
Joe Darion: Lyrics

I MARRIED AN ANGEL   (RH)
Richard Rodgers, Lorenz Hart: Music, Book, Lyrics
Book adapted by Lois Jacoby
(Agent informs that orchestration has been lost.)

INTO THE FIRE   (SF)
(Follow-up to Francis Swann's *Out of the Frying Pan*
Albert Moritz: Music, Lyrics
Francis Swann: Book

IRMA LA DOUCE   (TW)
Marguerite Monnot: Music
Alexander Breffort: Book, Lyrics
Julian More, David Heneker, Monty Norman: English Book and Lyrics

IT'S A BIRD, IT'S A PLANE, IT'S SUPERMAN (TW)
Based on comic strip "Superman"
Charles Strouse: Music
David Newman, Robert Benton: Book
Lee Adams: Lyrics

JAMAICA   (TW)
Harold Arlen: Music
E. Y. Harburg, Fred Saidy: Book
E. Y. Harburg: Lyrics

JO   (DPS)
Based on *Little Women* by Louisa May Alcott
William Dyer: Music
Don Parks, William Dyer: Book, Lyrics

KING AND I, THE   (RH)
Based on Margaret Landon's *Anna and the King of Siam*
Richard Rodgers: Music
Oscar Hammerstein II: Book, Lyrics

KISMET   (MTI)
Based on play by Edward Knoblock
Robert Wright, George Forrest: Lyrics, Music from themes of Alexander Borodin
Charles Lederer, Luther Davis: Book

KISS ME KATE   (TW)
Cole Porter: Music, Lyrics
Bella and Samuel Spewack: Book

KITTIWAKE ISLAND   (S)
Alec Wilder: Music
Arnold Sundgaard: Libretto

LADY BE GOOD   (TW)
George Gershwin: Music
Guy Bolton, Fred Thompson: Book
Ira Gershwin: Lyrics

LADY IN THE DARK   (DPS)
Kurt Weill: Music   (TW *)
Moss Hart: Book
Ira Gershwin: Lyrics

LAST SWEET DAYS OF ISAAC, THE (MM)
Nancy Ford: Music
Gretchen Cryer: Book, Lyrics

LEAVE IT TO JANE   (TW)
Based on *College Widow* by George Ade
Jerome Kern: Music
Guy Bolton, P. G. Wodehouse: Book, Lyrics

LEAVE IT TO ME   (TW)
Cole Porter: Music, Lyrics
Bella and Samuel Spewack: Book

LI'L ABNER   (TW)
Johnny Mercer, Gene dePaul: Music, Lyrics
Norman Panama, Melvin Frank: Book

LITTLE MARY SUNSHINE   (MM)
A musical about operettas
Rick Besoyan: Music, Book, Lyrics

LITTLE ME   (TW)
Based on novel by Patrick Dennis
Cy Coleman: Music
Neil Simon: Book
Carolyn Leigh: Lyrics

LOOK TO THE LILIES   (MM)
Jule Styne: Music
Leonard Spigelgass: Book
Sammy Cahn: Lyrics

LOVE FROM JUDY   (TW)
Hugh Martin: Music

* Professional groups only.

Original cast of Promenade *(l. to r.)*: *Pierre Epstein, Margot Albert, George S. Irving, and Michael Davis.*

Eric Maschwitz, Jean Webster: Book
Hugh Martin, Jack Gray: Lyrics

LUTE SONG   (D)
Raymond Scott: Music
Will Irwin, Sidney Howard: Book
Bernard Hanighen: Lyrics

* *MAGGIE FLYNN*   (SF)
Hugo Peretti, Luigi Creatore, George David Weiss:
   Music, Book, Lyrics

* *MAME*   (TW)
Based on novel by Patrick Dennis and play *Auntie Mame* by Lawrence and Lee
Jerry Herman: Music, Lyrics
Jerome Lawrence, Robert E. Lee: Book

* *MAN OF LA MANCHA*   (TW)
Mitch Leigh: Music
Dale Wasserman: Book
Joe Darion: Lyrics

MAN WITH A LOAD OF MISCHIEF, THE
   (MM)
John Clifton: Music
Ben Tarver: Book
John Clifton, Ben Tarver: Lyrics

* *ME AND JULIET*   (RH)
Richard Rodgers: Music
Oscar Hammerstein II: Book, Lyrics

ME NOBODY KNOWS, THE   (MM)
Gary W. Friedman: Music

Stephen M. Joseph: Book
Will Holt: Lyrics
Original idea and additional lyrics by Herbert Shapiro

MEET ME IN ST. LOUIS   (TW*)
Based on movie
Hugh Martin, Ralph Blane: Music, Lyrics
Sally Benson: Book

* MILK AND HONEY   (TW)
Jerry Herman: Music, Lyrics
Don Appell: Book

MINNIE'S BOYS   (MM)
Based on lives of the Marx Brothers
Larry Grossman: Music
Arthur Marx, Robert Fisher: Book
Hal Hackady: Lyrics

MONEY   (DPS)
Sam Pottle: Music
David Axelrod, Tom Whedon: Book, Lyrics

* MOST HAPPY FELLA   (MTI)
Based on Sidney Howard's play They Knew What They Wanted
Frank Loesser: Music, Lyrics, Book

MOTHER GOOSE NOW
Gilbert M. Martin: Music
John Jakes: Book, Lyrics

* MR. PRESIDENT   (MTI)
Irving Berlin: Music, Lyrics
Howard Lindsay, Russel Crouse: Book

MR. SCROOGE   (D)
(Christmas musical)
By Richard Morris, Dolores Claman, Ted Wood

MR. WONDERFUL   (MTI)
Jerry Bock, Larry Holofcener, George Weiss: Music, Lyrics
Joseph Stein, Will Glickman: Book†

MUSIC IN THE AIR   (TW)
Jerome Kern: Music
Oscar Hammerstein II: Book, Lyrics

* MUSIC MAN, THE   (MTI)
Based on story by Meredith Willson, Franklin Lacey
Meredith Willson: Music, Book, Lyrics

* MY FAIR LADY   (TW)
Adapted from G. B. Shaw's play and Gabriel Pascal's motion picture Pygmalion
Frederick Loewe: Music
Alan Jay Lerner: Book, Lyrics

NAUGHTY-NAUGHT   (MM)
Richard Lewine: Music

John Van Antwerp: Dialogue
Ted Fetter: Lyrics

* NEW GIRL IN TOWN   (MTI)
Based on Eugene O'Neill's Anna Christie
Bob Merrill: Music, Lyrics
George Abbott: Book

* NO STRINGS   (RH)
Richard Rodgers: Music, Lyrics
Samuel Taylor: Book

NOW   (MM)
Dennis Eliot: Book
Gilbert M. Martin: Music, Lyrics

NOW IS THE TIME FOR ALL GOOD MEN   (SF)
Nancy Ford: Music
Gretchen Cryer: Book, Lyrics

OF THEE I SING   (SF)
George Gershwin: Music
Ira Gershwin: Lyrics
George S. Kaufman, Morrie Ryskind: Book

OH BOY!   (TW)
Jerome Kern: Music
Guy Bolton, P. G. Wodehouse: Book, Lyrics

OH CAPTAIN!   (TW)
Based on film Captain's Paradise by Alec Coppel
Jay Livingston, Ray Evans: Music, Lyrics
Al Morgan, José Ferrer: Book

OH! KAY   (TW)
George Gershwin: Music
Guy Bolton, P. G. Wodehouse: Book
Ira Gershwin: Lyrics

OH! LADY, LADY   (TW)
Jerome Kern: Music
Guy Bolton, P. G. Wodehouse: Book, Lyrics

OH! SUSANNA   (SF)
Based on songs by Stephen Foster
Ann Ronell: Music, Lyrics
Florence Ryerson, Colin Clements: Book

* OKLAHOMA!   (RH)
Richard Rodgers: Music
Oscar Hammerstein II: Book, Lyrics

OLDEST TRICK IN THE WORLD   (SF)
(See Double Entry)

* OLIVER!   (TW)
Lionel Bart: Music, Book, Lyrics

O MARRY ME!   (MTI)
Based on She Stoops to Conquer by Oliver Goldsmith
Robert Kessler: Music
Lola Pergament: Book, Lyrics

* ON A CLEAR DAY YOU CAN SEE FOREVER   (TW)
Burton Lane: Music
Alan Jay Lerner: Book, Lyrics

---

* Professional groups only.
† (Heritage Music Press, 501 E. Third Street, Dayton, O. 45402)

Roland Winters (E. F. Albee) is invaded by the Marx Brothers (l. to r.) Irwin Pearl (Chico), Alvin Kupperman (Zeppo), Lewis J. Stadlen (Groucho), and Daniel Fortus (Harpo), the original cast of Minnie's Boys.

* *ONCE UPON A MATTRESS*   (MTI)
Mary Rodgers: Music
Jay Thompson, Marshall Barer, Dean Fuller: Book
Marshall Barer: Lyrics

110 IN THE SHADE   (TW)
Based on *The Rainmaker* by N. Richard Nash
Harvey Schmidt: Music
N. Richard Nash: Book
Tom Jones: Lyrics

ONE TOUCH OF VENUS   (TW)
Kurt Weill: Music
S. J. Perelman, Ogden Nash: Book
Ogden Nash: Lyrics

ON THE TOWN   (TW)
Leonard Bernstein: Music
Betty Comden, Adolph Green: Book, Lyrics

OUR HEARTS WERE YOUNG AND GAY
  (D)
Based on book by Cornelia Otis Skinner and Emily Kimbrough
Gerald Alters, Herbert Hartig: Score
Lois Corey: Libretto

OUR MISS BROOKS   (D)
David Rogers, Mark Bucci: Score
Christopher Sergel: Book

OUR NIGHT OUT   (SF)
Mary Elizabeth Briggs: Score
Robert and Lillian Masters: Book

OUT OF THIS WORLD   (TW)
Cole Porter: Music, Lyrics
Dwight Taylor, Reginald Lawrence: Book

* *PAINT YOUR WAGON*   (TW)
Frederick Loewe: Music
Alan Jay Lerner: Book, Lyrics

* *PAJAMA GAME, THE*   (MTI)
Based on novel *7½ Cents* by Richard Bissell
Richard Adler, Jerry Ross: Music, Lyrics
George Abbott, Richard Bissell: Book

* *PAL JOEY*   (TW)
Richard Rodgers: Music
John O'Hara: Book
Lorenz Hart: Lyrics

PANAMA HATTIE   (TW)
Cole Porter: Music, Lyrics
Herbert Fields, B. G. DeSylva: Book

PEACE   (MM)
Al Carmines: Music
Tim Reynolds: Book

PENNY   (D)
John Coates, Jr.: Music
Anne Coulter Martens: Book
Liz Martens, Louise Coates: Lyrics

* *PETER PAN*   (SF)
Based on play by Sir James M. Barrie
Mark Charlap, Jule Styne: Music
Carolyn Leigh, Betty Comden, Adolph Green:
Lyrics

PIGSKIN AND PETTICOATS   (SF)
Tom Margitan: Music
Bill Thompson: Book, Lyrics

PIPE DREAM   (RH)
Based on John Steinbeck's novel
Richard Rodgers: Music
Oscar Hammerstein II: Book, Lyrics

* *PLAIN AND FANCY*   (SF)
Albert Hague: Music
Joseph Stein, William Glickman: Book
Arnold B. Horwitt: Lyrics

* *PORGY AND BESS*   (TW*)
Based on *Porgy* by Dorothy and DuBose Heyward
George Gershwin: Music
DuBose Heyward: Libretto
DuBose Heyward, Ira Gershwin: Lyrics

PRESENT ARMS!   (TW)
Richard Rodgers: Music
Herbert Fields: Book
Lorenz Hart: Lyrics

PROMENADE   (MM)
Al Carmines: Music
Maria Irene Fornes: Book, Lyrics

* *PROMISES, PROMISES*   (TW)
Burt Bacharach: Music
Neil Simon: Book
Hal David: Lyrics

(TW*) Professional groups only.

* *PURLIE*   (SF)
Gary Geld: Music
Ossie Davis, Phillip Rose, Peter Udell: Book
Peter Udell: Lyrics

RAGS TO RICHES   (AP)
Developed from Horatio Alger
By Aurand Harris

* *REDHEAD*   (MTI)
Albert Hague: Music
Herbert and Dorothy Fields, Sidney Sheldon, David
  Shaw: Book
Dorothy Fields: Lyrics

RIO RITA   (TW)
Harry Tierney: Music
Guy Bolton, Fred Thompson: Book
Joe McCarthy: Lyrics

* *RIVERWIND*   (MTI)
John Jennings: Music, Book, Lyrics

* *ROAR OF THE GREASEPAINT—THE SMELL
  OF THE CROWD, THE*   (TW)
Leslie Bricusse, Anthony Newley: Music, Book,
  Lyrics

ROBERTA   (TW)
Adapted from Alice Duer Miller's story
Jerome Kern: Music
Otto Harbach: Book, Lyrics

SACRAMENTO FIFTY MILES   (AP)
Americanized version of *The Brementown
  Musicians*
By Eleanor and Ray Harder

SALAD DAYS   (TW)
Julian Slade: Music
Julian Slade, Dorothy Reynolds: Book, Lyrics

SALLY   (TW)
Jerome Kern: Music
Guy Bolton, Clifford Grey: Book, Lyrics

SAY DARLING!   (TW)
Based on novel by Richard Bissell
Betty Comden, Adolph Green, Jule Styne: Music,
  Lyrics
Richard Bissell, Abe Burrows, Marian Bissell: Book

SECRET LIFE OF WALTER MITTY, THE
  (SF)
Based on story by James Thurber
Leon Carr: Music
Joe Manchester: Book
Earl Shuman: Lyrics

SENTIMENTAL SCARECROW, THE   (SF)
(Fantasy)
Musical version of play by Rachel Field
Nathan Brown: Music
S. Charles Shertzer: Book, Lyrics

SEVENTEEN   (SF) (TW*)
Novel by Booth Tarkington

Stars Shirley Booth (far right) and Al Freeman, Jr., in a scene from Look to the Lilies.

Walter Kent: Music
Sally Benson: Book
Kim Gannon: Lyrics

* *1776*   (MTI)
Sherman Edwards: Music, Lyrics
Peter Stone: Book

* *SHE LOVES ME*   (TW)
Based on play by Miklos Laszlo
Jerry Bock: Music
Joe Masteroff: Book
Sheldon Harnick: Lyrics

* *SHOW BOAT*   (RH)
Based on Edna Ferber's novel
Jerome Kern: Music
Oscar Hammerstein II: Book, Lyrics

---

* Professional groups only.

* *SILK STOCKINGS*   (TW)
Based on movie "Ninotchka" by Melchior Lengyel
Cole Porter: Music, Lyrics
George S. Kaufman, Leueen MacGrath, Abe Burrows: Book

SIMPLY HEAVENLY   (DPS)
Based on novel *Simple Takes a Wife* by Langston Hughes
David Martin: Music
Langston Hughes: Book, Lyrics

* *SKYSCRAPER*   (SF)
Based on *Dream Girl* by Elmer Rice
James Van Heusen: Music
Peter Stone: Book
Sammy Cahn: Lyrics

SONG IN THE WIND   (D)
Score by authentic folk-song writers, names no longer known

* *SONG OF NORWAY*   (TW)
Based on life and music of Edvard Grieg from
  story by Homer Curran
Adaptation by Robert Wright, George Forrest:
  Music, Lyrics
Milton Lazarus: Book

* *SOUND OF MUSIC, THE*   (RH)
Based on Maria Trapp's *The Trapp Family Singers*
Richard Rodgers: Music
Oscar Hammerstein II: Lyrics
Howard Lindsay, Russel Crouse: Book

* *SOUTH PACIFIC*   (RH)
Based on James A. Michener's *Tales of the South
  Pacific*
Richard Rodgers: Music
Oscar Hammerstein II, Joshua Logan: Book
Oscar Hammerstein II: Lyrics

* *STOP THE WORLD—I WANT TO GET OFF*
  (TW)
Leslie Bricusse, Anthony Newley: Music, Book,
  Lyrics

STREETS OF NEW YORK, THE   (SF)
Based on play by Dion Boucicault
Richard B. Chodosh: Music
Barry A. Grael: Book

STUDENT GYPSY, THE   (MM)
(or *THE PRINCE OF LIEDERKRANZ*)
Rick Besoyan: Music, Book, Lyrics

SUNNY   (TW)
Jerome Kern: Music
Otto Harbach, Oscar Hammerstein II: Book, Lyrics

* *SWEET CHARITY*   (TW)
Based on original screenplay by Federico Fellini,
  Tullio Pinelli, Ennio Plaiano
Cy Coleman: Music
Neil Simon: Book
Dorothy Fields: Lyrics

* *TAKE ME ALONG*   (TW)
Based on *Ah Wilderness* by Eugene O'Neill
Bob Merrill: Music, Lyrics
Joseph Stein, Robert Russell: Book

* *TENDERLOIN*   (TW)
Based on novel by Samuel Hopkins Adams
Jerry Bock: Music
George Abbott, Jerome Weidman: Book
Sheldon Harnick: Lyrics

* *THREEPENNY OPERA, THE*   (TW)
English adaptation by Marc Blitzstein
Kurt Weill: Music
Bertolt Brecht: Book, Lyrics

THREE WISHES FOR JAMIE   (SF)
Ralph Blane: Music, Lyrics
Charles O'Neal, Abe Burrows: Book

THIRTEEN CLOCKS, THE   (MTI)
Based on James Thurber's fairy tale

Marc Bucci, James Thurber: Music, Lyrics
Fred Sadoff: Book

13 DAUGHTERS   (MTI)
Eaton Magoon, Jr.: Music, Book, Lyrics

TIP TOES   (TW)
George Gershwin: Music
Guy Bolton, Fred Thompson: Book
Ira Gershwin: Lyrics

TOM SAWYER   (MTI)
Based on the Twain classic, *The Adventures of
  Tom Sawyer*
Frank Luther: Music, Lyrics

TOP BANANA   (TW)
Johnny Mercer: Music, Words
Hy Kraft: Book

TREE GROWS IN BROOKLYN, A   (MM)
Arthur Schwartz: Music
Betty Smith, George Abbott: Book
Dorothy Fields: Lyrics

TRIAD   (MTI)
Three one-act operas
By Mark Bucci
(*SWEET BETSY FROM PIKE, TALE FOR A
  DEAF EAR, THE DRESS*)

TWO BY TWO   (RH)
Richard Rodgers: Music
Peter Stone: Book
Martin Charnin: Lyrics

* *UNSINKABLE MOLLY BROWN, THE*
  (MTI)
Meredith Willson: Music, Lyrics
Richard Morris: Book

VERY GOOD EDDIE   (TW)
Jerome Kern: Music
Phillip Bartholomae, Guy Bolton: Book
Schuyler Greene: Lyrics

* *WALKING HAPPY*   (SF)
Based on *Hobson's Choice* by Harold Brighouse
James Van Heusen: Music
Roger O. Hirson, Ketti Frings: Book
Sammy Cahn: Lyrics

* *WEST SIDE STORY*   (MTI)
Based on a conception of Jerome Robbins
Leonard Bernstein: Music
Arthur Laurents: Book
Stephen Sondheim: Lyrics

WHAT MAKES SAMMY RUN?   (TW)
Based on novel by Budd Schulberg
Ervin Drake: Music, Lyrics
Budd and Stuart Schulberg: Book

* *WHERE'S CHARLEY?*   (MTI)
Based on Brandon Thomas' *Charley's Aunt*
Frank Loesser: Music, Lyrics
George Abbott: Book

* *WILDCAT* (TW)
Cy Coleman: Music
N. Richard Nash: Book
Carolyn Leigh: Lyrics

* *WISH YOU WERE HERE* (MTI)
Based on Arthur Kober's *Having a Wonderful Time*
Harold Rome: Music, Lyrics
Arthur Kober, Joshua Logan: Book

WIZARD OF OZ (TW)
By L. Frank Baum
Adapted by Frank Gabrielson, Harold Arlen, E. Y. Harburg: Music, Lyrics of MGM motion picture score

* *WONDERFUL TOWN* (TW)
Based on *My Sister Eileen* by Joseph Fields, Jerome Chodorov and stories by Ruth McKenney
Leonard Bernstein: Music
Joseph Fields, Jerome Chodorov: Book
Betty Comden, Adolph Green: Lyrics

YOUNG ABE LINCOLN (one act) (MTI)
Victor Ziskin: Music
Richard N. Bernstein, John Allen: Book
Joan Javits: Lyrics
Special dialogue and Lyrics by Arnold Sungaard

YOUNG TOM EDISON (SF)
Martin Kalmanoff: Music, Lyrics
Robert K. Adams: Book

* *YOU'RE A GOOD MAN, CHARLIE BROWN* (MM)
Based on "Peanuts" by Charles M. Schultz
Clark Gesner: Music, Lyrics

* *YOUR OWN THING* (TW)
Hal Hester, Danny Apolinar: Music, Lyrics
Donald Driver: Book

* *ZORBA* (MM)
Adapted from *Zorba the Greek* by Nikos Kazantzakis
John Kander: Music
Joseph Stein: Book
Fred Ebb: Lyrics

MUSICALS NOT GENERALLY AVAILABLE

The musicals listed in this section are not generally available from leasing agents. They appear in this chapter because no one thought them worthy of the investment in multiple production materials, reproduction, and promotion to nonprofessional or stock groups. Getting the performance rights for one of these shows should be attempted well in advance.

Even if a title of interest does not appear on the list of shows mentioned, basic information from the show's program or other source of author's billings, plus the procedure described herein should uncover the necessary production material.

Since this is largely an unfamiliar area a little background is in order. Once the original production closes, all rights (unless specified otherwise by the production contract) and production materials revert to the show's authors. Those materials include production scripts, orchestrations, and individual instrumental parts as well as any material written for the show but later eliminated during rehearsals, tryouts, or previews.

Pride of authorship would indicate that the materials for most shows still exist in a dusty trunk, a library, a musical agent's filing drawer, or in family memoirs.

The production company or educational group looking for a real production plum would do well to study discarded shows for available gems to save from oblivion by mounting a successful production. A show such as *All American* by Strouse and Adams offers much of the success of the same team's *Bye Bye Birdie*. Of course it would take some tailoring of the Prof. Fordorsky part, dialogue, and production (the New York production was inhibited by an unworkable set) but it could be raised to the same level of the hit song "Once Upon a Time," which is included in the show's score. The only trouble is *All American* is not currently available.

HOW TO SECURE PRODUCTION RIGHTS

If a musical is not available through a leasing agent, the process of obtaining rights is similar to that which the New York producer goes through to obtain production rights for the Broadway production. Predictably the task will be more difficult than dealing with a leasing agent to obtain rights for an available show.

Arrangements must be made through the author's agent (usually his lawyer, literary agent, or music publisher) or maybe in some cases directly with the author or his heirs. Reference to the author's agent can often be found in published

Harry Secombe as Pickwick confronts Mrs. Bardel (Hattie Jacques) in Pickwick.

201

volumes of his more successful works. If unsuccessful, the next best place to check for the author is The Dramatists Guild, Inc., 234 West 44th Street, New York, N.Y. 10036. There are also professional directories published that can be found in some libraries and the offices of local theatrical booking agents. Both *Variety* and *Billboard* publish annuals in which some agents are found in ads or directory listings. The staff at Drama Book Shop, 150 West 52nd Street, New York, N.Y. 10019 might be able to help.

The most foolproof method to reach the composer is through the royalty-collections firms of ASCAP (American Society of Composers, Authors, and Publishers) and BMI (Broadcast Music Incorporated). Those firms can furnish the address of the composer's agent, who, if not also the agent for the author, probably knows who he is. They may be reached at regional offices in larger cities or at their headquarters at:

ASCAP, 575 Madison Avenue, New York, N.Y. 10022

BMI, 589 Fifth Avenue, New York, N.Y. 10017

Results from inquiries are sure to vary. Some material may be lost forever. Some authors may prefer that the work stay buried. Others may welcome the opportunity for another forum. Perhaps in the quiet of the post-production they have reassembled a work of merit that was ruined by a heavy-handed producer or director. Perhaps the original authors would be interested in working with a local group to rewrite or restage the show. The idea offers some interesting possibilities.

The hit-or-perish reality of modern Broadway economics is ravenous of too much creativity and good ideas that turned bad or were turned down by the critics. The tendency to trample the near-miss is a peculiarly inhuman trait found too often in musical theatre. There is smash hit material in almost every musical. *A Time for Singing* played several weeks of preview performances to appreciative capacity audiences. The show opened, and critics turned thumbs down. Ticket sales took a nose dive, and the show folded. The British musical *Pickwick* played to many SRO houses in a cross-country prior-to-Broadway tour. When it opened, the critics said Dickens wouldn't have wanted it this way. The producer soon closed the show despite the fact that a longer run would have surely been more profitable. *Pickwick* ran almost four years in England, but closed after only 56 performances on Broadway.

Those are but two titles on the following list.

Many other works bear the label of flop or were considered financially risky to import from successful West End (London's "Broadway") runs, yet still contain valuable and entertaining material. Producing one of them could be an exciting, special, and rewarding experience.

Currently no convenient method or procedure exists for a theatrical group to obtain rights and production materials for musicals available only from British leasing agents and vice versa. It is hoped by presenting this material that the world of musical theatre may become more enriched.

Inquiries about the possibility of producing a currently playing London show should be directed to the manager of the theatre where the show is playing. The theatre manager is always a good place to start for a show since closed. London theatre managers are much more influential than in the United States. Many are on the same level as a producer. Reference should also be made to the appendix of *Let's Do a Musical* by Peter A. Spencer (Studio Vista Ltd., London, 1968) for a comprehensive list of London shows and addresses of British leasing agents.

* * *

SELECTED UNAVAILABLE MUSICALS OF POTENTIAL VALUE

ALL AMERICAN
Charles Strouse: Music
Mel Brooks: Book
Lee Adams: Lyrics

ANYA
(Based on *Anastasia* by Marcelle Maurette and Guy Bolton)
Robert Wright, George Forrest: Music, Lyrics
(Based on themes of Sergei Rachmaninoff)
George Abbott, Guy Bolton: Book

AS THE GIRLS GO
Jimmy McHugh: Music
William Roos: Book
Harold Adamson: Lyrics

BAJOUR
(Based on *The New Yorker* stories by Joseph Mitchell)
Walter Marks: Music, Lyrics
Ernest Kinoy: Book

* BLITZ
Lionel Bart: Music, Lyrics
Lionel Bart, Joan Maitland: Book

BRAVO GIOVANNI
(Adapted from the novel by Howard Shaw)
Milton Schafer: Music
A. J. Russell: Book
Ronny Graham: Lyrics

* Musical that premiered in London.

BY JUPITER
(Based on *The Warrior's Husband* by Julian F. Thompson)
Richard Rodgers: Music
Lorenz Hart: Lyrics
Richard Rodgers, Lorenz Hart: Book

* CHARLEY GIRL
(Based on conception by Ross Taylor)
David Heneker, John Taylor: Music, Lyrics
Hugh and Margaret Williams: Book

DARLING OF THE DAY
(Based on Arnold Bennett's *Buried Alive*)
Jule Styne: Music
E. Y. Harburg: Lyrics

DEAR WORLD
(Based on *The Madwoman of Chaillot* by Jean Giraudoux as adapted by Maurice Valency)
Jerry Herman: Music, Lyrics
Jerome Lawrence, Robert E. Lee: Book

GAY LIFE, THE
Howard Dietz, Arthur Schwartz: Music, Lyrics
Fay and Michael Kanin: Book

HOUSE OF FLOWERS
Truman Capote: Book
Harold Arlen: Music
Capote, Arlen: Lyrics

I HAD A BALL
Jack Lawrence, Stan Freeman: Music, Lyrics
Jerome Chodorov: Book

JENNIE
(Suggested by the life of Laurette Taylor)
Arthur Schwartz: Music
Arnold Schulman: Book
Howard Dietz: Lyrics

* JORROCKS
(Based on the novels of R. S. Surtees)
David Heneker: Music, Lyrics
Beverly Cross: Book

KEAN
(From a comedy by Jean-Paul Sartre, based on play by Alexander Dumas)
Robert Wright, George Forrest: Music, Lyrics
Peter Stone: Book

LA STRADA
(Based on Federico Fellini film)
Lionel Bart: Music, Lyrics
Charles K. Peck, Jr.: Book

LET IT RIDE
(Based on *Three Men on a Horse* by John Cecil Holm and George Abbott)
Jay Livingston, Ray Evans: Music, Lyrics
Abram S. Ginnes: Book

* LOCK UP YOUR DAUGHTERS
(Based on *Rape Upon Rape* by Henry Fielding)
Laurie Johnson: Music
Lionel Bart: Lyrics
Bernard Niles: Adaptation

MISS LIBERTY
Irving Berlin: Music, Lyrics
Robert E. Sherwood: Book

* ROBERT AND ELIZABETH
(From original idea by Fred G. Moritt, based on *The Barretts of Wimpole Street* by Rudolph Besier)
Ron Grainer: Music
Ronald Millar: Book, Lyrics

* PICKWICK
(Based on Dickens' Posthumous Papers of the Pickwick Club)
Cyril Ornadel: Music
Wolf Mankowitz: Book
Leslie Bricusse: Lyrics

SHERRY
(Based on *The Man Who Came to Dinner* by George S. Kaufman and Moss Hart)
Laurence Rosenthal: Music
James Lipton: Book, Lyrics

A TIME FOR SINGING
(Based on *How Green Was My Valley* by Richard Llewellyn)
John Morris: Music
Gerald Freedman, John Morris: Book, Lyrics

UP IN CENTRAL PARK
Sigmund Romberg: Music
Herbert and Dorothy Fields: Book
Dorothy Fields: Lyrics

Scene from Sigmund Romberg's The Desert Song.

Section IV

OTHER MUSICAL SHOWS

Many people don't realize that it is possible to go back into the archives of musical theatre and dig out the production materials for shows dating back to the 1800's.

In England it is a rather common practice. Audiences there seem to treasure and enjoy such historic works as Italians cherish the works of grand opera—both classic titles and obscure ones.

American critics and audiences have developed a snobbish attitude toward what is often termed an "outdated" show. That is unfortunate, but an apparent fact of life for which a solution looks dim. Budgets for such educational ventures have far outdistanced audience reception in the few cases in which a schedule of historical works has been offered. Perhaps when Americans achieve the often-predicted increase in leisure-time activities, more "antiquated" musical theatre works will be produced anew just to rediscover the part they played in the development of the art form.

Single shows, mostly operettas, such as *The Student Prince, The Desert Song, The Great Waltz*, the comic operas of Gilbert and Sullivan, and others remain popular and are produced on a regular basis. Modern operas such as *The Ballad of Baby Doe* are also included in the following list. A full description and address for the leasing agents' abbreviations will be found at the beginning of SECTION II on page 187.

A number of these shows are now in public domain. Where royalties still exist they will probably be low. Getting hold of production materials might be more expensive than normal because the scripts and orchestrations may have been packed away in warehouses and require a special effort to locate. When a title of interest does not appear in the agent's current catalog it would be wise to verify production material availability prior to scheduling a performance. If the agent has dropped the show refer to the procedures mentioned in Section III.

* * *

AESOP'S FALABLES   (AP)
(rock musical)
Ed Graczyck

ALADDIN, JR.   (TW)
(operatic extravaganza)
J. Cheever Goodwin: Book
Music: Various composers

ALASKAN, THE   (TW)
(comic opera)
Revised and reconstructed by Richard F. Carroll, Gus C. Weinburg

Harry Girard: Music
Joseph Blethen: Book, Lyrics

ALGERIA (ROSE OF ALGERIA)   (TW)
Victor Herbert: Music
Glen MacDonough: Book, Lyrics

ALI BABA (or *MORGIANA AND THE FORTY THIEVES*)   (TW)
Harry B. Smith, David Henderson: Book
Music: Various composers

ALMA, WHERE DO YOU LIVE?   (TW)
Jean Briquet: Music
From the German of Adolf Phillipp
English version by George V. Hobart

AMEER, THE   (TW)
Victor Herbert: Music
Frederick Ranken, Kirke LaShelle: Book

AMERICAN BEAUTY, AN   (TW)
Gustave Kerker: Music
C. M. S. McLellan: Libretto

ANGEL FACE   (TW)
Victor Herbert: Music
Harry B. Smith: Book
Robert B. Smith: Lyrics

ANNABELLE BROOM, THE UNHAPPY WITCH   (MTI)
Eleanor and Ray Harder

APPLE BLOSSOMS   (TW)
(operetta)

Fritz Kreisler, Victor Jacobi: Music
William LeBaron: Book, Lyrics

ARCADIANS, THE   (TW)
Lionel Monckton, Howard Talbot: Music
Mark Ambient, A. M. Thompson: Book
Arthur Wimperis: Lyrics

BABES IN TOYLAND   (TW)
Victor Herbert: Music
Glen MacDonough: Book

BABETTE   (TW)
Victor Herbert: Music
Harry B. Smith: Book, Lyrics

BACHELORS, THE   (TW)
E. L. Darling: Music
D. Delinore, F. C. Payne: Book

BALALAIKA   (TW)
George Posford, Bernard Grum: Music
Eric Maschwitz: Book, Lyrics

BALKAN PRINCESS, THE   (TW)
Paul Rubens: Music
Frederick Lonsdale, Arthur Curzon: Book
Paul A. Rubens, Arthur Wimperis: Lyrics

BALLAD OF BABY DOE, THE   (TW)
Douglas Moore: Music
John Latouche: Book

BALLET GIRL, THE   (TW)
Carl Kieffert: Music
James Tanner: Book
Adrian Ross: Lyrics

BARTERED BRIDE, THE   (TW)
(comic opera)
Bedřich Smetana: Music
Karel Sabina: Libretto
English translation by Libushka Bartusek

BELLE OF NEW YORK   (TW)
Gustave Kerker: Music
C. M. S. McLellan

BITTERSWEET   (TW)
Noel Coward: Music, Book, Lyrics

BLOSSOM TIME   (CL)
(operetta)
Franz Schubert: Music, adapted by Sigmund Romberg
Dorothy Donnelly: Book, Lyrics

BLUEBEARD JUNIOR   (TW)
Music: Various composers
Clay M. Green: Book

THE BLUE MOON   (TW)
Howard Talbot, Paul A. N. Rubens: Music
Harold Ellis: Book
Percy Greenbank, Paul A. N. Rubens: Lyrics

BLUE PARADISE, THE   (TW)
Edgar Smith: Book

Edmond Eysler: Music
Additional numbers by Sigmund Romberg
Austrian Book by Leo Stein, Bela Jenbach
Herbert Reynolds: Lyrics

CANARY COTTAGE, THE   (TW)
Earl Carroll: Music, Lyrics
Oliver Morosco, Elmer Harris: Book

CANDIDE   (S)
(comic operetta based on Voltaire)
Leonard Bernstein: Music
Lillian Hellman: Book
Richard Wilbur: Lyrics
John Latouche, Dorothy Parker: Additional Lyrics

CASTLES IN THE AIR   (TW)
Percy Wenrich: Music
Raymond W. Peck: Book, Lyrics

CAT AND THE FIDDLE, THE   (TW)
Jerome Kern: Music
Otto Harbach: Book, Lyrics

CHAPERONES, THE   (TW)
Isidore Witmark: Music
Frederick Ranken: Book, Lyrics

CHIEFTAIN, THE   (TW)
(comic opera)
Sir Arthur Sullivan: Music
F. Burnand: Libretto

CHINESE HONEYMOON, A   (TW)
Howard Talbot: Music
George Dacne: Libretto

CHOCOLATE SOLDIER, THE   (Mrs. Helen
    Bartsch, 1 East 42nd St., New York, N.Y. 10017)
Oscar Straus: Music
Rudolph Bernauer, Leopold Jacobson: Book, Lyrics

CINDERELLA (or *THE PRINCE AND THE
    FAIRY*)   (TW)
(extravaganza)
Music: Various composers
Harry B. Smith, David Henderson: Book

CINGALEE, THE   (TW)
Lionel Monckton: Music
James Tanner: Book
A. Ross, P. Greenbank: Lyrics

CLINGING VINE, THE   (TW)
Harold Levy: Music
Zelda Sears: Book, Lyrics

THE CONSUL   (S)
(opera)
Gian Carlo Menotti: Music, Book, Lyrics

CORSAIR, THE   (TW)
(operatic burlesque)
E. E. Rice, J. J. Braham: Music
J. Cheever Goodwin: Book

COUNTESS MARITZA   (CL)
(operetta)
Emmerich Kalman

COUNTRY GIRL, A   (TW)
L. Monckton: Music
James T. Tanner: Book
Adrian Rosa: Lyrics
P. Greenbank, Paul Rubens, additional lyrics and
    numbers

CYRANO   (SF)
(operetta: *Cyrano de Bergerac*)
Charles George: Music, Lyrics
Jacques Deauville: Book

DANCING YEARS, THE   (SF)
(operetta)
Ivor Novello, Christopher Hassall

DEAR MISS PHOEBE   (TW)
Musical adaptation of *Quality Street*
Harry Parr Davies: Music
Christopher Hassall: Book, Lyrics

DEBUTANTE, THE   (TW)
(operetta)
Victor Herbert: Music
Harry B. Smith, Robert Smith: Book, Lyrics

DESERT SONG, THE   (SF) (TW *)
(operetta)
Sigmund Romberg: Music
Otto Harbach, Oscar Hammerstein II, Frank Man-
    del: Book

DICK TURPIN   (TW)
(opera)
Bowness Briggs: Music
Gratton Donnelly: Book

DOLLAR PRINCESS   (TW)
Leo Fall: Music
N. M. Willner, F. Greenbaum: Book
American version by George Grossmith, Jr.

DOLL GIRL, THE (DAS PUPPENMAEDEL)
    (TW)
Leo Fall: Music
Leo Stein, A. M. Willner: Book
American adaptation by Harry B. Smith

DORCAS   (TW)
By Harry and Edward Paulton
C. Lockname, Watty Hydes: Original music

DREAM CITY   (TW)
Victor Herbert: Music
Edgar Smith: Book, Lyrics

DREAM GIRL, THE   (TW)
Victor Herbert: Music
Rida Johnson Young: Book, Lyrics

EARL AND THE GIRL, THE   (TW)
Ivan Caryll: Music
Seymour Hicks: Book
Percy Greenbank: Lyrics

EAST WIND   (TW)
Sigmund Romberg: Music
Oscar Hammerstein II: Lyrics

_____
* Professional groups only.

ECHO, THE   (TW)
Deems Taylor: Music
William LeBaron: Book, Lyrics

EILEEN   (TW)
(comic opera)
Victor Herbert: Music
Henry Blossom: Book, Lyrics

ENCHANTRESS, THE   (TW)
(comic opera)
Victor Herbert: Music
Fred DeGressac, Harry B. Smith: Book, Lyrics

ENGLISH DAISY, AN   (TW)
Alfred Mueller-Norden: Music
Seymour Hicks, Walter Slaughter: Book
Percy Greenbank: Lyrics

ERMINIE   (TW)
(comic opera)
Jakobowski: Music
Edward Paulton: Book

EVANGELINE   (TW)
(American opera bouffe)
E. E. Rice: Music
J. Cheever Goodwin: Book

EXCELSIOR, JR.   (TW)
R. A. Barnett

FANTANA   (TW)
Raymond Hubbell: Music
Sam S. Shubert, Robert B. Smith: Book, Lyrics

FASCINATING FLORA   (TW)
Gustave Kerker: Music
R. H. Burnside, Jos. Herbert: Book

50 MILES FROM BOSTON   (TW)
George M. Cohan

FILIBUSTER, THE ("A Tropical Romance")
    (TW)
(comic opera)
William Loraine: Music
J. P. Wilson: Book, Lyrics

FIREFLY, THE   (CL)
(operetta)
Rudolf Friml

FLEUR DE LYS   (TW)
(comic opera)
Adapted from the French of Chivot and Duru
J. Cheever Goodwin: Book
William Furst: Music

FLORABELLA   (TW)
(operetta)
Charles Cuvillier, Milton Schwarzwald: Music
Pearcy Maxman: Lyrics
Adapted by Cosmo Hamilton and Dorothy Don-
    nelly

FLORADORA   (TW)
Leslie Stuart: Music
Owen Hall: Libretto

FOLLOW THRU (TW)
Laurence Schwab, B. G. DeSylva: Book
DeSylva, Brown, Henderson: Songs
Bobby Connolly: Music

1492 (TW)
Carl Pfluger, E. E. Rice: Music
R. A. Barnett: Libretto

FORTUNE TELLER, THE (TW)
Victor Herbert: Music
Harry B. Smith: Book

45 MINUTES FROM BROADWAY (TW)
George M. Cohan

FRENCH MAID, THE (TW)
Walter Slaughter: Music
Basil Hood: Book

GAIETY GIRL, A (TW)
Sidney Jones: Music
Owen Hall: Book
Harry Greenbank: Lyrics

GAY HUSSAR, THE (EIN HERBST-MANOEVER) (TW)
(operetta)
Emmerich Kalman: Music
F. Bakony: Book

GAY'S THE WORD (SF)
(operetta)
Ivor Novello, Alan Melville

GEORGE WASHINGTON, JR. (TW)
George M. Cohan

GINGHAM GIRL, THE (SF)
Albert Von Tilzer: Music (TW)
Daniel Kusell: Book
Neville Fleeson: Lyrics

GIRL FROM DIXIE, A (TW)
Theodore Northrup: Music
Harry B. Smith: Book

GIRL FROM KAY'S, THE (TW)
Ivan Caryll: Music
Owen Hall: Book
Adrian Ross, Claude Aveling: Lyrics

GIRL FROM PARIS, THE (TW)
Ivan Caryll: Music
George Dacne: Book

GIRL IN THE TRAIN, THE (DIE VERSCHIEDEN FRAU) (TW)
(operetta)
Leo Fall: Music
Victor Leon: Book
American adaptation by Harry B. Smith

GIRL WHO DARED, THE (TW)
Alfred G. Robyn: Music
T. T. Bailey: Book, Lyrics

GOING UP (TW)
(Founded on *The Aviator* by James Mongomery)
Louis A. Hirsch: Music
Otto Harbach: Book, Lyrics

GONDOLIERS, THE (TW) (S)
Arthur S. Sullivan: Music
William S. Gilbert: Book, Lyrics

GOOD GRIEF, A GRIFFIN (AP)
(Based on Frank Stockton's legend)
Eleanor and Ray Harder

GOOD NIGHT, PAUL (TW)
Harry H. Olsen: Music
Roland Oliver, Charles Dickson: Book, Lyrics

GOOD WITCH OF BOSTON, THE (or *The Strange Case of Mother Goose*) (AP)
Pamela and Edward Borgers

GOVERNOR'S SON, THE (TW)
George M. Cohan

GREAT WALTZ, THE (TW)
Johann Strauss (father and son): Music
Moss Hart: Book
Desmond Carter: Lyrics

GREEK SLAVE, A (TW)
Sidney Jones: Music
Owen Hall: Libretto
P. Greenbank, A. Ross: Lyrics

GYPSY BARON (TW)
Johann Strauss arranged and adapted by Ronald Hanmer: Music
Phil Park, Conrad Carter: Book
Phil Park: Lyrics

GYPSY LOVE (TW)
(operetta)
Franz Lehar: Music
Harry B. and Robert B. Smith: English Book, Lyrics

GYPSY PRINCESS (TW)
Emmerich Kalman: Music
Adaptation by Conrad Carter, Phil Park, and Ronald Hanmer

HARMONY HALL (SF)
(operetta)
Harry B. Smith, Geoffrey O'Hara: Book, Lyrics

HAVE A HEART (TW)
Jerome Kern: Music
Guy Bolton, P. G. Wodehouse: Book, Lyrics

HAWAII (TW)
Theodore Northrup: Music
Thorton Cole: Book, Lyrics

HEN-PECKS, THE (TW)
A. Baldwin Sloane: Music
Glen McDonough: Words
E. Ray Goetz: Rhymes

HER REGIMENT   (TW)
(operetta)
Victor Herbert: Music
William LeBaron: Book, Lyrics

HIGH JINKS   (CL)
(operetta)
Rudolf Friml

HIGHROLLER, THE   (TW)
Wilford Herbert: Music
Archie Morrow: Book, Lyrics

HIS LITTLE WIDOWS   (TW)
William Schroeder: Music
Rida Johnson Young, Wm. Drury Duncan: Book,
    Lyrics

H.M.S. PINAFORE   (TW) (S)
Arthur S. Sullivan: Music
William S. Gilbert: Book, Lyrics

HONEYDEW   (TW)
Efrem Zimbalist: Music
Joseph W. Herbert: Book

HOTEL TOPSY-TURVY   (TW)
Victor Roger, Lionel Monckton: Music
Arthur Sturgess: Libretto

IDOL'S EYE, THE   (TW)
Victor Herbert: Music
Harry B. Smith: Book

IMAGE OF BIZ BIZ, THE   (TW)
George D. Clews: Music
S. V. Brewster: Book

IN GAY NEW YORK   (TW)
Gustave Kerker: Music
Hugh Morton: Words

IN MEXICO   (TW)
(opera)
Oscar Weil: Music
C. T. Dazey, Oscar Weil: Words

IOLANTHE   (TW)
Arthur S. Sullivan: Music
William S. Gilbert: Book, Lyrics

IRENE   (TW)
Harry Tierney: Music
James Montgomery: Book
Joseph McCarthy: Lyrics

*I SINCERELY DOUBT THAT THIS OLD
    HOUSE IS VERY HAUNTED*   (AP)
Paul Crabtree

ISLE OF CHAMPAGNE   (TW)
W. W. Furst: Music
Charles A. Byrne, Louis Harrison: Book

IT HAPPENED IN NORDLAND   (TW)
Victor Herbert: Music
William LeBaron: Book, Lyrics

IT'S UP TO YOU   (TW)
Manuel Klein: Music

Augustin McHugh, A. Douglass Leavitt: Book
Edward A. Paulton: Lyrics

JACK AND JILL   (TW)
Robert A. Keiser: Music
Sidney P. Levy: Book, Lyrics

JULY WOOING, A   (TW)
Wilford Herbert: Music
Archie Morrow: Book, Lyrics

JUST SO STORIES   (AP)
(Adapted by Aurand Harris from three of Rudyard
    Kipling's *Just So Stories*)

KHAN OF KATHAN, THE   (TW)
Herman W. Albert: Music
Kenneth Seymour Webb: Book, Lyrics

KATINKA   (CL)
(operetta)
Rudolf Friml

KING'S RHAPSODY   (SF)
(operetta)
Ivor Novello: Book
Christopher Hassall: Lyrics

KISMET   (TW)
(Turkish lyric comedy)
Gustave Kerker: Music
Richard F. Carroll: Libretto

KNIGHTS OF SONG   (TW)
(musical about Gilbert and Sullivan)
Glendon Allvine

LADY LUXURY   (TW)
William Schroeder: Music
Rida Johnson Young: Book, Lyrics

LADY SLAVEY, THE   (TW)
(operatic comedy)
John Crook and others: Music
George Dacne: Libretto
Additional lyrics and music by Hugh Morton and
    Gustave Kerker

LAND OF SMILES   (TW)
Franz Lehar: Music
Conrad Carter, Hans May, and Fred S. Tysh:
    Adaptation

LEGEND OF SLEEPY HOLLOW   (SF)
(Classic by Washington Irving)
Herbert S. French, Jr.: Music
John P. Donaldson: Book, Lyrics

LILAC DOMINO, THE   (TW)
(operetta)
Charles Cuvillier: Music
Emerich Von Gatti and Bella Jenbach: Book, Lyrics
English book by Harry B. Smith
English lyrics by Robert B. Smith

LINDA   (TW)
(one-act opera)
Roland Fiore: Music
Richard Reddy: Libretto

LISTEN LESTER   (TW)
Harold Orlob: Music
Harry L. Cort, George E. Stoddard: Book, Lyrics

LITTLE BOY BLUE (LORD PICCOLO)
  (TW)
(operetta)
Henri Bereny: Music
Rudolph Schanzer, Karl Lindau: Book
American adaptation by A. E. Thomas, Edward A.
  Paulton

LITTLE CHRISTOPHER COLUMBUS   (TW)
Ivan Caryll: Music
George B. Smith, Cecil Raleigh: Book

LITTLE HOST, THE   (TW)
William T. Francis, Thomas Chilvers: Music
Edgar Smith, Louis DeLange: Book, Lyrics

LITTLE JESSIE JAMES   (TW)
Harry Archer: Music
Harlan Thompson: Book, Lyrics

LITTLE JOHNNY JONES   (TW)
George M. Cohan

LITTLE MILLIONAIRE, THE   (TW)
George M. Cohan

LITTLE NELLY KELLY   (TW)
George M. Cohan

LITTLE RED RIDING HOOD   (TW)
G. Serpette: Music
Blum and Toche: Libretto
Revised by Al Henderson

LITTLE TROOPER, THE   (TW)
(French vaudeville operetta)
Raymond and Mars: Book
Adapted by Clay M. Greene
Wm. Furst, V. Roger: Music

LITTLE TYCOON, THE   (TW)
(comic opera)
Willard Spencer: Words, Music

LITTLE WHOPPER, THE   (TW)
Rudolf Friml: Music
Otto Harbach, Bide Dudley: Book

LITTLE WOMEN   (SF)
Geoffrey O'Hara: Music
John Ravold: Book
Frederick Howard: Lyrics

LOLLIPOP   (TW)
Vincent Youmans: Music
Zelda Sears: Book
Zelda Sears, Walter DeLeon: Lyrics

LOOK OUT   (TW)
George D. Clewis: Music
S. V. Brewster: Book

LOST, STRAYED OR STOLEN   (TW)
Woolson Morse: Original Music
Adapted from French by J. C. Goodwin

LOVE CURE, THE (KUNSTLERBLUT)
  (TW)
(operetta)
Edmund Eysler
by Leo Stein, Carl Lindau

MADCAP DUCHESS, THE   (TW)
(comic opera)
Victor Herbert: Music
David Stevens, Justin Huntly McCarthy: Libretto

MADELEINE   (TW)
(opera)
Victor Herbert: Music
Grant Stewart: Book

MAID AND THE MUMMY, THE   (TW)
Robt. Hood Bowers: Music
Richard Carle: Book, Lyrics

*MAIDS OF ATHENS (KING OF THE
  MOUNTAINS)*   (TW)
(operetta)
by Victor Leon
Carolyn Wells: English Book, Lyrics
Franz Lehar: Music

MAM'SELLE 'AWKINS   (TW)
Alfred Aarons: Music
Richard Carle: Book

MAN FROM CHINA, THE   (TW)
John W. Bratton: Music
Paul West: Book, Lyrics

MAN WHO OWNS BROADWAY, THE
  (TW)
George M. Cohan

MARRIAGE BY LANTERN   (TW)
Jacques Offenbach: Music
Andrew MacMillan: English Lyrics

MARTHA   (TW)
(opera)
By Friedrich von Flotow
Vicki Baum, Ann Ronell: American stage adaptation

MARY   (TW)
Louis Hirsch: Music
Otto Harbach, Frank Mandel: Book, Lyrics

MARY'S LAMB   (TW)
(Adapted from French *Madame Mongodin*)
Richard Carle: Music, Book, Lyrics

MAYOR OF TOKIO, THE   (TW)
(farcical opera)
William Frederick Peters: Music
Richard Carle: Book

MEDAL AND THE MAID, THE   (TW)
Sidney Jones: Music
Owen Hall: Book
C. H. Taylor: Lyrics

THE MEDIUM　(S)
(opera)
Gian Carlo Menotti: Music, Book, Lyrics

MERRY MONARCH, THE　(TW)
(comic opera)
J. Cheever Goodwin (from the French): Book
Woolson Morse: Music

MERRY PEASANT, THE (DER FIDELE
　BAUER)　(TW)
(operetta)
Victor Leon, Leo Fall

MERRY WIDOW, THE　(CL) (SF) (TW)
(operetta)
Franz Lehar: Music
(Based on London version by Christopher Hassall)
Milton Lazarus: Book revisions
Froman Brown: New Lyrics

MIKADO, THE　(TW) (S)
Arthur S. Sullivan: Music
William S. Gilbert: Book, Lyrics

MILES AROON　(TW)
by George H. Jessop, Horace Townsend
W. J. Scanlan and others: Music

MISFIT MAN, THE　(TW)
(comedy opera)
T. J. Lindorff, H. C. Schuyler, G. F. Pond, J. F.
　Bradley: Music
J. F. Hirshfeld, J. E. O. Winslow: Book

M'LLE MODISTE　(TW)
Victor Herbert: Music
Henry Blossom: Book, Lyrics

MISS DOLLY DOLLARS　(TW)
Victor Herbert: Music
Harry B. Smith: Book

MISS PRINCESS　(TW)
(operetta)
Alex Johnstone: Music
Frank Mandel: Book
Will B. Johnstone: Lyrics

MISS SIMPLICITY　(TW)
(comic opera)
H. L. Heartz: Music
R. A. Barnett: Book

MR. PICKWICK　(TW)
Manuel Klein: Music
Charles Klein: Book
Grant Stewart: Lyrics

MOCKING BIRD, THE　(TW)
(comedy opera)
A. Baldwin Sloane: Music
Sidney Rosenfeld: Book

MODERN EVE, A　(TW)
Adapted by William M. Hough, Benjamine Hap-
　good Burt; Jean Gilbert, Victor Hollander: Music
Jerome Kern: Interpolations

MONTE CARLO　(TW)
Thoard Talbot: Music
Sidney Carlton: Book
Harry Greenbank: Lyrics

MOROCCO BOUND　(TW)
F. Osmond Carr: Music
Arthur Branscombe: Book
Adrian Ross: Lyrics

MY BEST GIRL　(TW)
Augustus Barratt: Music
Channing Pollock, Rennold Wolf: Book, Lyrics

MY CHINA DOLL　(SF)
Charles George

MY HOME TOWN GIRL　(TW)
Louis A. Hirsch: Music
Frank M. Stammers: Book, Lyrics

MY MARYLAND　(CL)
(operetta)
Sigmund Romberg

NATOMA　(TW)
(opera)
Victor Herbert: Music
Joseph D. Redding: Libretto

NAUGHTY MARIETTA　(TW)
(comic opera)
Victor Herbert: Music
Rida Johnson Young: Book, Lyrics

NEVERHOMES, THE　(TW)
A. Baldwin Sloane, Glen McDonough: Music
E. Ray Goetz: Rhymes

NEW MOON　(TW)
Sigmund Romberg: Music
Oscar Hammerstein II, Frank Mandel, Lawrence
　Schwab: Book, Lyrics

NIGHT IN VENICE, A　(TW)
Johann Strauss
Ruth and Thomas Martin: English Book, Lyrics

NINA ROSA　(TW)
Sigmund Romberg: Music
Otto Harbach: Book
Irving Caesar: Lyrics

NO, NO, A MILLION TIMES NO!　(SF)
(or *Only A Farmer's Daughter*)
Bud Tomkins: Music, Lyrics
Eskel Crawford: Book

NO, NO, NANETTE　(TW)
Vincent Youmans: Music
Otto Harbach, Frank Mandel: Book
Irving Caesar, Otto Harbach: Lyrics

O'BRIEN GIRL, THE　(TW)
Loius Hirsh: Music
Otto Harbach, Frank Mandel: Book, Lyrics

OLD KING COLE (SF)
Haakon Perderbach: Music
Joe Edward Grenzeback: Book

OLD LADY SHOWS HER MEDALS, THE
(SF)
David Rogers, Mark Bucci

ONLY GIRL (TW)
(Adapted from Frank Mandel's comedy *Our Wives*)
Victor Herbert: Music
Henry Blossom: Book

ORANGE BLOSSOMS (TW)
Victor Herbert: Music
Fred DeGressac: Book
B. G. DeSylva: Lyrics

ORPHEUS IN THE UNDERWORLD (TW)
Jacques Offenbach: Music
Hector Cremieux: Libretto
John M. Glowach: Revision

PARISIAN MODEL, THE (TW)
Max Hoffman: Music
Harry B. Smith: Book, Lyrics

PATIENCE (TW) (S)
Arthur S. Sullivan: Music
William S. Gilbert: Book, Lyrics

PEARL OF PEKIN (TW)
(Adapted from *La Fleur de The*)
Lacocq: Music (some original numbers by G. Kerker)

PEGGY FROM PARIS (TW)
William Loraine: Music
George Ade: Book, Lyrics

PEOPLE AND ROBBERS OF CARDEMON TOWN (AP)
By Thorbjorn Egner
Translated from Norwegian

PIFF, PAFF, POUF (TW)
Jean Schwartz: Music
Stanislaus Stange: Book
William Jerome: Lyrics

PINK LADY (TW)
Ivan Caryll: Music
C. M. S. McLellan: Book, Lyrics

PIRATES OF PENZANCE, THE (TW) (S)
Arthur S. Sullivan: Music
William S. Gilbert: Book, Lyrics

PISTOL-PACKIN' SAL (SF)
Bud Tomkins: Music, Lyrics
Eskel Crawford: Book

PITTER PATTER (TW)
William B. Friedlander: Music, Lyrics
Will M. Hough: Book

POM POM (TW)
(comic opera)

Hugh Felix: Music
Anne Caldwell: Book, Lyrics

PRIMA DONNA, THE (TW)
(comic opera)
Victor Herbert: Music
Henry Blossom: Book

PRINCE ANANIAS (TW)
(comic opera)
Victor Herbert: Music
Francis Nellson: Libretto

PRINCE PRO TEM (TW)
Lewis S. Thompson: Music
Robert E. Barnet: Libretto

PRINCESS BONNIE, THE (TW)
(comic opera)
Willard Spencer: Words, Music

PRINCESS IDA (TW)
Arthur S. Sullivan: Music
William S. Gilbert: Book, Lyrics

PRINCESS NICOTINE, THE (TW)
(comic opera)
William Furst: Music
C. A. Byrne, Louis Harrison: Book

PRINCESS PAT (TW)
(comic opera)
Victor Herbert: Music
Henry Blossom: Book

PURPLE ROAD, THE (TW)
(operatic romance)
W. F. Peters: Music
Fred DeGressac, W. Cary Duncan: Book, Lyrics

PYGMALION AND GALATEA (TW)
Ambroise Thomas: Music
Oscar Weil: Libretto
(Based on W. S. Gilbert's comedy)

QUEEN HIGH (TW)
Lewis Gensler: Music
Lawrence Schwab, B. G. DeSylva: Book
B. G. DeSylva: Lyrics

QUEEN OF THE MOVIES (TW)
Jean Gilbert: Music
Glen McDonough: Book

RED MILL, THE (TW)
Victor Herbert: Music
Henry Blossom: Original Book
Milton Lazarus: New Book
Forman Brown: Additional Lyrics

RED ROSE, THE (TW)
Robert Hood Bowers: Music
Harry B. Smith, Robert B. Smith: Book, Lyrics

RED WIDOW, THE (TW)
Charles J. Gebest: Music
Channing Pollock, Rennold Wolf: Book, Lyrics

REGINA (TW)
(opera based on *The Little Foxes* by Lillian Hellman)
Marc Blitzstein: Text and Music

RISE OF ROSIE O'REILLY, THE (TW)
George M. Cohan

ROBIN HOOD (CL)
(operetta)
Reginald De Koven

ROLLICKING GIRL, THE (TW)
W. T. Francis: Music
Sidney Rosenfeld: Book, Lyrics

ROSALIE (TW)
Sigmund Romberg, George Gershwin: Music
William Anthony McGuire: Book
P. G. Wodehouse, Ira Gershwin: Lyrics

ROSALINDA (TW)
Johann Strauss: Music
Gottfried Reinhardt, John Mehan, Jr.: Book
Paul Kerby: Lyrics
Erich Wolfgang Korngold: Musical Adaptation

ROSE MAID, THE (TW)
(operetta)
Bruno Granichstaedten: Music
Harry B. Smith: Book

ROSE MARIE (CL)
(operetta)
Rudolf Friml, Herbert Stothart

ROYAL CHEF, THE (TW)
Ben M. Jerome: Music
George E. Stoddard, Chas. S. Taylor: Book, Lyrics

ROYAL ROGUE, A (TW)
(comic opera)
William T. Francis: Music
Charles Klein: Book
Grant Stewart: Lyrics

ROYAL VAGABOND, THE (TW)
Dr. Anselm Goetzl: Music
Stephen Ivor Szinney, Wm. Cary Duncan: Book,
Lyrics

RUDDIGORE (TW) (S)
Arthur S. Sullivan: Music
William S. Gilbert: Book, Lyrics

RUNAWAYS, THE (TW)
Raymond Hubbel: Music
Addison Burkhardt: Book, Lyrics

SAID PASHA (TW)
(comic opera)
Richard Stahl: Music
Scott Marble, Richard Stahl: Libretto

THE SAINT OF BLEEKER STREET (S)
Gian Carlo Menotti: Music, Book, Lyrics

SALLY, IRENE AND MARY (CL)
(operetta)
J. Fred Coots

SAMBO GIRL, THE (TW)
Gustave Kerker: Music
Harry B. Smith: Book, Lyrics

SAN TOY (TW)
Sid Jones: Music
Edward Morton: Book
H. Greenbank, A. Ross: Lyrics
L. Monckton: Additional Musical Numbers

SARI (DER ZIGEUNERPRIMAS) (TW)
(operetta)
Emmerich Kalman: Music
Julius Wilhelm, Max Grunbaum: Book
C. C. S. Cushing and E. P. Heath: English Adaptation

SCHOOL GIRL, THE (TW)
Leslie Stuart: Music
Henry Hamilton, Paul Potter: Book
Charles H. Taylor: Lyrics

SEESAW (TW)
Louis A. Hirsh: Music
Earl Derr Biggers: Book, Lyrics

SERENADE, THE (TW)
Victor Herbert: Music
Harry B. Smith: Book

SHIP AHOY (TW)
Miller and Northrup: Music
H. Grattan Donnelly: Book
Campbell and Skinner: Revision

SHOW GIRL, THE (TW)
H. L. Heartz, E. W. Corlias: Music
R. A. Barnett: Book
D. K. Stevens: Lyrics

SILVER SLIPPER, THE (TW)
Leslie Stuart: Music
Owen Hall: Book
W. H. Risque: Lyrics

SINBAD (or THE MAID OF BALSORA)
(TW)
(extravaganza)
W. H. Batchelor: Music
Harry B. Smith: Book

SINGING GIRL, THE (TW)
Victor Herbert: Music
Stanislaus Stange: Book
Harry B. Smith: Lyrics

SLEEPY HOLLOW (TW)
George Lessner: Music
Russell Maloney: Book, Lyrics

SONG BIRDS, THE (TW)
(operatic travesty)
Victor Herbert: Music
George V. Hobart: Lyrics

SONS O'GUNS   (TW)
J. Fred Coots, Henry Davis: Music
Fred Thompson, Jack Donahue: Book
Arthur Swanstrom: Lyrics

SORCERER, THE   (TW)
Arthur S. Sullivan: Music
William S. Gilbert: Book, Lyrics

SPRING MAID, THE   (TW)
(from the German by Wilhelm and Willner)
Heinrich Reinhardt: Music
Harry B. Smith, Robert B. Smith: Book, Lyrics

STUDENT PRINCE IN HEIDELBERG, THE
   (CL)
(operetta)
Sigmund Romberg

SUE DEAR   (TW)
Frank H. Grey: Music
Bide Dudley, Joseph Herbert, C. S. Montanye:
   Book, Lyrics

SULTAN OF SULU, THE   (TW)
Alfred G. Wathall: Music
George Ade: Book, Lyrics

SUZETTE   (TW)
(comic opera)
Oscar Weil: Music, Libretto
French source by Oscar Weil

SWEETEST GIRL IN TOWN, THE   (SF)
Charles George

SWEET GIRL   (TW)
(Adapted from the German of Alex Landesberg
   and Leo Stein by A. Demain Grace)
H. Reinhardt: Music

SWEETHEARTS   (TW)
(operetta)
Victor Herbert: Music
Harry B. Smith, Fred DeGressac: Book

TAKE IT FROM ME   (TW)
Will R. Anderson: Music
Will B. Johnstone: Book, Lyrics

TALES OF HOFFMAN   (SF)
(operetta version of opera by Jacques Offenbach)
Charles George

TALK OF NEW YORK, THE   (TW)
George M. Cohan

TANGERINE   (TW)
(Adapted by Guy Bolton from a play by Phillip
Bartholomae and Lawrence Langner)
Carolo Sanders: Music
Howard Johnson: Lyrics

TAR AND TARTER   (TW)
(comic opera)
Adam Itzel, Jr.: Music
Harry B. Smith: Book

TATTOOED MAN, THE   (TW)
(comic opera)

Victor Herbert: Music
Harry B. Smith, A. N. C. Fowler: Book

THE TELEPHONE   (S)
(opera)
Gian Carlo Menotti: Music, Book, Lyrics

TELEPHONE GIRL, THE   (TW)
Gustave Kerker: Music
Hugh Morton: Book

TENDERFOOT, THE   (TW)
(operatic comedy)
H. L. Heartz: Music
Richard Carle: Book

THREE LITTLE LAMBS   (TW)
Edward W. Corliss and others: Music
R. A. Barnett: Book

THREE MUSKETEERS   (TW)
Rudolf Friml: Music
P. G. Wodehouse, Clifford Grey: Lyrics
William Anthony McGuire: Adaptation

THROUGH THE YEARS   (TW)
Vincent Youmans: Music
Brian Hooker: Book
Edward Heyman: Lyrics

TILLIE'S NIGHTMARE   (TW)
A. Baldwin Sloane: Music
Edgar Smith: Book, Lyrics

TIME, PLACE AND THE GIRL   (TW)
Joseph E. Howard: Music
Adams and Hough: Book, Lyrics

TOOT TOOT   (TW)
(Adapted from Rupert Hughes's farce *Excuse Me*)
Jerome Kern: Music
Edgar Allan Woolf: Book
Berton Braley: Lyrics

TOURISTS, THE   (TW)
Gustave Kerker: Music
R. H. Burnside: Book, Lyrics

TRIAL BY JURY   (TW) (S)
Arthur S. Sullivan: Music
William S. Gilbert: Book, Lyrics

TRIP TO WASHINGTON, A (or *THE LONE-
STAR GIRL*)   (TW)
(Based on Charles H. Hoyt's *A Texas Steer*)
Ben Jerome: Music
Henry Blossom: Book, Lyrics

TROUBLE IN TAHITI   (S)
(opera)
Leonard Bernstein: Music, Book, Lyrics

TUXEDO   (TW)
(minstrel farce)
Various Composers: Music
Richard Marble: Book

---

* Professional groups only.

UMPIRE, THE   (TW)
Joe Howard: Music
Will M. Hough, Frank Adams: Book, Lyrics

VAGABOND KING, THE   (SF) (TW *)
(Based on *If I Were King* by Huntley McCarthy)
Rudolph Friml: Music
W. H. Post, Brian Hooker: Book, Lyrics

VELVET LADY, THE   (TW)
Victor Herbert: Music
Fred Jackson: Book
Henry Blossom: Musical Adaptation

VERY GOOD EDDIE   (TW)
Jerome Kern: Music
Phillip Bartholomae, Guy Bolton: Book
Lorenz Hart: Lyrics

VICEROY, THE   (TW)
(comic opera)
Victor Herbert: Music
Harry B. Smith: Libretto

WANG   (TW)
(operetta)
Woolson Morse: Music
J. Cheever Goodwin: Book

WAY UP EAST   (TW)
Richard Carlo

WAYWARD WAY (THE DRUNKARD)
  (TW)
(musical adaptation of *The Drunkard*)
No authors listed

WHEN LOVE IS YOUNG   (TW)
William Schroeder: Music
Rida Johnson Young, William Cary Duncan: Book,
  Lyrics

WHEN REUBEN COMES TO TOWN   (TW)
Herman Perlet

WHEN SHAKESPEARE'S LADIES SING
  (SF)
(operetta)
Charles George

WHEN SWEET SIXTEEN   (TW)
(song play)

Victor Herbert: Music
George V. Hobart: Book, Lyrics

WHIRL OF THE TOWN, THE   (TW)
Gustave Kerker: Music
Hugh Morton: Words

WHITE EAGLE, THE   (TW)
Rudolf Friml: Music
W. H. Post, Brian Hooker, Russell Janney: Book,
  Lyrics

WHITE HORSE INN   (SF)
(musical version of play by Hans Muller and Erik
  Charell)

WILDFLOWER   (TW) (CL)
Vincent Youmans, H. Stothart: Music
Otto Harbach, Oscar Hammerstein II: Book, Lyrics

WIZARD OF THE NILE, THE   (TW)
Victor Herbert: Music
Harry B. Smith: Book

WIZARD OF OZ, THE   (TW)
(musical extravaganza)
Paul Tietjens, A. Baldwin Sloane: Music
L. Frank Baum: Book, Lyrics

WONDERFUL WALTZ   (SF)
(operetta)
Victor Herbert: Music (selected from two early
  works)
Charles George: Book, Lyrics

WONDERLAND   (TW)
Victor Herbert: Music
Glen MacDonough: Book

YANKEE CONSUL, THE   (TW)
Alfred Robyn: Music
Henry M. Blossom: Book, Lyrics

YANKEE TOURIST, A   (TW)
Alfred Robyn: Music
Richard Harding Davis: Book
Wallace Irwin: Lyrics

YEOMAN OF THE GUARD   (TW) (S)
Arthur S. Sullivan: Music
William S. Gilbert: Book, Lyrics

YOU NEVER KNOW   (CL)
(operetta)
Cole Porter